Federalism and Social Policy

Federalism and Social Policy focuses on a crucial question: Is a strong and egalitarian welfare state compatible with federalism? In this carefully curated collection, Scott L. Greer, Heather Elliott, and contributors explore the relationship between decentralization and the welfare state to determine whether decentralization has negative consequences for welfare. The contributors examine a variety of federal nations, including Spain, Canada, and the United Kingdom, asking four key questions related to decentralization: (1) Are there regional welfare states (for example, Scotland and Quebec)? (2) How much variation exists in the structures of federal welfare states? (3) Is federalism bad for welfare? (4) Does austerity recentralize or decentralize welfare states? By focusing on money and policy instead of law and constitutional politics, the volume shows that states shape regional governments and policies even in federal states.

Scott L. Greer is Professor of Health Management and Policy, Global Public Health, and Political Science at the University of Michigan.

Heather Elliott is a doctoral candidate and research associate in the Departments of Health Management and Policy and Political Science at the University of Michigan.

Federalism and Social Policy

Patterns of Redistribution in 11 Democracies

Edited by Scott L. Greer and Heather Elliott

UNIVERSITY OF MICHIGAN PRESS

Ann Arbor

Published in the United States of America by the
University of Michigan Press
Manufactured in the United States of America
Printed on acid-free paper
First published May 2019

A CIP catalog record for this book is available from the British Library.

Library of Congress Cataloging-in-Publication Data

Names: Greer, Scott L., editor. | Elliott, Heather, editor.
Title: Federalism and social policy : patterns of redistribution in 11 democracies / edited by
    Scott L. Greer and Heather Elliott.
Description: Ann Arbor : University of Michigan Press, 2019. | Includes bibliographical
    references and index. |
Identifiers: LCCN 2019000219 (print) | LCCN 2019008964 (ebook) | ISBN 9780472124633
    (E-book) | ISBN 9780472131174 (hardcover : alk. paper)
Subjects: LCSH: Federal government—Case studies. | Comparative government. |
    Social policy—Cross-cultural studies.
Classification: LCC JC355 (ebook) | LCC JC355 .F3724   2019 (print) | DDC 339.5/2—dc23
LC record available at https://lccn.loc.gov/2019000219

Cover image: "Exactitude," poster by Pierre Fix-Masseau (1929).

Acknowledgments

The workshops underlying this book were funded with generous support from the University of Michigan Office of the Provost and the Rackham Graduate School as their Social Science Annual Institute. Teresa Ramirez, Connie Rockman, and Jean Steppe and their colleagues in the Department of Health Management and Policy at the University of Michigan provided crucial administrative support and good cheer. Jenna Bednar, Daniel Halberstam, and Barry Rabe of the University of Michigan were enormously helpful discussants at our second workshop; Holly Jarman of the University of Michigan was a very helpful colleague and critic throughout; and Marta Arretche of the University of São Paulo was extremely helpful in helping us understand the task we faced and how to think about it. Two anonymous readers for the University of Michigan Press helped us sharpen the analysis and draw out the comparative implications of the book. Elizabeth Demers, Danielle Coty, Kevin Rennells, and Ellen Goldlust of the Press showed great patience and technical skill, both of which were needed! We thank them all.

When we were finishing this book, we were saddened to learn of the death of one of our collaborators, Gebhard Kirchgässner. We remember him with this volume.

Contents

Digital materials related to this title can be found on
the Fulcrum platform via the following citable URL:
https://doi.org/10.3998/mpub.9993201

Introduction

Comparative Federalism, Public Policy, and Money

Scott L. Greer

Is a strong and egalitarian welfare state compatible with federalism?

Some say no. How can it be, when federalism seems to almost automatically demand different treatment for people based on where they live, when it causes a newborn baby to be treated differently based on where in a country her parents live (Banting and Kymlicka 2006b)? Further, how can a strong welfare state or social democracy, with its tamed capitalism and commitment to welfare, coexist with federalism when federalism fragments the polity, empowers local elites, and makes it difficult to pass expansive social programs? How can it be good for a welfare state to create a race to the bottom in which jurisdictions have incentive to compete away their taxes, social policies, and regulations? And how can it be good for a welfare state to fragment finances so that poorer jurisdictions have less money and more need?

Some say yes. Federalism does not just enable experimentation, it also confines political aberrations. It allows countries to circumvent gridlock in one government, so that there are always some developments. It can enable some regions to have more social democratic policies if they want and even can create competition among regions and tiers of government to have higher social standards. But above all, the hazards of federalism to the welfare state, say federalist social democrats, lie in specific rules. Federalism need not impede legislation, fragment risk pools, or create downward competition. The relationship between social democracy and federalism is all in the rules, and a well-designed federal system, like a well-designed electoral or legal system, can support egalitarian policies while still permitting experimentation and local adaption.

This conversation matters because those rules, always under revision, are under particular strain since the start of the global financial crisis in 2008. Authority has been migrating from central states toward regional government for decades, but that might be changing as we write under the pressure of revenue shocks, debt crises, and the bitter politics of hard times as well as the course of partisan, generational, and class politics (Gerber and Kollman 2004; Hooghe, Marks, and Schakel 2010; Kazepov and Barberis 2013). It matters for countries that are restructuring their systems: changing the balance of responsibility and power between central and local might also make certain social policies and groups of people more or less vulnerable. It matters for political activists debating which level of government will introduce new and redistributive social policies, as in the United States (Béland, Rocco, and Waddan 2016; Greer and Jacobson 2010). It matters for federations whose basic sustainability is in question, as in Belgium and the United Kingdom, since the ability of their regional governments to pursue distinctive agendas is part of their politics of multinational statecraft. And it matters for the crisis-ridden European Union as it stumbles through its new fiscal governance arrangements toward a more dominant role in its member states' policies.

Like most very simple questions, the answer to the question of whether federalism is good or bad for the welfare state is *It depends* (Pierson 1995). A strong, well-financed, and sustainable and egalitarian interpersonally redistributive welfare state depends on policy design, politics, and institutions. It depends on underlying social and economic formations, on institutions, on programmatic design and policy legacies, and on the political coalitions that sustain or undermine them. Comparative federalism scholarship rarely takes into account the design of policies and their financing, and policy scholarship often has a very narrow take on the nature and operation of federalism.

We seek to understand the variation in redistribution and generosity within federal states as a function of *both* federal politics and institutions *and* the design and funding of policies. This book is the fruit of a five-year international project whose goal was to better understand the relationships between territory, money, and the structure of programs and the variability of the welfare state within countries and between policy areas. The project makes it easier to understand the impact of different forms of decentralization on inequality and social investment in good and bad economic times.

Theories of Federalism and Inequality: What Is the Relationship between Decentralization and the Welfare State?

As might befit a topic that has long been discussed and has real political stakes, there are many theories about the relationship between decentralization and the welfare state. We focus here on theories that address the relationship between decentralization and social policy, particularly expenditures (the welfare state). The question of what decentralization does to the welfare state has preoccupied most people who think about federalism and social policy, just as expenditures rather than tax schemes or private welfare have been the focus of most welfare state research. Future research agendas should take into account the interaction of private welfare, public welfare, and labor market regulation that our country chapters discuss but that is not part of our framework.

The starting point for most discussions of the topic is what initially appears to be a solid correlation in the literature between decentralization and lower welfare state expenditure (Huber and Stephens 2001; Swank 2001; Castles 1999). The consensus has been that decentralized countries do not develop extensive welfare states. Even if that consensus is not necessarily well-founded methodologically (Greer, Elliott, and Oliver 2015) or empirically (Kleider 2015; Scruggs and Allan 2006),[1] it is still the starting point for much literature.

The four families of theory we identify have different methodological approaches and preoccupations, but all seek to rebut, explain, or go beyond this simple correlation between decentralization and lower welfare state expenditure. They also focus on the distinction between shared rule and self-rule that was developed by Elazar (1987). Self-rule is the ability of jurisdictions to make their own decisions (e.g., about taxes, policies, priorities), and shared rule is the ability of jurisdictions to influence the central state (e.g., through votes in an upper house). In general, many more countries are marked by self-rule than by shared rule, a phenomenon that a look beyond federalism to local government makes even clearer (Hooghe, Marks, and Schakel 2010; Kazepov and Barberis 2013). So what is the relationship between decentralization and the welfare state?

Regional Welfare States

One approach, particularly common in Europe but also popular in Canada (Greer 2019), focuses on self-rule (Keating and McEwen 2005; Moreno and McEwen 2005; Keating 2009). Just as welfare states are part of state building, perhaps they are part of nonstate enterprises of nation building or territorial distinction. Authors in this approach focus on regional welfare states—on the actions of regional governments themselves and their ability to redistribute between their citizens, insure their citizens against misfortune, and use social policy to structure a distinctive society. At its core, this literature is interested in the extent to which a distinctive society (or at least one with a distinctive national identity) is reflected in mobilization for greater control over social policy and the extent to which that national distinctiveness translates into distinctive social policies. This literature occasionally overlaps with authors who are concerned about the different politics and preferences of regional governments in rich and poor areas (Beramendi 2012), which is best understood by taking their constitutional power into account as well (Dyson 2015).

Part of the reason researchers have been interested in regional welfare states is precisely their connection with national agendas (especially since the core business of regional governments is the welfare state rather than, for example, foreign, defense, or monetary policy). Multinational states open up the possibility of competing welfare nationalisms. Separating nation, state, and welfare state creates the possibility of a distinctive Flemish, Basque, or Welsh welfare state (Béland and Lecours 2005, 2008; McEwen 2002). Multinational states also create competition between different levels of government seeking to show their relevance to ordinary voters through social programs, a phenomenon that has been particularly pronounced in Canada under the Liberals but that is also visible in other decentralized countries.

A second reason for the interest in regional welfare states is that they are sources of experimentation and comfort for those who are out of power. Even in relatively homogeneous countries or countries whose salient political cleavages are not territorial, such as the United States or Mexico, there are partisans of decentralization—typically because they are dissatisfied with the content of federal policies. While this impulse has in American history often been driven by southern resentment of federal policies that undermine racist institutions (Riker 1964; Lieberman and Lapinski 2001; Lieberman 1998; Katznelson 2005; Bateman, Katznelson, and Lapinski 2018), many Americans have despaired of politics in Washington, DC, seeking ingenuity and solutions at the state or local level (Katz and Bradley 2013). Federal states, which can be quite large and sophisticated, indeed often develop innovative policies (Teaford 2002; Fox 2010), as do local governments. Even if we do not care about policy innovation, federal states have been redoubts of key political forces in times of adversity (e.g. the PRI in Mexico [Green and Ibarra-Rueda 2017]) or parties that are out of power in the central governments of Spain or the UK.

This literature is rich in political analysis and in a few jurisdictions has come together into a convincing picture of politics and policy. But its characteristic focus on regional protagonists—on the actions of regional governments and the politics behind those actions—also means that it presents at most an incomplete picture of the relationships among state, welfare state, and redistribution.

The first problem is the common bias toward a few cases—that is, places with stateless nations that have nationalist parties and politics as well as the size, money, and sophistication to develop an ensemble of distinctive policies. This category includes Scotland, Catalonia, and Quebec, followed at a great remove by Wales and Flanders, with surprisingly little attention to the Basque experience and almost none to more "normal" regions. Even within these regions, nationalist parties and center-left parties with autonomist leanings tend to receive the attention. Andalusia is a major policy actor with a population similar to Sweden, but literature on the stateless nation of Galicia outweighs it. Galicia is a redoubt of the Spanish Popular Party, but literature about Galicia focuses on the smaller nationalist movement. Italy is a spectacular case of most issues in territorial politics, but its lack of large stateless nations leaves it relatively unrepresented in this literature.

The second problem is that as a strategy for scholarship, it tends to cede control of the research agenda to the regional politicians themselves. It leads research on territorial politics to follow regional politicians in focusing on distinctive policies in areas under regional control and on contests over control of given policy areas rather than on the region's overall welfare state, much of which might be run centrally (as with pensions), or which might not be framed by any significant actor as being primarily an issue of territorial politics. In some cases, this means that small budget items with high symbolic impact, such as cultural policy, loom very large.

Third, there is a problem of baseline: not only is there no clear standard of distinctiveness, but there is also no comparative standard by which we can say that one region in one country has more or less latitude or distinctiveness relative to another region in another country. Most of the issues that fascinate students of regional politics may be less signs of distinctive regional welfare states than of divergent implementation, by divergent people, of essentially similar systems.

In other words, this literature is to be valued for its cumulative, politically focused, understanding of how distinctive welfare regimes develop in particular places, but it does not coalesce into an understanding of the comparative place of regions in welfare states and redistribution, and its regional lens means that it is not always strong on the interaction between broader systemic issues such as economic crisis or Eurozone rules and the behavior of individual governments. The lack of baselines for identifying regional welfare particularity—Do the policy variations really matter within the country or in comparative perspective?—undercuts the usefulness of the often-fascinating case studies.

Federalism as a Market for Government

The essential model of territorial politics in economics is of a market for government, a model formulated by Charles Tiebout in which mobile factors of production choose a government with a desirable level of taxes and benefits—that is, the price and product that governments, modeled like firms, sell to people and companies (Tiebout 1956). In such a model, there is a tendency to equilibrium, with governments selling a package of services at every price point.

The simplifying assumptions of Tiebout's model immediately disqualify it as a picture of government in practice. Not all factors of production are mobile (skilled labor concentrates in certain cities, natural resources are not evenly distributed), there are costs to mobility (textile factories are more mobile than, for example, universities), and governments' decision making is influenced by a wide range of internal and external factors that can outweigh the discipline of competition. Governments can ignore marginal failure (population loss) for a long time, and governments routinely subsidize or bail each other out in ways that undermine the pure competitive model. In some places such as the United States, there is evidence that people vote with their feet for lower taxes and higher benefits, but the impact is limited since people are hemmed in by reliance on family networks, available housing, labor markets, and firm- or industry-specific skills. In many countries, including Spain, Belgium, the UK, and Canada, issues of language and cultural differences also impede mobility. Further, firms go bankrupt and die out, although governments typically do not. Even when there is something like bankruptcy, the jurisdiction and its government and certainly the place and people do not drop off the map. In other words, even if Tiebout correctly identified *a* dynamic of intergovernmental finance, he clearly did not provide a general theory.

Tiebout clearly identified *a* logic at work; Paul Peterson transformed it into the thesis that the competitive situation of state and local governments in the United States would lead them to focus on economic development, including education, rather than on redistributive functions the federal government would take on, and the data seem to bear him out (Peterson 1981, 1995; Adolph, Greer, and Massard da Fonseca 2012).

Economists' models also started to take advantage of the fact that democratic governments are subject not only to market discipline but also to electoral discipline. This led to more of a focus on institutions, which manifested in three different ways. First, it led to analyses of how intergovernmental financial arrangements can redistribute resources to reduce inequalities between territories in the name of equity (Boadway and Shah 2009; Oates 1999). Second, it led to efforts to incorporate democracy as a variable disciplining governments—voters, before leaving, could also make sure governments had a suitable balance of taxes and spending.[2] This led to, for example, Musgrave's (1959) principle of "assignability"—that each government should have its own taxes and responsibilities so that voters could know who to blame for high taxes or poor services. Adding democratic discipline to competition also created a dual case for decentralization—since voters could observe things going wrong in small jurisdictions, and because smaller jurisdictions would be price (tax) takers rather than setters. Third, it led to political analyses about how we could structure institutions to make the real world more like Tiebout's model, which would mean "market-preserving federalism" (Weingast 1995, 2009; Rodden and Rose-Ackerman 1997).

The economic argument tends to settle into an analysis of a market with a potentially Pareto-optimal equilibrium in which interjurisdictional competition and voters' discipline keep public services from being inefficiently provided or overprovided (a word that is almost impossible to define without tautology). In short, competition between governments for factors of production impedes the rent seeking by employees and local interests, to which all politics is vulnerable. As in life, some individual actors—for example, London, Orlando, and Venice—are just lucky in that they have immobile assets that allow them to charge higher taxes than they otherwise might. Governments and institutions can introduce market failure, so the question is how to avoid intergovernmental financial schemes and debt that undermine the joint discipline of interjurisdictional competition and tax-sensitive electorates. The public sector and its complexity are recast as an impediment to markets clearing. Predictably, since China is growing, we are asked to believe that Chinese growth must be driven by markets and therefore that Chinese local government should be admired for inferred conformity to its market-preserving federal principles (Qian and Weingast 1997; Montinola, Qian, and Weingast 1995). Not all scholars agree, of course (Shih, Adolph, and Liu 2012).

This approach has four general problems. The first is that, like all models, economic models abstract, and it is possible to confuse a partial model containing a few mechanisms with an actual description of the system. Second, all the key mechanisms—intergovernmental competition and electoral discipline—are highly variable depending on institutions and politics. The models' basic applicability can vary between substantial and almost none.[3]

The third problem is that the model incorporates normative biases. There is simply no reason to expect that intergovernmental competition or the kind of democracy modeled in these studies actually produce a desirable level of welfare by any definition. Excessive spending and provision exist only in relation to a hypothesized market equilibrium, which cannot exist in a real institutional setting. The common result is a simple manifesto for smaller government in which tax competition that might seem destructive is applauded because smaller government is better (Riker 1982; Weingast 1995). This liberal approach is more often assumed than justified (Gray 2010).

Finally, the models that move away from the pure competitive logic of Tiebout to introduce assumptions about democratic accountability and responsiveness introduce strong assumptions about the quality and operation of democracy that are not obviously valid (Treisman 2007). A more local government could be more accountable and transparent—or it could be an authoritarian enclave (Gibson 2012; Mickey 2015). If local and regional governments are not more transparent, accountable, or responsive as a result of their smaller sizes, then models assuming that they are will fare badly. What use is assignability if the government in question is unaccountable?

The "market for government" argument would be strengthened if we had a better, more comparative, and less judgmental understanding of the relationships among institutions, finances, and expenditure. Many studies of uncertain cumulativeness find or do not find competition and discipline, but integrating policy areas, institutions, and fiscal decisions into one comparative framework has proven a challenge.

Federalism as a Veto Point

Economic authors tend to celebrate decentralization for the (potential) virtues of interjurisdictional competition and accountability; students of the welfare state are much less likely to celebrate it or to focus on competition or the democratic virtues of self-rule at the local and regional levels. Rather, those in the latter field tend to start by assuming basic correlation between decentralization and smaller welfare states and focus on how the political dynamics and institutions of decentralized states interfere with both welfare state expansion and productive retrenchment (e.g., to address "new social risks" such as those faced by women and precarious workers; see Bonoli 2005; Jensen et al. 2014; Taylor-Gooby 2004). This approach generally focuses on federalism as an institutional feature that prevents policies that have democratic support (Greer, Elliott, and Oliver 2015). The classic social policy scholarship is mostly skeptical of the benefits of federalism for variations on this reason: for example, Heidenheimer (1973) notes the drag created by fragmentation, Scharpf (1988) points to the "joint-decision traps" that intergovernmental relations produce, and major later works include federalism as a drag on welfare state development so uncontroversial as to be essentially a control (Swank 2001; Hicks 1999). The key writers in this tradition today, arguing coherently that federalism diminishes the chances and impact of egalitarian social policy, are Evelyn Huber and John Stephens and Juan Linz and Alfred Stepan.

Huber and Stephens (2001) offer a broad analysis of the development of the welfare state in Europe, regarding federalism as part of a constellation of institutional variables that can multiply veto points, giving minority interests opportunities to weaken or block redistributive legislation (following on Immergut 1992). They create a *Fragmentation* variable that incorporates various institutional veto points such as bicameralism, referenda, and federalism. The distinction is broadly similar to the one drawn by Arend Lijphart (1984), though he incorporates more variables, or the centripetal/centrifugal democracy concept developed in the masterful work of Gerring and Thacker (2008). Huber and Stephens's composite *Fragmentation* variable, in their regressions, reduces the size of the welfare state in countries with higher fragmentation scores.

The problem with Huber and Stephens's approach is that while it captures a basic insight—more veto points diffuse and often defeat pressure for expansive social policies—it lumps together a variety of very different institutional features. Bicameralism, referenda, and federalism have similar origins in polities such as Switzerland and the United States and often covary, but they need not go together. Huber and Stephens's (2001) qualitative discussion justifying *Fragmentation* focuses on Australia, arguing that the Australian Senate is a function of federalism and responsible for the relative lack of generosity of the Australian welfare state. It is not clear, however, that the Australian Senate reflects federal politics in any clear way, that it is responsible for the shape of the Australian welfare state, or that the Australian welfare state's limited generosity therefore results from federalism (Galligan 1995; Castles 2001, 1985; Brenton, this vol.).

Furthermore, there is a problem with temporality. Even if federalism impedes welfare state growth in the countries where it preceded the welfare state, that tells us little about what to expect from cases in which federalism and the welfare state grew together (Spain) or ones in which the story of federalism is the story of decentralization of an established welfare state (Belgium, the UK, and arguably Italy).

In general, *Fragmentation* is a needlessly simple variable that combines too many different and often unrelated things. It mixes shared and self-rule along with other issues. It contends that veto points interfere with expansive policy but tells us little about the impact of federalism or the other kinds of institutional devices discussed.

Stepan and Linz shared the basic insight that federal political institutions constrain the forces of welfare state expansion (Stepan and Linz 2011; Stepan 2001). They discuss federalism as a "demos-constraining" institution that limits the ability of the people (demos) to have its preferences reflected in policy. The more veto points in a system, the more demos-constraining it is. Federalism is a major veto point in this analysis; federal polities are demos-constraining in that they prevent voters from getting what they would prefer. Linz and Stepan here assume a demos; as they know well, many if not most federal states are constructed as they are precisely to cope with the absence of an agreed-upon demos (Stepan 1999). For them, a weaker welfare state might be the price of keeping a country together.

Both Huber and Stephens and Linz and Stepan treat federalism as a feature of the country as a whole. They focus on shared rule, the impact of regional politics on the central state, rather than taking an interest in the impact of regional politics on regional welfare arrangements. Both accounts also attribute to federalism a related but quite different issue, which is the extent of self-rule. Countries such as Canada, Spain, and the UK have a high level of self-rule among their regional governments, but the regional governments have very little formal say in their central governments' decisions. The United States has representation for its states, but its Senate treats states as electoral circumscriptions rather than giving state governments a formal role in federal politics. In Germany and Austria, where regional governments are directly represented in the upper house, scholars have argued that the effect is to induce a party system that nationalizes regional politics, with votes for state governments shaped by preferences for federal policy (Katzenstein 1987; Jeffery 2003). The structure of the central government has no necessary relationship with the organization of regional government. Self-rule and shared rule can vary independently.

In short, this argument starts with an apparent correlation between institutional veto points and lower welfare expenditures (and less welfare state reform), but its chosen mechanism is unclear because of the handling of the data. In an example of what Snyder (2001, 100) calls "mean-spirited thinking," the relationship pairs an aggregate country-level independent variable, *Veto Points*, with an average country-level dependent variable, *Expenditure*, and thereby obscures both institutional and policy variation. Both pairs of authors treat federalism as a feature of the state that explains state-level welfare expenditures, focusing on central state policymaking as the explanation for average outcomes and downplaying the variable relations between federalism and central government policymaking. Focusing on shared rule also directs this literature's attention away from the variation between regions (self-rule). This literature would benefit from a more nuanced approach that distinguishes shared rule, self-rule, and other things such as referenda and that could discuss the scale of divergence within a country as a result of self-rule.

Meso-Level Institutional Theories

Insufficient attention to the workings of political institutions is the kind of problem that political scientists tend to remedy, and the problems of both the economists and the comparative sociologists seem to involve lack of specificity about institutions. The result has been an efflorescence of political science work on federalism. These authors are usually most interested in the robustness of federalism rather than its public policy implications, and they tend to treat public policy mostly in terms of fiscal sustainability and threats to federal bargains. Nonetheless, their work is some of the most interesting research taking place on federalism and territorial politics.

One approach dates back to at least William Riker (1964; see also Volden 2004) and focuses on political parties. The basic argument of the parties literature is that statewide parties can hold fissiparous political systems together by aggregating different interests, facilitating bargaining, and aligning politicians' incentives toward a statewide rather than more sectional solution (Huntington 1968; Aldrich 1995; Mair 1997). Logically, therefore, the creation of statewide parties stabilizes new democracies (Linz and Stepan 1992), and the operation of statewide parties contributes to their ongoing robustness (Filippov, Ordeshook, and Shvetsova 2004). Quite a bit of empirical literature indeed associates statewide parties with integration, coordination, and conflict resolution within federations (Katzenstein 1987), though the direction of the causality is not clear since centralizing or decentralizing political institutions can contribute to centralizing or decentralizing the party system (Chhibber and Kollman 2004; Hopkin 2009; Lago-Peñas and Lago-Peñas 2011; Elkins and Simeon 1980). A second approach is to refocus on institutions, identifying the incentives they create for politicians and solving the problem of economic theories that posit nonexistent competition or underspecify governments' incentives (Rodden 2006; Beramendi 2010; Rogers 2016).

The first two approaches are synthesized in Bednar's *The Robust Federation*, which canvasses the range of safeguards against defection from basic federal bargains by either central or regional governments. These safeguards include judicial review, political parties, and popular support for a stable federal balance. In a robust federation, governments that start to defect—for example, by irresponsible fiscal policy, secessionist mobilization, or encroachment on each other's authority—will be blocked by those safeguards. Bednar is unusual in paying equal attention to defection by regional and central governments as a threat to the federation.

Naturally, identification of putatively desirable, incentive-compatible, institutional arrangements directs our attention to the rather large number of existing institutional arrangements that are not desirable. The result is a third approach that focuses on the bargains that lead to particular federal arrangements. These authors focus on the reasons why rational and self-interested politicians might create inefficient, unstable, inegalitarian, or otherwise problematic political institutions (Beramendi 2011; Rodden and Rose-Ackerman 1997).

The origins and evolution of political institutions, including federal ones, is a long-standing preoccupation of many disciplines, including political science. This approach is noteworthy for its focus on the interaction of incentives, bargaining strategies, and institutions as well as the tendency to motivate research by pointing to the distance between existing political institutions and a more efficient or otherwise desirable ideal. In this it reflects a common approach in political science that accepts much of the basic conceptual framework of economics, including rational choice theory and normative assumptions about the desirable liberal state, but emphasizes the limits of economic models that ignore the complexity of the incentives and institutional arrangements facing policymakers. For these researchers, the success of federations rests on getting the right institutions, but the politics of constitution writing can produce the wrong institutions.

This preoccupation with reducing political and institutional impediments to regional overspending then produces a characteristic preoccupation with soft budget constraints on regional governments that permits them to issue too much debt in the confidence that the central government will bail them out (Rodden 2005, 2014; Mclean 2015). There are two logical solutions to this problem of the soft budget constraint (Dyson 2014). One is to make regional governments as vulnerable as possible to the hard budget constraint of debt markets, as is said to be the case with American states, which generally have balanced budget constraints and are disciplined by bond markets (Rodden 2005). Problems—for example, the procyclicality this induces, the difficulty of establishing economically and socially beneficial automatic stabilizers under such a regime, and the excessive dependence on complex accounting determinations that these policies entail (Mabbett and Schelkle 2013)—are less commonly discussed. The other solution is to simply make it impossible for regional governments to access the debt market by putting their debt under the control of a presumably more prudent and technocratic central government. The politics of this option and its impact on investment are also downplayed.

A salient characteristic of the literature on the relationship between federalism and the welfare state is that its approach to public policy essentially comes from economics as practiced in international financial institutions. Its dialogue with (or responsiveness to) economics means that it tends to adopt preferences from public choice with regard to the importance of some issues, notably regional debt and soft budget constraints (Peterson and Nadler 2014; Rodden 2005), small government (Weingast 1995), and general compliance with the Washington consensus (Wibbels 2000, 2005). The focus, with regard to public policy, is on the fiscal sustainability of the state, not the impact of its public policies.

This political science version of IMF surveillance narrows the range of motivations and issues in politics. This literature would benefit from a better understanding of the regional expenditures and policies in relation to federal ones, which would expand its understanding of the political economy of federalism so that policy becomes something more nuanced than spending. As it stands, the sophistication of this institutional analysis rests on assumptions from 1970s public choice in which politicians witlessly spend unless constrained. It also depends on the typically unstated assumption that bond markets are, if not right, at least so powerful as to dominate politics. Neither assumption seems tenable. Politicians balance multiple issues and preferences, and bond markets clearly have problems of gaming, imperfect information, herd behavior, and ideology.

The result is a structural bias in this literature toward austerity. Debt, for example, is conceptualized as involving only the numerator (debt) and not the denominator (GDP) of a debt-to-GDP ratio, and social investment or demand-side policies are made hard to imagine. That would scarcely be a legitimate approach if debt-reduction policies reliably produced growth (Alesina and Ardagna 2010), but they do not (Guajardo, Leigh, and Pescatori 2011). Authors in this school have a curious faith in the wisdom of bond markets and to a lesser extent central governments as well as a matching lack of faith in voters and politicians. That is a reasonable, or at least explicable, stance for employees of the IMF who address central governments on behalf of creditors, but it seems rather a narrow preoccupation for social scientists.

Federalism as a Social Fact: A Historicist Approach

In contrast to the rationalist and institutionalist approaches of most political scientists and essentially all economists, some scholars focus on the historical context, without which most territorial politics is hard to understand (Erk and Anderson 2009; Erk and Koning 2009; Livingston 1952). This school of authors generally makes a two-step argument. The first step, which coincides with Linz and Stepan's work, is that decentralization is frequently a response to a divided or multiethnic society (Stepan 1998). In such societies, different nations might have different preferences, different political classes might have incentive to seek divergence, and different nations' voters or elites might not trust each other enough to want to pool resources and redistribute. In Belgium, perhaps a paradigmatic case, the two major units, Flanders and Wallonia, have substantially different economies, governments with very different projects and problems, and a completely fragmented political system that creates incentives to run against the other national group. The result is increasing decentralization from a unitary state to a highly decentralized, complex, federal one.

The second step, then, is to point out that in such states, it is overdetermined that the welfare state will be less generous and will be particularly unlikely to initiate redistributive programs. According to this hypothesis, low trust in other people reduces support for redistribution (Crepaz 1998, 2008; Banting and Kymlicka 2006a). The hypothesis looks attractive. Belgium inherited a very redistributive welfare state and political economy, but it is now under attack from Flemish politicians who regard it as a mechanism to redistribute from them to Walloons. Voters in a diverse place might vote for less redistribution because they are disinclined to support any program that redistributes to a group they do not like or trust. On the other side, the few largely homogeneous decentralized countries—Austria, Australia, and Germany stand out—do have highly nationalized politics, with federalism incorporated into their national party politics. If federalism is generally a response to a diverse society, we should not be surprised that federal welfare states are weak. The same fundamental cause of social fragmentation is at work in both institutional design and social politics, creating a fundamental endogeneity problem (Rodden 2004). For these authors, looking to institutions misses the point if the problem is federalism's endogeneity to history and society.

Which Leaves Us Where?

What, then, is the relationship between federalism and a strong welfare state? While paths toward social and politically egalitarian policies are visible in each, whether because of majorities that overwhelm veto points, social democratic nationalist projects in stateless nations, or superb fiscal management that endures competition, it is also easy to see multiple ways in which federalism would tend to be bad for social democracy. In other words, the answer is *It depends*. But on what?

The most ambitious comparative effort to sort through the relationship produced a series of valuable historical case studies that demonstrated the complexity and intertwined nature of any explanation of federalism (Obinger, Leibfried, and Castles 2005). They find that timing and history matter—a salutary corrective to much current writing in economics and political science but not an effective hypothesis for stimulating further comparative inquiry.

Meanwhile, the largest share of literature about regional government and policy since the crisis began has focused on the quite narrow issue of how regions can be prevented from overspending. Even if the budgeting decisions of regional governments were not the cause of the crisis in any country, financial constraints and soft budgets combined to leave many regional governments with insuperable debt burdens. The result is an argument about whether regional governments and Eurozone member states should be tightly controlled by (wiser? more accountable?) central governments, or whether budgetary constraints should be hardened with powerful no-bailout rules so that bond markets provide the discipline. Debt crises are hardly distinctive to regional governments. Eurozone member states are in the same predicament, and plenty of sovereign governments have debt crises, but remarkably little attention has gone to making this point or developing a comparative framework that incorporates politics beyond a preoccupation with soft budget constraints (though see Dyson 2014). Just as the relationships among federalism, social policy, expenditure, and society have become especially important and changeable and comparative federalism scholarship has become more theoretically sophisticated (Bednar 2011), many scholars have narrowed their focus down to that of the IMF (Mclean 2015; Rodden 2014).

Questions about Federalism and the Welfare State

The preceding sections led us to a series of empirical questions that would help to explain how federalism and the welfare state interact in good and bad economic times.

Do Regional Welfare States Exist?

Part of the case for a social democratic federalism or any federalism is diversity. Whether it is economists arguing that different tastes matter or social democrats defending decentralization on the grounds that Scotland, Minnesota, and Navarre can have better welfare states, the kind and quantity of variation is a crucial and often unspecified factor. This question directly addresses the preoccupation of the regional welfare states literature. Just how distinctive are regional welfare states from one another within a country? How much do their spending levels, sources of financing, and priorities vary? Is it actually realistic to expect different "worlds of welfare" within a country? Secondarily, how much variation happens between countries? To what extent do countries' different political, economic, and institutional environments permit or encourage the development of distinctive regional welfare states? Answering these questions would shed light on the extent to which self-rule can produce quantitative and qualitative variations in welfare states—that is, the extent to which different federations permit or encourage different levels of diversity. Insofar as self-rule produces diversity, it calls into question the averages and aggregates of welfare effort that underpin many comparative studies. These answers would allow us to start to identify the mechanisms that promote or constrain divergence across countries and would suggest the limits to literatures that focus on regional governments as protagonists and on the dynamics of regional politics. If regional welfare states are not very distinctive or seem to be shaped by the state, then the literature focused on regional welfare state politics might need to reconsider its often case-specific findings.

How Much Variation Exists in the Structures of Federal Welfare States?

The question that logically flows from the question about the existence of regional welfare states—distinctiveness within one country—is how and how much the internal structures of federal welfare states vary. A variety of theories, notably those of economists, suggest that only a few kinds of functional territorial welfare state exist in equilibrium (Hooghe and Marks 2009). More variation occurs in the political scientist's concept of robust welfare states, but there are still clear boundaries on how much they can diverge while being robust (Bednar 2009). Other theories—notably the regional welfare states approach and the historicist approach—might suggest more variation since they posit political arguments that might not be particularly driven by functional political economy. A study of the health sector structured in this manner found a great deal of similarity, with states pooling risk and regulating centrally in a way that suggested insurance logics and a response to externalities and focusing delivery on more local levels (Adolph, Greer, and Massard da Fonseca 2012). This pattern, quite compatible with basic fiscal federalism, was broken mostly in the case of stateless nations, highlighting the importance of interactions between states and the challenging politics of stateless nations.

Is Federalism Bad for Welfare?

This is perhaps the oldest and most frequently asked question, since it arises any time the establishment of a welfare program is proposed or whenever anyone suggests transferring responsibility for some element of social policy from one level to another. There are a variety of basic arguments: that there will be a race to the bottom as regional governments compete away their tax bases; that the welfare state will bloat as politicians buy support with soft budgets; that there will be innovation; that there will be greater horizontal inequity as richer areas keep their own revenue or the central state redistributes their revenues. Understanding the interplay of regional distribution between programs and between countries would start to address this problem: for example, do programs become weaker or less countercyclical if they are the responsibility of regional governments? The answer will clearly depend on program design and financing, but if we can identify the financial and institutional prerequisites for different kinds of egalitarian or competitive finances, we can start to identify better the situations in which federalism is good or bad for the welfare state and its promises of greater equality and social insurance. In other words, rather than try to focus on comparing federal and nonfederal states, we focus on identifying and explaining the considerable variation within the range of federal states because their outcomes are quite different and not always well understood.

Does Austerity Recentralize or Decentralize Welfare States?

Finally, most of the states in our sample have been emerging from a giant fiscal and economic crisis. What is the effect of crisis—or growth—on federal welfare states? Part of the answer to this question depends on the answer to the previous one: if policies managed and financed by regional governments are more vulnerable to economic downturns, then the distribution of specific responsibilities and financing would matter greatly. But there is also a second-order political question, which is whether the political and fiscal strains of crisis lead to decentralization (as central governments seek to shed responsibilities onto regional governments) or centralization (as central governments seek to gain control over regional governments, taking advantage of law and vertical fiscal imbalance in a crisis atmosphere). Both might be reasonable expectations for authors in our traditions, whether they are expecting a new chapter of an ongoing struggle between stateless nations and central states or a push toward an equilibrium with hard regional budget constraints. But equally, the veto points theory suggests that federal states will be less likely to change in any circumstance, and a high degree of self-rule might produce divergence that does not change the composition or levels of welfare spending everywhere.

A New Approach to Decentralization and Social Policy: Expenditures and Responsibilities in Cross-National Perspective

The different theories, with the partial exception of regional welfare state theories, are addressing the same basic correlation: between federalism and welfare state expenditure in each country. A whole country is coded fragmented, federal, or otherwise, and that coding is incorporated into an explanation of its overall average welfare expenditure.

This state-focused approach has some problems that might explain the impasse. First, the approach depends on binary variables (e.g., federal or not) or indexes made up of different attributes (e.g., federalism and referenda) such as Huber and Stephens's *Fragmentation* variable. Second, authors typically rely on OECD data, which presents total regional and local government expenditure within the state. It does not reliably distinguish regional and local government expenditure, and it does not distinguish variation in various kinds of expenditure within a country. A poor region might have a small budget of its own but be the site of large central state expenditures through programs such as pensions or social health insurance. The approach therefore cannot shed much light on the many and complex systems of interpersonal and interterritorial redistribution. It further does not distinguish between policy sectors. The comparative welfare state literature has long had a tendency to focus on pensions, which as this book shows tends to be the most centralized policy area and are easiest to measure. But health, education, and other social policies such as active labor market policy are enormous items of expenditure with variable and potentially important effects on public finances, inequality, and people's lives. Benefits, services, and policies aimed at the 18–65 age groups are particularly tricky in terms of intergovernmental relations and policy coordination and have also been a major site of authority migration and policy change in many countries (López-Santana 2015). Social policy can shape societies, as nationalist governments know well, and are also areas of policy that are frequently wholly or partly the charge of regional governments. The extent of variation between policy areas within and between countries is relatively underexplored and is unavailable in OECD data.

Further, those who try to do quantitative statistical analysis in this kind of area face some basic problems. A number of older pieces have tried to quantify the impact of federalism in regressions (Castles 1999; Huber and Stephens 2001). The initial problem was that of a small N that made quantitative results, in even the most conceptually interesting study, fundamentally unconvincing (Cameron 1978). A plausible response was to use time-series analysis, but this encounters a different problem. Institutions are quite stable. Most of the control variables one might use in explaining welfare state generosity, such as labor market centralization, GDP per capita, and demographic profile, are also quite stable from year to year. As a result, time series analysis sits badly with differences that are primarily cross-sectional. Autocorrelation problems are inevitable with such persistent variables.[4] Given the difficulties of using time-series analysis for essentially cross-sectional differences, the problem of a small N reappears, as does the problem of omitted variables that comes when we try to separate out the impact of any one stable feature of a country from every other possibly relevant omitted variable. The result is an intractable problem from a frequentist statistical point of view, which might be part of the reason that despite far better datasets and statistical methods, there has been only one effort to replicate and extend the correlation since Castles (1999). (The closest the literature has come since then is Kleider 2015, which is far better done.)

In many cases, the response has been country case studies, and such case studies are the mainstay of the literatures that focus on individual regions and the literatures that focus on the historical and social fundamental causes of federalism and ungenerous welfare states. The problem is that country case studies do not just have a tendency to focus on party politics and institutions rather than actual money and policy. They also lack a basic descriptive quantitative and policy baseline that tells us what kind of money is being spent by whom on what. Increasingly rich detail about politics and policymaking does not tell us how much regional welfare states differ.

Data and Country Chapters

Our response was to embark on a multinational effort, with the generous help of the University of Michigan, to collect data on policies and money in the decentralized states of the OECD: Austria, Australia, Belgium, Canada, Germany, Italy, Mexico, Spain, Switzerland, the United States, and the United Kingdom. Table 1 presents the Regional Authority Index (RAI) for the different countries, showing their different degrees of self-rule and shared rule in 2010. The RAI is by far the biggest, most systematic, and most comprehensive framework for evaluating regional authority and supersedes the various other frameworks that have been proposed but never really fleshed out (Hooghe et al. 2016).

After a 2013 workshop, the authors collected data in standardized templates: one reporting on the basic characteristics of their country's different regional governments; one focusing on the fiscal characteristics of those different regions, such as debt and own-source revenue; and one on expenditure by policy area, distinguishing as much as possible between regional governments' expenditures out of their own resources, regional governments' expenditures driven by federal matching funds (e.g., Medic-

TABLE 1. Regional Authority Index Scores, 2010

This box shows the Regional Authority Index scores for each of our countries (Hooghe and Marks 2015). For our purposes, these scores provide a broad guide to the type and extent of decentralization in each country. Institutional depth (regional government autonomy, distinguishing a region from a deconcentrated office), policy scope, fiscal and borrowing autonomy and representation are all attributes of self-rule and denote a high level of regional autonomy. Participation in lawmaking, control of the central state's executive, borrowing, and fiscal policy as well as role in constitutional reform are all aspects of shared rule.

Country	Inst. depth	Policy scope	Fiscal auton.	Borrowing auton.	Rep.	Self-Rule	Law-making	Exec. ctrl	Fisc. ctrl	Borrowing ctrl	Constit. ref.	Shared Rule	RAI
Australia	2.9	4	2	2	4	14.9	1.5	2	2	2	3	10.5	25.4
Austria	3	3	2	2	4	14	1	1	1	2	3	9	23
Belgium	4.8	4.8	4.8	1.9	6.7	23.1	2	2	2	1	3	10	33.1
Canada	3.7	3.7	4.2	3.4	4.9	19.9	.1	1	1	0	4	6	26
Germany	5.6	4.8	2.6	3.8	8.1	25	2	2	2	2	4	25	37
Italy	5	5	4	3	7	24	0	1	.2	0	2	3.2	27.3
Mexico	3	3	3	2	4	15	2.5	0	0	0	4	5.5	20.5
Spain	4.8	4	4.5	1.7	6.6	21.6	1.3	2	1.1	2	6.2	12.6	34.3
Switzerland	3	4	4	3	4	18	1.5	2	2	0	3	8.5	26.5
UK	2.8	2.1	.7	1.3	3.2	10.1	.2	.2	0	0	.6	1	11.2
United States	3.8	3.8	5.1	3.8	5.6	22.1	1.5	2	0	0	4	7.5	29.6

Source: Data from Regional Authority Index, http://www.unc.edu/~gwmarks/data_ra.php; Hooghe et al. 2016.

aid in the United States), and federal expenditures in different regions (e.g., the amount of state pension in the different parts of the UK). The authors compiled publicly available data, marking a major step beyond the existing available OECD data. Pragmatically, 2010 was the year in which every country had some data, though some could have longer series. A longer discussion of coding and data is posted on the University of Michigan's Deep Blue website (https://deepblue.lib.umich.edu/). The data collected by Kleider (2015) would also be valuable but are not used here. As the conclusion discusses, our effort started to show serious data limitations and interesting patterns in the unavailable data.

The chapters link expenditure and revenue data with policy and politics. They explain the programmatic, legal, and policy contexts for expenditures and their consequences, thereby both contextualizing the data and bringing public policy fully into comparative federalism studies. One of the most striking problems with the existing comparative literature is the frequent lack of integration between analyses of public policy and federalism. The *Oxford Handbook of Regional and Local Democracy in Europe* (Loughlin, Hendriks, and Lidström 2011), for example, sticks to high-level law and politics accounts, leaving the reader unclear about who does what in a given country and how it is financed. Such fuzziness about the way decentralization works in public policy interferes with our ability to understand the conflicts, decisions, stakes, and effects of federal politics. Innumerable single-country studies and a number of policy area studies with several countries start to redress the problem, but structured comparisons that link politics and policy, such as are found in the chapters here, remain rare.

We confronted the trade-off of all comparative politics research between respect for national idiosyncrasies and comparison across countries. Thus, for example, the RAI can be critiqued for failing to capture changes in the way federalism works (waivers to states to modify policies in education and health in the United States have big policy effects but would not show up). The RAI chose comparison and legalism over the nuances of policymaking in each country. After much work with problematic data, we opted for the reverse. Since subnational quantitative data are generally poor in their own right and are mostly not fit for direct comparison, the nuanced approach to public policies missing in most federalism research is the strength of this book. Chapter authors use quantitative data and policy analysis to portray the interaction of federalism and the welfare state, with a special focus on redistribution and change.

The template for each country chapter was therefore designed to elicit information about programmatic structure and redistributive effects that would allow answers to comparative questions while presenting the countries' welfare states and federalism coherently and using what quantitative data exist. Within the template, authors were encouraged to highlight what was important and comparatively interesting about their countries.

Simply identifying the cases in this book is a contentious matter. On one hand, our concern is with the welfare state and how welfare states work in a number of countries. On the other, we have chosen a selection of states that could, depending on inclination, be described as *territorialized, decentralized, regionalized, devolved,* or *federal* or with even more bespoke terms such as the Spanish *state of the autonomies.* Each of these terms has many meanings used in extensive academic literatures, and arguably none applies to all the countries under consideration. All of them involve some form of decentralization of political authority, policymaking, and finance to a substate government.

In choosing cases to illustrate a phenomenon with so many names, our starting point is formal institutional structures, which also determine many other features of government and public policy within a political system, and the existence of permanent, general-purpose government. Regionalized and decentralized authorities may, however, fail some of these criteria. They might not be democratic, permanent, or general purpose. We have chosen systems and the midlevel (regional) governments within systems that fulfill the following criteria:

1. They include two (or more) tiers of directly elected governments with multiple or general purposes, each acting directly on the citizen and not dependent on the other for permission or authority to do so.
2. These governments are territorially based.
3. The constitutional foundations of those governments are such that one tier cannot be unilaterally abolished by another.

Our concern is therefore with systems that include multilevel, democratic governments that are constitutionally protected, unlike, for example, local government, which even if it is constitutionally recognized is capable of being reformed or restructured by another tier of government. Thus, the principle of the division of functions is permanent, even if those functions or the boundaries of the units might change. This, in turn, affects the dynamics of both politics and policymaking in such systems; each tier of government must accept the existence of the other as part of the reality of how that country works and as a practical matter coordinate if governance is to be at all successful.

We selected as cases all systems that appeared to satisfy these criteria and were members of the OECD. For many long-established (and often self-described) federal systems, such as the United States, Canada, Switzerland, Australia, and Germany, little difficulty arises. In some cases, however, the selection is more contentious. The UK is highly asymmetrically decentralized, and its "devolved" tier of government does not affect the approximately 85 percent of its population and economy in England, while its unwritten constitution means that the devolved tier also lacks constitutional protection, at least by some standards. We nonetheless included it because of the strong element of self-rule for Northern Ireland, Scotland, and Wales and because devolution is about as entrenched as any other norm in the UK. Belgium has a complex system of government that includes a consociational element, with the substate governments comprising territorially based "regions" as well as language-based "communities." Austria's intricate form of cooperative federalism has always raised questions about the autonomy of the *Länder* and the ways in which Austria is in fact "federal." Belgium and Austria are nonetheless formally federal and so were included. We excluded France on the grounds that its regions, while they have scope to engage in many different activities, have such minimal social welfare functions in practice that they are not really general-purpose governments (Jones 2013). French regions have limited self-rule, and France is not formally federal.

We focus on the politics and welfare states of federations rather than comparing between federal and nonfederal countries for three reasons. First, the variation within federal countries is so impressive as to highlight a need for explanation. Second, drawing any inferences about the nature of the welfare state by comparing federal and nonfederal countries is hard; politics is very different, and there are other awkward problems, such as the generally smaller size of nonfederal countries and the role awkward geography plays in shaping much in addition to the likelihood of federalism (Adolph, Greer, and Massard da Fonseca 2012). Third, given the ongoing decentralization of many countries (Hooghe and Marks 2016), the lessons drawn from variation within federations might prove applicable to formally nonfederal countries.

Our data vary by region, by expenditure category, and by policy. That means that we avoid the biases that come from examining policies that are frequently centralized (pensions) or frequently decentralized (education) and taking them as representative of the whole welfare state. Sometimes, as with Austria, entire policy fields in a juridically federal country are run in such a centralized manner as to produce no territorially relevant data. Our approach also avoids using an average of expenditure, which flattens out the impact of self-rule and fiscal financial structures, and instead highlights the variability in financial mechanisms and political economy within countries. And finally, our data direct our attention from country-level correlations at the start, giving us a fuller and richer picture of the real impact of state structures on policy.

The country chapters are written to focus on how the welfare states engage in redistribution in five policy areas: primary and secondary (under-18) education; higher education (direct funding from governments); health; 18–65 benefits and services, which covers diverse areas such as unemployment benefits, disability policies, and active labor market measures; and finally pensions. The five policy areas are as precise as we could make them while incorporating subnational data and data on central expenditures broken down by territory. We did not try to judge a priori whether a particular policy area is about investment or redistribution. Particularly in the area of education, such a judgment can drive results overall, as happened in Peterson's (1995) work. Such a judgment also can be somewhat artificial, since almost every social policy can be an investment as well as a form of redistribution: health care is an investment in a healthier workforce; income replacement and pensions are economic stabilizers, reducing the amount of unpaid informal care needed; day care both constitutes a human capital investment and allows more parents into the labor force; and so forth. Parsing out the extent to which a policy area is about social investment or redistribution is a task better done at the country and program level if the data permit.

Each chapter works through the different policy areas and ends with a discussion and explanation of the country's current trajectory. The result is a set of chapters that allow us to provide a conclusion in which we answer the four questions posed here based on comparable policy and financial information. Broadly, we find that regional welfare states' distinctiveness is limited, the variation between the structures of federations is limited, decentralization is not clearly bad for welfare, and there is no automatic way in which economic adversity leads to centralization or decentralization.

NOTES

1. In fact, there is literature showing that decentralization can reduce inequality by creating a more equal distribution of public goods across territory. See Martinez-Vazquez, Lago-Peñas, and Sacchi 2017; Grossman, Pierskalla, and Dean 2017; Costa-Font and Greer 2016.

2. If government is a good that people purchase, we presume that it reflects their "taste" in an economic model. The use of that word shows how far these scholars are from the ones who focus on nationalism and regional welfare states.

3. For example, studies of intergovernmental policy change are as likely to find emulation or coordinated lobbying as to find competition behind diffusion (Füglister 2012; Boushey 2010). The United States has seen some particularly striking examples of networks that span governments and operate opportunistically across jurisdictions (Hertel-Fernandez 2014).

4. The most obvious way to update and replicate these quantitative studies would be to use the Regional Authority Index, which is the best quantitative comparable study we have of decentralization and the Comparative Welfare States dataset, the best one on general political and economic variables related to welfare states. There are 22 countries that have basically complete data in both. Among them, the mean change in self-rule in a given year since 1980 is .09 and in shared rule is .02 in an index that runs 0–20 for each (Hooghe et al. 2016; Brady, Huber, and Stephens 2014; Castles 1999). In 95.27% of cases (year/country), there was zero change in the shared rule score, and in 89.36% of the cases there was zero change in self-rule. The data point to a cross-sectional answer to the question of how federalism mattered, which in turn highlights problems of a small N, highly persistent autocorrelated variables, and likely omitted variables.

REFERENCES

Adolph, Christopher, Scott L. Greer, and Elize Massard da Fonseca. 2012. "Allocation of Authority in European Health Policy." *Social Science and Medicine* 75 (9):1595–603. https://doi.org/10.1016/j.socscimed.2012.05.041

Aldrich, J. H. 1995. *Why Parties? The Origin and Transformation of Political Parties in America*. Chicago: University of Chicago Press.

Alesina, Alberto, and Silvia Ardagna. 2010. "Large Changes in Fiscal Policy: Taxes versus Spending." In *Tax Policy and the Economy*, 24:35–68. Chicago: University of Chicago Press/NBER.

Banting, Keith G., and Will Kymlicka. 2006a. "Introduction: Multiculturalism and the Welfare State: Setting the Context." In *Multiculturalism and the Welfare State: Recognition and Redistribution in Contemporary Democracies*, edited by Keith G Banting and Will Kymlicka, 1–47. Oxford: Oxford University Press.

Banting, Keith G., and Will Kymlicka. 2006b. *Multiculturalism and the Welfare State: Recognition and Redistribution in Contemporary Democracies*. Oxford: Oxford University Press.

Bateman, David A., Ira Katznelson, and John S. Lapinski. 2018. *Southern Nation: Congress and White Supremacy after Reconstruction*. Princeton: Princeton University Press.

Bednar, Jenna. 2009. *The Robust Federation: Principles of Design*. Cambridge: Cambridge University Press.

Bednar, Jenna. 2011. "The Political Science of Federalism." *Annual Review of Law and Social Science* 7 (1): 269–88.

Béland, Daniel, and André Lecours. 2005. "The Politics of Territorial Solidarity: Nationalism and Social Policy Reform in Canada, the United Kingdom, and Belgium." *Comparative Political Studies* 38 (6): 676–703.

Béland, Daniel, and André Lecours. 2008. *Nationalism and Social Policy: The Politics of Territorial Solidarity.* Oxford: Oxford University Press.

Béland, Daniel, Philip Rocco, and Alex Waddan. 2016. *Obamacare Wars: Federalism, State Politics, and the Affordable Care Act.* Lawrence: University Press of Kansas.

Beramendi, Pablo. 2011. *Regions and Redistribution: The Political Geography of Inequality.* Cambridge: Cambridge University Press.

Boadway, Robin, and Anwar Shah. 2009. *Fiscal Federalism: Principles and Practice of Multi-Order Governance.* Cambridge: Cambridge University Press.

Bonoli, Giuliano. 2005. "The Politics of the New Social Policies: Providing Coverage against New Social Risks in Mature Welfare States." *Policy and Politics* 33 (3): 431–49.

Boushey, Graeme. 2010. *Policy Diffusion Dynamics in America.* Cambridge: Cambridge University Press.

Brady, David, Evelyne Huber, and John D. Stephens. 2014. *Comparative Welfare States Data Set.* Chapel Hill and Berlin: University of North Carolina and WZB Berlin.

Cameron, David R. 1978. "The Expansion of the Public Economy: A Comparative Analysis." *American Political Science Review* 72 (1): 1243–61.

Castles, Francis G. 1985. *The Working Class and Welfare: Reflections on the Political Development of the Welfare State in Australia and New Zealand, 1890–1980.* Wellington, NZ: Allen and Unwin.

Castles, Francis G. 1999. "Decentralization and the Post-War Political Economy." *European Journal of Political Research* 36 (1): 27–53.

Castles, Francis G. 2001. "A Farewell to Australia's Welfare State." *International Journal of Health Services* 31 (3): 537–44. https://doi.org/10.2190/e6w8-3hyy-ehj5-7vfk

Chhibber, Pradeep K., and Ken Kollman. 2004. *The Formation of National Party Systems: Federalism and Party Competition in Canada, Great Britain, India, and the United States.* Princeton: Princeton University Press.

Crepaz, Markus. 1998. "Inclusion versus Exclusion: Political Institutions and Welfare Expenditures." *Comparative Politics* 31 (1): 61–80.

Crepaz, Markus. 2008. *Trust beyond Borders: Immigration, the Welfare State, and Identity in Modern Societies.* Ann Arbor: University of Michigan Press.

Dyson, Kenneth H. F. 2014. *States, Debt, and Power: "Saints" and "Sinners" in European History and Integration.* Oxford: Oxford University Press.

Elazar, Daniel. 1987. *Exploring Federalism.* Tuscaloosa: University of Alabama Press.

Elkins, David, and Richard Simeon, eds. 1980. *Small Worlds: Parties and Provinces in Canadian Political Life.* Agincourt, ON: Methuen.

Erk, Jan, and Lawrence Anderson. 2009. "The Paradox of Federalism: Does Self-Rule Accommodate or Exacerbate Ethnic Divisions?" *Regional and Federal Studies* 19 (2): 191–202.

Erk, Jan, and Edward Koning. 2009. "New Structuralism and Institutional Change: Federalism between Centralization and Decentralization." *Comparative Political Studies* 42 (11): 1–23.

Filippov, M., P. C. Ordeshook, and O. Shvetsova. 2004. *Designing Federalism: A Theory of Self-Sustainable Federal Institutions.* Cambridge: Cambridge University Press.

Fox, Daniel M. 2010. *The Convergence of Science and Governance: Research, Health Policy, and American States.* Berkeley: University of California Press.

Füglister, Katharina. 2012. *Policy Laboratories of the Federal State? The Role of Intergovernmental Cooperation in Health Policy Diffusion in Switzerland*. Baden-Baden: Nomos.

Galligan, Brian. 1995. *A Federal Republic: Australia's Constitutional System of Government*. Melbourne: Cambridge University Press.

Gerber, Elisabeth R., and Ken Kollman. 2004. "Introduction—Authority Migration: Defining an Emerging Research Agenda." *PS* 37 (3): 397–400.

Gerring, John, and Strom C. Thacker. 2008. *A Centripetal Theory of Democratic Governance*. Cambridge: Cambridge University Press.

Gray, Gwendolyn. 2010. "Federalism, Feminism, and Multilevel Governance: The Elusive Search for Theory?" In *Federalism, Feminism, and Multilevel Governance*, edited by Melissa Haussman, Marian Sawer, and Jill Vickers, 19–34. Farnham: Ashgate.

Greer, Scott L. 2019. "Health Policy and Territorial Politics: Disciplinary Misunderstandings and Directions for Research" In *Handbook of Territorial Politics*, edited by Klaus Detterbeck and Eve Hepburn, 232–45. Cheltenham: Edward Elgar.

Greer, Scott L., Heather Elliott, and Rebecca Oliver. 2015. "Differences That Matter: Overcoming Methodological Nationalism in Comparative Social Policy Research." *Journal of Comparative Policy Analysis: Research and Practice* 17 (4): 408–29. https://doi.org/10.1080/13876988.2015.1060713

Greer, Scott L., and Peter D. Jacobson. 2010. "Health Policy and Federalism." *Journal of Health Politics, Policy, and Law* 35 (2): 203–26.

Grossman, Guy, Jan H. Pierskalla, and Emma Boswell Dean. 2017. "Government Fragmentation and Public Goods Provision." *Journal of Politics* 79 (3): 823–40.

Guajardo, Jaime, Daniel Leigh, and Andrea Pescatori. 2011. *Expansionary Austerity: New International Evidence*. IMF Working Paper, International Monetary Fund.

Heidenheimer, Arnold J. 1973. "The Politics of Public Education, Health, and Welfare in the USA and Western Europe: How Growth and Reform Potentials Have Differed." *British Journal of Political Science* 3 (3): 315–40.

Hertel-Fernandez, Alexander. 2014. "Who Passes Business's 'Model Bills'? Policy Capacity and Corporate Influence in US State Politics." *Perspectives on Politics* 12 (3): 582–602.

Hicks, Alexander. 1999. *Social Democracy and Welfare Capitalism: A Century of Income Security Politics*. Ithaca: Cornell University Press.

Hooghe, Liesbet, and Gary Marks. 2016. *Community, Scale, and Regional Governance*. Vol. 2 of *A Postfunctionalist Theory of Governance*. Oxford: Oxford University Press.

Hooghe, Liesbet, Gary Marks, and Arjan H. Schakel. 2010. *The Rise of Regional Authority: A Comparative Study of 42 Democracies*. London: Routledge.

Hooghe, Liesbet, Gary Marks, Arjan H. Schakel, Sandra Chapman Osterkatz, Sara Niedzwiecki, and Sarah Shair-Rosenfield. 2016. *Measuring Regional Authority*. Vol. 1 of *A Postfunctionalist Theory of Governance*. Oxford: Oxford University Press.

Hopkin, Jonathan. 2009. "Party Matters: Devolution and Party Politics in Britain and Spain." *Party Politics* 15 (2): 179–98.

Huber, Evelyne, and John D. Stephens. 2001. *Development and Crisis of the Welfare State: Parties and Policies in Global Markets*. Chicago: University of Chicago Press.

Huntington, Samuel P. 1968. *Political Order in Changing Societies*. New Haven: Yale University Press.

Immergut, Ellen M. 1992. *Health Politics: Interests and Institutions in Western Europe*. Cambridge: Cambridge University Press.

Jeffery, Charlie. 2003. "The German Laender: From Milieu-Shaping to Territorial Politics." In *Germany, Europe, and the Politics of Constraint*, edited by Kenneth Dyson and Klaus Goesz, 97–108. Oxford: Oxford University Press for the British Academy.

Jensen, Carsten, Christoph Knill, Kai Schulze, and Jale Tosun. 2014. "Giving Less by Doing More? Dynamics of Social Policy Expansion and Dismantling in 18 OECD Countries." *Journal of European Public Policy* 21 (4): 528–48.

Jones, David K. 2013. "Politiques de Sante: The Regional Centralization of French Health Policy." In *Decentralization and Federalism in European Health and Social Care*, edited by Joan Costa i Font and Scott L Greer, 208–27. Basingstoke: Palgrave.

Katz, B., and J. Bradley. 2013. *The Metropolitan Revolution: How Cities and Metros Are Fixing Our Broken Politics and Fragile Economy*. Washington, DC: Brookings Institution Press.

Katzenstein, Peter. 1987. *Policy and Politics in West Germany: The Growth of a Semisovereign State*. Philadelphia: Temple University Press.

Katznelson, Ira. 2005. *When Affirmative Action Was White: An Untold History of Racial Inequality in Twentieth-Century America*. New York: Norton.

Kazepov, Yuri, and Eduardo Barberis. 2013. "Social Assistance Governance in Europe: Towards a Multilevel Perspective." In *Minimum Income Protection in Flux*, edited by Ive Marx and Kenneth Nelson, 217–48. London: Palgrave Macmillan.

Keating, Michael. 2009. "Social Citizenship, Solidarity, and Welfare in Regionalized and Plurinational States." *Citizenship Studies* 13 (5): 501–13. https://doi.org/10.1080/13621020903174654

Keating, Michael, and Nicola McEwen. 2005. "Devolution and Public Policy: A Comparative Perspective." *Regional and Federal Studies* 15 (4).

Kleider, Hanna. 2015. "Decentralization and the Welfare State: Territorial Disparities, Regional Governments and Political Parties." PhD diss., University of North Carolina at Chapel Hill.

Lago-Peñas, Ignacio, and Santiago Lago-Peñas. 2011. "Decentralization and the Nationalization of Party Systems." *Environment and Planning C: Government and Policy* 29:244–63.

Lieberman, Robert C. 1998. *Shifting the Color Line: Race and the American Welfare State*. Cambridge: Harvard University Press.

Lieberman, Robert C., and John S. Lapinski. 2001. "American Federalism, Race and the Administration of Welfare." *British Journal of Political Science* 31 (2): 303–29.

Lijphart, Arend. 1984. *Democracies: Patterns of Majoritarian and Consensus Government in Twenty-One Countries*. New Haven: Yale University Press.

Linz, Juan J., and Alfred Stepan. 1992. "Political Identities and Electoral Sequences: Spain, the Soviet Union, and Yugoslavia." *Daedalus* 121 (2): 123–39.

Livingston, W. S. 1952. "A Note on the Nature of Federalism." *Political Science Quarterly* 67 (1): 81–95.

Loughlin, J., F. Hendriks, and A. Lidström. 2011. *The Oxford Handbook of Local and Regional Democracy in Europe*. Oxford: Oxford University Press.

Mabbett, Deborah, and Waltraud Schelkle. 2013. "Searching under the Lamp-Post: The Evolution of Fiscal Surveillance." Paper presented at the 20th International Conference of Europeanists—Crisis and Contingency: States of (In)Stability.

Mair, P. 1997. *Party System Change: Approaches and Interpretations*. Oxford: Clarendon.

Martinez-Vazquez, Jorge, Santiago Lago-Peñas, and Agnese Sacchi. 2017. "The Impact of Fiscal Decentralization: A Survey." *Journal of Economic Surveys* 31 (4): 1095–1129.

McEwen, Nicola. 2002. "State Welfare Nationalism: The Territorial Impact of Welfare State Development in Scotland." *Regional and Federal Studies* 12 (1): 66–90.

Mclean, Iain. 2015. "Spending Too Much, Taxing Too Little? Parliaments in Fiscal Federalism." *European Political Science* 14 (1): 15–27.

Montinola, Gabriella, Yingyi Qian, and Barry R. Weingast. 1995. "Federalism, Chinese Style: The Political Basis for Economic Success in China." *World Politics* 48 (1): 50–81.

Moreno, Luis, and Nicola McEwen. 2005. "Exploring the Territorial Politics of Welfare." In *The Territorial Politics of Welfare*, edited by Nicola McEwen and Luis Moreno, 1–40. London: Routledge.

Musgrave, Richard A. 1959. *The Theory of Public Finance*. New York: McGraw-Hill.

Oates, Wallace E. 2005. "Toward a Second-Generation Theory of Fiscal Federalism." *International Tax and Public Finance* 12 (4): 349–73.

Obinger, Herbert, Stephan Leibfried, and Francis G. Castles, eds. 2005. *Federalism and the Welfare State: New World and European Experiences*. Cambridge: Cambridge University Press.

Peterson, Paul E. 1981. *City Limits*. Chicago: University of Chicago Press.

Peterson, Paul E. 1995. *The Price of Federalism*. Washington, DC: Brookings Institution.

Peterson, Paul E., and Daniel J. Nadler, eds. 2014. *The Global Debt Crisis: Haunting U.S. and European Federalism*. Washington, DC: Brookings Institution Press.

Qian, Yingyi, and Barry R. Weingast. 1997. "Federalism as a Commitment to Preserving Market Incentives." *Journal of Economic Perspectives* 11 (4): 83–92.

Riker, William. 1964. *Federalism: Origins, Operation, Significance*. Boston: Little, Brown.

Riker, William. 1982. *Liberalism against Populism: A Confrontation between the Theory of Democracy and the Theory of Social Choice*. Prospect Heights, IL: Waveland.

Rodden, Jonathan A. 2004. "Comparative Federalism and Decentralization: On Meaning and Measurement." *Comparative Politics* 36 (4): 481–500.

Rodden, Jonathan A. 2005. *Hamilton's Paradox: The Promise and Peril of Fiscal Federalism*. Cambridge: Cambridge University Press.

Rodden, Jonathan A. 2014. "Can Market Discipline Survive in the U.S. Federation?" In *The Global Debt Crisis: Haunting U.S. and European Federalism*, edited by Paul E. Peterson and Daniel Nadler, 40–61. Washington, DC: Brookings Institution Press.

Rodden, Jonathan A., and Susan Rose-Ackerman. 1997. "Does Federalism Preserve Markets?" *Virginia Law Review* 83 (7): 1521–72.

Rogers, Melissa Ziegler. 2016. *The Politics of Place and the Limits of Redistribution*. New York: Routledge.

Scharpf, Fritz. 1988. "The Joint Decision Trap: Lessons from German Federalism and European Integration." *Public Administration* 66 (3): 239–78.

Scruggs, Lyle, and James P. Allan. 2006. "The Material Consequences of Welfare States: Benefit Generosity and Absolute Poverty in 16 OECD Countries." *Comparative Political Studies* 39 (7): 880–904.

Shih, Victor, Christopher Adolph, and Mingxing Liu. 2012. "Getting Ahead in the Communist Party: Explaining the Advancement of Central Committee Members in China." *American Political Science Review* 106 (1): 166–87. https://doi.org/10.1017/S0003055411000566

Snyder, Richard. 2001. "Scaling Down: The Subnational Comparative Method." *Studies in Comparative International Development* 36 (1): 93–110.

Stepan, Alfred. 1998. "Modern Multinational Democracies: Transcending a Gellnerian Oxymoron." In *The State of the Nation: Ernest Gellner and the Theory of Nationalism*, edited by John A Hall, 219–41. Cambridge: Cambridge University Press.

Stepan, Alfred. 1999. "Federalism and Democracy: Beyond the U.S. Model." *Journal of Democracy* 10 (4): 19–34.

Stepan, Alfred. 2001. *Arguing Comparative Politics*. Oxford: Oxford University Press.

Stepan, Alfred, and Juan J. Linz. 2011. "Comparative Perspectives on Inequality and the Quality of Democracy in the United States." *Perspectives on Politics* 9 (4): 841–56. https://doi.org/10.1017/S1537592711003756

Swank, Duane. 2001. "Political Institutions and Welfare State Restructuring: The Impact of Institutions on Social Policy Change in Developed Democracies." In *The New Politics of the Welfare State*, edited by Paul Pierson, 197–236. Oxford: Oxford University Press.

Taylor-Gooby, Peter, ed. 2004. *New Risks, New Welfare: The Transformation of the European Welfare State*. Oxford: Oxford University Press.

Teaford, J. C. 2002. *The Rise of the States: Evolution of American State Government*. Baltimore: Johns Hopkins University Press.

Tiebout, Charles M. 1956. "A Pure Theory of Local Expenditure." *Journal of Political Economy* 64 (5): 416–25.

Vampa, D. 2016. *The Regional Politics of Welfare in Italy, Spain, and Great Britain*. New York: Springer.

Volden, Craig. 2004. "Origin, Operation, and Significance: The Federalism of William H. Riker." *Publius: The Journal of Federalism* 34 (4): 89–108.

Weingast, Barry R. 1995. "The Economic Role of Political Institutions: Market-Preserving Federalism and Economic Development." *Journal of Law, Economics, and Organization* 11 (1): 1–31.

Weingast, Barry R. 2009. "Second Generation Fiscal Federalism: The Implications of Fiscal Incentives." *Journal of Urban Economics* 65 (3): 279–93.

Wibbels, Erik. 2000. "Federalism and the Politics of Macroeconomic Policy and Performance." *American Journal of Political Science* 44 (4): 687–702.

Wibbels, Erik. 2005. *Federalism and the Market: Intergovernmental Conflict and Economic Reform in the Developing World*. Cambridge: Cambridge University Press.

The Secret Life of Territorial Politics

Social Policy in Belgium

Janet Laible

Belgium is a federal system that has devolved considerable authority over social policy to substate actors but that retains an extensive social insurance system at the federal level. Yet Belgium appears to be at a crossroads with respect to funding its social security system and to funding social expenditure more broadly.[1] The social welfare system that initially emerged under a centralized state has been radically transformed by constitutional reforms and the collapse of postwar bargaining patterns, and it has faced more recent challenges from austerity measures. The federalization of Belgium that hived off elements of social welfare to regions and language communities has also empowered them to make policy choices that have undercut central government priorities and that have upset carefully agreed jurisdictions of social policy authority. Thus, while Belgian social welfare was long understood to embody universalistic elements and statewide commitments to social solidarity, distinctive welfare patterns have now emerged across the substate terrain of territorial and linguistic politics. These distinctions reflect substantive policy differences that can matter to citizens' lived experiences of the welfare state. These differences have increasingly been politicized by regionalist and separatist movements in Belgium as well as by pro-Belgium political actors. Regional actors now claim even the basic functions of social security as part of a continuing struggle over the parameters of decentralization. Austerity appears neither to have pushed the state toward a recentralization of social policy nor to have contributed to its further decentralization (or to the subsequent offloading of its costs onto substate budgets), but austerity has amplified existing conflicts over entitlement to central state resources and has illuminated the differential impact of fiscal tightening on the Belgian regions. Across the Belgian state, austerity is replacing the long-standing social policy narratives of equality and social solidarity with a new narrative of efficiency that may do far more to recast the ideological and institutional underpinnings of social welfare than have the decades-long battles over the Belgian constitution.

Furthermore, at a time when the stakes of social welfare politics are high, the patterns of welfare expenditure in Belgium remain difficult to discern, even for the political actors who are contesting those patterns. A discussion of social welfare that focuses solely on the structural characteristics of the welfare state and on the formal policy jurisdictions of the federal constitution is inadequate for capturing the flows of funding and the delivery of benefits in Belgium. Instead, two characteristics of Belgian politics require further attention. First, the properties of the social insurance system obscure the territorial dimensions of social welfare. Some policy differences among substate entities cannot be inferred from published data, and efforts to assign territorial or community responsibility for contributions or outflows run aground on a lack of appropriate information. Second, statutory and informal political bargains may operate with different assumptions and goals than do constitutional pacts regarding social policy, further disguising the tracks of social welfare policymaking. These factors suggest that a straightforward assessment of the impact of decentralization on the welfare state is impossible. In the absence of federalism, the central state certainly would dominate the economics and politics of social welfare. But the development of federalism has created the arenas in which territorial and language politics can get enacted around social policy questions, and it has incentivized policy entrepreneurs to frame social welfare politics in regional and linguistic terms, compounding the challenges of reading social welfare policy directly from a formal institutional script.

Institutional and Political Characteristics

Belgium has been described as a "holding together" federation that emerged subsequent to a process of devolution and in which the substate entities were themselves generated by the dynamics of linguistic politics within a formerly centralized state (Deschouwer 2012, 11). Hence, Belgium possesses unusual institutional characteristics that combine the multilevel properties of a federal system with a variegated substate structure. Although Belgium was created as a unitary state in 1830, political pressure from linguistic and later territorial interests led to a series of major reforms of the state beginning in 1970. Demands for cultural autonomy led to the creation of constitutionally defined cultural (language) communities (Dutch-speaking or Flemish, French-speaking, and German-speaking), and calls for greater autonomy over economic and social policy were met with a new constitutional principle of regional autonomy for three territorial units: Flanders, Wallonia, and the Brussels-Capital Region.[2] When its 1993 constitution came into effect, Belgium became a formally federal state with separately directly elected representative bodies of the regions (the Dutch and French communities have indirectly elected parliaments and executives; the twenty-five members of the German community parliament are directly elected).

Social policy in Belgium is thus produced and implemented in a federal state that has atypical constituent units and highly complex territorial relations. The federalization of the Belgian state has included the extensive devolution of authority over many areas of social policy that were once under the purview of the central (now federal) government to the regions and communities; the federal government retains only a limited policy role for Belgium as a whole. The policy jurisdictions of the regions are those that have a territorial basis, broadly construed to include economic affairs and a degree of fiscal policy (but excluding monetary policy), land use and planning, housing, the environment, agriculture, water policy, transportation, public works and infrastructure, industrial policy, rural development, some aspects of energy policy, and employment policy (see Belgium.be). Regional social policy expenditure should thus largely be found in employment policy and in aspects of infrastructure such as housing. The language communities were granted authority over policies with cultural and "personalizable" aspects, including cultural policy, tourism, media, and the use of languages. This authority also gives the communities a sizable role in social policy, including vocational training and most other forms of education, areas of health policy, and aid to people (youth, families, immigrant accommodation, and social aid). The federal government retains authority over the traditional areas of high politics—that is, defense and foreign affairs. Regions and communities may make foreign treaties on subjects that fall under their jurisdiction. Social security, including the social insurance system of health care, and some other areas of public health remain under federal jurisdiction.

The already-complex constitutional framework has generated a number of institutional asymmetries, resulting in observations that Belgium represents a strong case of both formal (juridical) and informal and political (de facto) asymmetries as a federal system (Swenden 2002). These asymmetries complicate the picture of social policy expenditure, obscuring expenditure flows in certain respects and making explicit comparisons across similar types of units (i.e., across regions or communities) impossible in many cases.

First, Brussels is formally the only bilingual region in Belgium, with the practical effect that residents of the Brussels-Capital Region may opt for public services to be provided in either French or Dutch. The exercise of community responsibilities in Brussels is conducted by three community commissions.[3] However, there is no linguistic census of Brussels, nor are residents assigned to a community or required to remain in the same one (although candidates for party electoral lists must specify a community and cannot later change that choice) (Deschouwer 2006, 904). Thus, comparisons of expenditures by the two communities on "their" constituents in the Brussels-Capital Region must rely on population estimates: most sources converge on an estimate of a 90 percent French-speaking population and a 10 percent Dutch-speaking population. However, the absence of a linguistic census means that all estimates of per capita social welfare expenditure by community must be interpreted with care (Fédération Wallonie-Bruxelles 2015, 34). Nor is it possible directly to compare the policy authority of the community commissions: the French Community Commission has a degree of legislative autonomy granted by the French Community and may legislate in areas such as curative health care and personal welfare, while the Flemish Community Commission cannot.

Second, substate politics have driven asymmetric institution building in ways that can make expenditure flows even more opaque. Each region and community initially had its own legislative body. However, the Flemish Region and the Dutch-speaking community fused their authorities because these populations are largely coterminous, and the Flemish Region now manages the combined budgets for regional and community matters. The French-language community and the Walloon Region are not coterminous. Thus, comparing social welfare expenditure in the French Community and the Dutch Community (or in Wallonia and the Flemish Region) becomes either an impossible task or an exercise in forensic accounting. The Flemish budget does not separate "regional" from "community" expenditures, and only an effort to extract precise budget items attributable to either a "territorial" or a "personalizable" policy domain would enable comparisons with other subunits. (The published data rarely take a form that could support such comparisons.) In practice,

Flemish politicians have the freedom to shift money between budget items in ways that their counterparts in other territorial subunits do not. In theory, Flemish leaders could therefore respond to a reduction in the federal grants to either regions or communities by moving funds between purportedly regional and community priorities as politically desirable—for example, from health care infrastructure to the delivery of personal welfare services.

Third, the authority of the French-language community does not extend to the areas of Wallonia that are under the jurisdiction of the German-language community (which is geographically contained within the borders of Wallonia) but does extend to French-language institutions of the Brussels-Capital Region. (The authority of the Dutch-language community similarly extends to analogous institutions in the Brussels-Capital Region.) Expenditure data from Wallonia often separate statistics for the German Community to the extent that regional policy jurisdiction extends over this community.

Finally, in a number of linguistically complex areas, so-called facilities are provided if the members of the nonmajority language community constitute a large share of the local population: they may seek primary education as well as some public services and documents in their language. Thus the assertion of personalizable rights may contribute to a variegated social welfare map within certain areas of the country.

In addition to its complex institutional terrain, Belgium has long been an arena in which an intricately balanced set of political mechanisms governs policymaking at the center of the state (now the federal level). Belgian social welfare was managed for decades under the logic of consociational bargaining, with the country's ideological and later linguistic "pillar" parties as the stewards of social welfare policymaking and administration.[4] In a twist that makes Belgian consociationalism uniquely complex, the postwar ideological pillars—Catholic, Social Democrat, and Liberal—and their party analogues were overlain with linguistic and territorial politics, tendencies that grew increasingly important in the electoral arena by the 1970s.[5] Constitutional reforms in 1970 cemented consociational practices in the federal arena, institutionalizing bargaining by linguistic groups. After this point, increasing segmentation occurred along language lines, producing a bipolar system in which the two main language groups were "condemned to find a negotiated way out of all conflicts," with few remaining institutions to bridge the divide between communities (Deschouwer 1999, 105; Deschouwer 2006, 902).[6] Federal elections often produced unwieldy coalitions of up to six parties, with the larger parties insisting on the inclusion of their linguistic sisters as a condition for coalition formation. This contributed to stability (and predictability) in coalition governments until the twenty-first century, but it also empowered minor parties as veto players within coalition governments and brought language issues into the heart of federal politics.

Despite the erosion of the traditional pillars and their related political parties (and the increasing fragmentation of party politics at the federal level), consociationalism remains crucial for decision making (Deschouwer 2006). The old pillar parties remain deeply entrenched in public administration, with the management of social welfare and social security largely in the hands of these parties and their parastatal organizations. Christian, social democratic, and liberal organizations remain key agents in the delivery of social services and education, and the pillar parties serve key roles in recruiting and promoting personnel in the administration of social policy (Deschouwer 2009; Swenden, Brans, and De Winter 2006).

Financing the Welfare State(s) in Belgium

Belgium is generally categorized with the social-insurance model welfare states, similar to Germany and the Netherlands, although its social security system also has NHS-style elements and it has a significant amount of private expenditure specifically in health care. Social security in Belgium remains under the authority of the federal government and includes a variety of social insurance programs that are intended to promote social solidarity: in principle, the federal government retains jurisdiction over income-replacing and cost-covering benefits.[7] The system technically has three "tracks" (for salaried workers, the self-employed, and civil servants), but in all cases the payment of benefits is made through a range of functionally specific parastatal organizations. The system for salaried workers is the largest: the National Office for Social Security collects the social charges assessed on employers and employees and directs funds to the relevant parastatal payment institutions. Benefits include family allowances, unemployment benefits, pensions, sickness and disability insurance, workplace injury insurance, occupational disease insurance, and annual vacation funds. Some variations exist between manual workers and white-collar workers. Belgian social security is financed by social security contributions and general taxation, which may be used by the federal government to make up the difference between projected expenses and actual social security contributions. (For more details on health care financing, see Laible 2013.)[8] As of January 1, 2015, the total contribution of a salaried private sector employee was 13.07 percent of gross salary, and the total basic contribution of the employer was 24.92 percent; Belgium has the highest labor tax wedge in the OECD (Service Public Fédéral, Social Security 2016, 22; IMF 2015). There is also some limited federal spending on social welfare outside the social security system.

The funding of substate governments is a complex mix. The fiscal autonomy of regions and communities ranks low in comparison to substate actors in other federal systems (although this been shifting toward greater autonomy for the regions in recent years). However, substate units possess a high degree of financial autonomy and can allocate their resources as they choose within the boundaries of their legal competencies (Van Rompuy 2010, 117; Swenden 2009, 8). Beginning with the state reforms of 1980, regions and communities were granted the right to tax, although community and regional finances derived almost entirely from federal transfers until the 1988 reforms (Hooghe, Schakel, and Marks 2008a, 212). With the extension of new policy competencies to the substate level from 1989, the financing of regions and communities also received an overhaul. Regions received authority over a range of regional taxes, with different degrees of autonomy.[9] More important, after 1995, regions were granted the autonomy to change the tax base, tax rate, and exemptions of personal income tax within certain limits. However, the regions secured their largest sources of revenue from a tax-sharing arrangement based on federal personal income tax (PIT). Community financial sources were newly transformed with a share of PIT and value-added tax (VAT), and they received a federal grant linked to the share of foreign students receiving a university education in either community.[10]

State reforms after 2001 were premised on maintaining vertical budgetary neutrality; with the increased tax autonomy of the regions and the transfer of revenue from what would become new regional taxes, the federal government reduced the PIT transfer to the regions and shifted it to the communities (Algoed 2009, 3). The regions gained additional power to set the base and rate of some new taxes, achieving full fiscal autonomy over twelve taxes, and received broader authority to change the rate of PIT. However, the Special Majority Law on the Funding of the Communities and Regions established that regardless of their powers and policy jurisdictions, the regions should not take actions that would lead to unfair tax competition. The complex negotiations to form a Belgian government in 2011 led to additional reforms. In 2014 the regions gained greater fiscal autonomy when they, along with federal and municipal authorities, received the ability to impose personal income taxes. This amount was initially equal to an amount mitigated by the federal level but in the future could be adjusted within limits. Regions can also grant tax reductions in limited areas.

Reforms have also affected community revenues. By 2008, effectively all community revenues were derived from VAT and PIT transfers (Swenden 2009, 6). The VAT transfer, like the PIT transfer, was linked to inflation (and after 2012 to a percentage of the growth rate of national income), which would then be adjusted to reflect school-age populations. Finally, about a fifth of VAT transfers would be linked to the communities taxraising capacity following the *juste retour* principle that "tax receipts should correspond to a community's contributions to the shared tax" (Hooghe, Schakel, and Marks 2008a, 212).

Currently, substate finances rely heavily on a PIT grant from the federal level, including an equalization mechanism across the regions, with VAT revenue also transferred to the communities.[11] Flanders still derives most of its revenue from federal transfers, as Wallonia did until 2009, when its proportion of regional spending from federal government transfers dipped below 50 percent; only a little more than a third of regional spending in Brussels comes from transfers from central government (see table 1). In all three regions, reliance on central government transfers for spending initially declined slightly after the onset of the recession. However, the complicated history of substate financing in Belgium suggests caution in comparing data over time, particularly given recent changes to the fiscal autonomy of the regions and the evolving spending responsibilities of the substate actors. The comparative interpretation of expenditure data is complicated by the fusion of the Flemish Region and the Dutch-Speaking Community, which makes Flemish Regional spending incommensurable with that of the other regions.

TABLE 1. Proportion of Regional Spending from Central Government Transfers

	2008 (%)	2009 (%)	2010 (%)	2011 (%)
Flemish Region	69.5	66.8	65.3	68.0
Walloon Region	51.3	49.3	49.0	48.3
Brussels-Capital Region	36.7	34.3	36.0	35.1

Source: Based on BISA/IBSA, *Perspectives Régionales 2015–2020: Annex Statistique* (2015), Spreadsheet Tab 17.

Note: To calculate central government transfers, the author combined the categories "Transfers of Fiscal Receipts," "Other Transfers—From the Federal Power," and "Other Transfers—From Social Security" from "Receipts" in Regional Accounts (Categories D1, D2a, and D2c).

Equalization and Redistribution

Like many federal systems, Belgium operates a system of equalization transfers to promote horizontal equity across regions. After the 1989 funding reforms, an equalization grant was introduced to compensate for changes from the previous formula and for regional inequalities. Specifically, because the new system of financing would work to the benefit of Flanders, the wealthiest region, a solidarity payment was introduced. If a region has per capita PIT revenue lower than the national average, it receives annually €11.6 (inflation-adjusted) per inhabitant, multiplied by the percentage difference of regional PIT per capita from the national average (Algoed 2009, 2). Technically this is a vertical transfer, not a horizontal one. Wealthier regions do not contribute to this payment; rather, the federal government withholds it from the PIT transferred annually to the regions. In practice, Wallonia has remained a receiving region since the creation of the equalization mechanism,, the Brussels-Capital Region became a receiving region in 1997, and Flanders has never been a receiving region (Van Rompuy 2010, 112). Swenden (2009) has argued that the shares of PIT and VAT that remain with the federal government constitute an equalization mechanism, given that for more than two decades Flanders has contributed more and it ultimately gets redistributed to the other regions. Thus, despite the decrease over time of the equalization grants per se, equalization continues through the federal government's role as a mechanism for promoting solidarity. A final form of equalization exists in a federal special-purpose grant to regions as a form of compensation for labor market policy success: the grant is given for each unemployed person for whom the region creates a job.[12]

Data on the distribution and redistribution of social benefits also serve as indicators of how the state and parastatal institutions respond to inequality and risk. Expenditure data from Belgium between 2008 and 2011 indicate that while the central state is the dominant provider of social security, some of this expenditure is managed by regional and community governments, enabling a reading of where and for whom insurance against risk is directed. The data also draw attention to the ways in which substate governments use central and their own resources to structure different welfare experiences for their constituents. Citizens' needs for social benefits may reflect social or economic characteristics of their region or community, yet their ability to secure equal access to benefits may also be shaped by these variables. The data also hint at the ways in which differing expenditure patterns among regions and communities can be difficult to interpret.

The category of benefits and services directed toward those between the ages of 18 and 64 illustrates the underlying tendencies in the
Belgian welfare state.[13] This category represents the third-largest area
of social welfare expenditure after health and pensions. Per capita
spending in this category confirms the predominance of the central
state as the core of social security: from funding provided by the central state, the center itself distributes the largest share, although this
share has declined since the onset of the economic crisis of 2008 relative to the share of central state funding spent by the regions (see table
2). This funding largely derives from social insurance charges, and
central-state-attributed expenditure is disbursed by insurance parastatals as well as by the federal government to individuals. Of the three
regions, Flanders spends the smallest share of central state funding on
18–64 benefits, with the shares spent by Brussels and Wallonia con-
verging since 2008. No clear pattern of change in the expenditure of
regionally derived revenues in this category is evident in the four years
following the onset of economic contraction: spending by the Flemish
government increased, spending by Wallonia fluctuated, and spending
by the Brussels-Capital Region initially increased but later declined.
The initial impression is that the central state redistributes a greater
share of its resources in this area of benefits and services to Wallonia
and Brussels and that Flanders spends far more of its own resources

TABLE 2. Per Capita Expenditures for Benefits and Services, Ages 18–64 (€)

	Central State Sources				Regional Sources			
	2008	2009	2010	2011	2008	2009	2010	2011
Federal/Central Government	4,461.55	3,087.99	3,115.87	3,322.60				
Flemish Region	1,246.15	1,462.47	1,484.39	1,486.39	842.32	907.26	928.44	960.67
Walloon Region	1,701.41	1,876.52	1,917.53	1,945.59	373.60	444.31	402.88	412.96
Brussels-Capital Region	1,640.58	1,759.25	1,870.52	1,928.20	552.15	570.63	464.04	502.02

Source: Author calculations, based on data from the following: Service Public Fédéral Budget et Contrôle
de la Gestion, Base Documentaire Générale, Rapport Annuel (Brussels: 2009, 2010, 2011, 2012); Office
National des Pensions, Statistique annuelle des bénéficiares des prestations (Brussels: 2011); Service des Pensions du Secteur Public (online); OECD Social Protection and Well-Being Statistics online, Belgium; IN-
AMI, Statistiques Indemnités 2012 (Brussels: INAMI, Service des indemnities—Direction finances et statistiques, 2012); ONEM, Rapport Annuel 2011 (online); ONAFTS/Famifed, Activités (Brussels: 2008, 2009,
2010, 2011) and Le régime des allocations familiales des indépendants 2009–2010 (Brussels: 2011).

Note: Results are reported per population aged 18–64 in each region and in Belgium for the Federal/
Central category. In the calculations for expenditure per capita in the regions, all of the community commissions are added to the expenditure of the Brussels-Capital Region, and the total is divided by the population of the Brussels-Capital Region.

per capita on benefits for its regional 18–64 age-group than do either Wallonia or Brussels (around twice as much).

A closer examination of this category of benefits reveals deeper dynamics. In some areas such as survivor benefits, guaranteed income, and benefits for the handicapped, no regional expenditures occur, meaning that distribution occurs directly from the central state or federal level to those who are entitled to these social insurance benefits. In other areas, the redistributive tendencies of social welfare over territory appear justified by the geographical concentration of populations entitled to benefits. For example, per capita spending on active labor market policy, unemployment, and related benefits is higher in Wallonia and Brussels than in Flanders (see table 3): these funds are directed from the main social insurance parastatal to the regions, and expenditures overall have increased since 2008. (Benefits from the federal government are negligible and in fact declined from 2008 through 2011.) Yet unemployment is also much higher in Wallonia and Brussels during this period; it is unremarkable that areas with higher unemployment might spend more per capita on labor market activation and related policies than a region with lower unemployment. The population of Flanders is also older than that of the other two regions, so a smaller share of the population requires this support. Furthermore, beyond its funding from the central government, the Flemish Region spends an additional amount on its regional population—from €132 per capita in 2008 to €149 per capita in 2011—on labor market activation and related services (Service Public Fédéral Budget et Contrôle de la Gestion 2009, 2010, 2011, 2012). Thus, while one can make the case that the central state redistributes resources to areas with higher unemployment and younger populations, these regions, Wallonia and Brussels, may also lack the ability to invest their own resources in labor market support,

TABLE 3. Per Capita Active Labor Market Policy, Unemployment, and Related Benefits Expenditures from Central-Attributed Resources (€)

	2008	2009	2010	2011
Flemish Region	1173.80	1387.77	1408.91	1412.33
Walloon Region	1670.53	1845.05	1886.37	1914.01
Brussels-Capital Region	1599.79	1718.93	1830.73	1891.99

Source: Service Public Fédéral Budget et Contrôle de la Gestion, Base Documentaire Générale, *Rapport Annuel* (Brussels: 2009, 2010, 2011, 2012); ONEM, *Rapport Annuel 2011*, 107 (data for 2011 are estimates).

Note: Per capita figures are author calculations, with reference to population between the ages of 18 and 64.

and the relative advantages of Flanders enable it to invest in social services to an extent that the other regions cannot.

The structural weakness of Wallonia's economy is a telling comparative aspect of its social welfare profile. The relative indebtedness of the Walloon regional government as a percentage of regional GDP is strikingly and persistently higher than that of Flanders or the Brussels-Capital Region. In 2011, regional government debt in Wallonia reached 19.2 percent of regional GDP, compared to 8.1 percent in Flanders and 6.0 percent in Brussels (Banque Nationale de Belgique/National Bank of Belgium, BelgoStat; Institut des Comptes Nationaux 2014, 26). In this context, Wallonia's ability to respond to the social vulnerability of its population may be constrained, and the redistributive capacity of the Belgian state through social security thus plays a critical role in mitigating social risk in the region.

Yet the welfare state's function in underpinning Belgium-wide social solidarity has come under increasing political pressure in recent decades. Postwar Belgian elites agreed on the principle that the social security system should be universal and identical across the country and that its protections would represent and promote *national* interpersonal solidarity (Dandoy and Baudewyns 2005). However debates about the overall equity of the system, including the principles by which social welfare is financed and allocated, have more recently focused on regional differences in welfare expenditure and Wallonia's "disproportionate" reliance on central state resources. Flemish nationalists seeking greater autonomy or independence for Flanders have argued that their region contributes more to public finances and specifically to social welfare funds; an economically weaker Wallonia, with its more vulnerable population, is depicted as more dependent on the redistributive welfare state (and thereby on Flemish contributions). Flemish political actors have also argued in favor of decentralizing social security on grounds of efficiency: structural differences between regions could be better accommodated with appropriate policies. Nationalism thus represents a claim about distributional politics and economic sovereignty as much as an assertion of political sovereignty (Béland and Lecours 2005a, 2005b).

Walloon and Francophone politicians respond with appeals that social security is intrinsic to Belgian social and ultimately political citizenship. The Francophone political parties overwhelmingly support the continuation of a national system of universal benefits, and the main trade unions and business associations have also largely supported national social security (Dandoy and Baudewyns 2005). Data depicting implicit transfers among the Belgian regions bear out the argument that Wallonia and Brussels receive a net implicit transfer: approximately .74 percent of GDP for Wallonia and .24 percent of GDP for Brussels in 1999. Flanders at this time was a net payer of implicit transfers of .98 percent of GDP (Dandoy and Baudewyns 2005, 157). The dynamics of constitutional reform in Belgium have rendered this conflict in starker terms at the opening of the twenty-first century. Social security remains one of the few major policy areas under the jurisdiction of the central state; any claims for further decentralization that serve the interests of Flemish political actors inevitably invoke questions about the fairness of Walloon claims on what are argued to be Flemish resources.

Interpreting Social Welfare Expenditure

Despite the apparently clear picture that emerges about de facto equalization and redistribution across Belgian regions, inequalities in the social welfare system may be more difficult to interpret than most observers recognize. The characteristics of Belgian social policy and its financing mechanisms suggest that expenditures can be separated into three distinct areas: funds spent directly by the federal government on a limited range of welfare objectives; regional and community expenditures on social welfare; and expenditures by the social insurance parastatals. However, both the social insurance system and territorial politics at the substate level complicate efforts to analyze the functional and spatial distributions of welfare expenditure. Social insurance in particular blurs the territorial dimensions of welfare expenditure, first with its requirement that observers distinguish between *federal* policy outputs and *central* government outputs in the form of social insurance parastatal activity, and second in its inconsistent acknowledgment of the roles of regions or communities in the distributional politics of welfare.

Belgium's federal tier of government is conceptually and practically distinct from the administrative bodies of the state that manage the country's social insurance. At the federal level, revenue from social charges is specifically transferred to central parastatals (e.g., the National Office for Social Security for salaried workers). Thus, arguments that equate federal spending on social benefits with social security expenditures will significantly underestimate total expenditures by omitting federal transfers to parastatals: functionally specific *federal* spending categories such as health reveal nothing about the ultimate expenditure targets of the billions of euros generated by social charges and transferred to the social security administrations. These transfers are nested within the broader federal budget category of "Transfers of Revenue to the Social Security Administrations" in the annual reports of the Service Public Fédéral Budget et Contrôle de la Gestion.[14] The details of the ultimate disbursal of these transfers are provided in the annual reports of the social insurance parastatals. Table 4 illustrates the challenges of assuming that federal data capture the whole story of central government spending on health. Federal spending in recent years represents less than 15 percent of total central government spending on health care.

The social insurance system also challenges efforts to assign territoriality or language community to social insurance expenditures. A reading of parastatal documents demonstrates that these categories are inconsistently applied as parameters in publicly available data. The public's ability to raise questions about the distributional politics of social security is thus hobbled by a lack of detail about who receives certain types of benefits and where beneficiaries are located. Nuanced arguments about who is financing whom and about whether certain regions or communities contribute more to (or benefit more from) particular categories become challenging or impossible.

An overemphasis on Belgium's social insurance characteristics may lead observers to overlook spending by other levels of government. In areas such as health and old-age benefits, social insurance represents the bulk of expenditures. However, the federal government, regions, and communities all have nontrivial spending commitments in these areas. This may be particularly surprising with respect to old-age spending, given the entrenchment of pensions at the heart of the national insurance system: the three regions, the German community, and the Joint Community Commission in Brussels all record spending on old-age benefits.

TABLE 4. Central Government Expenditures on Health (Thousands of €)

	2009	2010	2011
Federal government expenditure	2,999,036.00	3,808,540.00	3,069,026.00
Social insurance expenditure	22,940,333.28	23,347,281.81	24,557,130.72
Total central government expenditure	25,939,369.28	27,155,821.81	27,626,156.72
Federal expenditure as share of total central expenditure	11.6%	14.0%	11.1%

Source: For federal government spending, see Service Public Fédéral Budget et Contrôle de la Gestion, Base Documentaire Générale, *Rapport Annuel* (Brussels: 2010, 2011, 2012); for social insurance expenditure, see INAMI, *Statistiques des soins de santé* (2009–2010, 2011–2012; FMP, *Rapport annuel statistique* (Brussels: Fonds des Maladies Professionelles, 2009, 2010, 2011); and Banque Nationale de Belgique, www.nbe.be/fr/statistiques

In the category of benefits available to those aged 18–64, substate authorities act alongside the social security parastatals to fulfill jurisdictional obligations—for example, for family benefits, incapacity benefits, and a range of uncategorized benefits. In housing, the data indicate that regions are uniquely responsible for expenditures; in other areas (e.g., active labor market and related benefits), one region may take action while the others do not. (In this case, the Flemish Region records expenditures along with the federal government and the employment parastatal ONEM, but the other regions do not.) A focus on Belgium-wide social insurance is justified given the proportion of spending on social benefits that occurs at this level. However, ignoring substate expenditures means losing the ability to analyze how regions and communities respond to social risks given their jurisdictions and resources as well as the ability to understand how they prioritize social policy choices.

Politics at the substate level similarly complicates efforts to plot the trajectories of social welfare expenditures. Federal constitutional bargains that purported to structure responsibilities for social spending have been upended by regional or community bargains that may ignore the preferences of federal actors in favor of substate priorities. These priorities blur neat divisions between regional and community jurisdictions and have reintroduced a territorial dimension to federal agreements that were carefully crafted to protect "personalizable" policy areas at the community level, thereby raising questions about the functions that the complex architecture of Belgian federalism is intended to serve.

The de facto asymmetries described earlier in this chapter represent aspects of a highly dynamic federal system in which the substate units continue to renegotiate and shift authority horizontally, even across types of subunits. Actions by the Walloon Region, for example, raise questions about the meaningfulness of linking territory (space) and areas of social policy. In 2005, Wallonia transferred to the German Community the "regional" competency of employment policy for its constituents. (Other regional competencies outside of social policy have also been transferred, including rural planning and the management of monuments and sites.) The Walloon government retains jurisdiction over these issues on the residual parts of its territory. The fact that many German speakers happened to live in areas with structural unemployment as a consequence of the decline of heavy industry challenged the neat distinction between territorial and personalizable politics envisioned by federal constitutional arrangements. Instead, efforts to implement appropriate policy solutions drove a pragmatic response: the transfer of labor market activation policies to administrators who were linguistically and territorially best placed to deliver them to German speakers.

In another subversion of the territory/community distinction, the French Community has transferred extensive competencies to Wallonia, including vocational training (considered an aspect of education) and a range of personalizable policy areas such as health policy (except for university hospitals), most family policy, aspects of social welfare, and the integration of immigrants, the disabled, and the elderly. However, Wallonia has jurisdiction in these areas only for French speakers, not for German speakers. Again, arguments about adjusting policy jurisdictions to resolve on-the-ground challenges won out over earlier claims that had established territory and personhood as distinct principles.

The intermeshing of linguistic and territorial politics featured in Belgian politics even before the emergence of the current federal system. Deschouwer (2012, 11) notes that debates about language use have "been settled in a more or less territorial way, which resulted after many piecemeal changes . . . in something that came to be labeled a federation." The 1963 legal construction of the language border, which established a formal demarcation line between language communities and the bilingual area of Brussels, illustrates the complexity of trying to keep community and territorial policymaking distinct. The fusion of the Flemish Region and Dutch Community parliaments is the clearest case of a substate settlement that dissolves the conceptual and political distinctions between territory and language community. However, the German Community represents a subtler example of how efforts to recognize community jurisdictions can depend on and activate territorial understandings of politics.

Beyond the transfer of regional jurisdictions from Wallonia to the German Community, efforts to respect the personalizable rights of German speakers consistently invoke *territorial* attributes of this community. Walloon policies that pertain to French speakers are understood to operate on territory outside the areas where German speakers live. Walloon and French Community documents refer specifically to policies that do or do not operate on the nine cantons of the German Community (Fédération Wallonie-Bruxelles 2012, 9). These understandings of territory shift policy debates from who German speakers are—that is, their personalizable rights and interests—to where they live. Supposedly personalizable rights get recast as territorial ones, calling into question the idea of a distinct domain of rights adhering to people as members of a language community. From a perspective of analyzing social policy, this conceptual murkiness indicates not only that straightforward comparisons among substate units should be approached with caution but also that the basic categorical framework of social policy jurisdictions in Belgium may have limited utility.

The substate bargains that produce these jurisdictional shifts also leave traces in social welfare expenditure data that escape straightforward interpretation. Apparently odd expenditure patterns seem to contradict the general framework of established policy jurisdictions. Substate entities in some circumstances have chosen to remit funds horizontally to the region or community that has taken on a policy responsibility. In these cases, social policy revenue derives not from regular funding sources but from a transfer from another region or community; expenditures reflect similar horizontal transfers from the remitting entity.[15] In addition, there are cases where a Belgian parastatal has taken over the payment of benefits from one substate entity but not the others. For example, FAMIFED/ONAFTS (family benefits for salaried workers) reports taking over the payment of certain family benefits from the Flemish Community, ranging from 335 million euros to 387 million euros. Interpreting social welfare expenditure therefore involves recognizing the formal distribution of policy jurisdictions over space and over people; the political bargains that substate actors have concluded among one another; and policy legacies that stretch back in time and that impose commitments even after jurisdictional changes have occurred.

Change (at What Cost?)

In the wake of global and regional economic slowdown, the amenability of the Belgian social welfare system to change has become an increasingly salient political concern. Although governments have attempted to reduce public spending since Belgium committed to joining the eurozone in the 1990s, social expenditure has been stubbornly resistant to change, and only recently have federal budgetary politics appeared likely to break the impasse. Belgium confronts multiple policy challenges with a need to address high public debt and spending obligations and with intensifying debate over the impact of high tax rates on growth and competitiveness. While Belgium significantly reduced its debt-to-GDP ratio from 131 percent in 1995 to 87 percent in 2007, expenditures outstripped GDP growth for more than a decade and were only modestly reduced during the peak of the economic crisis (IMF 2015, 15). At the beginning of 2017, public debt stood at 103 percent of GDP (Berns 2018).

After nearly a decade of recession, the commitments of eurozone membership continue to pressure Belgian governments to manage debt with structural reform. In late 2014, the European Commission cautioned Belgium that its draft budget for 2015 indicated noncompliance with the debt rule of the Stability and Growth Pact (i.e., a debt ratio of less than 60 percent of GDP) and that it could face a debt-based excessive deficit procedure (European Central Bank December 2014, 82–84). Nonetheless, taking into account a range of factors, the commission concluded in May 2015 that Belgium "should be considered" in compliance with the debt criterion and that it was "close" on excess deficit. The commission predicted that the debt ratio would peak at 106.9 percent in 2015 and then decline in the medium term but noted that sustained structural changes would be necessary to avoid "slippage" (European Commission 2015, 3–4).

International institutions have also focused on Belgium's need to cut expenditures, particularly on entitlement programs, and to undertake wide-ranging reforms to meet debt and deficit targets, to promote competitiveness, and to create a climate for sustainable growth. Public expenditures remain high by European standards, driven largely by social spending: aggregate social expenditure in Belgium measured 26.7 percent of GDP in 2008, 29.1 percent of GDP in 2009, 28.8 percent of GDP in 2010, and 29.4 percent of GDP in 2011—the third-highest in the OECD in 2011 after France and Denmark (OECD Stats Extracts). When Charles Michel's government was formed in 2014, social benefits still absorbed more than 25 percent of GDP, the second-highest level in the EU after France (IMF 2016). The IMF has noted that during the economic crisis, social spending growth in Belgium was driven by health care, pensions, and sickness benefits, as opposed to unemployment benefits (although unemployment benefits in 2010 represented nearly 4 percent of GDP, the highest in the OECD). Furthermore, spending on social protection and health care grew more than it did in other European countries during the first years of the economic crisis and continued to rise even after fiscal tightening was introduced (IMF 2015, 23). As an additional challenge, the aging population of Belgium will continue to require increased spending on care under the current system: in 2013, the commission reported that the costs of long-term care, health, and pensions would increase by 2 percent of GDP from 2010 to 2020 (European Commission 2013, 4; see also IMF 2016).

Both the OECD and the commission have criticized the weight of social spending in the federal budget, noting that in Belgium, as in a number of other eurozone countries, insufficient progress has occurred in shifting expenditures toward more growth-friendly areas (European Central Bank December 2014, 84; European Central Bank August 2015, 53; OECD 2017). These institutions have also urged Belgium to foster a more entre-preneurial business climate by reforming its tax structure and wage-setting system, singling out Belgium's labor taxes as a long-term drag on the country's competitiveness and its job creation potential, although the OECD notes that progress has been made since 2015 (European Commis-sion 2013, 4; European Commission 2015, 3; OECD 2017, 32, 34).

Belgium's political dynamics might suggest that the social welfare sys-tem can be highly responsive to political demands for restructuring. How-ever, at the level of federal politics, legacies of consociational bargaining cemented protections for the language communities that could block painful changes in policies or spending. Nonetheless, although the central state retains control of key areas of social security, the ability of the tradi-tional pillar parties to dominate its management has given way under the weight of new electoral coalitions and voting patterns. Federal politics since the summer 2014 elections signals that in some ways, consociational bargaining has been upended: new players that have entered the political arena are intent on permanently burying the old bargaining mechanisms. As early as 1990, Liberal leaders had argued that Belgian public adminis-tration was a closed system that was divided between the Catholic and Socialist pillars and that greater democracy and market influence were needed to break down those privileges (Deschouwer 2009, 12). The gov-ernment formed by Michel in October 2014 represented a coalition of center-right and liberal parties that committed itself to significant eco-nomic reforms, including austerity measures, to achieve its priorities of job creation and competitiveness. It is notable that the Parti Socialiste (the Socialist Party of the French community)—once the most vocal in favor of maintaining Belgium's commitment to an extensive, redistributive social security system—was not represented in the federal government coalition for the first time in twenty-five years. Furthermore, the coalition deal that brought the Flemish nationalist N-VA party into government was pre-mised on an agreement *not* to pursue further institutional reform and to focus on economic reform (Sinardet 2014). The coalition was described as the first in decades that could pursue a free-market agenda and implement major economic reforms ("Brussels Protests" 2014).

The coalition's argument about the importance of structural reforms for improving the overall health of the Belgian economy drew on concerns about the tax structure of the state and on arguments that growth in public spending was unsustainable. Proposed fiscal measures for 2015–18 included spending cuts of 1.9 percent of GDP, falling mostly on social security spending: of the planned 8 billion euros in spending cuts, nearly 65 percent came from social security (5.2 billion euros). Within social security, approximately 2.9 billion euros was cut from health care, with smaller amounts cut from pensions (including early retirement), unemployment benefits, sickness and disability benefits, child benefits, and other areas, including operating costs. A reduction in labor taxes of 2.8 billion euros (about 0.7 percent of GDP) would be offset by revenue increases from some excise taxes, early taxation of retirement savings, broadening the VAT base, taxation of the financial sector and financial transactions, and some other measures (IMF 2015, 21).

The government's announcement of its intention to balance the budget by 2018, largely through austerity measures and tax reform, set off protests by labor unions and their supporters, who had particular concerns about government plans to raise the pensionable age, to freeze public sector wages through temporary deindexation, and to cut public services. These protests reemerged following subsequent annual budgets. By 2016, even the IMF cautioned that further reforms should be sensitive to protecting social cohesion (IMF 2016). Economic reforms would also have an impact at the substate level to an extent that did not occur with previous efforts at economic reform. Given the variations in dependence of the regions and communities on transfers from the federal government, solutions to the economic challenges faced by the central state would reverberate across the territorial units but would not do so equally. A burden-sharing agreement reached before the current government was installed committed the regions and communities to contributing 0.6 percent of GDP in 2015–16 for the consolidation of public finances, with additional commitments possible with the 2015 Stability Program.

Conclusions

By creating and empowering substate actors in social policy, federalism has enabled these actors to introduce a degree of flexibility into the priorities of social welfare. This flexibility, however, has produced regional differentiation that challenges the egalitarian ethos of social security. Some aspects of differentiation derive from the choices of substate actors regarding funding priorities. Other aspects emerge from demographic or other local conditions over which political authorities may have little control. While the equalization mechanisms of social security are intended to mitigate this outcome, the dynamics of federalism acknowledge that differences exist and will continue to do so.

The ways in which the federated entities have engaged in asymmetric jurisdiction swapping also challenge the constitutional bargains intended to protect equality. Here again, regions and communities are responding pragmatically to local interests in ways that may be unavailable to the central state may. The results may contribute to inequality (or may constrain actors because of existing inequalities), but the alternative would be a central state that is hamstrung by the multiple, complex bargains required to strike deals under consociationalism. Thus, federalism pulls decision making about social policy out of the domain of consociationalism, with the exception of in the Brussels region, suggesting the possibility of greater flexibility and responsiveness.

While federalism was initially a response to the linguistic mobilization of the 1960s, the federalization of social policy has now become a tool enabling regionalist actors to press their claims about social justice in the Belgian state. Federalism did not necessarily intend to enlarge the scope of welfare state activity as much as it sought to widen its scale by incorporating Belgium's regions and language communities into the social welfare arena with a degree of financial and increasingly fiscal autonomy. Yet in doing so, federalism has had consequences for the ideals underlying the postwar welfare bargain and for the likelihood that those ideals will ever again be at the center of statewide consensus on the goals of the welfare state. Aside from the politics of regional conflict, a close accounting of social welfare expenditure is crucial for informed policymaking and for valid assessments of the character and scope of distributional politics at different levels of the Belgian state. This is even more important in times of economic constraint, when expenditure levels are likely to come under further scrutiny, with the potential consequences borne—and felt— unevenly across Belgian territory. Ultimately, such an accounting should also permit a more nuanced comparison of Belgium with other decentralized systems.

NOTES

1. As discussed later in the chapter, in Belgium, *social security* includes seven areas of social insurance. *Social assistance* refers to residual support, including supplemental income, guaranteed income for the elderly, guaranteed family benefits, and benefits for the disabled.

2. Belgium possesses an additional tier of government, provinces, that implements federal, regional, and community laws; administers roads, secondary education, and social welfare; and has some tax-raising capacity. At the risk of oversimplifying Belgian territorial politics but with a view to prioritizing larger-scale policy questions, I exclude the role of provinces from this study. On provinces, see Hooghe, Schakel, and Marks 2008a, appendix A, 211.

3. The French and Flemish (Dutch) Community Commissions were initially devolved from their respective language communities and have authority on initiatives relating to their communities, while the Common Community Commission is responsible for affairs that are not exclusive to either of the other community commissions. For a discussion of the Brussels community commissions, see http://www.ccc-ggc.brussels/

4. A scholarly consensus exists on the importance of power sharing among the elites of the country's pillars; a high degree of autonomy for the pillars in a range of social domains; nonmajoritarian elements, including proportional representation; and veto powers for political minorities. See Deschouwer 1999, 2006; Sinardet 2010.

5. By 1978, all "Belgian" parties outside of a small Marxist party had disappeared, and party politics had been reconfigured entirely along linguistic lines.

6. Power-sharing arrangements included linguistic parity in the cabinet (excluding the prime minister) and proportional representation in the Senate and Chamber of Deputies. Special protections were created for the francophone minority. In the Chamber, under the "alarm bell" procedure, if three-quarters of a language group's members claim that legislation would harm their interests, the parliamentary procedure is stopped and the government has thirty days to find a solution; if there is no solution, the government falls (Deschouwer 2012, 54).

7. The introduction of Flemish care insurance was deemed by the Court of Arbitration of Belgium to be a "supplementary scheme" that legitimately falls under community jurisdiction. Although this was challenged by the French Community, it was ruled constitutional, marking the first instance of regionalizing the scope of social insurance (Cantillon et al. 2006, 1036; Bouteca et al. 2013, 298–99).

8. I do not track private welfare expenditures (for example, individuals' private outlays for health care copayments).

9. These included "control over base and rate (e.g. gambling taxes), rate only (e.g. inheritance tax), rate within limits (e.g. registration fees on property transfer), or no control (e.g. vehicle registration)" (Hooghe, Schakel, and Marks 2008a, 212). Some environmental taxes were also transferred to the regions at this time.

10. The allocation of VAT was calculated from a 1989 baseline that was adjusted annually to take into account inflation and the number of students in elementary and secondary school per community, given the communities' new responsibilities in education. The proportion of VAT that was directed to the French and Dutch communities also reflected student numbers, with 57.55 percent of the total amount allocated to the Dutch community and 42.45 percent to the French community. The baseline of PIT allocated to the communities (as well as to the regions) was also set in 1989 but was adjusted based on changes in inflation and growth in national income (Swenden 2009, 5–6).

11. The allocation among regions is based on the localization principle (i.e., taxpayers are understood to be localized to the region in which they live, not where they work).

12. However, there is some debate on how to categorize this grant: Algoed (2009)

considers it a form of equalization (a "closed-ended grant"); Swenden (2009), conversely, argues that it has de facto become an unrestricted grant.

13. This category includes expenditures on survivor benefits, incapacity benefits, active labor market policy, unemployment and related benefits, housing benefits, family benefits, guaranteed income support, benefits for the handicapped, and other social benefits.

14. For further discussion of the dispersion of these transfers among the different social security branches, see the annual general budget proposals presented in the Belgian Chamber of Deputies.

15. General categories of revenue transfers among the substate public administrations are found in the Service Public Fédéral Budget et Contrôle de la Gestion annual reports, tables IV.1. The budgets of the individual public authorities include more detailed discussion of these transfers.

REFERENCES

Accord de Gouvernement. 2014. Brussels. October 10.

Algoed, Koen. 2009. *The Incentive Effects of the Belgian Equalization Scheme: Proposals for Reform.* Leuven: VIVES.

Behendt, Christian. 2013. "The Process of Constitutional Amendment in Belgium." In *Engineering Constitutional Change*, Ed. Xenophon Contiades, 35–50. London. Routledge.

Béland, Daniel, and André Lecours. 2005a. "Nationalism, Public Policy, and Institutional Development: Social Security in Belgium." *Journal of Public Policy* 25 (2): 265–85.

Béland, Daniel, and André Lecours. 2005b. "The Politics of Territorial Solidarity: Nationalism and Social Policy Reform in Canada, the United Kingdom, and Belgium." *Comparative Political Studies* 38 (6): 676–703.

Berns, Dominique. 2018. "L'Équilibre Budgétaire à Portée de Main: Pas Si Simple." *Le Soir*, 2 February.

Bisciari, P., W. Melyn, and L. Van Meensel. 2014. "Outlook for the Finances of the Communities and Regions." *NBB Economic Review*, September, 7–24.

Bouteca, N., C. Devos, and M. Mus. 2013. "The Future of Belgian Federalism as Seen through the Eyes of the Social Partners: A Continuing Obstacle to Social Policy Decentralization." *Regional and Federal Studies* 23 (3) 293–309.

"Brussels Protests End in Violence." 2014. *The Guardian*, 6 November.

Cantillon, Bea, Veerle de Maesschalck, Stijn Rottiers, and Gerlinde Verbist. 2006. "Social Redistribution in Federalised Belgium." *West European Politics* 29 (5): 1034–56.

Cendrowicz, Leo. 2014. "Belgium Grinds to a Halt for One-Day General Strike." *Guardian*, 15 December.

Centre de Recherche et d'Information Socio-Politiques (CRISP). 2015. "Public Authorities in Wallonia." www.crisp.be/wallonie/en/pouvoirs/region_wallonne.html

Dandoy, Régis, and Pierre Baudewyns. 2005. "The Preservation of Social Security as a National Function in the Belgian Federal State." In *The Territorial Politics of Welfare*, ed. Nicola McEwen and Luis Moreno, 148–67. London. Routledge.

Deschouwer, Kris. 1999. "From Consocation to Federation: How the Belgian Parties

Won." In *Party Elites in Divided Societies: Political Parties in Consociational Democracy*, ed. Kurt Luther and Kris Deschouwer, 74–107. London. Routledge.

Deschouwer, Kris. 2006. "And the Peace Goes On? Consociational Democracy and Belgian Politics in the Twenty-First Century." *West European Politics* 29 (5): 895–911.

Deschouwer, Kris. 2012. *The Politics of Belgium: Governing a Divided Society.* 2nd ed. London: Palgrave Macmillan.

European Commission. 2013. *Recommendation for a Council Recommendation on Belgium's 2013 National Reform Programme and Delivering an Opinion on Belgium's Stability Programme for 2012–2016.* COM(2013) 351 final. Brussels: 29 May.

European Commission. 2015. *Recommendation for a Council Recommendation on the 2015 National Reform Programme of Belgium and Delivering a Council Opinion on the 2015 Stability Programme of Belgium.* COM(2015) 252 final. Brussels: 13 May.

Hooghe, Liesbet, Gary Marks, and Arjan H. Schakel. 2008. "Operationalizing Regional Authority: A Coding Scheme for 42 Countries, 1950–2006." *Regional and Federal Studies* 18 (2–3): 123–42.

Hooghe, Liesbet, Arjan H. Schakel, and Gary Marks. 2008a. "Appendix A: Profiles of Regional Reform in 42 Countries (1950–2006)." *Regional and Federal Studies* 18 (2–3): 183–258.

Hooghe, Liesbet, Arjan H. Schakel, and Gary Marks. 2008b. "Appendix B: Country and Regional Scores." *Regional and Federal Studies* 18 (2–3): 259–74.

International Monetary Fund (IMF). 2015. *Belgium: Selected Issues.* IMF Country Report No. 15/71 (March). Washington, DC.

International Monetary Fund (IMF). 2016. *Belgium: Selected Issues.* IMF Country Report No. 16/78 (March). Washington, DC.

Laible, Janet. 2013. "Devolution, Nationalism, and the Limits of Social Solidarity: The Federalization of Health Policy in Belgium." In *Federalism and Decentralization in European Health and Social Care*, ed. Joan Costa-Font and Scott L. Greer, 228–49. Basingstoke: Palgrave-Macmillan.

OECD. 2017. *OECD Economic Surveys: Belgium 2017.* Paris.

Schokkaert, Erik, and Carine Van de Voorde. 2005. "Health Care Reform in Belgium." *Health Economics* 14:S25–S39.

Schokkaert, Erik, and Carine Van de Voorde. 2010. "Belgium's Health Care System: Should the Communities/Regions Take It Over? Or the Sickness Funds?" Paper presented at the Fourth Public Event of the Re-Bel Initiative, Brussels, 16 December.

Sinardet, David. 2010. "From Consociational Consciousness to Majoritarian Myth: Consociational Democracy, Multi-Level Politics, and the Belgian Case of Brussels Halle-Vilvoorde." *Acta Politica* 45 (3): 346–69.

Sinardet, David. 2014. "New Era Saddles Wallonia's Rulers with a Dilemma." *Financial Times*, 6 November.

Swenden, Wilfried. 2002. "Asymmetric Federalism and Coalition-Making in Belgium." *Publius* 32 (3): 67–87.

Swenden, Wilfried. 2009. *Territorial Finance in Belgium: Balancing Autonomy and Solidarity.* Working paper, University of Edinburgh.

Swenden, Wilfried, Marleen Brans, and Lieven De Winter. 2006. "The Politics of Belgium: Institutions and Policy under Bipolar and Centrifugal Federalism." *West European Politics* 29 (5): 863–73.

Van Rompuy, Paul. 2010. "Measurement and Practice of Fiscal Flows: The Case of Belgium." In *The Political Economy of Interregional Fiscal Flows: Measurement, Determinants, and Effects on Country Stability*, ed. Núria Bosch, Marta Espasa, and Albert Solé Ollé, 108–24. Cheltenham: Edward Elgar.

OFFICIAL DATASETS, PUBLICATIONS, AND ONLINE RESOURCES

Banque Nationale de Belgique/National Bank of Belgium—BelgoStat, www.nbb.be
Belgian Government Portal, www.belgium.be
BISA/IBSA (Brussels Institute for Statistics and Analysis) www.statistics.irisnet.be/ themes and www.ibsa.irisnet.be/publications
Brussels—Capital Health and Social Observatory, www.observatbru.be
Brussels—Capital Region Portal, www.be.brussels
European Central Bank. *ECB Monthly Bulletin* (December 2014, June, August 2015), ecb.europa.eu
FAMIFED (Federal Agency for Family Benefits) (prior to 1 July 2014, ONAFTS [Office National d'Allocations Familiales pour Travailleurs Salariés]), www.famifed.be
FPB (Federal Planning Bureau), www.plan.be
Fédération Wallonie-Bruxelles. 2012, 2015. *La Fédération Wallonie-Bruxelles en Chiffres*. Brussels: Ministère de la Fédération Wallonie-Bruxelles, www.federation-wallonie-bruxelles.be
FMP (Fonds des Maladies Professionnelles), www.fmp-fbz.fgov.be
INAMI (Institute National d'Assurance Maladie-Invalidité), www.inami.fgov.be
Institut des Comptes Nationaux. 2010, 2011, 2012, 2013. *Comptes Régionaux*. Brussels: Banque Nationale de Belgique.
INASTI (L'Institut National d'Assurances Sociales pour Travailleurs Indépendents), www.inasti.be
OECD Stats Extracts, stats.oecd.org
ONEM (Office National de l'Emploi), www.onem.be/fr
SFP (Service Fédéral des Pensions) (formed by 1 April 2016 merger of the ONP [National Pensions Office] and SdPSP [Public Sector Pensions Service]), www.sfpd.fgov.be
Service Public Fédéral Budget et Contrôle de la Gestion. 2009, 2010, 2011, 2012. *Base Documentaire Générale: Rapport Annuel*. Brussels.
Service Public Fédéral, Social Security. 2013, 2016. "Social Security: Everything You Have Always Wanted to Know." Brussels: FPS Social Security (English language), socialsecurity.belgium.be/en/publications
Statistics Belgium, statbel.fgov.be

Spain

The Politics of Who Not What

Kenneth Dubin

In interpersonal terms, Spain has long been one of the least redistributive welfare states in Europe (Mari-Klose 2015). This dynamic dates back to the development of a residual welfare state during the Francoist dictatorship. Its persistence since the transition to democracy in the late 1970s is the result not of federalism itself but rather of conflicts over the territorial distribution of authority.

Spain's democratic-era constitution was approved overwhelmingly (87.7 percent) by referendum in December 1978. Despite this apparent consensus, the territorial model of the state was an issue of such sensitivity that the foundational text left it unresolved. Spain has subsequently been beset by conflicts surrounding the territorial distribution of authority, its fiscal model, and even the unity of the state.

Redistributive questions have consistently taken a backseat to partisan debates over the territorial distribution of authority. The central question regarding welfare is *Who (which administration) does what?* rather than *Who (which citizen) gets what?* or *What is to be done (how delivered)?* Clear answers to the latter two questions would shift the terms of debate toward policy outputs and outcomes—and who pays for them—and away from the distribution of competencies. Not surprisingly, data transparency is problematic.

Spain is a thus a case in which welfare politics are subordinated to territorial politics. The weakly redistributive patterns revealed by our data are a product of historical legacies rather than constitutional structures. Their persistence owes more to constitutional conflict than to federalist design. The contrasting welfare outcomes in the two regions in which "who does what" is largely settled—the Basque Country and Navarre—and in the remaining fifteen regions speaks eloquently to the welfare implications of constitutional conflict.[1]

The Policy Implications of Unsettled Federalism

The federalist system that emerged in the early 1980s—the *State of Autonomies* composed of seventeen autonomous communities (ACs)—was more a holding pattern than a stable settlement. The scope and breadth of the issues left unresolved was, in comparative terms, exceptional. The distribution of funds and competencies across levels of government has been repeatedly revised with shifts in the balance of power between national and regional parties.[2] Yet with most actors focused on the pace and scope of devolution, policy innovation and policy efficacy have rarely made it to the top of the regional policymaking agenda, as is demonstrated by the findings from the most exhaustive econometric analysis of spending across our three key policy areas from 2002 to 2013 (Pérez-García, Tormo, and Lahiguera 2015):

1. Large and persistent differences exist across the regions in need-adjusted per capita spending for education and health care.
2. These spending differences predate the devolution of these competencies, and the policy-by-policy rank ordering of expenditures has not changed significantly over time, even as spending rose rapidly before the crisis and fell sharply beginning in 2010.
3. Differences in spending across the regions are more attributable to resources available than to need.
4. While differences in intensity of services (as measured by employment levels) exist and that cannot be explained by spending levels (indicating relative differences in efficiencies), differences in spending are the principal factor underlying the relative intensity of services provided.[3]

The few qualitative policy analyses available largely support these quantitative findings. ACs differ significantly in the public/private mix of service delivery in education and health care (Gallego and Subirats 2011), reflecting both long-standing historical patterns and ideological choices.[4] Differences in management styles and service efficiencies appear to be much smaller (Parrado 2010) as a result of

1. relatively high levels of information sharing among technical staff (Colino 2013a; Arbós et al. 2009);
2. relatively low levels of professionalization among political leaders of regional social welfare departments, limiting their capacity to interfere in service organization (Cordero, Jaime-Castillo, and Coller 2016; Coller et al. 2011); and
3. an underdeveloped culture of evaluation at all levels, which limits benchmarking and its subsequent pressures for innovation and efficiencies.[5]

Relative inattention to the content of policy—outputs and outcomes—is facilitated by the soft budget constraint facing (at least until recently) all ACs except the Basque Country and Navarre. While those fifteen regions may enjoy somewhat less tax autonomy than U.S. states or Canadian provinces, their revenue-raising authority, at least since 2002, has been significant. Nevertheless, these *common regime* (CR) ACs have had few incentives either to raise taxes or to engage in a race to the bottom to attract or retain taxpayers. Because AC tax receipts steadily increased from 2002 to 2010 after the absolute majority People's Party (PP) government restructured the ACs' competencies and financing, they had little reason to make use of their new tax authority.[6] These conjunctional disincentives were reinforced by an expectation that the PP's "definitive" reform would be renegotiated in a manner more favorable for all regions (as had been the case in prior reforms) the next time a central government depended on the votes of regional nationalists.[7]

With regional political elites enjoying a soft budget restraint and limited institutional and cultural pressures for transparency and accountability, devolution's impact on the composition of expenditures in the organization and delivery of key welfare services has been muted. The CR ACs exercise authority over key welfare policies but have as yet few incentives to rethink inherited patterns of service delivery. It is a commonplace of the fiscal federalism literature that soft budget restraints reduce governments' accountability. Spain's unsettled constitutional order reinforces this dynamic and distracts attention from the *Who gets what and how?* bread-and-butter questions of welfare state politics. In a contested constitutional order, present inequalities are less important than the prospects for future opportunities to renegotiate the distribution of resources and competencies.

Unsettled Arrangements: Data Implications

Data regarding taxing and spending in Spain are a powerful weapon in partisan debates regarding issues such as cross-class and interterritorial solidarity, the role of the church in a putatively nonconfessional polity, and the relationships among state, territory, and nation. Not surprisingly, few politicians work to make data more transparent or dig too closely into the affairs of their counterparts in other administrations. Given the deep reach of the political appointment process into the senior civil service ranks and the ease with which senior civil servants move back and forth between politics and their posts, much of the bureaucracy also has no interest in providing more complete data (Dahlström and Lapuente 2012). As a result, our data are often problematic.

For some questions, the data we seek are unavailable; for others, our confidence in their quality is limited. As authority for more policies has been devolved to the regions, so, too, has responsibility for data collection and reporting. Devolution of data collection has exacerbated long-standing problems with government statistics: data collection is uneven, changes in methodology are frequent, and scandals regarding data reporting are unexceptional.[8] These issues are a constitutive feature of Spanish federalism. Data clarity might well pose a substantive political challenge to existing settlements.

The current crisis appears to have created an opportunity space for reforms that force these long-unresolved issues to the fore. Nevertheless, their resolution would appear to require politically untenable shifts in the balance of power.

The Spanish Federalist System

The potentially federal arrangements sketched out in the Spanish Constitution were inspired by holding together impulses (Stepan 1999). During the Constitutional Convention, only the far right, Spanish nationalist AP (precursor to today's somewhat more centrist PP) and the center-right regional nationalists—the Catalan CDC and the Basque PNV—prioritized the territorial structure of authority. Catalans and Basques sought to recapture historic institutions of self-governance, while the AP, supported by the governing center-right UCD, wanted to preserve a unitary administration with 50 provincial units. The Socialists and Communists were supportive of a more federalist structure but prioritized social rights, while the UCD was primarily interested in preserving capitalist ownership of the means of production and expanding managerial discretion (Colomer 1998).

The final compromise permitted the creation of ACs through the convening of "constitutional" assemblies in seventeen regions to develop autonomy statutes that would then require parliamentary ratification. Two paths were defined: a fast track for the "historic" communities of Catalonia, the Basque Country, and Galicia, and a slower one for the rest. The fast track sought to accommodate Catalans and Basques; the constitution's call for a quasi-federal regime across the entire national territory and the promise that all ACs could eventually enjoy the same competencies and the preservation of the provincial administrations reflected conservatives' concerns that Spain's territorial integrity might be in jeopardy (Colomer 1998).

Who Gets What?

The Spanish regional financing system stands out among our cases. First, it features two distinct systems, the common regime (CR), governing fifteen ACs, and the foral regime (FR), governing the Basque Country and Navarre. While in theory the two could provide similar levels of per capita financing, FR regions in practice enjoy an enormous resource advantage. FR welfare policies not only are better funded but also reveal important differences in the composition of spending. Second, the system is inherently unstable because CR regions have powerful incentives to renegotiate both the financing system and their competency levels. With central governments frequently reliant on regional parties to pass legislation and tax receipts rising from the mid-1990s, those governments have lacked incentives either to reject entirely demands for reforms or to negotiate a definitive settlement.

Regional nationalist parties' demands for asymmetric federalism and statewide parties' countervailing calls for uniform competencies across the ACs have informed devolutionary initiatives since the early 1980s. The ten slow-track regime ACs would not see their competencies fixed until 2001, after the basic policy designs were developed. With the subsequent near-total devolution of health and education, the increase in public monies managed by the regions over the new millennium's first decade was greater than that in any other developed federalist country. Spain now has one of the more decentralized EU health care systems, with the regions almost entirely responsible for health care delivery. However, it features the least decentralized social protection system among Europe's federalist member states.

Financing System Characteristics

Under the FR, the Basque Country's three provinces and the AC of Navarre collect all taxes owed in their regions (except social security contributions) and pass a percentage (the *cupo* or *concierto*) to the central government in compensation for state-provided services in the region (including national defense). This system, rooted in historical privileges enjoyed by these regions in their relations with the Spanish Crown, is not without risks: the amount owed the central government is based on the national budget for nonassumed competencies. If this budget grows faster than regional tax receipts, the region pays more. For this reason, other regions (including Catalonia) did not press for the model's generalization during the 1978 Constitutional Convention (Gray 2015, 69–70).

The FR's benefits are today clearly visible and a source of grievance for other relatively wealthy regions. The FR calculation formula and privileges with respect to specific taxes generate significantly greater fiscal revenues (and control over those revenues). Critically, the base used to calculate the FR contribution to central government spending excludes the equalization funds used to redistribute tax revenues among the CR regions.[9] This calculation is also based on GDP and trade data with a base year of 1985; because the two regions subsequently have grown faster than the national average, adjustments for GDP and VAT significantly underestimate the base. Finally, only these two regions have the capacity to change rates for corporate taxes (Zabalza 2012; Zabalza and López-Laborda 2017).

Until 2002, the CR was largely funded through transfers, including block grants for education and health care for those regions exercising these competencies. The reduction of central government transfers in favor of ceded and shared taxes after 2002—and the elimination of conditional grants—meant that transfers became as much a horizontal as a vertical phenomenon (see table 1). This raised politically vexing and interconnected questions regarding tax equalization: what is being equalized (resources per inhabitant unadjusted or adjusted for such questions as population dispersion, insularity, geography, and so forth), and how much (León et al. 2015, 54–55).

The CR regions have failed to make extensive use of their authority to increase revenues through taxes because the most politically efficient strategy—in a financing system widely viewed by the protagonists as conditional—has been to demand larger transfers from the center. Politically powerful regions can improve deals reached with the center and other regions at the intergovernmental Council for Fiscal and Financial Policy when their bilateral Mixed Commission with the central government reviews, amends, and gives final approval to the council's proposal. These improvements can take two forms: adjustments in the weighted population formula used to distribute resources, and ad hoc funds targeting specific attributes of the region. Even less politically powerful regions have few incentives to develop their own taxes, as every reform to date has included both specific monies (the guarantee formula) to ensure that no region would lose funding and larger transfers for all. These guarantees are reinforced by the repeated inclusion of modulation rules limiting the maximum and minimum resources to be enjoyed by each AC with respect to the others. (León et al. 2015, chapters 5–6).

General Conclusions Regarding the Financing System

Initial financing arrangements for the ACs were universally regarded as provisional. Their persistence highlights institutional path dependence in federal systems and the risks of temporary solutions that seek to obscure underlying system logics.

Funding provided to the newly created ACs was based on an analysis

TABLE 1. Common Regime Financing System, 2002–2008 and 2009 Reform

Authority to alter base, rates, and/or schedules
- Personal income tax: 33% of total collections for region (50% after 2009)
- Wealth tax
- Estate and gift tax
- Property transactions tax
- Stamp duties
- Gambling
- Fees for devolved government services
- Transportation
- Retail hydrocarbon sales

No authority to alter base, rates, and/or schedules
- Value-added tax: 35% of total collections for region (50% after 2009)
- Excise taxes on alcohol, tobacco, and gas: 40% of total collections for region (58% after 2009)
- Electricity

Note: Region receives 100% of tax unless otherwise noted.

of the effective cost of the services being devolved (personnel and functions). The final figure was fixed through bilateral negotiations in the Mixed Commission for each AC. An Interterritorial Compensation Fund was created but then used to fund new investments in all the regions, distorting its purported objective of equalizing funding per capita across the regions. As central government spending on the newly devolved services had been highly unequal across regions, the effective cost approach reproduced and embedded in the new regional financing system the geographical biases of previous budgeting priorities (León 2009).

A weighted population formula was introduced in 1986, but the broader reform that year included elements that largely froze the prior regional ordering of central government disbursements on a per capita basis. It set minimum (the evolution of similar expenditures at the central government level) and maximum (nominal GDP growth) limits for AC resources. These brakes on changes in the relative distribution of funds across territories were reinforced by a guarantee that no region would be worse off under the new system, thus maintaining the original "transitory" financing system's relative distribution of resources.

In 2001, the PP government negotiated the "definitive" financing system in the context of the devolution of health care to the ten slow-track regions and the equalizing of competencies across all the regions (see tables 2 and 3). The regions would now receive 33 percent of income taxes (with capacity for altering rates), 35 percent of VAT (without authority for rates), and a host of minor excise taxes. The "definitive" system would prove to be as problematic as its predecessors. A real estate boom between 2002 and late 2007 brought an unprecedented flow of immigrants to Spain.[10] Population change was distributed unequally across the regions. Given that the regions were now responsible for both education and health spending, the model's inability to adjust funding accordingly generated important new interregional inequalities.

In 2009, with the economic boom turned to spectacular bust, the minority Socialist government revised the supposedly definitive 2002 reform (see table 4). The change was provoked not only by the technical problems just described but also by the political imperatives created by revisions of autonomy statutes in Catalonia, Valencia, Andalusia, Baleares, Aragón, and Castilla y León as well as by the government's desire to devolve administrative responsibilities for its ambitious 2007 dependent care policy. The reformed statutes, approved by the national Parliament, included newly devolved taxes and new rules for equalization across the regions. (Catalonia, Baleares, and Aragon, all losers under the previous equalization system, had incorporated revised equalization formulas into their statutes.) Surprisingly, the eurozone crisis was not a significant motivating factor for this reform; in fact, the reform's design failed to address many of the issues that made the crisis so challenging for the ACs' finances (Colino 2013b).

Each AC now receives 25 percent of its imputed tax load. If the financing required to provide essential services in a given region—education, health, and social services—is less (on an adjusted population basis) than the remaining 75 percent contributed to the general fund, the region receives the difference from the Guarantee Fund. While initially opposed by some of the poorer regions, this shift from full to partial equalization implied no dramatic changes. A complementary Sufficiency Fund was introduced to bring each region's total financing up to the initial level previously agreed in bilateral negotiations. Moreover, the Sufficiency Fund's growth is based on each year's total increase in central government receipts and is distributed to the regions irrespective of other variables governing tax flows. As a result, available financial resources for each AC continue to reflect the relative levels of the previous status quo (León et al. 2015, 156).

TABLE 2. Per Capita Adjusted Population Financing for Common Regime ACs

	2002	2003	2004	2005	2006	2007	2008	sist 01 2009	sist 09 2009	2010	2011	Δ 2002–11
Catalonia	99.8	99.4	100.5	99.8	99.3	96.5	97.1	101.0	103.8	99.3	99.6	−0.2
Galicia	100.8	100.5	98.9	99.5	98.9	101.8	105.2	102.4	100.1	105.5	105.9	5.1
Andalusia	99.4	100.7	101.2	100.5	101.7	102.6	100.2	96.0	92.4	95.9	95.9	−3.6
Asturias	103.4	104.1	102.5	101.3	101.4	105.2	109.2	107.8	103.1	107.4	107.4	4.0
Cantabria	116.7	117.6	116.5	119.6	118.6	119.7	119.7	124.8	118.0	117.9	119.1	2.4
La Rioja	115.2	115.6	115.9	115.3	115.3	116.1	118.4	115.5	110.3	115.8	120.0	4.8
Murcia	95.1	95.0	95.5	99.0	98.7	99.1	95.9	93.7	96.8	95.3	94.7	−0.4
Valencia	93.7	93.7	94.8	95.1	94.0	92.1	88.4	88.5	93.2	92.8	92.4	−1.2
Aragón	104.5	105.0	103.4	104.7	105.1	105.5	107.7	108.8	103.9	104.8	107.6	3.2
Castilla–La Mancha	96.7	96.9	96.4	99.0	100.0	101.6	101.1	97.6	95.1	98.7	98.3	1.6
Canarias	104.9	103.1	102.4	100.0	99.2	100.1	97.8	93.0	91.8	95.3	95.8	−9.0
Extremadura	106.9	108.5	106.2	106.6	106.8	110.6	113.0	108.0	103.7	112.9	109.8	2.8
Baleares	90.6	87.6	89.3	93.1	93.9	90.9	87.0	86.8	101.5	102.5	102.9	12.3
Madrid	99.2	98.7	98.6	97.9	98.4	97.2	100.6	107.6	109.9	100.7	100.2	1.1
Castilla y León	105.7	105.4	104.5	104.3	103.8	106.8	109.6	108.5	104.3	109.4	109.2	3.4
average	100.0	100.0	100.0	100.0	100.0	100.0	100.0	100.0	100.0	100.0	100.0	0.0
Std Dev	7.02	7.62	7.03	6.81	6.67	7.75	9.40	10.02	7.10	7.58	8.13	

Source: de la Fuente 2012a.
Note: Population adjustment based on formula used in 2009 Reform.

The 2009 reform did include advances. For the first time, need calculations incorporated the percentage of school-aged children and the elderly, a particularly important change given the demographic bias of the new expenditure pressures associated with the 2007 Dependency Law. Annual reviews were mandated for these demographic variables, addressing a serious lacuna in earlier agreements. Vertical tax imbalances were reduced through both an increase in ceded taxes (from 33 to 50 percent for personal income tax and VAT and from 40 to 58 percent for

TABLE 3. Resources per AC for Homogeneous Competencies under the Common Regimen (2010)

			Pre-equalization			Post-equalization		
	Normative Regional Tax Revenues[a] (€ millions)	Adjusted Population[b]	Fiscal Capacity per Capita (adj.) (€)	Fiscal Capacity per Capita (adj.) (as % of mean [100])	Rank/15 Regions	Final Resources per Capita (adj.) (€)[c]	Final Resources per Capita (adj.) (as % of mean [100])	Rank/15 Regions
Madrid	17,001	6,095,755	2,789	148	1	2,335	97	8
Baleares	2,677	1,104,358	2,424	129	2	2,331	97	9
Catalonia	17,163	7,434,588	2,309	123	3	2,281	95	11
Cantabria	1,248	590,968	2,112	112	4	2,734	114	1
Aragón	2,927	1,417,006	2,066	110	5	2,432	102	6
La Rioja	643	327,221	1,965	105	6	2,686	112	2
Asturias	2,190	1,124,410	1,948	104	7	2,492	104	5
Castilla y León	5,071	2,744,412	1,848	98	8	2,538	106	4
Valencia	9,016	5,020,576	1,796	96	9	2,134	89	15
Murcia	2,400	1,430,126	1,678	89	10	2,210	92	13
Galicia	4,884	2,968,169	1,645	88	11	2,421	101	7
Andalusia	13,161	8,220,687	1,601	85	12	2,224	93	12
Castilla–La Mancha	3,520	2,208,917	1,594	85	13	2,289	96	10
Extremadura	1,639	1,169,068	1,402	75	14	2,619	109	3
Canaries	2,211	2,192,893	1,008	54	15	2,209	92	14
Mean	5,717	2,936,610	1,879			2,396		

Source: De la Fuente 2012a, 2013c; Gray 2014.

[a]The tax revenue figures given here incorporate two of the adjustments to the official government figures recommended by De la Fuente (2012a, 2013c)—that is, to improve estimates of normative revenues across the 15 regions (i.e., to remove the effect of different rates being charged in different regions) and to account for the special tax regime in the Canaries region to facilitate interregional comparison.

[b]Adjusted for unit of need (based on demographic and geographic weightings).

[c]After application of the Guarantee Fund, Global Sufficiency Fund, Cooperation Fund, and Competitiveness Fund.

TABLE 4. Who Gets What? The Distribution of Competencies

	1980	1981	1982	1983	1984	1985	1986	1987	1990	1994	1995	1996	1997	1998	1999	2000	2001	2002	2003
Fast-track regions																			
Andalusia			E		H, S														U
Canary Islands				e		S	E			H					U				
Catalonia	e	H, S					E						U						
Galicia		e				S		E	H				U						
Navarre									H, e, S						U				
Basque Country						E		H, S											
Valencia				e		E, S		H						U					
Slow-track regions																			
Aragón												E, S		e			H	U	
Asturias											E, S			e			H,U		
Baleares												E, S	e				H,U		
Cantabria												E, S		e			H,U		
Castilla León											E, S			e			H	U	
Castilla la Mancha											S	E		e			H,U		
Estremadura											E, S			e			H,U		
Madrid											E, S				e	U	H		
Murcia											E, S				e		H		U
La Rioja												E		S	e		H,U		

Source: León 2010, 86.

Note: No significant expenditure transfers were granted to ACs between 1991 and 1993. e = primary and secondary education; E = university education; H = health care services; S = social services; U = unemployment (occupational training).

excise taxes) and the delegation of authority to alter tax rates and bands up to 10 percent. While the Sufficiency Fund largely thwarted the Catalans' equalization pretensions, analysis of the reform's impact suggests that the dispersion in adjusted per capita financing across regions has been reduced (de la Fuente 2012b). One indicator of persistent ambiguity in the Spanish system of regional finance—a reflection of disagreements over the constitutional model—is the fact that only with the 2009 reform was a technical evaluation committee created within the Council for Fiscal and Financial Policy.

Distributional Dynamics

Several factors limit the Spanish welfare state's overall impact on inequality. First, the insurance-based character of most retirement and unemployment pensions means that those with well-paid permanent positions receive the largest payouts from the social security system. The crisis has accentuated this bias, as universal benefits such as health and education have suffered greater cuts than social security. This is partially attributable to the fact that social security is a jealously guarded central government function; however, as health and education have far higher variable costs (personnel, levels of service), they may be easier (politically) to cut than legally recognized pension benefits.

The profound interpersonal and cross-regional inequalities that characterize the Spanish welfare state are not primarily a product of federalism. First and foremost, historically high interregional wealth differences were reinforced during the economic boom of the latter half of the dictatorship (1959–74). Ineffective industrial policy failed to counterbalance agglomeration dynamics in the historically most developed regions (and Madrid), and miserly welfare state spending (Spain spent a smaller percentage of GDP on welfare than any other OECD country in 1977) limited redistribution of the fruits of development. Landless peasants, smallholders, and unskilled laborers were forced to emigrate to the largest cities or to Northern Europe. The Spanish transition to democracy took place against a backdrop of high cross-regional differences in wages, in the penetration of state services, and, critically, in the availability of both educational and health services delivered in no small measure by the church.

Given the elite-negotiated nature of the transition, the church and its primary bases of support among the upper and middle classes (those most closely associated with the Francoist regime) ensured that church-based welfare institutions would not suffer the fate of the authoritarian regime. Rather, universalistic welfare provision was layered over existing modes of private provision (Moreno and Sarasa 1993). This approach was aggressively pursued by the center-right nationalists in Catalonia and to a lesser extent the Basque Country, the two regions leading the charge for greater regional autonomy (Rico Gómez 1996).

Two other biases further limited the urgency of redistribution on the policy agenda at the moment of federal construction. First, the Francoist regime's promotion of homeownership provided a safety net that muted demands for noncontributory pensions (Allen 2006). Second, the familial character of safety nets for infant and dependent care and the relatively low cost of private-sector personal services for the middle classes meant that there was no organized demand for public provision of such services.[11] The ACs enjoyed considerable policy autonomy with regard to these issues from early on but were primarily focused on delivering education and health care. The decentralization of welfare delivery did not keep these issues off the table, but it also did not encourage regional policymakers to address them.

The Distribution of Competencies and Data Issues

Pensions. The central government has exclusive power to regulate and manage all national pension schemes, including contributory pensions for unemployment, worker's compensation and retirement, and noncontributory old-age and unemployment pensions. Replacement rates for contributory pensions are quite generous, maximum pensions are quite high, and noncontributory pensions are very low.[12] The Spanish pension system's resulting limited redistributive effects affect both FR and CR regions. While the Social Security Administration clearly details regional spending on survivor and orphan benefits, it does not provide clear regional breakdowns of unemployment benefit payments. As a result, we have not been able to provide a breakdown of spending by regions for this category.

Employment Policy. Labor market legislation is an exclusive competency of the central government. However, the regions manage both the public employment service (job counseling and placement) and the labor inspection service. In 2013, the Annual Employment Policy Plan (€3.8 billion versus €7 billion in 2007) set aside 35 percent of total funding for the ACs and raised the percentage of those funds that were conditioned on performance from 15 to 40 percent. However, the performance criteria are largely oriented toward outputs rather than outcomes, meaning that it is difficult to evaluate the effectiveness of these policies (Bentolila and Jansen 2013). The budget for 2016 was €5.2 billion, with the same division of funds between the regions and the center (Ministry of Employment and Social Security 2016). Occupational training in the workplace, largely funded to date by EU funds, has been managed primarily by the main employer and union organizations in collaboration with the Ministry of Labor and the ACs' Labor Departments. We have been unable to obtain reliable data regarding participation in these programs, and the level of reporting for employment policies is of limited value. Not surprisingly, perhaps, Spanish active labor market policies have been beset by corruption problems at both the national and regional levels.[13]

Education. The central government's role in education is largely limited to setting basic minimum standards for education and running two nontraditional universities. Regions are responsible for managing all primary, secondary, and university education as well as vocational and continuing education. Publicly funded primary and secondary education is delivered by public schools and by private, mostly church-run schools agreeing to curricular oversight and limits on their ability to self-select students and charge additional fees (*escuelas concertadas*). Public spending per student in *concertado* schools is about half that in public schools. *Concertado* schools have significantly lower per-pupil costs because teacher salaries are lower, student-teacher ratios are higher, and education in rural areas, with its associated higher logistical costs, is almost entirely public (Rogero-García and Andrés-Candelas 2014).

Education spending is reported with care for children up to age three lumped in with primary and secondary educational spending. There is a varying mix of public and (publicly funded) private provision at this level. Coverage also varies widely from one region to another.

The AC's funding of university education is largely limited to public-sector universities. The central government provides framework legislation with respect to degrees and the certification of academic staff eligibility for civil service status. Most regions have created their own authorities for financing academic research, and some have even created their own career paths for academics in an effort to reduce bureaucratic restrictions on hiring and promotion.

Health. The sectoral intergovernmental conference sets a basic menu of health services that must be provided by all regions and defines which drugs are eligible for subsidy. However, the regions enjoy considerable discretion in the organization of health care, including the public/private mix. As in education, there is far greater public funding for private care in the historically wealthy regions, where private-sector health care systems were firmly entrenched before democracy. Our health data is the least problematic of the various welfare policies largely managed by the ACs.

Over-65 Benefits. Contributory pensions are the exclusive reserve of the state. Dependent care is managed by the regions. While we can be confident that the vast majority of the beneficiaries of these services are elderly, data on beneficiaries is not reported by age groups, making it impossible to report these benefits within this category.

Under-65 Social Benefits. Historically, the state provided nothing in the way of social assistance for working-age people. Whatever programs did exist were largely provided by municipal governments. After the eurozone crisis, the Socialists introduced a €400/month pension payment for those not (or no longer) eligible for unemployment benefits. The PP has formally maintained this benefit while greatly restricting eligibility.

The Crisis: The Emperor Has Nowhere to Hide

The ACs were particularly hard hit by the crisis as a result of their financing system, the central government's fiscal retrenchment strategy, and perhaps their inexperience in predicting and managing their fiscal flows. Although the financial crisis was clearly felt in Spain by early 2008, the ACs did not take steps to address the issue until 2010.

Just as the CR regions gained tax-setting authority over a significant portion of their revenue base in 2002, an economic boom generated windfall tax revenues, giving the regions few incentives to exercise their newfound authority. For those regions where the real estate bubble was concentrated (basically Madrid and the Mediterranean coast), there were huge receipts from ceded taxes on property transfers and related legal documentation services. In 2006 alone, more than 600,000 new residential units were built in Spain, more than the remaining 14 countries in the EU-15 put together. Revenues in real terms from these taxes increased eightfold from 1996 to 2006. These transactions also contributed to a spectacular rise in VAT receipts (León et al. 2015, 176–77). Revenues mushroomed even in regions largely bypassed by the real estate boom thanks to the structure of the Sufficiency Fund, which was linked to the growth in central government tax receipts.

The CR regions' situation was exacerbated by the two-year lag in the budget reconciliation process for income, VAT, and excise taxes. Calculations for revenue disbursements from the center are based on the central government's budget projections and the CR revenue-sharing formula.

Large central government errors in these calculations became the AC's problem only with the central government's reconciliation in 2010.

Under severe pressure from the troika composed of the European Commission, the ECB, and the IMF, the Zapatero government and the opposition PP agreed on a November 2011 amendment to the constitution imposing harsh balanced budget rules. The overall direction of the reform followed the precedent set by the German Parliament and EU budget reforms denominated the six pack (Albertí Rovira 2013; Medina Guerrero 2013). Previous governments had approved statutory budget stability rules in 2001 and 2006; however, both lacked effective sanctions regimes. More than a cosmetic measure to calm the troika and bond market sharks, the 2011 amendment transformed the federal balance of power. Timely reporting of budget information is now mandatory. The national Tax Ministry can recommend a course of action that must be followed by the region with oversight from the ministry. If an AC fails to convince ministry inspectors that the proposed reforms have been carried out, the ministry can even suspend ceded tax revenues and ultimately intervene in the regional government.

These reforms and other measures affecting the ACs' core activities, including health, education, and social services (particularly with respect to regulations governing public-sector employees), have provoked a flurry of jurisdictional claims by the regions to the Constitutional Court. AC claims of breaches in their constitutionally protected autonomy increased fivefold from 2011 to 2012 (Albertí Rovira 2013, n. 41).

The crisis and the 2011 constitutional reforms could reshape Spanish federalism in three fundamental ways. First, recent reports suggest that the ACs are starting to make significant use of their tax capacity for the first time (Solé-Ollé 2013). Co-responsibility no longer appears to be simply an unfulfilled promise of the Spanish fiscal regime. Second, the constitutional reform of budget rules, if applied, could bring about a sea change in budget transparency, both vertically and horizontally, encouraging more open and forthright discussions regarding the structure of the financing system. Third, if this new commitment to budget transparency is consolidated, it should facilitate more rigorous policy evaluation, which is a sine qua non for meaningful innovations in health, education, and social services.

To date, however, the evidence for change is underwhelming. Both the center and the regions have flouted the budgeting rules set out in Organic Law 2/2012. Only 3 of the 17 regions (Madrid, the Basque Country, and Navarre) met the 2014 debt-to-GDP limits, and total regional debt exceeded the target by more than 6 percent (22.4 percent versus a target of 21.1 percent) ("Sólo Madrid" 2015),[14] even though the government raised the target in September 2014.[15] In this context, it is hardly surprising that the Rajoy government chose to delay until the next legislature the revision of the current financing system. Politics, not institutional rules, apparently will continue to drive the evolution of the AC financing system.

The Impact of Federalism on the Spanish Welfare State

Education

Regional differences in educational outcomes are a persistent feature of the Spanish political economy: the correlation between a region's literacy rate in 1860 and the level of reading comprehension on the 2009 PISA test is 72 percent (Bagues 2013). While such long-standing variations suggest that structural explanations are critical for understanding contemporary differences in educational outcomes across the CAs, policy decentralization has also permitted increasing differences in regional approaches to education, particularly since the early 2000s. Large differences exist in the delivery structure, focus, and coverage of early child care, vocational education, and some lifelong learning programs (Gallego and Subirats 2011, 2012). However, we have precious little evidence on the efficacy of these programs (Bentolila and Jansen 2014).

Early Childhood, Primary, and Secondary Education

Public expenditures on early childhood, primary, and secondary education include both public schools and fully funded private schools (*escuelas concertadas*). When democracy returned to Spain, the country's public school system was so small that expanding mandatory education required collaboration with the large church-run system.[16] Private schools that sought public funding were required to offer free education, to hold nonprofit status, to admit students on the same basis as public schools, and to deliver at a minimum the same curriculum as public schools. While religious activities had to be voluntary, even today the Catholic Church educates about three-quarters of *concertado* school students.

While formally free and open to all students, *concertado* schools have often created barriers to entry through "voluntary" donations and higher fees for uniforms, materials, and optional activities. Some regions have even allowed *concertado* schools to privilege the children of alumni.[17] The result is a clear correlation between social class and *concertado* school attendance.[18] While students in *concertado* schools perform better on average than their public school peers, when controlling for social class, there is no difference in outcomes between the two systems.

Public expenditure per student in *concertado* schools is approximately 50 percent of that in public schools. Explanations for this enormous difference include often markedly lower salaries in *concertado* schools, the concentration of special needs and problem students in public schools, and the costs borne by the public system for transport in rural areas (Rogero-García and Andrés-Candelas 2014). The *concertado* system serves a larger percentage of students in the wealthiest regions of the country. The percentage of students in *concertado* schools is well above the national average in Baleares, Catalonia, La Rioja, and Valencia. It is highest in Madrid and the Basque Country, where it accounts for almost 50 percent of students. It is lowest in the two poorest regions, which lack big urban centers and their accompanying professional middle classes—Extremadura and Castilla La Mancha. In 2009, the ACs overall spent 16.6 percent of their total nonuniversity budget on subsidies to *concertado* schools. For Madrid, the figure was 24.3 percent, and for the Basque Country, it was 28.6 percent; in Castilla La Mancha, it was just 8.5 percent (Fernández Llera and Muñiz Pérez 2012).

Large disparities in the size of the *concertado* sector across ACs complicate interpretations of the significance of the broader trend toward more equal per-student spending across the ACs (Pérez Esparrells and Morales Sequera 2012).[19] As with other policy areas, comparative analysis of the Spanish regions' educational policy is problematic. A recent survey of the literature on inequality of opportunity in education revealed a lack of systematic data analysis, weak theoretical and analytical frameworks, and profound disagreements even when considering the same data (Fernández Mellizo-Soto 2014).

Some authors have argued that, particularly when the PP is in power, the central government has gone to great lengths to limit the regions' autonomy in educational policy (Losada and Maíz 2005). Both the Socialists and the Conservatives have indeed sought to impose a certain degree of uniformity through framework legislation that includes content for core curriculum, requirements for students to advance grades and to enter vocational or pre-university tracks, and criteria structuring the relationship between the ACs and public, *concertado*, and private schools. However, qualitative research reveals meaningful differences in the educational policies pursued by the ACs for primary and secondary education (del Campo and López Sánchez 2015).

Andalusia took control of its schools in 1984. Given the region's relative poverty, there were few *concertado* schools outside the main provincial capitals. The Socialists enjoyed an absolute majority in the region and set equal access as a fundamental priority. They focused on building public schools and ensuring minimal variation in content and standards. The Socialists were disinclined to license additional *concertado* schools and acceded quickly to union demands to harmonize salaries between public and *concertado* school teachers (del Campo and López Sánchez 2015).

The Community of Madrid, long controlled by the Conservatives, took over educational policy in 2000, inheriting a system of *concertado* schools that served approximately one-third of all students. As the region grew and new neighborhoods were built, the region offered *concertado* schools (particularly those whose promoters were ideologically close to the government) exclusive rights to build new schools. Not surprisingly, *concertado* schools came to represent approximately half of all available school places. Unlike the Socialists in Andalusia, the PP in Madrid has refused to equalize salaries across the two systems, resulting in considerable cost savings for the region. Also unlike Andalusia, Madrid has promoted differentiation over equality. Starting in 2006, it has introduced bilingual education in some schools, physically separated vocational and general education, and promoted an "excellence" system featuring four tracks, with students assigned according to standardized test results (del Campo and López Sánchez 2015). While the crisis and student resistance have limited implementation of these measures, the vast differences with Andalusia are clear.

Finally, the Basque Country is the region not only with the highest per-capita educational spending but also with the highest degree of independence for local school officials. This result is largely an unintended consequence of the policies pursued to extend use of the Basque language. The region inherited a large network of *concertado* schools that included almost 50 percent of all students. There were both church schools and a large number of parent-run cooperatives (*ikastolas*) created with the primary goal of recovering the Basque language repressed during the Francoist dictatorship. Unlike Madrid, the Basque government did not seek to expand the *concertado* system but rather promoted three models of language instruction—majority Spanish, majority Basque, and mixed—with the choice of instruction at the discretion of the school administration (generally in close consultation with parents).[20] This solution opened the door to greater local control than exists in other regions (del Campo and López Sánchez 2015).

The Basque Country is also the only AC to exercise total control over student aid grants for pre-university education (Pérez Esparrells and Morales Sequera 2014). For other regions, coverage rates for ministerial grants ranged from a low of 3 percent in Navarre and 3.3 percent in Catalonia to 8.5 percent in Extremadura. Coverage rates for subsidies offered by the ACs varied from 1.8 percent in Navarre and 2.2 percent in Aragon to 42 percent in Extremadura and 46.7 percent in Castilla y León. Until the early 2000s, only the wealthiest regions provided some complementary aid funding beyond that offered by the Ministry of Education. For academic year 2011–12, the ministry provided most ACs somewhere between 60 and 80 percent of all financing. The major exception is Madrid, which provides a high level of subsidization for 0–3 education through a large *concertado* school network.

The most important aid categories through age 16 are meals, books, and other educational materials as well as special needs education. For ages 16–18, more than 50 percent of total aid in each AC goes to compensatory funds providing incentives for at-risk students to stay in school (Pérez Esparrells and Morales Sequera 2014). While there is a strong negative correlation between levels of central government grants and regional wealth, this relationship has been weakened somewhat as some regions have pursued different policies. In the aggregate, some 26.8 percent of Spanish primary and secondary students benefited from some grant during the 2011–12 academic year. This figure is a far cry from the 40 percent EU average.

Universities

All ACs have managed their regional universities since the transfer of competencies for university and postgraduate education to the Baleares in 1997. Until the 2011–12 academic year, prices for official degrees were set by the AC within limits set by the sectoral conference (in recent years, a minimum of the consumer price index and a maximum of the index plus four percentage points). With Law 14/2012, the ACs were permitted to raise prices to reflect costs (15–25 percent of costs for EU citizens and up 100 percent for others) (Escardíbul et al. 2013). This limited liberalization of university fees has given rise to a rapid increase in fee dispersion across the ACs. Prior to the reform, the dispersion across the ACs was little more than 10 percent for undergraduate degrees and less than 20 percent for master's. One year later, fee dispersion for undergraduates had exceeded 23 percent and for master's students had topped 40 percent. Enormous fee increases in Catalonia and Madrid, homes of the country's leading public universities, explain a large part of this dispersion (Escardíbul et al. 2013). Given that both the percentage of Spanish university students receiving need-based grants and the level of funding for these grants are low by OECD standards, the liberalized financing system may well accentuate inequalities in access to higher education (OECD 2015a).

The three most highly ranked universities on most international indexes are Catalan (see, e.g., http://www.u-ranking.es/analisis.php). In 2001, Catalonia created a program to attract international researchers to its universities and a quality agency to evaluate and certify academics for promotion; the agency is more rigorous than its central government counterpart. Catalonia also concentrated resources in a small number of universities. The Community of Madrid, by contrast, created separate research institutes outside of the universities and did not concentrate resources in newer institutions such as the University Carlos III that had greater flexibility to innovate (Sánchez-Cuenca 2016).

Health

Decentralization of health care in Spain has been critical to system innovation. The Socialists promised to transform the social health insurance system inherited from the Franco regime into a publicly funded, universal, and free national health system. However, the 1986 Health Act included means testing, copayments, private insurance subsidies, and contracting out to private physicians and hospitals; the transformation of the social health insurance system into a national health system was driven by the regions. Catalan and Basque conservative nationalists secured important reductions in the central government's coordinating powers. The Basques then extended coverage to citizens not covered by social security, a measure quickly adopted by the other regions with devolved competencies and then by the state under pressure from unions. Subsequent early innovations by the regions with devolved competencies included public management reforms (Catalonia), coverage for mental care and child dental care (Basque Country), and primary care reforms (Andalusia and Navarre). The Catalans were also the first to introduce independent agencies overseeing contracting with public and private providers (Rico and Costa-Font 2005).

More recent health care innovations often focused on the governance model, particularly in PP-controlled regions. Public-private partnerships for hospital construction and the delivery of both specialist and in some cases primary care services have permitted lower salary costs by evading public-sector wage scales. However, a comprehensive study of hospitals in the Communities of Madrid and Valencia revealed that neither the ACs nor the concessionaires publish financial statements permitting evaluation of fees paid or the concessionaires' costs. In both ACs, regional savings banks—controlled by the regional governments—were key shareholders in the structuring of these deals; the lack of transparency is thus hardly surprising. Independent observers claim that the arrangements are beset by cherry-picking of profitable services, preferential interest rates that inflate profitability, and a lack of effective governance (Acerete et al. 2015).

Supplemental private insurance has also come to reinforce social cleavages in many of the most urbanized and wealthy regions (especially Madrid and Catalonia). Penetration rates of private health insurance in 2012 varied from a high of 27.9 percent in Madrid to a low of only 10.4 percent in Asturias (López i Casanovas and González López-Valcárcel 2016, 197). With the Spanish national health system now suffering the biggest cutbacks in its history, stratification in access to health care may well come to resemble the long-existing divisions in the educational system.

The significance of these cutbacks is difficult to evaluate. On the one hand, while health spending fell by 14 percent from 2009 to 2013, 2013 nominal spending was still double the 2001 amount (López i Casanovas and González López-Valcárcel 2016, 195). On the other, it is extremely hard to get a clear measure of the direction of travel of health spending across regions, as minor changes in the nominator or denominator lead to different outcomes in the comparisons. Given the limited transparency of data on efficiency and efficacy, cross-regional spending comparisons appear to put the cart before the horse (200–202).

Indeed, transparency and evaluation remain the Achilles' heel of the Spanish health system. Pérez-Durán (2015) has created a synthetic index of accountability for the 17 AC public health services. Her review of the statutes governing reporting, evaluation, and sanctioning reveals considerable obstacles. Only in Galicia does the regional body for evaluation and sanctioning enjoy political, administrative, financial, and personnel independence. Eleven ACs have no independent regional evaluator, including the Basque Country, Catalonia, and Navarre. The Ministry of Health does little to remedy this problem: Spanish hospital data are published anonymously, making it difficult to evaluate individual sites (Alonso et al. 2015).

15–64 Benefits and Services

Active Labor Market Policies

During the current crisis, the ACs have been largely responsible for the management of the public employment services (PES). While data on active labor market policies are woefully inadequate, if we consider labor market outcomes over time, decentralization does not seem to have made a significant difference. When Spain suffered deep economic crises in the mid-1970s and again in the early 1990s, the PES was totally or largely a central government function. Both then and now, however, economic adjustment was achieved largely through employment levels and precarious employment. To the extent that PES matter for employment outcomes, the Spanish PES has been a spectacular failure whatever level of government is responsible for its management.

Minimum Income Supports

Prior to the 2009 introduction of a nationwide, noncontributory, €426/month unemployment benefit, the only benefits available for healthy indigent adults were minimum-income programs offered by the regions and municipalities (Ayala Cañón 2012; Arriba 2014). Access to these AC and municipal programs has been quite restricted and benefit levels extremely low. The great exception to this rule is the Basque Country, which uniquely among the ACs provides a significant guaranteed minimum income. The Socialist government fiercely protested the Basque program when it was introduced by the center-right PNV in the late 1980s in response to widespread poverty occasioned by the collapse of heavy industries. In a clear indication of the ideological distance between the Basque Country and the rest of Spain, the program was supported by regional parties across the political spectrum, including the Basque PP.

Today, the Basque initiative accounts for more than 40 percent of all spending nationally on such programs. As table 5 indicates, the Basque Country in 2012 spent three times more on these programs than any other AC as a percentage of total public spending. In terms of per-person funding levels, only Navarre offers similar benefits. The number of beneficiaries of these programs doubled from 2007 to 2010, providing a clear measure of the intensity of the crisis. However, as the effects of the crisis on AC finances deepened, some ACs raised barriers to access and reduced both the quantity and duration of benefits. As several analysts have noted, important data-reporting problems make it hard to evaluate the impact of these programs (Ayala Cañón 2012, 122 n. 6).

Ayala Cañón (2012) reports that variations in the generosity of benefits across ACs in 2010 was on the order of 25–30 percent, depending on the number of persons in the household receiving benefits. These benefits increased sharply over the 2000s as some regions increased benefits significantly (always from a very low level), while others were much less ambitious. Leaving aside the Basque program, the differences across ACs, while surely reflecting partisan differences, generally reflect the relative wealth of the regions, with the less wealthy regions offering both lower benefits and lower coverage rates; however, both Madrid and Catalonia offer benefits below the national average.

Old-Age Benefits and Services

Dependent care services are the main old-age benefit provided by the ACs. Both contributory and noncontributory pensions are managed by the national Social Security Administration despite some ACs' longstanding demands for pension devolution. Pensions have largely been

TABLE 5. Proportion of Regional Budget Devoted to Minimum Income Supports

	2002 (%)	2006 (%)	2008 (%)	2010 (%)	2011 (%)	2012 (%)
Andalusia	0.15	0.13	0.12	0.19	0.19	0.22
Aragón	0.11	0.05	0.04	0.17	0.28	0.37
Asturias	0.56	0.29	0.59	0.71	0.87	1.03
Baleares	0.16	0.10	0.11	0.16	0.19	0.16
Canarias	0.18	0.13	0.07	0.22	0.25	0.26
Cantabria	0.18	0.07	0.15	0.29	0.64	0.62
Castilla–La Mancha	0.04	0.02	0.01	0.02	0.03	0.03
Castilla y León	0.26	0.16	0.13	0.17	0.32	0.40
Catalonia	0.30	0.26	0.27	0.49	0.52	0.43
Extremadura	0.14	0.02	0.03	0.04	0.03	0.03
Galicia	0.20	0.17	0.16	0.19	0.25	0.27
Madrid	0.34	0.27	0.22	0.31	0.38	0.38
Murcia	0.05	0.01	0.02	0.06	0.08	0.08
Navarre	0.20	0.18	0.24	0.70	0.86	0.79
País Vasco	1.39	2.01	1.98	3.03	3.09	3.28
Rioja	0.07	0.05	0.05	0.21	0.37	0.47
Valencia	0.07	0.04	0.02	0.11	0.12	0.10
Ceuta	0.00	0.00	0.00	0.06	0.09	0.16
Melilla	0.12	0.36	0.31	0.48	0.63	0.72

Source: Arriba 2014.

spared the crisis-related cutbacks suffered by other social welfare programs, a situation that is hardly surprising given that the governing PP's support is concentrated among older citizens.

Dependent Care: A Failure of Federalism or a Failure of Resources?

Perhaps the best example to conclude the analysis is the pressing policy issue of dependent care for the disabled and elderly. In 2006, the Zapatero government introduced a major dependent care initiative. It set national standards for evaluating disability but delegated to the regions the implementation and full regulation of dependent care systems. This ambitious reform has fallen victim to the crisis. In 2010, long-term care expenditures as a percentage of GDP were less than half the EU-27 average. Although spending on dependent care is low in all ACs, important differences exist among the delivery models (Arriba González 2014; Martínez-Buján 2014; Moreno Fuentes 2015).

The Socialists sought to create a national network of public-sector provision supported by third-sector organizations. While they initially proposed a program under the umbrella of the national social security system, pressures from the more nationalist regions and private-sector interests led to a hybrid program funded by the state but delivered through the regions and municipalities. The central government would provide a minimum level of funding to all regions based on assessed needs—in principle, about one-third of total funding—while the regions would enjoy both substantial autonomy in implementation and the capacity to increase spending should they desire. In 2009, with the program not scheduled to be completely rolled out until 2014, the central government provided approximately 50 percent of funding for the program, the ACs 40 percent, and beneficiaries 10 percent through needs-tested copayments.

While cash benefits were to have been largely residual in the model, they quickly came to comprise more than 50 percent of total spending as they were favored by most of the regional governments as well as by families. Some regions emphasize cash payments paid directly to families in recognition of their care for dependent relatives (Andalusia); in others, the primary model consists of cash payments for contracting nonprofessional care for dependent household members (Navarre); in still others (especially Madrid), the dominant model is one of professional home health care support. These differences reflect not only programmatic preferences but also differences in socioeconomic structures (Navarre vs. Andalusia) or levels of urbanization (Madrid). Other important differences between regions include the level of copayments required, the rapidity with which benefits are granted, and the likelihood that a given level of dependency will be recognized (CES 2013).

Cuts in funding introduced by the central government through reforms of the law in 2010, 2011, and 2012 reduced the state contribution to less than 20 percent of funding needs, leaving the ACs with responsibility for approximately 60 percent and beneficiaries another 20 percent. More important, the reforms restricted access to the program through stricter evaluative criteria—for example, the number of persons with the right to claim benefits was reduced by more than 100,000 (from 1.04 million) between January 2012 and December 2013. Not surprisingly, the regions have responded to the increased burdens on their resources by aggressively restricting access to benefits through more strict evaluations and delays in the granting of benefits. The law's limited impact can be seen in the fact that at no time since its introduction did the trend in spending on disability benefits in Spain exceed the trend in the EU-15 (and in fact, Spanish spending has been substantially lower than the EU-15 figure since 2011) (Zalacaín 2015).

Conclusions

The Spanish federalist system is plagued by uncertainty surrounding the distribution of authority and resources. This uncertainty is not a product of federalism; rather, the lack of political consensus regarding the distribution and structure of political power is the reason Spain is federalist. The problem is technically intractable because it requires a political solution.

The fundamental limitations of the Spanish welfare state—comparatively low funding, scant redistributive capacity, and a stunted capacity for policy evaluation and learning—are also not the result of its territorial institutions. All of the problems facing the Spanish welfare state today predate the emergence and consolidation of its federal institutions. Spain's limited fiscal capacity (low fiscal effort and high rates of tax evasion) is a failure of its central government, which continues to manage the bulk of tax legislation and collection for the fifteen CR ACs. Limited redistributive capacity and the absence of a culture of evaluation (and hence policy efficacy) are historic lacunae. Political contestation over the distribution of authority clearly discourages the transparency required to address these challenges. In this sense, federalism is again not the problem but the symptom. While it would be easier to address these issues in a unitary system, the sociopolitical cleavages endogenous to the design of Spanish federalist institutions obviously preclude the reestablishment of a unitary state.

Many authors (Colino and Kölling 2014, 257; Gray 2014, 22; León et al. 2015) have noted that Spain appears to support Jonathan Rodden's contention that where central governments collect the bulk of taxes but face constraints in controlling the spending and borrowing of the federation's member regions, fiscal discipline will be difficult to obtain. To overcome these constraints, it would be helpful to revisit an electoral system that privileges regionally concentrated parties over secondary, nationwide parties whose votes are more widely distributed. Even if a majority consensus could be reached regarding such a constitutional revision, it would surely entail unforeseen political consequences. In this sense, the Rodden claim is correct but provides Spanish political elites with few practical lessons.

This chapter has also highlighted another factor constraining fiscal discipline in Spain: the central government's relative indifference regarding regional spending and debt financing. Spain's current distribution of competencies between the center and the regions was set out only in 2002, coinciding with an enormous economic boom. Given the still-contested nature of the division of competencies and the resource slack associated with the boom, it is hardly surprising that fiscal discipline has been lacking. The evidence to date suggests that initiatives taken to rein in spending in the CR ACs since 2011 have met mixed success.[21] Once again, however, the problem is not the design of federalism but the contested nature of the polity. To apply the law in a way that is fair and transparent first requires a political consensus regarding the definition of fairness.

NOTES

1. Fernández-Albertos and Manzano (2012) claim that the lack of partisan conflict over the welfare state reflects the exceptional degree of consensus in public opinion regarding welfare state preferences, with voters of the two dominant parties having virtually identical preference orders for welfare state policies (health care > unemployment > education > pensions). Critically, voters' preferences vary considerably on the issue of decentralization.

2. This is less true for the Basque Country and Navarre, which have a distinct constitutional status. The discussion in this chapter focuses largely on the fifteen "common regime" ACs.

3. Pérez-García et al. 2015 claim that insufficient evidence currently exists to clarify the reasons underlying these relative differences in efficiencies. We reach much the same conclusion. Studies of cross-regional service quality in Spanish welfare services are few and far between.

4. Private delivery is more common in the historically more developed regions where church-related social services (for both health care and education) and private mutual insurance organizations (health care) were relatively well established before the transition to democracy in the late 1970s.

5. For example, profile data on the unemployed are virtually nonexistent at the national or AC level, making it impossible to design effective active labor market policies to address one of the country's most persistent socioeconomic problems (Felgueroso 2015).

6. The Great Recession—really a depression by any reasonable standard—began in Spain in 2008. However, the budget reconciliation process for most ACs features a two-year lag, meaning that the ACs were largely immune to the crisis until 2010.

7. Spain's d'Hondt electoral system rewards parties with strong national or regional bases and punishes parties with diffuse national bases. As a result, regional nationalist parties (particularly the Catalans) have played the kingmaker whenever one of the two dominant national parties has failed to gain an absolute majority.

8. Anomalies in the reporting of health spending data by the Community of Valencia led the European Commission to recommend the first fine of a member state for manipulating debt and deficit data under its new "six pack" powers (European Commission 2015).

9. As the FR regions are among the wealthiest, they would be net contributors if they were included in this fund. This issue has considerable economic and political salience.

10. Immigration grew from less than 2 percent to almost 15 percent of the population in less than ten years.

11. Much of the Left saw family care issues as "reactionary" concerns of the church. As a result, these kinds of welfare issues lacked champions across the ideological spectrum until the early 2000s (Guillén and León 2011; Valiente 1994, 2011).

12. Among OECD countries in 2015, Spain had the second-highest gross replacement rate at retirement, exceeded only by the Netherlands. The replacement rate was identical for average, half average, and 150 percent of average final pay (OECD 2015b).

13. For example, corruption that subsidizes political parties, employer associations, and unions is endemic in the Spanish program of workplace training coordinated through the CA's Public Employment Services (de Cózar and Álvarez 2014).

14. Debt according to the excessive deficit procedure (EDP) by regional (autonomous) government, as a percentage of GDP. http://www.bde.es/webbde/en/estadis/in foest/bolest13.html (see table 13.1 at the link).

15. Nothing in the law suggested that the central government could raise budget targets during the fiscal year, although it obviously did so (Conde-Ruiz and Rubio-Ramírez 2014).

16. In 1975, the year of Franco's death, Spain spent only 1.8 percent of GDP on education; OECD countries at the time were spending more than 5 percent, a level Spain did not reach until the late 2000s. In addition, only 45 percent of 15-year-olds were attending school, a figure that increased to 65 percent in 1980 and topped 97 percent by 2000 (Martínez Álvarez et al. 2013).

17. For an overview of the literature on the two systems and their outcomes, see Rogero-García and Andrés-Candelas 2014; Gortazar 2016.

18. Survey data show that parents choose *concertado* schools primarily for the social networks they offer rather than for religious reasons (Fernández Llera and Muñiz Pérez 2012).

19. The coefficient of variation in CA per-student spending on nonuniversity education fell from 17.5 percent in 2000 to 12.3 percent in 2008.

20. The contrast with Catalonia is notable. There, a nationalist government imposed (and subsequent Socialist governments did not alter) a system of linguistic immersion in which all public and *concertado* schools were required to make Catalan the main language of instruction, with Spanish taught almost as a foreign language.

21. For analyses of the evolution of AC finances since the crisis, see the FEDEA Observatorio Fiscal y Financiero de las CC.AA, http://www.fedea.net/category/observatorio-ccaa

REFERENCES

Acerete, Basilio, Mar Gasca, Anne Stafford, and Pamela Stapleton. 2015. "A Comparative Policy Analysis of Healthcare PPPs: Examining Evidence from Two Spanish Regions from an International Perspective." *Journal of Comparative Policy Analysis: Research and Practice* 17 (5). https://doi.org/10.1080/13876988.2015.1010789

Aja, Eliseo. 2003. *El Estado Autonómico: Federalismo y Hechos Diferenciales*. Madrid: Alianza.

Albertí Rovira, Enoch. 2013. "El Impacto de la Crisis Financiera en el Estado Autonómico Español." *Revista Española de Derecho Constitucional* 98:63–89.

Allen, Judith. 2006. "Welfare Regimes, Welfare Systems, and Housing in Southern Europe." *European Journal of Housing Policy* 6 (3): 251–77.

Alonso, José M., Judith Clifton, and Daniel Díaz-Fuentes. 2015. "The Impact of New Public Management on Efficiency: An Analysis of Madrid's Hospitals." *Health Policy* 119:333–40.

Arbós Marín, Xavier, César Colino Cámara, María Jesús García Morales, and Salvador Parrado Díez. 2009. *Las Relaciones Intergubernamentales en el Estado Autonómico: La Posición de los Actores*. Barcelona: Institut d'Estudis Autonòmics.

Arriba González de Druana, Ana. 2014. *El Papel de la Garantía de Mínimos Frente a la Crisis: VII Informe sobre Exclusión y Desarrollo Social en España 2014*. Madrid: Fundación FOESSA.

Ayala Cañón, Luis. 2012. "Los Sistemas de Garantía de Ingresos ante la Crisis: Una Perspectiva Territorial." *Ekonomiaz* 81 (3).

Bagues, Manuel. 2013. "Path Dependence." 29 May. http://nadaesgratis.es/bagues/path-dependence

Bentolila, Samuel, and Marcel Jansen. 2013. "Algo se Mueve . . ." 17 September. http://nadaesgratis.es/bentolila/algo-se-mueve-en-las-politicas-activas-de-empleo

Beramendi, Pablo. 2012. *The Political Economy of Inequality: Regions and Redistribution*. Cambridge: Cambridge University Press.

Beramendi, Pablo, and Ramón Máiz. 2004. "Spain: Unfulfilled Federalism." In *Federalism, Unitarism, and Territorial Cleavages*, ed. U. Amoretti and N. Bermeo, 123–54. Baltimore: Johns Hopkins University Press.

Colino, César. 2013a. "Intergovernmental Relations in the Spanish Federal System: In Search of a Model." In *The Ways of Federalism in Western Countries and the Horizons of Territorial Autonomy in Spain*, ed. A. López-Basaguren and L. Escajedo San Epifanio, 2:111–24. Berlin: Springer.

Colino, César. 2013b. *Responses to the Crisis and the Estado Autonómico in Spain: Governmental Strategies and Consequences on Power Relations and Stability*. Madrid: Universidad Autónoma de Madrid. http://www.uam.es/ss/Satellite/Derecho/es/1242658791834/listadoCombo/Working_Papers.htm

Colino, César, and Angustias Hombrado, 2015. "Territorial Pluralism in Spain: Characteristics and Assessment." In *Territorial Pluralism: Managing Difference in Multinational States*, ed. Karlo Basta, John McGarry, and Richard Simeon, 171–95. Vancouver: University of British Columbia Press.

Colino, César, and Mario Kölling. 2014. "Parallel Lives: Unsolved Problems and Reform Initiatives in Spanish and German Fiscal Federalism." In *Fiscal Federalism and Fiscal Decentralisation in Europe*, ed. S. Lutgenau, 198–223. Vienna: Austrian Studienverlag.

Coller, Xavier, Antonio M. Jaime, and Andrés A. Santana. 2011. "La Profesionalización de los Diputados Autonómicos en España (1980–2005): Análisis de Continuidades y Supervivencia." Paper presented at the annual conference of the Spanish Association of Political Science and Administration, Murcia.

Colomer, J. M. 1998. "The Spanish State of Autonomies: Non-Institutional Federalism." *West European Politics* 2l (4): 40–52.

Conde-Ruiz, José Ignacio, and Juan Rubio-Ramírez. 2014. "La Ley de Estabilidad Presupuestaria y las CC.AA." 26 December. http://nadaesgratis.es/rubio-ramirez/la-ley-de-estabilidad-presupuestaria-y-las-ccaa

Consejo Económico y Social (CES). 2013. *La Aplicación de la Ley de Dependencia en España.* Madrid.

Cordero, Guillermo, Antonio M. Jaime-Castillo, and Xavier Coller. 2016. "Candidate Selection in a Multilevel State: The Case of Spain." *American Behavioral Scientist* 60:853–68.

Dahlström, Carl, and Victor Lapuente. 2012. "Weberian Bureaucracy and Corruption Protection." In *Good Government: The Relevance of Political Science*, ed. S. Holmberg and B. Rothstein, 150–73. Cheltenham: Elgar.

de Cózar, Álvaro, and Pilar Álvarez. 2014. "30 Años de Estafa Continua." El País, 15 June. http://politica.elpais.com/politica/2014/06/15/actualidad/1402842749_308339.html

de la Fuente, Ángel. 2012a. *La Evolución de la Financiación de las Comunidades Autónomas de Régimen Común, 2002–2011*. Madrid: Fundación SEPI.

de la Fuente, Ángel. 2012b. *El Nuevo Sistema de Financiación de las Comunidades Autónomas de Régimen Común: Un Análisis Crítico y Datos Homogéneos para 2009 y 2010*. Madrid: Fundación BBVA.

de la Fuente, Angel, and José E. Bosca. 2014. *Gasto Educativo por Regiones y Niveles en 2010*. Madrid: Fundación BBVA.

del Campo, Esther, and Eliseo López Sánchez. 2015."Modelos Educativos y Políticas de Educación Secundaria en Andalucía, Madrid, y País Vasco: Problemas, Agendas, y Decisiones." *Gestión y Análisis de Políticas Públicas, Nueva Época* 13. http://dx.doi.org/10.24965/gapp.v0i13.10236

Dubin, Kenneth A. 2012. "Adjusting to the Law: The Role of Beliefs in Firms' Responses to Regulation." *Politics and Society* 40 (3): 389–424.

Durán-Cabré, José María, Alejandro Esteller-Moré, and Luca Salvadori. 2012. "Regional Competition on Tax Administration." Unpublished Manuscript.

Echebarría, Koldo, and Joan Subirats, 1998. "Descentralización y Coordinación de la Sanidad en el Estado Autonómico." *Papeles de Economia Española* 76:78–93.

Escardíbul, Josep-Oriol, Susana Morales, Carmen Pérez Esparrells, and Eva De La Torre. 2013. "Evolución de los Precios de Matrícula en las Enseñanzas Universitarias por Comunidades Autónomas (1992–2013): Un Análisis antes y después del Espacio Europeo de Educación Superior." Paper presented at the Association of Educational Economics, Coruña, Spain, 4–5 July.

European Commission. 2015. "Commission Recommends Imposing a Fine on Spain for Misreporting of Deficit Data in Valencia." 7 May. http://europa.eu/rapid/press-release_IP-15-4939_en.htm

Felgueroso, Florentino. 2015. "En el Pleistoceno de las Políticas de Empleo." 12 June. http://nadaesgratis.es/felgueroso/en-el-pleistoceno-de-las-politicas-de-empleo

Fernández-Albertos, José, and Dulce Manzano. 2012. "The Lack of Partisan Conflict over the Welfare State in Spain." *South European Society and Politics* 17 (3): 427–47.

Fernández-Llera, Roberto. 2011. "Descentralización, Deuda Pública, y Disciplina de Mercado en España." *Innovar* 21 (39): 67–82.

Fernández-Llera, Roberto, and Santiago Lago Peñas. 2011. "Ultraperiferia, Economía, y Finanzas Públicas de Canarias: Una Panorámica." [*Revista de Estudios Regionales* 90:17–44.

Fernández-Llera, Roberto, and Manuel Muñiz Pérez. 2012. "Colegios Concertados y Selección de Escuela en España: Un Círculo Vicioso." *Presupuesto y Gasto Público* 67:97–118.

Fernández-Llera, Roberto, Santiago Lago Peñas, and Jorge Martínez Vázquez. 2013. "La Autonomía Tributaria de las Comunidades Autónomas y Su (Des)Uso: Presencia de una Restricción Presupuestaria Blanda." Paper presented at the Encuentro de Economía Pública Conference, Seville, 31 January–1 February.

Fernández Mellizo-Soto, María. 2014. "The Evolution of Inequality of Educational Opportunities: A Systematic Review of Analyses of the Spanish Case." *Revista Española de Investigaciones Sociológicas* 147:107–20.

Gallego, Raquel, and Joan Subirats. 2011. *Autonomies i Desigualtats a Espanya: Percepcions, Evolució Social, i Polítiques de Benestar.* Barcelona: Institut d'Estudis Autonòmics.

Gallego, Raquel, and Joan Subirats. 2012. "Spanish and Regional Welfare Systems: Policy Innovation and Multi-Level Governance." *Regional and Federal Studies* 22 (3): 269–88.

Gortazar, Lucas. 2016. "Escuela Concertada: Un Mal Equilibrio." http://politikon.es/2016/06/07/escuela-concertada-un-mal-equilibrio/

Gray, Caroline. 2014. "Smoke and Mirrors: How Regional Finances Complicate Spanish-Catalan Relations." *International Journal of Iberian Studies* 27 (1): 21–42.

Gray, Caroline. 2015. "A Fiscal Path to Sovereignty? The Basque Economic Agreement and Nationalist Politics." *Nationalism and Ethnic Politics* 21 (1): 63–82.

Guillén, Ana Marta, and Margarita León, eds. 2011. *The Spanish Welfare State in European Context.* Farnham: Ashgate.

Heywood, Paul. 1998. "Power Diffusion or Concentration? In Search of the Spanish Policy Process." *West European Politics* 21 (4): 103–23.

Hopkin, Jonathan. 2009. "Devolution and Party Politics in Britain and Spain." *Party Politics* 15 (2): 179–98.

Lago Peña, Santiago, and Antonio Martínez-Vázquez. 2016. "El Gasto Público en España en Perspectiva Comparada: ¿Gastamos lo Suficiente? ¿Gastamos Bien?" *Papeles de Economía Española* 147:2–25.

Lapuente, Victor. 2012. "La Loca Historia del Estado Español." *El Diario*, 18 November. http://www.eldiario.es/piedrasdepapel/politicos-funcionarios-Molinas_6_6970 3039.html

Lázaro, Marta. 2015. "Sin Noticias de la Reforma de la Financiación Autonómica." 19 May. www.lne.es

León, Sandra. 2009. "¿Por Qué el Sistema de Financiación Autonómica es Inestable?" *Revista Española de Investigaciones Sociológicas (Reis)* 128:57–87.

León, Sandra. 2010a. "The Political Rationale of Regional Financing in Spain." In *The Political Economy of Inter-Regional Fiscal Flows: Measurement, Determinants, and Effects on Country Stability*, ed. Nuria Bosch, Marta Espasa, and Albert Solé, 249–70. Cheltenham: Elgar.

León, Sandra. 2010b. "Who Is Responsible for What? Clarity of Responsibilities in Multilevel States: The Case of Spain." *European Journal of Political Research* 50:80–109.

León, Sandra. 2012. "How Do Citizens Attribute Responsibility in Multilevel States? Learning, Biases, and Asymmetric Federalism: Evidence from Spain." *Electoral Studies* 31:120–30.

León, Sandra, et al. 2015. *La Financiación Autonómica: Claves para Comprender un (Interminable) Debate*. Madrid: Alianza Editorial.

López i Casanovas, Guillem, and Beatriz González López-Valcárcel. 2016. "El Sistema Sanitario en España: Entre lo Que no Acaba de Morir y lo Que no Termina de Nacer." *Papeles de Economía Española* 147:190–211.

López Laborda, Julio. 2011. "Beneficios y Costes del Estado Autonómico." *Cuadernos Manuel Jimeno Abad* 1:34–42.

Losada, Antón, and Ramón Maíz. 2005. "Devolution and Involution: De-Federalization Politics through Educational Policies in Spain (1996–2004)." *Regional and Federal Studies* 15 (4): 437–51.

Maiz, Ramon, Francisco Caamaño, and Miguel Azpitarte. 2010. "The Hidden Counterpoint of Spanish Federalism: Recentralization and Resymmetrization in Spain (1978–2008)." *Regional and Federal Studies* 20 (1): 63–82.

Marí-Klose, Pau. 2015. "Un Estado Que Favorece la Desigualdad." Ctxt.es, 12 February. http://tinyurl.com/oogoqfd

Martínez Álvarez, José Antonio, Cristina Sánchez Figueroa, and Pedro Cortiñas Vázquez. 2013. "Evolución de la Política Educativa en España: Instituto de Estudios Fiscales." *Papeles de trabajo del Instituto de Estudios Fiscales. Serie economía* 12:3–35.

Martínez-Vazquez, Jorge. 2014. "La Descentralización Tributaria a las Comunidades Autónomas en España: Desafíos y Soluciones." In *Por una Verdadera Reforma Fiscal*, ed. J. Duran and A. Esteller-Moré. Editorial Ariel.

Medina Guerrero, Manuel. 2013. "El Estado Autonómico en Tiempos de Disciplina Fiscal." *Revista Española de Derecho Constitucional* 98:109–47.

Ministry of Employment and Social Security. 2016. *El Gobierno Aprueba el Plan Anual de Política de Empleo 2016*. http://prensa.empleo.gob.es/WebPrensa/noticias/lab oral/detalle/2872

Moreno, Luis, and Sebastia Sarasa. 1993. "Génesis y desarrollo del Estado del Bienestar en España." *Revista Internacional de Sociología* 3 (6): 27–69.

Moreno Fuentes, Javier Francisco. 2015. *Challenges and Reforms in Long-Term Care Policy in Spain.* Madrid: Instituto Universitario de Investigación Ortega y Gasset.

OECD. 2015a. *Education at a Glance 2015: OECD Indicators.* http://dx.doi.org/10.1787/eag-2015-en

OECD. 2015b. *Pensions at a Glance 2015: OECD and G20 Indicators.* http://dx.doi.org/10.1787/pension_glance-2015-en

Parrado, Salvador. 2010. "The Role of Spanish Central Government in a Multi-Level State." *International Review of Administrative Sciences* 76 (3): 469–88.

Pérez Durán, Ixchel. 2015. "Assessing Formal Accountability for Public Policies: The Case of Health Policy in Spain." *International Review of Administrative Sciences.* https://doi.org/10.1177/0020852314565999

Pérez Esparrells, Carmen, and Susana Morales Sequera. 2012. "La Descentralización de la Enseñanza no Universitaria en España: Análisis de Convergencia desde la Perspectiva del Gasto." *Presupuesto y Gasto Público* 67:137–60.

Pérez Esparrells, Carmen, and Susana Morales Sequera. 2014. "Las Becas y Ayudas al Estudio en la Educación no Universitaria en España: Diagnóstico desde la Perspectiva Regional y Propuestas de Mejora." *Revista de Educación* 366:87–112.

Pérez-García, Francisco, Vicent Cucarella Tormo, and Laura Hernández Lahiguera. 2015. *Servicios Públicos, Diferencias Territoriales, e Igualdad de Oportunidades.* Bilbao: Fundación BBVA, IVIE.

Rico, Ana, and Joan Costa-Font. 2005. "Power Rather Than Path Dependency? The Dynamics of Institutional Change under Health Care Federalism." *Journal of Health Politics, Policy, and Law* 30 (1–2): 231–52.

Rico Gómez, Ana. 1996. "Regional Decentralization and Health Care Reform in Spain (1976–1996)." *South European Society and Politics* 1 (3): 115–34.

Rogero-García, Jesús, and Mario Andrés-Candelas. 2014. "Gasto Público y de las Familias en Educación en España: Diferencias entre Centros Públicos y Concertados." *Revista Española de Investigaciones Sociológicas* 147:121–32.

Ruíz-Almendral, Violeta. 2013. "Curbing the Deficit in Spain and Its Autonomous Communities: A Constitutional Conundrum." *Bij de Buren*, January, 68–77.

Sala, Gemma. 2013. "Federalism without Adjectives in Spain." *Publius: The Journal of Federalism* 44 (1): 109–34.

Sánchez-Cuenca, Ignacio. 2016. "La Ventaja Universitaria Catalana." *Infolibre*, 17 May. www.infolibre.es

Sanzo, Luis. 2015. "La Lucha Contra la Pobreza en España: La Excepción Vasca." *Agenda Pública*, 12 October. http://agendapublica.es/la-lucha-contra-la-pobreza-en-espana-la-excepcion-vasca/

Simón, Pablo, Santiago Lago-Peñas, and Alberto Vaquero. 2012. "On the Political Determinants of Intergovernmental Grants in Decentralized Countries: The Case of Spain." *Publius* 44 (1): 135–56.

Solé-Ollé, Albert. 2009. "Evaluating the Effects of Decentralization on Public Service Delivery: The Spanish Experience." In *Does Decentralization Enhance Service Delivery and Poverty Reduction?*, ed. Ehtisham Ahmad and Giorgio Brosio, 257–86. Cheltenham: Edward Elgar.

Solé-Ollé, Albert. 2013. "Regional Tax Autonomy in Spain: 'Words' or 'Deeds'?" Paper presented at workshop on Interaction between Local Expenditure Responsibilities and Local Tax Policy, Copenhagen, 12–13 September.

"Sólo Madrid, País Vasco y Navarra Cumplieron el Tope de Deuda en 2014." 2015. *El País*, 13 March. http://economia.elpais.com/economia/2015/03/13/actualidad/142 6233643_114434.html

Stepan, Alfred. 1999. "Federalism and Democracy: Beyond the U.S. Model." *Journal of Democracy* 10 (4): 19–34.

Valiente Fernández, Celia. 2011. "La Erosión del Familismo en el Estado de Bienestar en España: Las Políticas de Cuidado de los Niños desde 1975." In *Las Familias Monoparentales a Debate*, ed. Elisabet Almeda Samaranch and Dino Di Nella, 2:47–66. Barcelona: Copalqui.

Valiente Fernández, Celia. 1994. *El Feminismo de Estado en España: El Instituto de la Mujer, 1983–1994*. Madrid: Instituto Juan March de Estudios e Investigaciones.

Zabalza, Antoni. 2012. "Una Nota sobre el Ajuste del IVA en el Sistema Foral de Financiación: Marco Analítico y Propuesta de un Nuevo Mecanismo." *Hacienda Pública Española* 202:105–23.

Zabalza, Antoni, and Julio López-Laborda. 2011. "The New Spanish System of Intergovernmental Transfers." *International Tax and Public Finance* 18:750–86.

Zabalza Martí, Antonio, and Julio López Laborda. 2017. "The Uneasy Coexistence of the Spanish Foral and Common Regional Finance Systems." *Investigaciones regionales: Journal of Regional Research* 37:119–52.

Zalacaín, Joseba. 2015. "La Ley de Dependencia, una Oportunidad Perdida." El Diario, 11 January. http://www.eldiario.es/agendapublica/impacto_social/Ideas-valorar-situacion-Ley-Dependencia_0_344365622.html

Zubiri, Antoni. 2015. "Un Análisis del Sistema Foral de la Comunidad Autónoma del País Vasco y Sus Ventajas durante la Crisis." *Papeles de Economía Española* 143:205–24.

Immobilism by Design

Fiscal Devolution and Territorial Inequality in Italy

Julia Lynch and Rebecca Oliver

Even before decentralizing reforms that began in the late 1990s, the Italian welfare state was well known for large differences in the level of protection offered to residents across the country's twenty regions (Fargion 1996). When constitutional reforms devolved fiscal and policy autonomy to subnational regions, many observers expected this inequality in social provision to grow even wider (Arachi and Zanardi 2004; Franco 2010). A series of legislative reforms granted greater autonomy to regions and recalibrated domains of legislation and social service delivery mechanisms. Contrary to expectations, however, no noticeable increase in regional inequalities in social spending has occurred since the onset of these reforms. Particularly in light of the fact that the reforms are taking place in a context of pronounced regional differences in wealth, fiscal capacity, and economic development (Del Pino and Pavolini 2015), this is a surprising finding. Partisan competition and legislative gradualism have yielded an underlying stability in the inequality between regions on social spending.

There are several good reasons to expect that reforms aimed at creating greater regional autonomy and deepening fiscal federalism would generate increasing inequality in regional social spending. First, several cross-national studies have found that political decentralization is associated with increased regional spending disparities (Canaleta, Arzoz, and Garate 2004; Ezcurra and Rodríguez-Pose 2013; Kyriacou, Muinelo-Gallo, and Roca-Sagalés 2015).[1] Single case studies of Colombia and Australia, too, have found evidence pointing in this direction (Bird and Tarasov 2004; Bonet 2006).

Second, considerable research has documented historical differences in growth and productivity between Italy's wealthier northern regions and less affluent southern areas (Leonardi, Nanetti, and Putnam 1987; Triglia 1992). Numerous studies have identified a persistent "fiscal gap"—that is, a gap between expenditure needs and own revenues—in a number of regions (Unioncamera Veneto 2009, 2013). If historical patterns of revenues and spending remain in place, fiscal decentralization is likely to generate increasing inequality between regions in social spending.

Third, since the 1994 start of the Second Republic, which coincided with the rise to prominence of a political party that strongly criticized fiscal redistribution, decentralization has been a leitmotif of national politics. Many of Italy's devolutionary reforms were either spearheaded by or done in reaction to demands by the Northern League (Lega Nord), which has consistently campaigned against redistribution of tax revenues from North to South and in recent years has aggressively advocated a federal system and greater fiscal independence of the North (Groppi and Scattone 2006, 132). When in the ruling coalition, the Lega Nord has demanded that fiscal decentralization be a government priority. However, even initiatives occurring under center-left coalitions that excluded the Lega Nord were influenced by the political threat posed by the party.

A fourth reason to expect that the decentralization in Italy would create growing divergence in social spending patterns between regions is the specific nature of the decentralizing reforms, which consisted of measures devolving significant policy and fiscal autonomy to local governments. Prior to the first initiatives, regional prerogatives had been rather limited, with a strict hierarchical structure and limited delegation to regional authorities.[2] In 1997, the center-left government of Prime Minister Romano Prodi was the first to undertake decentralizing reforms. These reforms, known collectively as the Bassanini Laws, changed administrative structures and allocated a number of administrative functions and civil service positions to regions, provinces, and municipalities. The major constitutional reform of 2001, which modified Chapter V of the constitution, also introduced by a center-left government under Prime Minister Giuliano Amato, primarily involved a reallocation of legislative competences between the central government and the regions. Any function not reserved for the central government or shared between levels of government was granted to the regions.

Along with these new responsibilities for local administration, the amended Article 119 of the constitution also introduced some safeguards against too much regional divergence. One of the reserved powers that remained with the prerogative of the central government was the determination of "essential levels of services concerning civic and social rights which must be guaranteed across territory" (Cento Bull 2002, 187). The rewritten Article 119 stipulates the establishment of a financial equalization fund to compensate economic disequilibria between northern and southern regions (Alber 2014, 149). Nevertheless, the central government relinquished authority to suspend regional legislation, and the next law on fiscal federalism (42/2009) granted even greater revenue autonomy to regions and local authorities.

The 2009 law was introduced and passed by the center-right coalition government led by Silvio Berlusconi, which included the Lega Nord. Regional and municipal authorities were granted chief responsibility over social services and education (subject to providing an "essential level of provision" set by agreement with the central state). In an effort to further devolve the locus of fiscal responsibility, regions were granted a share of the nationally collected value-added tax and the entirety of revenues from and the right to modify (within bounds) the personal income tax and tax on business. Municipalities gained a segment of value-added tax, income tax, and the right to levy certain new property taxes. Law 42/2009 also specified that grants to the regions from the central government be cut in proportion to these increases in local fiscal capacity.

For all of these reasons—the theoretical expectations that federalism will produce growing divergence, the highly disparate economic bases and social provision patterns in Italy's regions prior to the reforms, the political impetus for greater regional autonomy in taxing and spending, and the significant fiscal and policy devolution implied by the reform legislation—it would be reasonable to expect that the decentralization of the Italian welfare state would result in growing inequalities between the regions in social spending. But this has not been the case.

Territorial Inequality in Social Spending

Several different levels of government and administrative entities undertake social protection in Italy. EU guidelines (which are reflected in the Italian accounts; see Istat 2011) classify social protection spending under a wide range of functions ranging from the quite marginal (social assistance to the elderly, parental leave benefits) to substantial expenditure items (old-age pensions, health care). In Italy prior to decentralization, subnational governments were generally responsible for providing social services and assistance for the neediest. The regional governments were

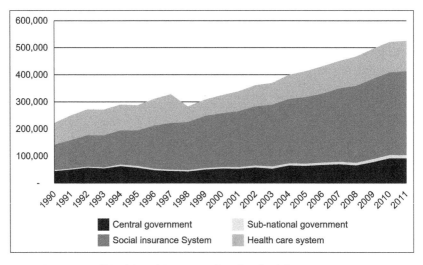

Fig. 1. Percentage of Total Social Protection Spending by Administrative Unit (millions of current euros)

Source: Data on social protection spending from Istat 2014b; data on health spending from Istat2014e.

charged with administering health services to be paid for largely by pass-through spending from the central government (details in France 2014; Toth 2014). The central state oversaw programs related to the labor market and some forms of disability. The social insurance system disbursed funds collected from employers, employees, and the self-employed to the major social insurance programs (old-age and widows' pensions, some disability pensions, family allowances, and a minimal unemployment insurance benefit). Primary, secondary, and postsecondary education is funded primarily by the Ministry of Education, University, and Research, which provides monies for teacher and staff salaries (86 percent of education spending in 2009) (Sibiano and Agasisti 2013, 14). The maintenance of school facilities and integrative projects, student aid, and vocational training are regionally funded.

Figure 1 shows the share of social spending in Italy carried out by the four administrative units from 1990 to 2011. The figure illustrates that the vast and rapidly increasing bulk of social spending in Italy is carried out through the social insurance system and not by either the national or subnational governments or even by the health care system. Subnational governments' share of social spending has risen since decentralizing reforms began in the late 1990s, but that increase has been very modest relative to

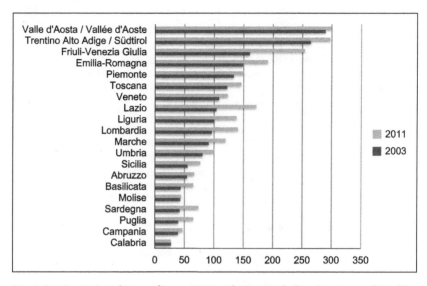

Fig. 2. Per Capita Social Expenditures, 2003 and 2011, Excluding Pensions and Health (current euros)
Source: Data from Istat 2014a.

the total amounts of spending—from 1.81 percent of total social spending in 1990 to a high of 2.29 percent in 2010.

Subnational governments nevertheless do have important roles in social spending. They are responsible for an increasing array of social and health services as well as for providing the basic social safety net. And marked variation in regional spending occurs within the competencies afforded to the regions, provinces, and municipalities. Figure 2 shows the variation across regions in social service spending and cash transfers by municipalities, which in many cases correspond to regional GDP (see Appendix for regional GDP figures).

Some version of figure 2 is the dominant image that most analysts appear to have in mind when they think about the pronounced regional variation in the welfare state across Italy. The coefficient of variation for overall social expenditures (excluding health and pensions) has a wide range between regions, with a slight decline from 0.70 in 2003 to 0.62 in 2011. Most of the larger increases in social spending during this period occurred in regions with lower overall spending, with the exception of Friuli-Venezia Giulia and Lazio, where spending rose by 58 and 65 percent, respectively.

While the data in figure 2 correspond to the dominant image of a frag-

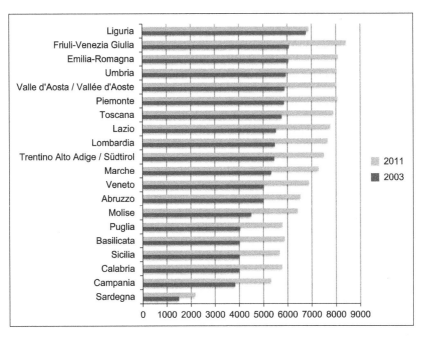

Fig. 3. Per Capita Social Expenditures, 2003 and 2011, Including Pensions and Health (current euros)

Note: Data refers to sum of per capita spending on social protection, health, and pensions. Pension per capita refers to population over 65.

Source: Pension data is from INPS (pension ai superstiti, pensione di vecchiaia, prestazioni assistenziali); data for health spending and other social spending are from Istat 2014b, d.

mented, regionally divergent welfare state in Italy, these figures are not adjusted for the size of the population at risk of needing services in different regions and exclude health and social insurance spending. Understanding the full spectrum of social spending available to residents in different regions requires a different approach. Figure 3 shows per capita social spending in the Italian regions including health and pensions and adjusting for population demographics. Regional variation in social spending is greatly attenuated when we include a broader swath of social spending: The coefficients of variation across regions are 0.24 in 2003 and 0.21 in 2011. Most regional increases in spending are quite similar to the average—a 37 percent increase (in euros per capita). Exceptions include Liguria, where per capita social spending increased by less than 2 percent between 2003 and 2011.

Relative stability in the amount of variation in total per capita social

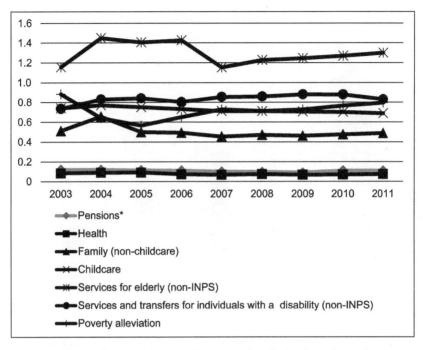

Fig. 4. Coefficient of Variation Between Regions in Standardized per Capita Social Expenditures, Including Pensions and Health, 2003–2011

Note: Coefficients of variation of per capita spending in each policy field were calculated across 20 regions for each year between 2003 and 2011. Spending per capita adjusted for appropriate population: pensions per capita based on the population 65 and over; child care per capita based on the 0–4 population; services and transfers for individuals with disabilities (which does not include spending on individuals over 65) based on the under-65 age group. "Pensions" line includes pension ai superstiti, pensione di veccahiaia, prestazioni assistenziali.

Source: Data from Istat 2014a, c, d.

spending between regions over time could obscure important changes in different policy areas. Figure 4 shows the coefficient of variation of spending among the regions in different policy domains, including those that are administered centrally and those delegated to the municipalities. Disaggregation by policy area allows for more appropriate population adjusters to estimate per capita spending. Within each of these policy areas, we measure the coefficient of variation between regions for a given year. This permits us to compare regional variation over time in a given spending area and across policy fields.

Overall, we observe considerable stability over time in the magnitude of regional differences in social spending. This trend is particularly salient in two of the largest spending areas, health and pensions, where cross-

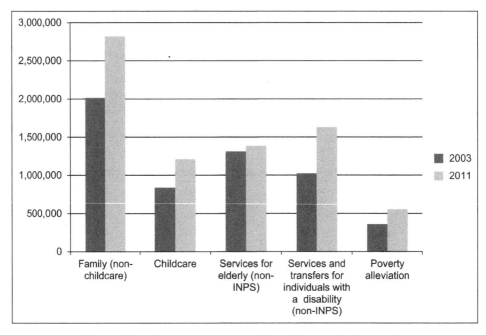

Fig. 5. Italian Total Spending on Assistance and Social Services by Municipalities, 2003 and 2011 (thousands of euros)
Source: Data from Istat 2014a, c, d.

regional differences in spending are both very low and very stable over time. Despite the fact that the Italian National Health Service is administered at the national level, it provides universal access to medical care that is funded via general revenues collected at the national level (Toth 2014). Old-age pensions are financed by social contributions levied on employers, employees, and the self-employed that are set at the national level and administered by the Instituto Nazionale Previdenza Sociale (the National Social Security Institute).[3] Perhaps not surprisingly given the centralized administration of financing in these two policy areas, regional inequality in health and pension spending is low once we adjust for the demographic structure of the population.

Social spending on assistance and social service provision at the municipal level (Istat 2014b) presents much greater cross-regional variation with distinct dynamics for different policy fields. Figure 5 illustrates the per capita spending on these different measures aggregated at the national level.[4] Those spending areas in which the regional differences are greatest (as seen in figure 4)—poverty alleviation and social assistance to the elderly—are also the policy areas that receive the fewest resources.[5]

Most spending on poverty alleviation is directed toward services and other direct interventions, including shelters for the homeless, services for domestic abuse and for former inmates, and some psychiatric services. The amounts are typically low, with high variation between years. Cross-regional variation in poverty alleviation has remained relatively stable with the exception of a low in 2005 and a high in 2003. Municipal services and transfers for users with physical, mental, or sensory disabilities (including people living with HIV or affected by TB) do not include spending directed toward the elderly and have been quite stable over time.[6] Absolute spending on these services has increased (figure 5) but has done so rather evenly across regions and thus with stable levels of regional dispersion (figure 4).

Municipalities finance a number of services and transfers directed toward the elderly, including social assistance, mobility assistance, and home care.[7] Outside of pensions, regions differ markedly in the scope and the type of services offered for the elderly. Variation is more substantial in this arena than in other policy fields, as signaled by the high starting point and persistently higher coefficient of variation (CV) than for other policy areas. Barbabella et al. (2013, 32–33) distinguish five regional profiles in terms of continuous care for the elderly, one of the main spending areas in elder care, based on the "intensity" of assistance offered and the use of residencies versus a reliance on cash for care and the employment of in-home attendants. They also note significant regional differences in the integration of health services with municipal care options: many wealthier regions have a stronger track record than less affluent ones. A close examination of the changes in the annual per capita expenditure amounts in a given region indicates that the decline in cross-regional variation in spending on services for the elderly stems not from broad spending increases as southern regions catch up to their northern counterparts but rather from stability, with minor increases in some southern regions and a modest decline in some northern regions (while others have stable expenditures).

Change over time in the degree of regional inequality in the field of family policy has generally been less pronounced than in the areas of services for the poor and elderly. Spending on both child care and other family policies rose considerably between 2003 and 2011 (figure 5). The decline in regional variation in child care spending, from a high of 0.77 in 2004 to 0.69 in 2011 took place in the context of an increase in overall spending on public child care across Italy (Oliver and Mätzke 2014). The number of municipalities offering child care services also broadened from 32.8 to 50.7 percent between 2003 and 2013 (Istat 2014c). Cross-regional variation in non-child-care family services, which include community centers, municipal shelters for teenagers, social work, home care for families with young children, foster care, and cash transfers (notably family income supplements and housing assistance) was quite stable over time with the exception of a peak in 2004 (Istat 2013, 8).

In sum, the fiscal and administrative decentralization of Italy's welfare state prompted many to fear and some to hope that increasing cross-regional inequalities in social provision would occur. In the context of a dualistic economy and strong political pressure for greater regional fiscal autonomy, these expectations have rarely been questioned. However, remarkably little increase has occurred in the differences between regions in social spending since 2003, the earliest date for which we have reliable data. One reason for this is that the vast bulk of social spending in the regions actually consists of health and pension spending, which is relatively invariant across regions (after adjusting for demographic structure) and quite stable over time.

What Has Caused Regional Inequalities to Remain Stable?

Despite the apparent priority placed by successive governments on pushing forward decentralization of the Italian state, devolution has in fact been delayed or deferred. This contrast between the rhetoric and the reality of decentralization bears partial responsibility for the stability in cross-regional social spending patterns in recent years. Partisan contestation and self-decelerating implementation measures have yielded a halting development of legislation and have ultimately sustained a pattern of cross-regional redistribution that limits growth in interregional inequality in social spending.

Partisan Wrangling over the Content of Reform

Throughout Italy's Second Republic, both the center-right and the center-left have been consistently committed to comprehensive devolution. The Lega Nord and several northern regions pressured all sides to include decentralization in their policy plans. For the center-right, a viable majority coalition necessitated the partnership of the Lega Nord. Center-left politicians, for their part, were unwilling to cede the issue of devolution, and with it possible support from voters in northern cities, to the center-right or the Lega Nord. However, even within the two main coalitions, let alone between them, there have been vastly different ideas about the appropriate articulation of such reform. Alternation in government between the center-left and center-right during the Second Republic has thus introduced multiple parallel paths to reform, delaying decisive progress toward devolution and postponing concrete implementation even of those reforms that have been passed. Painstakingly slow negotiations also occurred within coalitions, particularly those involving the Lega Nord, further contributing to delays in implementation.

The first major period of reform began in 1997 with the Bassani Laws and culminated in a 2001 constitutional reform. The center-left was in power at the national level but had recently suffered major electoral defeats in regional elections in the North, where the Lega Nord, allied with the center-right, performed strongly. Two northern regional presidents had proposed popular referenda to pressure the government to devolve fiscal and administrative power to the regions (Keating and Wilson 2010, 10). The timing of the center-left reforms suggests that they were unwilling to cede the issue of decentralization to the Lega Nord and its center-right allies (Mazzoleni 2009, 143–44), but the Italian Left had long supported some forms of decentralization, ensuring that these reforms did more than simply pay lip service to the issue (Massetti and Toubeau 2013, 366). At the closing of its term, in the spring of 2001, the center-left Amato government used its narrow majority to pass the constitutional reform through both houses of Parliament.

The reform passed without legislative support from Forza Italia, the Lega Nord, or other center-right parties, however, and when a center-right coalition claimed victory in the May 2001 elections, members of the coalition called for a referendum opposing the constitutional reform.[8] The parties of the center-right were divided, however, in their approach to decentralization. During the campaign leading up to the 2001 constitutional reform, Umberto Bossi, the leader of the Lega Nord, referred to the center-left's reform as "false federalism" (cited in Keating and Wilson 2010). Premier Berlusconi also opposed the reform while simultaneously committing to undertake a further devolutionary change (Keating and Wilson 2010, 11; Massetti and Toubeau 2013). But his Forza Italia party was decidedly split on the question, particularly at the regional level: some regional presidents supported the measure as a necessary incremental step (e.g., Roberto Formigoni in Lombardia, Raffaele Fitto in Puglia), while others actively opposed it (e.g., Giancarlo Galan in Veneto) (Keating and Wilson 2010, 13). And Alleanza Nazionale (National Alliance), the third member of the center-right coalition, opposed the 2001 reform because it had gone "too far and risked penalizing the less developed regions of the Mezzogiorno" (Massetti and Toubeau 2013, 368).[9]

These disagreements within the Right about the proper nature of decentralization would hinder effective action to overturn the center-left's 2001 reform. The center-left, having just lost the election, nevertheless managed a coherent rally to protect its reform from the referendum to overturn it. Moreover, in 2001, public opinion appeared to strongly favor a reform. In an Italian National Election Studies survey, almost 80 percent of respondents agreed that "more autonomy should be given to the regions" and 62 percent concurred with the statement that "tax money should be given to (and administered on their own by) the regions" (cited in Massetti and Toubeau 2013, 369).[10] In the October 2001 referendum, 64.2 percent of voters endorsed the constitutional reform, with majorities supporting the measure in every region except Val d'Aosta (where turnout, at 35.8 percent, was low).

After the referendum, the center-right's time in office was marked by difficulty negotiating an alternative reform plan as well as by some substantive work toward developing a law to implement the 2001 reform. However, the Berlusconi government, elected just after the reform went into effect, "did not show any interest in completing the constitutional framework inherited from its predecessor" (Palermo 2012, 242). Nevertheless, the minister for regional affairs wrote up a small part of the enabling legislation, clarifying the allocation of competencies and transferring some limited administrative responsibilities to regions (Laws 131/2003 and 11/2005). However, this legislation constituted a drop in the bucket of measures requiring legislative clarification before implementation could take place (Palermo and Wilson 2013, 10), and the center-right's main interest with regard to devolution during its 2001–5 term was devising an alternative to the center-left's reform.

Bossi, the leader of the Lega Nord and minister of institutional reform in the Berlusconi government, was in charge of developing the center-right's counterproposal, known in Italy as the "reform of the reform." Bossi's proposal was sweeping in scope, containing changes to 53 articles of the constitution (Palermo 2012, 243). Among other things, it proposed expanding the regions' exclusive competencies in the fields of health, education, and public safety and eliminating the central government's capacity to overrule regional laws.[11] In 2005, after long and tense intracoalition negotiations, members of the center-right coalition parties in Parliament approved the counterproposal—and then promptly lost power to Prodi's center-left coalition.

In 2005, the center-left sponsored a referendum on the reform of the reform, calling it "grossly incoherent and socially divisive" (Palermo and Wilson 2013, 11). Opposition to the counterreform extended beyond the traditional center-left constituents to include, among others, the regional president of Campania, who denounced it as "egotistic regionalism that lacks solidarity" (Keating and Wilson 2010, 13). In this referendum, 61.3 percent of voters opposed the counterreform: it received support from narrow majorities in the northern regions of Veneto and Lombardia but decisive opposition in central and southern regions (Keating and Wilson 2010). The center-right's attempt to rewrite the 2001 constitutional reform had failed.

When the center-left returned to power under Prodi, the government drafted a law aimed at executing the reform provisions to modify the system of regional equalization funds that determined the allocation of revenues controlled by the central government. The legislation was an essential step and was likely also motivated by acute concerns about losing electoral support in the North. Members of the center-left government emphasized that "the underlying principle of the draft was solidarity, contrary to the envisaged rather competitive federalism at variable speeds of the center-right" (Alber 2014, 148). The proposed legislation endeavored to balance concerns for administrative efficiency with those of interterritorial solidarity (Alber 2014, 147). While the measure was silent on questions of regional taxation, it set out clear language on equalization (Palermo and Wilson 2013, 11) and would have been an essential component of any substantive fiscal decentralization. However, when the government coalition lost support of a few small parties, snap elections were called in 2008, and the draft law was submitted to Parliament but never debated or adopted (Alber 2014, 147).

In 2009, Berlusconi's new center-right government began to formulate and pass its own legislation on fiscal federalism to fill in the framework laid out in the 2001 constitutional amendment. At the time, the Lega Nord's electoral support had surged, and Forza Italia promised devolution to secure a coalition with the regionalist party (Alber 2014, 148),[12] which had campaigned for a legislative slate for fiscal autonomy that would "safeguard the financial interests of northern taxpayers" (Palermo and Wilson 2013, 12). However, parties in the center-left coalition also supported the passage of fiscal federalism legislation, which they viewed as simply enacting the 2001 constitutional reform. The Berlusconi government managed to produce legislation on fiscal federalism, but during the arduous process of negotiating the law, the center-right faced splinter movements, particularly from representatives from southern regions (R. Lombardo, leader of the MpA, cited in Massetti and Toubeau 2013, 374). Further splits emerged when the leader of Alleanza Nazionale spoke out resolutely against the reform, "stressing the need to give more weight to the principle of solidarity" (Massetti and Toubeau 2013, 374). Division within the center-right meant that the government lost its majority within those committees charged with writing the legislative decrees to enact fiscal federalism, which in turn meant that measures underwent a more protracted negotiation process and were ultimately "diluted" (Massetti and Toubeau 2013, 375).

The center-left Democratic Party's Matteo Renzi revived constitutional questions relating to the structure of federalism immediately after becoming prime minister in 2014. Initial versions of the reform received support from Forza Italia, but this agreement fell through as the proposal evolved and it became clear that Renzi would seek a confirmatory referendum on the reform rather than attempting to piece together the two-thirds majority required to pass it without a popular consultation (Bianchi 2017).

Early versions of Renzi's proposal for constitutional reform made apparent his government's desire to boldly reimagine constitutional frameworks rather than merely completing the work begun by his predecessors. The final proposal represented a far-reaching overhaul of Italian political institutions and an "attempt to simplify the institutional circuit and to speed up the legislative process" (Pasquino and Valbruzzi 2017, 148). Most prominently, the sweeping proposal included eliminating symmetric bicameralism by reducing the scope of the Senate's legislative power, removing the Senate vote of confidence, and modifying the body's composition from 315 directly elected members to 100 indirectly elected members (councilors and mayors elected by regional councils). Other parts of the reform directly affected the relationship between regions and the central government strongly in favor or the latter by promoting legislation was that favored the principle of "state supremacy," thereby allowing the central government to intervene in regional jurisdiction when matters of "national interest" were involved (Cardilli 2016; Ceccarini and Bordignon 2017; Draege and Dennison 2017; Pasquino and Valbruzzi 2017). The proposed amendments also included abolishing provinces (the subnational unit below the region) and introducing a new electoral law.

Most important for territorial dynamics, the proposed amendment modified Article 119, which governs the allocation of resources to municipalities, cities, and regions to finance their assigned public functions. The proposed reform introduced a phrase explicitly linking resource allocation to reference cost indicators to "promote conditions of efficiency"

(Servizio Studi Camera dei Deputati 2016, 36). In other words, the proposed amendment constituted another in a long line of attempts to resolve how resource allocation should be affected by historical expenditure patterns versus desired levels of spending, with the attendant consequences for the distribution of resources across regions. This amendment could have launched a new round of implementation laws changing in the cross-regional distribution of resources tied to service provision, but the December 2016 referendum on the matter did not pass, with 59.1 percent of voters rejecting the packet of proposals.

Veneto and Lombardia held consultative referenda in October 2017 on the prospect of greater regional autonomy. In both cases, the initiative was taken by regional presidents from the Lega Nord who activated Article 116 of the constitution, under which regions may request more autonomy. After considerable back and forth on the phrasing, especially in Veneto, where an early version of the question was deemed unconstitutional, voters were asked if they would like their region to undertake institutional initiatives to further "forms and conditions of autonomy." In both cases, the results were broadly supportive, with 95 percent (38 percent turnout) in Lombardia and 98 percent (57 percent turnout) in Veneto (*Economist* 2017). These referenda offer a popular mandate for the initiation of negotiations on greater autonomy, thereby introducing a new moving part to the still-open issue of fiscal federalism.

Contrasting objectives and a lack of decisive political will have meant that the process of decentralization in Italy is being drawn out over a lengthy period. Leaders from both the Left and the Right have been constrained by the opposing pressures of, on the one hand, acknowledging the demands for change within wealthy northern regions (formulated decisively by the Lega), and on the other, avoiding blame for major disruption to the status quo. Differing views over the form devolution should take meant that initiatives by one coalition were often met with a consultative referendum aimed at reversing the initiative and/or a laboriously produced, comprehensive counterproposal. No single set of reforms had the broad cross-party endorsement that would avoid triggering lengthy consultative measures. In part as a consequence of protracted intracoalition negotiations, sometimes involving regional figures, reforms tended to be introduced at the tail end of a government's term, with enactment left to the opposing coalition, which was frequently unenthusiastic about building on its political opponents' initiatives. Thus, the enduring partisan wrangling on the precise content, scope, and goals of devolution produced astonishing time lags between devolution initiatives.

The political deadlock surrounding decentralization had important consequences for cross-regional inequalities in social spending. While each party sought to be associated with decentralization in some form, leaders were also wary of enacting decisive changes to the cross-regional redistribution of fiscal revenues that would lead to worsening provisions for less wealthy and efficient southern regions. A decisive, comprehensive reform of cross-regional fiscal allocation mechanisms has repeatedly been delayed. In the absence of a decisive reform, the existing mechanisms for allotting revenues from the center to the regions and compensating for economic differences between regions have remained the default practice. This has guaranteed a degree of de facto stability in the resources available to regions despite de jure changes in the degree of fiscal autonomy and responsibility of regional governments.

Self-Decelerating Mechanisms

Built into the process of decentralization in Italy were a series of mechanisms that deferred decision making, required varying levels of consultation, and ensured time delays that slowed the pace of real reform. No reform on fiscal devolution was self-implementing or even complete when passed as a law or a constitutional reform. In most cases, the legislation passed by the legislature was incomplete, necessitating a string of enabling laws and enactment decrees before the reform could take effect. This results in part from the Italian legislative process, which generally outlines broad principles in framework legislation but requires additional enacting legislation and legislative decrees to trigger the legal standing to begin implementation. Further, reform legislation often specified a time delay or a transitional phase, both of which may delay implementation. In the absence of an upper chamber representing regional interests, passing a reform relevant to regional prerogatives entailed consultation with a series of ad hoc committees and bodies with multiple veto players.[13] Finally, a legal vacuum resulting from the delayed implementation of devolution reforms opened space for regions to contest arrangements, taking matters to the Constitutional Court and entailing further delays.

Much of the reallocation of legislative powers between the central government and regional governments in the 2001 reform had immediate force of law (Palermo and Wilson 2013, 9–10). However, the vast bulk of the reform legislation was sufficiently vague that it could not go into effect without subsequent implementation law and enacting decrees that required nonbinding regional consultations and administrative regulations. In particular, Article 119.3 establishes that the state shall provide for a general equalization fund to support territories with lower per capita fiscal capacity, while Article 117 specifies that the central government's competencies include "determination of the basic level of benefits relating to civil and social rights that must be guaranteed throughout the national territory." Each of these concepts lacks concrete operationalization in the reform bill. As Barberis (2010) emphasizes, the constitutional text does not specify how essential levels of service should be constructed or whether they include levels of performance or a list of protected rights, either in principle or in practice (Barberis 2010, 97). Furthermore, there is no language regarding how the cost of provision of essential services will be offset by the equalization fund.

Two implementation laws related to the 2001 constitutional reform were passed in 2003 and 2005, but the bulk of enacting legislation was not initiated until 2009. For eight years, then, a legal void left open to interpretation how the amended Article 119 on fiscal federalism should take effect. Law 42/2009 was advanced to fill this void. However, this piece of legislation itself was only a "framework law," which meant that it contained key directive principles of fiscal federalism but that multiple subsequent enactment decrees were necessary to spell out the distributional allotment procedures.

The use of enactment decrees to flesh out the body of major legislative initiatives in Italy is common despite the original constitutional constraints requiring that decrees be reserved for exceptional circumstances.[14] The implementation law on fiscal federalism has required 9 enacting decrees and 70 administrative measures (Conpaff 2013). These decrees are themselves not self-executing: most do not come into effect without a series of consultations and executive rules that can take as long as seven years (Palermo and Wilson 2013, 14).[15] More often than not, the decrees also contained self-activating time delays, with a specified transitional phase and then a future date on which a given provision will be operational. For example, elements of fiscal federalism came into operation in 2016 after a transitional phase that began three years earlier (Palermo and Wilson 2013, 15; see also Valdescalici 2014, 79).[16]

The passage of an enacting decree related to decentralization is far from a simple task, requiring two or three levels of consultation. First, all members of the governing coalition must support the decree, a proviso that has proven particularly difficult in instances where the Lega Nord has staked out an extreme position. Second, *any* government decree necessitates "the compulsory, but not binding, opinion of parliamentary committees" (Capano 2005, 19). With a decree regarding regional matters, there is an additional obligation to consult with regional bodies. The 2001 constitutional amendment specifies that until the completion of the reform of the Senate, regions and local governments must be consulted through parliamentary committee (Keating and Wilson 2010).

Further complicating implementation, several additional consultative committees exist for such subject matter that involves the joint participation of representatives from central, regional, and local levels of government (Ceccherini 2008, 219): the Conference of the State, Regions, and Autonomous Provinces (Conferenza Stato-Regioni), the State–Municipalities–Local Autonomies Conference, and the State–Regions–Autonomous Provinces–Municipalities–Local Autonomies Conference (Ceccherini 2008). The Constitutional Court has deemed consultation with these bodies compulsory in a number of instances, particularly policies "concerning areas of regional competence and expertise" (Ceccherini 2008, 223). Between 2002 and 2010, the court issued 23 decisions on the subject of fair collaboration (Ceccherini 2008, 220).

The joint conferences have been instructed to consult on matters beyond legislative degrees involving regional provisions, including matters

> on the state legislative guidelines pertaining to matters of immediate regional interest; on the national economic planning objectives for financial policy and State budget; on the general criteria affecting the exercise of the programming and coordinating power (in which case the Conference's opinions were binding) . . . drafting process of several guideline documents (if only to reach a weak agreement). (Ceccherini 2008, 223)

In some instances, mandatory but advisory and nonbinding consultation has meant that the central government has adopted initiatives despite the position expressed by the conference.[17] Yet extensive and lengthy consultations on contentious distributional issues have often delayed legislation or administrative regulation on matters related to devolution.

One of the most important sources of delay is that the concepts of essential levels of service (LEPs) and equalization around which legislation on fiscal federalism has been constructed have not been adequately defined. These concepts were cited in and were central to the 2001 constitutional reform. Regions were to provide essential levels of social, educational, and health services derived from the 1948 constitution, but fiscal equalization between regions would be carried out by the central government to provide additional financing when a region's revenues proved inadequate. However, the reform did not define or establish methods for measuring LEPs or specify precisely how or how much equalization between regions ought to occur.

Only in May 2009 did the law on fiscal federalism (42/2009) broach the subject of how to implement the LEP. In attempting to allocate greater autonomy and fiscal responsibility to regions, this law specified that the costs or "allowable" expenditures for LEPs should be based not on a region's previous spending for service provision (historic expenditure) but rather on a metric of "standard costs"—that is, the costs that would be required by a well-functioning government to produce such services. While the expression evokes notions of uniformity and efficiency, the law itself was resolutely silent on how standard costs for essential levels of services were to be established and measured. The definition of LEPs, especially outside of health, remained unsettled.[18] Examining the period from 1985 to 2009, Buglione (2014, 321) underscores that despite the increased taxing capacity of northern regions, "the solidaristic character of the Italian fiscal federalism model has so far been safeguarded" as GDP per capita resources for a given region are derived from the sum of equalization transfers (higher for southern regions) and tax revenue (approximately double for northern regions).

Legislative decree 216/2010, passed by center-right government in November 2010, took a step toward clarifying these concepts but did not actually define the essential levels of services or establish measures to evaluate standard cost (Disposizioni in Materia 2010). Rather, the decree set out a detailed set of steps that were required to establish metrics for LEPs. The decree identifies the "basic functions" of local government and a provisional list of services. It enunciates a methodology for determining the LEP and the related cost analysis without using the criterion of historic expenditure. The decree specifies that the standard requirements for each basic function will be determined through a five-step process involving the identification of information and data required for accounting through questionnaires to be completed by municipalities, individuating quantitative levels of performance, cost analysis, statistical model development, and a definition of indicators to access adequacy of services (Disposizioni in Materia 2010; see also Vitiello 2014). The decree established 2013 as the deadline for determining essential levels of service, which would then be used to generate payments to regions during a three-year transitional period beginning in 2014.

At this stage, the full severity of the financial crisis was becoming apparent. In August 2011, leaders from the European Central Bank urged the Italian government to take far-reaching measures to redress shortfalls in public finances (Lynch 2014, 384). In December, the newly appointed technocratic government led by Prime Minister Mario Monti (which also included representatives from center-right and center-left parties) put forward the €30 billion "Save Italy" austerity plan designed to reduce the national debt (De la Porte and Natali 2014; Del Pino and Pavolini 2015, 257; León, Pavolini, and Guillén 2015, 195–96; Gianesini 2014, 160–61). It included important pension reforms (increasing the retirement age and introducing more stringent conditions for early retirement) and launched major labor reform negotiations (Agostini and Sacchi 2015; De la Porte and Natali 2014, 744; Lynch 2014, 383; Picot and Tassinari 2015).

Despite swift action in other realms, the enactment of the LEPs continued to wind its way slowly through the process. Slides from a July 2013 meeting with the IMF delegation indicate that the central execution measures were still absent at that point (Conpaff 2013, 18). Only at the eleventh hour, on 23 December 2013, did the Commissione Tecnica Paritetica per l'Attuazione del Federalismo Fiscal (Joint Technical Commission for the Implementation of Federalism) approve and publish 10 methodological notes for the implementing decree (Disposizioni in Materia 2010). The methodological notes individuate precisely which services fall into the category of fundamental function, establish formulas for determining service needs for local entities, and include calculations for defining standard costs (Conpaff 2013, 21). However, a 2014 decree (16/2014) delayed the beginning of transitional application of the standard requirement to 2015. And an April 2015 legislative report explicitly states that, with respect to determination of LEPs and the essential performance level, "State law required by the provision in question has not so far intervened" (Camera dei Deputati 2015, 12). Not until December 2016 was the methodological note determining the calculation procedure for the estimated tax capacity of each municipality adopted (Commissione Bicamerale 2018).

In the legislative session that ended in January 2018, methodological notes for calculating standard needs and requirements for functions related to education and social services were approved by decree of the President and Council of Ministers. While no implementation can take place without these lengthy methodological notes, the completion of the notes does not itself bring to an end the process of adopting changes to the practice of fiscal federalism.

During this period of acute austerity, even seemingly stringent budgetary constraints that pushed regions toward greater fiscal self-reliance contain language on equalization. For example, the balanced budget rule enacted in 2012 (243/2012) requires central, regional, and local governments to maintain balanced budgets (Ministero dell'Economia e Finanze 2012, 2), in line with the debt rule from the European Union Stability and Growth Pact, which requires an annual reduction in debt-to-GDP ratio (OECD 2013, 22). At the same time, the law stipulates that "in downturns, the Central Government activates a system of transfers to balance the decrease in local revenue with reference to the local expenditure functions for which the Central Government sets minimum standards." Thus, in addition to built-in delays, much of the recent Italian lawmaking on fiscal decentralization continues to expressly require rather extensive cross-regional redistribution.

In February 2014, Prime Minister Renzi entered office, planning swiftly to take on reforms geared at promoting economic recovery and placating European Commission officials. In October 2014, Renzi rolled out the draft of his first budget bill, which included more than €15 billion in cuts to government spending, with €4 billion of that amount directed toward regions, from 2015–2018 (Del Pino and Pavolini 2015, 257; Disposizioni per la Formazione 2014). The prime minister's office pressed for budgetary reductions to largely take the form of 3 percent across-the-board cuts to regions, municipalities, and ministries (Rogari 2014). The rhetoric surrounding the bill depicted unilateral deep cuts to regional spending, and regional leaders adamantly objected, claiming that the cuts were entirely untenable (Rubino 2014; Del Pino and Pavolini 2015, 258). The president of Piemonte renounced cuts, arguing that they were unsustainable without addressing health care spending, and the president of Lombardia underscored that the budget did not apply standard costs, which would have "favored and rewarded the virtuosity of the Lombard region" (Regioni.it 2014). The budget law passed in late December 2014, which included a reduction of the development and cohesion fund by €750 million, affected available resources for social spending in poorer regions. But the largest budget cuts in this area targeted health spending (Mobili, Trovati, and Turno 2014). The budget called for the implementation of the 2014–16 Health Pact, a three-year agreement between the government and the regions that would allocate funds for health policy in accordance with the "standard cost" procedures established by legislative decree 68/2011 (Ministero dell'Economia e Finanze 2015, 23; see also France 2014).[19] In February 2015, the text of the agreement between the central government and the regions (Intesa Stato-Regioni sui Tagli) finalized budget cuts, specifying recalculated regional contributions and central allocations (Conferenza Permanente 2015) while nevertheless ensuring that essential levels of assistance be maintained across regions.

Austerity budgets have brought about cuts to spending but do not appear to have hastened or circumvented the long-delayed implementation of essential levels of services. Long-standing practices of cross-regional subsidization consequently buffered the potential for growing interregional inequality in service provision. The enactment of the 2001 constitutional reform and 2009 law on fiscal federalism turned on the designation of standard cost requirements for essential levels of social service provision. The operationalization of the fiscal autonomy of regions in line with their respective fiscal capacity requires that these cost metrics take on a legal enunciation.[20] Constitutional reforms and critical legislation on decentralization either failed to specify or delayed to a future date decisions on core parameters relating to cross-regional distribution.

The preface to the January 2018 report of the Bicameral Parliamentary Commission on the Implementation of Fiscal Federalism (Commissione Parlementare per l'Attuazione del Federalismo Fiscale) included minutes of an 18 January 2018 meeting. The president of the commission began by discussing how the report documents all modifications to fiscal federalism from the previous report and constitutes "a very useful recognition of the various open questions" (Commissione Bicamerale 2018, 3). Other members of the commission are even more explicit about the unfinished nature of implementation. One member cites multiple concerns, noting that "completion the implementation of Article 119 of the Constitution is still lacking" and that the regional consultative referenda represent a "sudden acceleration of alternating opposing signals" (Commissione Bicamerale 2018, 4). Perhaps unsurprisingly, the report's first subtitle is "An Enduring Transition [Una Perdurante Transizione]." The section concludes by stating that "the basic challenge remains: to complete the process of implementing Article 119 and put the word *end* on the enduring transition" (Commissione Bicamerale 2018, 12). In closing, the report references the multiple "open questions," such as the financing of municipalities, ordinary regions, and special regions and harmonization of budgets and standard requirements and fiscal capacities that remain to be resolved before fiscal federalism can be truly achieved.

In sum, Italian decentralization reforms have contained explicit self-decelerating mechanisms—time lags and transitional periods, lengthy consultative mechanisms with nebulous requirements about adhering to decisional outcomes, and an apparently intentional lack of key conceptual details that would be needed to enact implementation legislation. As a result, although the constitutional reform and major legislation on devolution are often referred to as framework legislation, the apt parallel seems less a construction frame than an unfastened tarp: present but decidedly nebulous in form.[21]

In the case of fiscal devolution, the devil is indeed in the details, which were systematically delegated to forthcoming deliberation. The 2001 constitutional reform and 2009 law on fiscal federalism turn on the implementation and thus designation of standard cost requirements for LEPs with respect to social services. The operationalization of regional fiscal autonomy in line with fiscal capacity requires that these cost metrics take on legal definition, which has yet to occur. In the absence of such definitions, previous budgetary practices were simply carried forward, with equalization funds directed toward regions that had fiscal gaps regardless of whether these gaps would have been justified under a system of LEP. The lag in specification of important details related to decentralization thus has important consequences for social spending in the Italian regions. It has allowed regional budgets generally to default to existing practices and spending levels and has likely prevented major divergence among regions' social spending.

Conclusion

With heavy pressure from supporters of greater fiscal autonomy for Italy's wealthy northern regions, governments of both the right and the left during the Second Republic have mounted what promised to be sweeping reforms toward fiscal federalism. Given that Italy's regions are marked by deep and long-standing differences in per capita wealth and economic development, there is every reason to expect that a more locally based welfare funding and administration would quickly give rise to growing regional inequality in social spending.

The onset of the financial crisis might well have been expected to accelerate the pace of change of devolution and/or to heighten existing inequalities between regions. If the poorest regions are seeing their resources cut and lack alternative means of generating funds, regional spending differences might grow. Conversely, reductions in overall social spending budgets might lessen regional inequalities if wealthier regions have less means to pursue discretionary measures. Despite forecasts of an imminently transformed map of regional power and responsibility, though, Italy has not yet witnessed the expected growing divergence among regional welfare states. The combination of partisan divisions over the form of decentralization and extensive built-in self-decelerating mechanisms in the reforms that have been adopted have meant that bold announcements of transformation do not and likely cannot yield sharp upsurges in inequality between the wealthy regions with strong fiscal capacity and those without. Instead, a pattern of immobilism and reversion to the status quo ante of significant regional redistribution has emerged.

Without any strong veto points resisting decentralization, such stasis is surprising, especially given the support from both left and right coalitions for fiscal devolution. But while each party sought to be associated with decentralization, in large part as a consequence of direct or indirect pressure from the Lega Nord, no single reform received comprehensive cross-party endorsement. Reform proposals were frequently met with equally detailed and laboriously produced counterproposals following elections. The lack of broad cross-partisan support also meant that each reform attempt elicited lengthy consultative measures. The legal ambiguity stemming from partially completed or suspended reforms prompted a number of court cases brought by regional leadership, further slowing the implementation of the reform's basic principles.

The reforms also contained numerous examples of deferred decision making and built-in delays. In particular, the most contentious dimensions of reforms, those with potentially stark distributional consequences for wealthier versus poorer regions, were repeatedly underspecified and delegated to forthcoming deliberation. Leaders appeared wary of completely underwriting decisive changes on the cross-regional redistribution of fiscal revenues that would lead to a reduced share of revenues for less wealthy southern regions. The 2001 constitutional reform and 2009 law on fiscal federalism turn on designating the "standard costs" associated with providing "essential levels" of social and health services. The operationalization of the fiscal autonomy of regions in line with their fiscal capacity requires that these standard costs and essential levels be defined in law. But these matters have been tied up in broad and lengthy consultations that have yet to be concluded. And so the allotment of the regional equalization fund and real constraints on local spending, the most distributionally contentious matters, remain unstipulated.

Outside of the domain of social insurance and health, social policy across regions has historically presented differences in scope of policy development, institutional structure, and degree of spending. These differences have been all the more pronounced in the more expensive areas of social service provision—child care and elder care—where many wealthy northern regions have pioneered high-quality assistance for elders and innovative and extensive public child care. Yet despite these initial differences, the ongoing fiscal decentralization in Italy has yet to yield a notable increase in inequality in regional welfare spending. To date, and running counter to both lay expectations and political science theories, devolution has not led to an escalation of spending inequality across Italian regions. The immobilizing influences on policy have concatenated to form a decidedly pronounced bias toward stability in the regional distribution of social spending.

APPENDIX

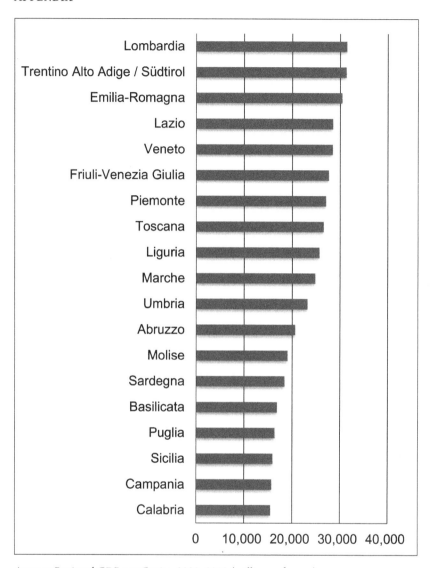

Average Regional GDP per Capita, 2000–2012 (millions of euros)
Source: Istat 2015.

NOTES

1. These findings are contingent on the measure of political decentralization and factors such as the quality of regional governance. Other work has found the opposite relationship (Lessmann 2009).

2. Sicily, Sardinia, Valle d'Aosta, and the autonomous provinces of Trento and Bolzano are designated as "special statute" regions and had somewhat more extensive policy autonomy prior to the decentralization.

3. We extracted data on three major types of pensions: the old-age (over-65) pension (*vecchiaia*), survivor's pension (*pension ai superstiti*), and the assistance pension (*prestazioni assistenziali*), also referred to as social allowance (only distributed to individuals over the age of 65)(EMN 2014, 20).

4. Child care per capita figures refer to the 0–4 population and thus appear comparatively quite large. To place this figure in context, public spending on child care amounted to 34 percent of municipal spending on family policies in 2011.

5. Given the debate on the wide regional variation in standard costs of provision, differences in per capita spending do not fully capture differences in provision.

6. Unlike the Istat per capita calculations, we limit the denominator to those under 65, since these services are targeted at that group.

7. Although central health services are not included, these amounts include services and transfers to elderly patients of Alzheimer's disease (Istat 2014b).

8. "Constitutional reforms approved by less than 2/3 of the parliament can be subject to a binding confirmative referendum in Italy, and this took place for the constitutional reform in October 2001" (Palermo and Wilson 2013, 9).

9. In addition, "FI's ideological flexibility, combined with its personalistic and centralised organization, allowed Berlusconi to [attempt to] bridge the divide between the LN on the one hand and the . . . AN on the other, but this was not an easy feat" (Massetti and Toubeau 2013, 360)

10. In the survey, 73.7 of respondents disagreed with the statement that "poor regions should count on own forces."

11. This centralizing element was seen as a means "to balance the concessions to the Northern League" (Keating and Wilson 2010, 12).

12. Similarly, Massetti and Toubeau (2013, 361) argue that the "advancement of the LN's goal has been conditioned, first, by its capacity to set the political agenda through its exercise of blackmail and coalition 'potential.'"

13. Approximately 65 percent of new policies require ministerial decrees to be implemented and consequently "often lag behind either because of the resistance of ministerial bureaucracies and pressure groups or because of internal incongruences in the law" (Maurizio Cotta and Colino 2015, 31).

14. According to the 1948 constitution, the use of decree laws is permitted only in exceptional circumstances, however the practice has become routine (Capano 2005, 19).

15. "Indeed most of the decrees are not self-executing: either they need further integration by means of executive rules or they postpone the definition of essential aspects" (Valdescalici 2014, 79).

16. Palermo and Wilson (2013, 14) argue that "this dilution in time was the political compromise needed to guarantee strong parliamentary support."

17. In such instances, the central government need only "provide adequate reasons,

which constitute the 'minimum requirement validating the State's unilateral decision' (Constitutional Court decision n.116 of 1994)" (Ceccherini 2008, 219).

18. According to the 2009 law on fiscal federalism, services need be considered in two categories. "Essential services" (health, administrative spending on education, social assistance, and capital expenditures for public transportation) (Valdescalici 2014, 87) are to be provided throughout the territory, with the equalization fund covering 100 percent of any eventual difference between the region's fiscal capacity and standard requirement costs. The provision of these services accounts for more than 80 percent of regional budgets (Valdescalici 2014, 87). For nonessential services, which constitute 15–20 percent of regional budgets, including matters such as administrative expenses and public transportation delivery costs, the equalization fund covers only 75 percent of the difference between the region's fiscal capacity and the cost of services.

19. According to Lynch and Ceretti (2015, 244), "Standard costs . . . determined by the cost of provision in several regions with virtuous efficient healthcare systems. However, the Monti government left the standard cost provisions unimplemented. . . . As a result, the financing of regional health budgets remains in limbo until cost benchmarks can be worked out."

20. Similarly, Valdescalici (2014, 90) points out that "the emphasis given to accountability can be challenged by the number of parachutes which the system has introduced in order to remedy the regional imbalances and to guarantee cohesion. Additional grants for extra-ordinary circumstances as well as infrastructural equalization have been conceived for this purpose."

21. This is in line with Mangiameli (2014, 20), who concludes that "there have also been obstacles to the completion of fiscal federalism because of some vagueness in the constitutional rules regarding public finances, particularly in the matter of equalisation. Indeed, while Article 119(3), assigns the task of issuing legislation to set up the equalisation fund to the State, and Article 117(2) (e) vests the State with the (exclusive) responsibility for equalising financial resources, no provision is made to indicate any way of financing the equalisation fund or to specify what type of equalisation is to be chosen, with the result that all he institutional stakeholders involved view the implementation of Article 119 Const. to be a pathway fraught with uncertainty and pitfalls."

REFERENCES

Agostini, C., and D. N. S. Sacchi. 2015. The Europeanisation of the Italian Welfare State: Channels of Influence and Trends. In *The Italian Welfare State in a European Perspective: A Comparative Analysis*, ed. Ugo Ascoli and Emmanuele Pavolini. Bristol: Policy Press.

Alber, E. 2014. Italy's Piecemeal Path towards Fiscal Federalism: One Step Forward, Two Steps Back? In *Fiscal Federalism and Fiscal Decentralization in Europe*, ed. S. A. Lütgenau. Innsbruck: Transaction.

Arachi, G., and A. Zanardi. 2004. Designing Intergovernmental Fiscal Relations: Some Insights from the Recent Italian Reform. *Fiscal Studies* 25 (3): 325–65.

Barbabella, F., Carlos Chiatti, Mirko Di Rosa, and Laura Pelliccia. 2013. *Alcuni Profili dell'Assistenza nelle Regioni*. Rimini: Maggioli Editore.

Barberis, E. 2010. Rapporti Territoriali e Coordinamento: Una Contestualizzazione della Governance Sociale in Italia. *La Rivista delle Politiche Sociali* 1:79–101.

Bianchi, D. G. 2017. "I Missed a Penalty": The Constitutional Referendum and Matteo Renzi's Mistakes. *Modern Italy* 22 (3): 315–29.

Bird, R. M., and A. V. Tarasov. 2004. Closing the Gap: Fiscal Imbalances and Intergovernmental Transfers in Developed Federations. *Environment and Planning C: Politics and Space* 22 (1): 77–102.

Bonet, J. 2006. Fiscal Decentralization and Regional Income Disparities: Evidence from the Colombian Experience. *Annals of Regional Science* 40 (3): 661–76.

Buglione, E. 2014. Regional Finance in Italy: Past and Future. In *Italian Regionalism: Between Unitary Traditions and Federal Processes*, ed. Stelio Mangiameli, 307–34. New York: Springer.

Camera dei Deputati. 2015. *Documentazione e Ricerche il Federalismo Fiscale lo Stato di Attuazione della Legge n. 42 del 2009 al 1° aprile 2015: Schede di Lettura, n. 134/1(XVII Legislatura)*. http://documenti.camera.it/Leg17/dossier/Pdf/FI0250a.pdf

Canaleta, C. G., P. P. Arzoz, and M. R. Garate. 2004. Regional Economic Disparities and Decentralisation. *Urban Studies* 41(1): 71–94.

Capano, G. 2005. The Italian Parliament: A Powerful Institution That Performs in an Erratic Way. Paper presented at the ECPR Joint Sessions Workshop 7: Evaluating, Comparing and Classifying Legislatures. Granada, Spain, April 14.

Cardilli, M. 2016. Note sulla Riforma Costituzionale. *Amministrativ@mente* 5–6. www.amministrativamente.com/article/download/12135/11082

Ceccarini, L., and F. Bordignon. 2017. Referendum on Renzi: The 2016 Vote on the Italian Constitutional Revision. *South European Society and Politics* 22 (3): 281–302.

Ceccherini, E. 2008. La Colaborazione fra Stato ed Enti Territoriali negli Stati Composti dell'Unione Europea. *Cuestiones Constitucionales* 18:39–69.

Cento Bull, Anna. 2002. "Towards a Federal State? Competing Proposals for Constitutional Revision." *Italian Politics* 17 (1): 185–202.

Commissione Bicamerale. 2018. *Commissione Parlamentare per l'Attuazione del Federalismo Fiscale: Relazione Semestrale ai Sensi dell'Articolo 3, Comma 5, della Legge 5 Maggio 2009, N. 42*. Rome: Parlamento Italiano.

Conpaff. 2013. *Meeting with the IMF Delegation*. http://www.tesoro.it/ministero/commissioni/copaff/documenti/Incontro_COPAFF-FMI_del_3.7.2013.pdf

De la Porte, C., and D. Natali. 2014. Altered Europeanisation of Pension Reform in the Context of the Great Recession: Denmark and Italy Compared. *West European Politics* 37 (4): 732–49.

Del Pino, E., and E. Pavolini. 2015. Decentralisation at a Time of Harsh Austerity: Multilevel Governance and the Welfare State in Spain and Italy Facing the Crisis. *European Journal of Social Security* 17 (2): 246–70.

Disposizioni in Materia di Assistenza in Favore delle Persone Affette da Disabilità Grave Nonché delle Persone Disabili Prive del Sostegno Familiare (Proposte di Legge). 2014. *Gazzetta Ufficiale*, 19 March.

Disposizioni in Materia di Determinazione dei Costi e dei Fabbisogni Standard di Comuni: Città Metropolitane e Province. 2010. *Gazzetta Ufficiale*, 17 December. http://www.tesoro.it/ministero/commissioni/copaff/fabbisogni_standard.html

Disposizioni per la Formazione del Bilancio Annuale e Pluriennale dello Stato. 2014. *Gazzetta Ufficiale*, 23 December.

Draege, J. B., and J. Dennison. 2017. Making Sense of Italy's Constitutional Referendum. *Mediterranean Politics* 23:403–9.

Economist. 2017. Northern Italy Votes for More Autonomy: Unlike Catalonia, No One Is Asking for Independence, Yet. 26 October.

European Migration Network (EMN). 2014. *Migrant Access to Social Security and Healthcare in Italy: Policies and Practices*. https://ec.europa.eu/home-affairs/sites/homeaffairs/files/what-we-do/networks/european_migration_network/reports/docs/emn-studies/emn_synthesis_report_migrant_access_to_social_security_2014_en.pdf

Ezcurra, R., and A. Rodríguez-Pose. 2013. Political Decentralization, Economic Growth, and Regional Disparities in the OECD. *Regional Studies* 47 (3): 388–401.

Fargion, V. 1996. Social Assistance and the North-South Cleavage in Italy. *South European Society and Politics* 1 (3): 135–54.

France, G. 2014. The Italian Health Care System and the Economics of the Right to Health. In *Italian Regionalism: Between Unitary Traditions and Federal Processes*, ed. Stelio Mangiameli, 335–52. New York: Springer.

Franco, D. 2010. Mezzogiorno: Redistribuzione e Servizi Pubblici. *QA Rivista dell'Associazione Rossi-Doria* 21:131–51.

Gianesini, G. 2014. Family Patterns of Change in Italy: Challenges, Conflicts, Policies, and Practices. In *Handbook of Family Policies across the Globe*, ed. Mihaela Robila, 155–74. New York: Springer.

Groppi, T., and N. Scattone. 2006. Italy: The Subsidiarity Principle. *International Journal of Constitutional Law* 4:131–37.

Istat. 2011. *Classificazione Internazionale della Spesa Pubblica per Funzione (Cofog) secondo il Sistema dei Conti Europei SEC95*. https://www.istat.it/it/files/2011/01/cofog.pdf

Istat. 2013. *Gli Interventi e Servizi Sociali dei Comuni Singoli o Associati*. https://www.istat.it/it/salute-e-sanità

Istat. 2014a. *Indagine sugli Interventi e i Servizi Sociali dei Comuni Singoli o Associati*. https://www.istat.it/it/salute-e-sanità

Istat. 2014b. *Interventi e Servizi Sociali dei Comuni Singoli o Associati*. https://www.istat.it/it/salute-e-sanità

Istat. 2014c. *L'Offerta Comunale di Asili Nido e Altri Servizi Socio-Educativi per la Prima Infanzia*. https://www.istat.it/it/salute-e-sanità

Istat. 2014d. *Spesa Sanitaria Pubblica Corrente*. http://www.istat.it/it/salute-e-sanità

Istat. 2014e. *Spesa Totale Consolidata delle Amministrazioni Pubbliche al Netto degli Interessi per Funzione di Spesa*. https://www.istat.it/it/salute-e-sanità

Keating, M., and A. Wilson. 2010. Federalism and Decentralisation in Italy. Paper presented at the UK Political Studies Association Conference.

Kyriacou, A. P., L. Muinelo-Gallo, and O. Roca-Sagalés. 2015. Fiscal Decentralization and Regional Disparities: The Importance of Good Governance. *Papers in Regional Science* 94 (1): 89–107.

León, M., E. Pavolini, and A. M. Guillén. 2015. Welfare Rescaling in Italy and Spain: Political Strategies to Deal with Harsh Austerity. *European Journal of Social Security* 17 (2): 182–201.

Leonardi, R., R. Nanetti, and R. D. Putnam. 1987. Italy: Territorial Politics in the Post-War Years. *West European Politics* 10 (4): 88–107.

Lessmann, C. 2009. Fiscal Decentralization and Regional Disparity: Evidence from Cross-Section and Panel Data. https://papers.ssrn.com/sol3/papers.cfm?abstract_id=936874

Lynch, J. 2014. The Italian Welfare State after the Financial Crisis. *Journal of Modern Italian Studies* 19 (4): 380–88.

Lynch, J., and P. Ceretti. 2015. From Bismarckian Beginnings to Crisis and Reform. In *The Routledge Handbook of Contemporary Italy: History, Politics, Society*, ed. Andrea Mammone, Ercole Giap Parini, and Giuseppe A. Veltri. London: Routledge.

Mangiameli, Stelio. 2014. The Regions and the Reforms: Issues Resolved and Problems Pending. In *Italian Regionalism: Between Unitary Traditions and Federal Processes*, ed. Stelio Mangiameli. New York: Springer.

Massetti, E., and S. Toubeau. 2013. Sailing with Northern Winds: Party Politics and Federal Reforms in Italy. *West European Politics* 36 (2): 359–81.

Maurizio Cotta, R. M., and César Colino. 2015. *Sustainable Governance Indicators: 2015 Italy Report*. http://www.sgi-network.org/docs/2015/country/SGI2015_Italy.pdf

Mazzoleni, M. 2009. The Italian Regionalisation: A Story of Partisan Logics. *Modern Italy* 14 (2): 135–50.

Ministero dell'Economia e Finanze. 2012. *Italy's Major Structural Reforms: Progress Report, December 2011–November 2012*. Rome: Ministry of Economy and Finance.

Ministero dell'Economia e Finanze. 2015. *Draft Budget Plan*. Rome: Ministry of Economy and Finance.

Mobili, M., G. Trovati, and R. Turno. 2014. The Stability Law from Beginning to End. *Il Sole 24 Ore*, 22 December. http://www.italy24.ilsole24ore.com/art/public-finance/2014-12-26/the-stability-law-from-beginning-to-end-191541.php?uuid=ABGEKlVC

OECD. 2013. *OECD Economic Surveys: Italy 2013*. http://dx.doi.org/10.1787/eco_surveys-ita-2013-en

Oliver, R. J., and M. Mätzke. 2014. Childcare Expansion in Conservative Welfare States: Policy Legacies and the Politics of Decentralized Implementation in Germany and Italy. *Social Politics: International Studies in Gender, State and Society* 21 (2): 167–93.

Palermo, F. 2012. Italy: A Federal Country without Federalism. In *Constitutional Dynamics in Federal Systems: Sub-National Perspectives*, ed. M. Burgess and G. A. Tarr. Montreal: McGill-Queen's University Press.

Palermo, F., and A. Wilson. 2013. *The Dynamics of Decentralization in Italy: Towards a Federal Solution?* European Diversity and Autonomy Papers, EDAP Working Paper 4/2013. http://aei.pitt.edu/41705/

Pasquino, G., and M. Valbruzzi. 2017. Italy Says No: The 2016 Constitutional Referendum and Its Consequences. *Journal of Modern Italian Studies* 22 (2): 145–62.

Picot, G., and A. Tassinari. 2015. Politics in a Transformed Labor Market: Renzi's Labor Market Reform. *Italian Politics* 30 (1): 121–40.

Regioni.it. 2014. L.Stabilità: Maroni "Governo Non Ha Accolto Nessuna Richiesta Regioni" [press release]. Retrieved from http://www.regioni.it/news/2014/12/19/l-stabilita-maroni-governo-non-ha-accolto-nessuna-richiesta-regioni-381182/ (no longer accessible).

Rogari, M. 2014. Expansionary 2015 Budget Still Aims for €15 Bn in Spending Cuts. *Il Sole 24 Ore*, 16 October.

Rubino, M. 2014. Stabilità, le Regioni Insorgono: "Manovra Insostenibile: Sanità e Trasporti a Rischio." Renzi: "Pensate a Ridurre gli Sprechi." *Repubblica*, 16 October.

Servizio Studi Camera dei Deputati. 2016. *La Riforma Costituzionale: Disegno di Legge*

Costituzionale A.C. 2613-D, Testo a Fronte con la Costituzione Vigente n. 216/12 Parte Seconda—Aprile 2016. https://documenti.camera.it/leg17/dossier/pdf/ac0500n.pdf

Sibiano, P., and T. Agasisti. 2013. Efficiency and Heterogeneity of Public Spending in Education among Italian Regions. *Journal of Public Affairs* 13 (1): 12–22.

Toth, F. 2014. How Health Care Regionalisation in Italy Is Widening the North–South Gap. *Health Economics, Policy, and Law* 9 (3): 231–49.

Triglia, C. 1992. *Sviluppo senza Autonomia: Effetti Perversi delle Politiche nel Mezzogiorno.* Bologna: Il Mulino.

Unioncamera Veneto. 2009. *Responsibility and Federalism: Figures, Ideas, and Remarks to Speed Up the Realization of Fiscal Federalism in Italy.* http://www.osservatoriofederalismo.eu/wp-content/uploads/2015/01/Ultima_Quad_11_inglese.pdf

Unioncamera Veneto. 2013. *Spending "Centre" Role and Dynamics of Public Finance in Italy and in Europe.* http://www.ven.camcom.it/pubblicazioni.asp?ID=76

Valdescalici, A. 2014. Features and Trajectories of Fiscal Federalism in Italy. In *Fiscal Federalism and Fiscal Decentralization in Europe*, ed. S. A. Lütgenau. Innsbruck: Transaction.

Vitiello, B. 2014. L'Attuale Sviluppo della Definizione dei Costi Standard. In *I Livelli Essenziali delle Prestazioni Sociali e Sanitarie*, ed. C. Bottari. Santarcangelo di Romagna: Maggioli.

The United Kingdom

Territorial Tension

Alan Trench

The United Kingdom (UK) joined the "decentralized/federal countries' club comparatively recently. While the UK has long traditions of local government and administrative decentralization, the creation of meso-level political institutions with their own electoral mandate dates back only to the late 1990s. This process has been known as *devolution*, and its extent was such that without quite being aware of it, the UK moved from one of the most centralized countries in the OECD to one of the most decentralized, at least in terms of the proportion of public spending by substate governments.

In addition to having rapidly decentralized, the UK is distinctive in another major respect: it is highly asymmetric. Devolution has extended to three geographically peripheral parts (Scotland, Wales, and Northern Ireland) with small populations totaling about 10 million people, while leaving England—where about 85 percent of the UK's population lives— largely untouched.[1] The arrangements for Scotland, Wales, and Northern Ireland differ significantly, but each has a devolved government and legis- lature and a division of powers between devolved and UK tiers that in many ways resemble that in federal systems, and the devolved functions include key elements of welfare provision, including health and education services. England continues to be governed by the UK government and Parliament, whose functions also include nondevolved matters such as foreign affairs, economic policy, and (largely) social security for the whole of the UK.

Devolution is best understood as a response to the multinational char- acter of the UK. It is affected (if not caused) by substate nationalism. The

123

UK in its present form consists of an absorbing union between England and Wales that received legal form in 1536 and refused to recognize the Welsh language or other institutions; a 1603 personal union between England and Scotland that led to a parliamentary union in 1707; and an 1801 parliamentary union with Ireland, which failed to treat the Catholic majority as equal citizens with the Protestant minority. The differences among the unions are significant (Jackson 2012), and the resulting state is best understood as a "state of unions" (Mitchell 2007). Nevertheless, the UK was widely regarded both at home and overseas as a unitary state for most of the twentieth century, and key institutions and public policies were developed for the UK as a whole.

The Union's meaning differed in each part of it. England largely ignored the other parts or regarded them as places of interest for tourism, folklore, or folk culture. Scotland's national identity was preserved under the Union by a variety of means, including distinctive religious and legal systems and banking and educational institutions. Wales's distinctiveness was very limited on the institutional level until the 1960s but was preserved culturally largely thanks to the Welsh language, even if it received little official recognition. (For further discussion of predevolution policy variations, see Checkland 1985.) In Wales and Scotland, political nationalism emerged as a significant force capable of winning parliamentary seats (particularly in by-elections) in the 1960s. Northern Ireland's development was rather different. The entity was created in 1922 when the island of Ireland was partitioned following the establishment of the southern part of the island as the Irish Free State (later the Republic of Ireland). The northern six counties remained in the United Kingdom, and extensive powers were devolved to a Parliament of Northern Ireland and were used to entrench the dominance of the Protestant majority, which maintained extensive discrimination against the Catholic minority. Devolved government broke down in the late 1960s following civil unrest between the two ethnonationalist communities and the outbreak of the violent conflict known as the Troubles. Direct rule from London was subsequently established. After the 1998 Good Friday/Belfast Agreement, devolved government was reestablished with large elements of consociational power sharing between unionist and nationalist communities.[2]

Devolution was also a response to economic changes to the UK during the 1980s and 1990s, among them deindustrialization in Scotland, Wales, and northern England; increasing reliance on services, particularly in southern England; and welfare state retrenchment. All three devolved parts of the UK are poorer than the UK as a whole—Scotland only to a limited degree now, but significantly so for Wales (which has all the problems of a postindustrial economy that has not been rebuilt) and Northern Ireland (where the legacy of the Troubles is added to a largely rural economy and a weak private sector).

Devolution implied profound changes to public policy as well as to political institutions. A large number of distributive welfare state functions, including health, education, public housing, and personal social services became the responsibility of the devolved governments and legislatures. So did important nonwelfare functions such as environmental and planning matters, culture and language, and for Scotland (and Northern Ireland after 2007) policing, the courts, and the justice system. Nonetheless, the welfare-related functions are by far the most important in financial terms—in 2012–13, health and education accounted for about 66 percent of Scottish government spending, 71 percent of Welsh government spending, and 63 percent of the spending by the Northern Ireland executive. Before 1999, these functions had been administratively decentralized to secretaries of state for Scotland (established 1885), Wales (established 1964), and (under direct rule) Northern Ireland. The existence of these administrative arrangements meant that the initial process of political devolution was remarkably smooth, because it built on existing structures and policy frameworks. However, it also enabled the UK at the center to avoid having to think hard about the nature and implications of devolution, constitutionally or in other ways.

The Territorial Organization of the Welfare State

While devolution is a novel constitutional experience for the UK, a developed welfare state is not. The roots of the present system go back to the early years of the twentieth century and the introduction following the 1909 People's Budget of a system of national insurance providing unemployment insurance and old-age pensions. After the Second World War, the model of the present welfare state was established by the 1945 Labour government following the recommendations of Sir William Beveridge. The welfare state's features included a large public housing sector; the National Health Service, which provided universal health care for everyone free at the point of use; compulsory free schooling for all children between ages 5 and (initially) 15; and "public assistance" in the form of cash benefits for the unemployed and low-income families. In addition, existing pensions and unemployment insurance received a boost. The Beveridge welfare state proved considerably more expensive than expected, particularly for health services, but was also hugely popular and attracted political support from all major parties, the Conservatives included. It also proved remarkably durable as a structure. Even faced with serious financial constraints in the late 1970s and 1980s, the underlying approach to welfare remained intact even as the amounts spent were limited (though even in real terms this stalled their rate of growth rather than resulted in any substantial reduction).

That model is distinctive in a number of ways. Based on 1980s data, Esping-Andersen (1989) characterized it as a "liberal" welfare state, like that of Anglo-Saxon countries such as the United States or Australia, though the UK had a more extensive welfare state than those countries did at the time. It is also largely (and contrary to Beveridge's proposals) noncontributory. While old-age pensions and some unemployment benefits are related to contributions through the national insurance system, other benefits cover those with inadequate contribution records. Key elements are funded from general tax revenues and are provided on the basis of need, not contribution records. Payments or care provided also relate to need rather than criteria such as previous income. Rationing mechanisms include a system of "priority need" for allocating social housing and the gatekeeper role of family doctors for nonurgent health care. Administration and provision of services has often been decentralized or deconcentrated, however. Local authorities were responsible for providing education for under-18s and social housing; frequently reorganized local boards ran the National Health Service. The responsibilities of central government for these services were exercised by the Scottish Office, the Welsh Office after 1964, and the Northern Ireland departments in general accord with UK government policy as implemented for England but with local variations.

Devolution's implications for the welfare state (or more widely) received little consideration before it was enacted. Constitutional anomalies relating to England within the devolved UK remain and have been the subject of debate.[3] The welfare state's impact on the constitutional structure of the UK has been subject to some academic discussion, pitting "welfare nationalist" arguments against ideas of a union that had guaranteed welfare rights but that was now starting to fragment. On the welfare nationalist side (see, e.g., McEwen 2002; Keating 2007), the arguments largely concern Scotland. They posit that Scotland is more inclined to support collectivist or social-democratic state provision of a generous welfare state, that the success of the post-1945 welfare state helped cement Scotland's place in the Union, but that retrenchment by Conservative governments in the 1980s and 1990s put this under pressure, weakening Scots' attachments to the Union as such and strengthening support for forms of distinctive provision and nationalism. Welfare debates certainly played a part in the arguments made by the pro-independence side in the 2014 referendum on Scottish independence. Such arguments have much less resonance in Wales or Northern Ireland, however, despite strong opposition to Conservative welfare changes there as well.

Many social policy scholars have reflexively assumed that welfare was uniform in nature and rooted in a shared form of UK-wide "social citizenship" (Marshall [1950] 1992) and have lamented the short-, medium-, and longer-term changes brought about by devolution and the pursuit of different policies in different parts of the UK. Such assumptions have often been based on a failure to understand variations inherent in the welfare state, but the trend has been aggravated by the failure to consider the wider implications of changes, many small in themselves, but becoming cumulatively significant. With few exceptions (notably Greer 2009), there have been few attempts to consider the implications of devolution for the welfare state in a way that reflects the more complex reality of the changes under way.

The Financing of Devolved Government

The financing of the UK's devolved governments is a direct continuation of the system used to fund the territorial departments (Scottish and Welsh Offices and Northern Ireland departments) before devolution, though some adjustments have occurred in recent years. Again, this simplified the process of making devolution happen by emphasizing administrative continuity but at the price of creating difficulties later.

The system is based on funding of the devolved governments by a block grant from the UK government from general tax revenues. The recipient governments are free to allocate the funds as they see fit. The grant is calculated on the basis of what is known as the Barnett formula, named for Joel Barnett (chief secretary to the treasury—effectively, budget minister) and devised in 1976, a time of considerable pressure on public spending caused by the need for the UK to receive a bailout loan from the IMF. The formula was initially used only for certain elements of the Scottish Office's budget, but its administrative simplicity and its potential to short-circuit political debate about comparatively small amounts of spending meant that its use was expanded to a wider range of functions and to spending by the Welsh Office and Northern Ireland departments. It therefore minimized the scope of arguments about finance with the territorial secretaries of state for Scotland, Wales, and Northern Ireland—arguments that the Treasury had tended to lose with Scotland. The formula remained a private part of the machinery of government, however, and its existence was not revealed in academic writing until 1980 (Heald 1980), when its inner workings remained confidential. Only in 1999, with the formula's adoption to fund the devolved administrations, were its workings officially published (HM Treasury 1999).

The formula works by giving devolved governments a share of changes in spending on "comparable functions" that are the responsibility of the UK government for England. If spending on schools or health in England goes up, so does the grant for Scotland and Wales; if spending is cut, the grants are reduced. The size of the share of the adjustment for England is determined by two factors: the share of the population of Scotland, Wales, and Northern Ireland in relation to England and the extent to which the English departmental spending is comparable—that is, the extent to which the function is devolved. Health and (under-19) education are regarded as almost wholly devolved, so their comparability percentages are 99.1 percent and 100 percent, respectively. Other functions, such as the environment and justice, are mixed and thus have varying percentages; percentages also vary for the different parts of the UK. The formula is therefore

Change in departmental spending × population factor
× comparability percentage

Both the population factors and departmental comparability percentage are reviewed periodically—usually every five years—as part of the process of UK government spending reviews.

The devolved governments are free to decide how to spend the block grants. There is no obligation to spend particular amounts on particular functions or to allocate increases resulting from higher spending on English schools on Scottish schools, though there may be political pressures to do so. The Barnett formula system therefore grants considerable spending autonomy to the devolved governments. However, the system is also based on the assumption that the devolved governments will accept broadly the same structure of public services as applies in England. They lack the ability to do something radically different—for example, more generous spending on health, which would mean taking resources from other spending areas, or cutting spending and having a smaller state, which would not result in reduced taxation. A major change by the UK government for England—such as an insurance-based approach to health care provision—would have major implications for devolved policy.[4] The approach encoded into the Barnett formula may make sense in the context of allocating resources within a single government. Whether it is appropriate for separate governments with their own electoral mandates and political priorities is more debatable. It was, however, one of the parameters of devolution and not an accidental choice (Trench 2007b, 89–92).

The Barnett formula system does not do two important things that are normally considered important elements of systems of finance in federal and regionalized systems. First, it does not assure or even seek to assure any sort of territorial equity. The formula's allocations are a product of simple (if not straightforward) arithmetic. There is no attempt to assess social or spending needs as part of the process. In any case, the formula applies only to incremental adjustments, not to the total amount allocated or the underlying baseline to which those increments are added. The formula has been widely criticized on these grounds (see, e.g., Heald and McLeod 2002; McLean 2005; House of Lords Select Committee on the Barnett Formula 2009). As all three devolved parts of the UK get more than the UK average of public spending through the formula (Scotland appears to get roughly 118 percent of the UK average, Wales 110–114 percent, and Northern Ireland 120 percent for devolved services), it is little surprise that less favored regions in England have objected to what they see as unduly generous treatment.

These criticisms may have considerable merit, but it is very hard to tell. There have been no published official attempts to estimate levels of spending need since 1979 (that is, the amount that would need to be provided to ensure that all parts of the UK had similar levels of public services given the underlying demand, such as levels of ill health) and the costs of provision.[5] The treasury's 1979 needs assessment exercise (HM Treasury 1979) involved both substantial if concealed political judgments (about the appropriate levels of public services) and a large-scale, complex, time-consuming, and data-intensive administrative undertaking. It is no wonder that there has been little appetite to repeat it, even if the consequence of not doing so is the preservation of substantial anomalies. Different approaches have been suggested as means of assessing relative spending needs in a less complicated way—that is, by using a small number of reliable proxy indicators (House of Lords Select Committee on the Barnett Formula 2009; Independent Commission on Funding and Finance 2009).

The version of this approach recommended by the Welsh government's Holtham Commission suggested appropriate "needs-related" figures of spending for devolved services of 114 percent of English spending for Wales, 105 percent for Scotland, and 121 percent for Northern Ireland (Independent Commission on Funding and Finance 2009, 22, 24). While this suggests that higher levels of funding for the Scottish, Welsh, and Northern Ireland governments compared to the English average are justified, implementing a fairer system would involve some politically painful changes, with substantial cuts for Scotland. Protecting Scotland's long-established generous funding through the Barnett formula has long been a major goal for Scottish politicians of all parties. Changing the system in a way that worked to Scotland's disadvantage has long been regarded as impossible, whether before the 2014 Scottish independence referendum (for fear of boosting support for independence) and afterward (because of the preelection "vow" to maintain the Barnett formula).

Another omission from the Barnett formula system has been fiscal devolution. Practically all the money spent by devolved governments comes from the UK government and general UK-wide tax receipts. There are therefore substantial but disguised interregional transfers within the system that owe their political origins to post-1945 assumptions about fairness within the welfare state. Although much American fiscal federalism literature emphasizes the "moral risk" of systems of federal financing based on transfers (see the introduction to this book) there are also some arguments in its favor—most notably, efficiency in the setting of tax rates and collection of taxes as a consequence of reduced opportunities for avoidance or evasion. As established in 1999, the devolved institutions had two small fiscal levers. One was general control of rates of local taxation (the nondomestic rate, for business premises, and the council tax, for residential premises). By reducing the grant payable to local authorities and allowing or requiring them to increase the revenues raised, devolved governments could increase the overall funding available to them. (In practice, this has not happened to any noticeable degree.) The second, for Scotland only, was a limited power to vary the standard rate of personal income tax by up to 3 percent. This power would have raised very little revenue if used and would have imposed considerable political costs; it appears to have been designed to preempt a political argument rather than as any serious sort of fiscal lever.

Nonetheless, since 2007, an active debate has concerned fiscal devolution for all three devolved governments. This has taken different forms for each part but has been most far-reaching for Scotland, where it was triggered by the election of the pro-independence Scottish National Party government in 2007, albeit as a minority. Debates about both independence and further devolution (Scottish Executive 2007; Scottish Government 2009; Commission on Scottish Devolution 2009) led to the partial devolution of personal income tax (10 points, across all three rates then in force) and devolution of some small land taxes, with a proportional reduction in the block grant. Coupled with the indirect control of local taxation, the Scottish government then became responsible for raising about 20 percent of devolved public spending. This approach was rooted not so much in demands for autonomy as in the need to ensure that the Scottish government was fiscally accountable. The land tax measures started in 2015, with income tax devolution taking effect in 2016, but they had already been superseded by more far-reaching proposals adopted following the 2014 referendum for devolution of all personal income tax and assignment of half of VAT receipts generated in Scotland (Smith Commission 2015, enacted by Scotland Act 2016). The Smith Commission proposals (which originated in work by the left-of-center Institute for Public Policy Research and had been adopted by the Scottish Conservative Party [Trench 2013; Scottish Conservatives 2014]) mean that the Scottish government is expected to receive about 50 percent of devolved spending from devolved or assigned taxes, again including its indirect control of local government spending.

For Northern Ireland, air passenger duty has been devolved on long-distance flights, principally to safeguard the direct flight between Belfast and Newark in the United States (though it proved uneconomic and was canceled in January 2017). More significant has been the agreement to devolve corporation tax (the tax on company profits) to Northern Ireland, subject to conditions about the political processes there, compliance with EU state aid rules, and avoidance of the use of Northern Ireland as a base for tax evasion without stimulating economic growth. The agreement was enacted in the Corporation Tax (Northern Ireland) Act of 2015, but implementation has been stalled by political difficulties within Northern Ireland, including suspension of the Assembly as well as substantial administrative problems.

For Wales, there is to be devolution of 10 points of personal income tax and some small land taxes, as was initially proposed for Scotland and largely endorsed by the Holtham and Silk Commissions. This plan was enacted in the Wales Act of 2017, with income tax devolution due to begin in April 2019. The weak Welsh tax base meant that this change was expected to raise about 25 percent of devolved spending including local taxation, 15 percent without (Commission on Devolution in Wales 2012, 143–44).

This extensive and rapid program of fiscal devolution has been accomplished at high speed, with little consideration by the government of the full economic implications (see House of Lords Select Committee on the Constitution 2015; House of Lords Select Committee on Economic Affairs 2015). In some cases, such as corporation tax devolution for Northern Ireland, the measures taken raise difficult EU legal issues regarding state aid. In virtually no cases have there been attempts to take a UK-wide view of the implications of fiscal devolution for the UK as a whole. (For a rare exception, see Bingham Centre for the Rule of Law 2015.) Rather, fiscal devolution has been driven by a range of political imperatives, reflecting the fragmented politics of the postdevolution UK and the different political dynamics (and relationships with the UK government) of each subunit.

Although the changes to financing devolution reveal a complicated and unsatisfactory approach to fiscal devolution, one key institution has retained and perhaps even strengthened its position: HM Treasury, the UK government's finance and economics department and the strongest domestic department by some considerable measure. The Statement of Funding Policy, on which the operation of the Barnett formula rests, is simply a statement of its policy. It has no legal or constitutional standing despite its importance, and it hands all key decisions about the operation and application of the formula to the treasury. These decisions are made based on data that are often not in the public domain and are made in private, with weak accountability to the public or the UK Parliament. The appeals and dispute-resolution mechanisms are weak and incapable of providing impartial mediation or arbitration. Fiscal devolution in fact increases the authority of the treasury in two ways. First, income tax, VAT, and corporation tax (if it is in fact devolved to Northern Ireland) will continue to be collected by the UK's tax collection agency, HM Revenue and Customs (HMRC), and details of how much is collected and collection and enforcement policy are matters for HMRC alone.[6] Arrangements for the accountability of HMRC to the devolved legislatures are weak and largely depend on courtesy rather than on formal or legal rights.

Second, the Barnett formula remains at the center of the financing of the UK's devolved governments. The most important decision following fiscal devolution is how much the block grant should be reduced to allow for devolved tax-raising capacity. This is a difficult issue both technically and politically. While a formula-based approach is proposed, much remains unclear about the formulas to be used and how they will be applied and updated in practice. Those decisions remain in the hands of HM Treasury. Nothing has constrained its control of UK public finances overall or their administration. Little has been done to make public finance more transparent, although to some extent, more data are published now than 10 years ago. The main mechanism for ensuring fairness and transparency remains the ability of the devolved governments to create a political argument. That ability benefits Scotland in particular, since it has the greatest capacity to damage the UK government by such arguments. It does little for the rights of citizens in any part of the UK to enjoy comparable or clearly expressed rights as a citizen of the Union or to scrutinize the means by which those rights are given effect.

The Impact of Devolution on Welfare Policies

It is unsurprising that devolution has changed public policy. It would be a great surprise if the creation of new political forces and arenas, coupled with nationalist politics, did not do so. Because preexisting administrative arrangements and structures formed the basis of political devolution, policies had extensive scope for variation. Indeed, perhaps the great surprise is that variation has not happened to a greater extent.

Welfare policies are unlike many other areas of public policy in one important respect. Under the devolution arrangements, they are entirely the responsibility of one tier of government. Unlike, say, transportation or environmental policy, there is no overlap between devolved and UK-level functions (although there are often points at which one tier's policies rub against those of another). Moreover, even if the Westminster Parliament's formal sovereignty still extends to health matters in Scotland, Wales, and Northern Ireland, the UK government lacks any legal powers or administrative capacity to intervene. Despite the lack of normal constitutional guarantees, devolved governments are genuinely autonomous in making and implementing policy.

Health

The UK's system of public health care is based on the National Health Service (NHS), established in 1948 on the principle of universal health care for all funded by general tax revenues and free at the point of use. The NHS is hugely popular, and most voters see it as the most important British institution, to the point that former Conservative chancellor Nigel Lawson famously described it as "the closest thing the English people have to a religion." Devolving responsibility for its workings was perhaps the most significant transfer of policy functions in 1998, made all the more significant for being undertaken by a Labour government: Labour has had a close political relationship with the NHS since its establishment.

As a single-payer system, the NHS distinguishes strongly between primary and other forms of care. General practitioners (family doctors) provide primary care to their patients as well as referrals for nonemergency specialist inpatient and outpatient treatment at the secondary or tertiary level. Access to specialists without a referral from a GP is impossible within the NHS (though it is possible for private patients). GPs therefore play a pivotal role as gatekeepers for the system as well as providing primary care. Historically, this has resulted in two broad levels of organization to run the NHS: a local or area health board responsible for organizing and managing primary care and a regional or strategic authority responsible chiefly for hospital provision, including ensuring a range of specialist care. The boundaries, size, and internal organization of the units have varied from time to time (few decades have passed without a major reorganization), but the essential structure has remained remarkably stable until recently.

Devolution took a remarkably open form. There were no legal constraints whatever for Scotland or Northern Ireland (or Wales, after 2006). In particular, there was no obligation to maintain universal care free at the point of use. While political commitments to that have been made, they were rather belated, coming first in 2007, and at the initiative of devolved ministers rather than the UK government. Nevertheless, policy change materialized relatively late, at least outside Wales, and again, the policies pursued by the UK government for England have been the most radical and most active.

English health policy has been underpinned by two different forms of marketization. One is the use of market-style mechanisms to determine what specialist (secondary and tertiary) treatments are provided and by whom. The emphasis has been on systems that enable individual patients or GPs to manage overall care, to identify the cost of hospital referrals, and to negotiate quasi-contractual arrangements for treatment within limited budgets. Policies therefore seek to deliver patient choice and competition among providers. The second has been to encourage the use of private-sector capital and management for the provision of facilities, including whole hospitals as well as clinics providing specialist treatments such as orthopedic surgery. These goals may be mutually contradictory, as privately funded hospitals are viable only with an assured revenue stream, and quasi-markets in health care imply that hospitals may lose their autonomy or go bankrupt if they cannot offer treatments at appropriate cost. Nonetheless, governments of all political complexions have pursued both goals since the 1980s, with varying degrees of emphasis and change. Under the 1997–2010 Labour governments, further innovations for treatment included walk-in clinics for minor conditions and telephone advice services. The most radical policy change was that under the 2010 coalition, which abolished the local-level commissioning organizations in favor of handing all control to GPs (who were expected to band together but could choose whether to do so and how), while all hospitals would become autonomous trusts and could go bankrupt if the market so determined. These changes implied a limited and shrinking role for politicians or the Department of Health at the center.

Welsh policy has also been highly dynamic, though in different ways. In 2003, reforms created local health boards with boundaries that corresponded with Wales's 22 local authorities. Local councils would also nominate a majority of members of the local health boards so that they would integrate the services they provided and emphasize public health while receiving some democratic input. This approach proved hopeless in practice, as local health boards oversaw areas that were simply too small for planning health services. Hospital trusts continued to exist as well. A 2009 reorganization created a structure of seven single-tier health boards organized around major hospitals, and that system remains largely in effect. Wales lacked the walk-in or telephone services provided in England and had much less use of private funding for facilities, which as a result were not modernized to the same extent.

Both Scotland and Northern Ireland have seen little organizational change. Both are comparatively well funded, thanks to the generosity of the Barnett formula arrangements and political pressures to maintain health spending. Scotland has made considerable use of private finance initiative arrangements and sought to innovate with partial election of health boards, which made little practical difference.

Judging policy effectiveness is harder for health than for other policy areas not. There is no official UK-wide effort to assess health services' performance, and data difficulties bedevil comparative work by outside bodies. The two most recent large-scale efforts (by the Nuffield Trust [Bevan et al. 2014] and by the OECD [2016]), concluded that there is little substantive difference in actual health outcomes across the UK despite organizational and policy difference. This contrasts with some earlier studies (notably one by the Nuffield Trust [Connolly, Bevan, and Mays 2010]) that suggested that the performance-management approaches pursued in England were more effective than those elsewhere.

Under-19 Education

Before devolution, compulsory schooling across the UK started at the age of 5. In most areas of England, Wales, and Northern Ireland, children moved to nonselective comprehensive secondary schools at age 11 and remained there at least until the legal school-leaving age of 16. In that final year, they would sit regulated external examinations (known since the 1980s as GCSEs). Those who wished would continue in full-time education until the age of 18, whether at those schools or in sixth-form or further education colleges. Additional education would often involve the A-level examinations used for university entrance and entry to other careers. Otherwise, pupils might leave at 16 to start work or pursue vocational training. Arrangements in Scotland were broadly similar, but public examinations were taken at ages 15 and 17, and admission to university was a year earlier for a four-year (not three-year) degree. National curriculums for each of the four parts of the UK were introduced in the 1980s. Schools were mostly organized and managed by elected local authorities. In some localities in England as well as in Northern Ireland, there was selective secondary education—pupils sat an examination at the age of 10 or 11 to determine whether they were suited to the more academically oriented grammar schools or should go to other secondary schools (often called "secondary modern" schools). In addition, England and parts of Scotland have a long-established tradition of better-off families using fee-paying private education (mostly at what are confusingly called *public schools*) for part or all of their children's upbringing.

Devolution has led to a number of reform programs in Scotland and Wales if less so in Northern Ireland; England has seen radical changes. Under the Labour governments (1997–2010), English policy saw an energetic and costly program of school building or rebuilding, Building Schools for the Future, that relied heavily on private-sector finance and contracting arrangements.[7] The curriculum was repeatedly revamped, first to put greater emphasis on basic skills (literacy and numeracy) and then to prescribe in considerable detail what pupils across the country should learn. The post-16 examinations were restructured from a single two-year course (A levels) to two one-year courses (A2 and A levels), each examined at its end, although the two-year course was later reestablished. Schools were subject to close performance monitoring, with regular reviews by the Office for Standards in Education, an independent inspectorate appointed by central government. Pupils were subject to regular assessments of progress from the age of 7 onward, and both the examination results and the inspections were used to rank schools. Each of these policies was subject to change from time to time. Some schools were encouraged to break away from local education authority control and establish themselves as "academies," a policy supported by the UK government, particularly in inner-city areas where established schools were performing weakly. Under the coalition (2010–15) and Conservative (2015–) governments, most of these policies have been continued and in some cases expanded. (The exception has been the school-building program.) The National Curriculum has become more detailed and prescriptive. Examination requirements for GCSEs have changed, but the education departments for Wales and Northern Ireland rejected those changes, so different examinations are now taken in each part of the UK, with consequent problems for recognition of qualifications by universities and employers. The greatest changes, however, have been to school organization, with a determined effort to undermine local education authorities and encourage schools to opt out of local control. Support has increased for the linkage of autonomous academics and the establishment of "academy chains" that bring multiple schools into one organizational framework. There has also been support for allowing parents to establish a new form of school, the "free school," again outside the purview of local authorities. (There has been a slow and reluctant acknowledgment of the problems these approaches can cause. For example, the absence of an overarching body with responsibility for overall planning of educational provision has led to a lack of schools in some areas and surplus in others. In addition, the accountability mechanisms for academies and free schools are quite weak.)

The idea of undermining local education authorities has been unpopular outside England and has not been pursued in Scotland or Wales. On the whole, Scottish policy has been the least active, with a schools building/rebuilding program (using private finance initiative contracts) in the 2000s but limited changes to curriculum, school organization, and vocational training. There have been efforts to enhance teaching as a career and an attempt to move away from the use of league tables, though they have moved somewhat back into favor. Instead, energy and funding have been devoted to higher education and in particular to eliminating tuition fees for Scottish-resident students attending universities in Scotland.[8] Wales has experienced limited attempts to reshape the post-16 curriculum through establishment of a "Welsh baccalaureate" and a wholesale abandonment of regular testing and league tables. Northern Ireland has seen relatively little change with the exception of a controversial attempt by a Sinn Fein (nationalist) education minister to abolish selection at 11 for secondary education, which was divided by the ethnoreligious communities.

Education policy has the unique benefit of an authoritative cross-national evaluation framework in the form of the triennial Programme for International Student Assessment (PISA), which also differentiates between each of the four parts of the UK. PISA therefore provides a means of assessing the relative success of education policy not just within the UK but in comparison with all OECD members. It also offers the benefits of comparison over time. Table 1 shows the UK scores on the PISA for 2006 and 2015.

The UK as a whole has performed at or slightly above the OECD average in each subject area each time the exercise has been carried out. Beyond that, these figures suggest that both England (with a very dynamic but consistently performance-oriented policy) and Northern Ireland (where changes have been minimal) have fared best in the PISA assessments, showing both improvements over time and sitting slightly above OECD averages, particularly in science. The more humane and pro-teacher approaches of both Scotland and Wales, with less demanding inspection regimes, less emphasis on regular testing of pupils, and much less or no use of league tables, have not produced similar results; in fact, Wales has seen a deterioration of student attainment. Moreover, more detailed aspects of the PISA data suggest that these problems are particularly serious for poorer performers and in less affluent areas, especially in Wales.

TABLE 1. PISA Results, 2006 and 2015

	Science		Math		Reading	
	2006	2015	2006	2015	2006	2015
UK average	515	509	495	492	495	498
OECD average	499	493	498	490	492	493
England	516	512	495	493	496	500
Scotland	515	497	506	491	499	493
Wales	505	485	484	478	481	477
Northern Ireland	508	500	494	493	495	497

Source: Data from Bradshaw et al. 2007.
Note: Figures are mean scores for each subject area.

Pensions and Welfare Benefits

Pensions and welfare benefits generally were reserved as part of the devolution arrangements for Scotland and Wales in 1998. They therefore remained UK-wide, and devolved legislatures have no power to alter welfare arrangements legally and no capacity to deliver welfare administratively. Two welfare benefits (the housing benefit, to support the housing costs of low-income households, and the council tax benefit, to support the local government tax costs of people receiving the housing benefit) were administered through local authorities but fell outside the devolved powers despite the fact that local government generally formed part of the devolved responsibilities. This division of functions and the problems of managing the interface with devolved responsibilities for "personal care" led to considerable difficulties when the Scottish Parliament decided to provide personal care free of charge to all older people in need of it.[9]

For Northern Ireland, the situation was more complicated, since welfare was formally devolved under the Belfast/Good Friday Agreement. Social security was, however, made subject to a parity requirement, so that levels of welfare benefits and the circumstances under which they were payable would resemble those in Great Britain and would be paid for directly from the UK Exchequer even though it was administered by a separate agency in Northern Ireland. The different institutional structures of Northern Ireland would require considerable differentiation in the detail of welfare policy.

Until roughly 2013, the Labour Party treated the UK-wide welfare system as of fundamental and totemic significance without offering any clear explanation of the principles behind this view. There are some practical reasons for this approach: economic and demographic factors mean that all three devolved parts of the UK make higher-than-average claims on the welfare bill and are net recipient regions overall.[10] A uniform welfare system may have appeared to offer a way of rewarding traditionally Labour-supporting areas.

Faced with the 2010–15 coalition government's austerity program, however, this judgment was less clear-cut. The coalition embarked on a program of public-spending austerity in which welfare spending was a prime target (and from which health and schools spending were sheltered). It also sought to deliver sweeping changes in welfare provision designed to promote work wherever possible as well as reduce the costs of welfare. Protections on spending on health and education in real terms and guarantees for the growth of old-age pensions by advantageous index measures meant that the cuts to other aspects of welfare were severe. Working-age benefits—particularly the tax credits for working families introduced by the post-1997 Labour governments—were substantially cut. Benefits for those unable to work because of poor health or disability were reduced and the criteria for those conditions were made more stringent. Limits were placed on the rents and size of properties for which the housing benefit could be paid, the total amount of benefit payable to each individual household, and the overall welfare budget. Many key benefits were restructured, with a new "universal credit" planned to incorporate most existing specific benefits and "make work pay," though the introduction of this credit has been riddled with problems, particularly related to computer systems.

These changes resulted not just in a narrower and less generous welfare system skewed heavily in favor of pensioners but also a more fragmented one. While Wales has demonstrated no interest at all in welfare devolution, the idea has had significant political implications in both Scotland and Northern Ireland. In Northern Ireland, welfare cuts played a part in two of the periodic crises that have engulfed devolved government there, with Sinn Fein's refusal to implement them leading to a reduction in the UK Treasury's grant for the welfare system and to questions about what exactly "parity" in welfare means. In Scotland, the welfare cuts fueled debates during the 2014 independence referendum campaign. It was little surprise that the Smith Commission adopted recommendations (also stemming from proposals made by the Institute for Public Policy Research and largely endorsed by the Scottish Conservatives [Lodge and Trench 2014; Scottish Conservatives 2014]) for partial devolution. Such recommendations include the devolution of specific benefits relating to disability and care for frail and disabled people and the housing element of the new universal credit as well as a general power to supplement nondevolved UK welfare benefits if the Scottish Parliament wishes and can find funds to do so.

Certain trends can be seen in the impact of devolution generally. One is a process of slow differentiation in welfare provision and increasing and uncontrolled variation in the UK's welfare state (see Birrell 2009). This makes the welfare state and the rights its citizens enjoy increasingly hard to set out or explain in any cogent way. The second is that the key driver of change is English practices and preferences for both market-oriented policies and the use of techniques of performance management. These phenomena appear to deliver better policy outcomes in some respects but do so to only a limited extent and at considerable cost. By contrast, devolved governments can largely maintain preexisting policies with limited adjustments—devolved governments are not so much laboratories of democracy as laboratories of policy conservatism while England innovates in risky ways.

The Future of the UK's Welfare State and Brexit

Prognostication is always difficult. For the UK's welfare state, it is even more hazardous than normal. Despite that, some key questions about its development can usefully be raised.

The UK faces a range of major challenges. Some are the mainstay of discussions in territorial politics: the implications of decentralizing reforms for public policy and for shared institutional frameworks as well as national identity; the need for accommodation of national diversity and the implications of doing so. The UK continues to face these challenges. There is limited demand for further substantive devolution from Wales or Northern Ireland, particularly of welfare functions, and no appetite for such debates at the center. Scotland is different, but the mechanisms for welfare and tax devolution in the Scotland Act of 2016 have yet to take effect and are likely to reshape those arguments.

These political challenges are not the only ones the UK faces or even the most important. One is the burden of an aging population and the associated costs for health and social care. Despite attempts to protect health spending, these efforts are widely regarded as failing to keep pace with growing demand for health care. Nothing has been done to address social care costs despite repeated inquiries (Royal Commission on Long Term Care 1999; Commission on Funding of Care and Support 2011) and a clear need for a solution. Instead, the political response to date has been to protect or enhance the value of the state pension and reduce the impact of inheritance tax (which is only payable on large estates). Since 2010, austerity measures have primarily affected those of working age who have low incomes or who are dependent on state benefits. These measures may be popular with older Conservative voters but ultimately increase the cost of dealing with the problem and contribute to a substantial transfer of resources from working-age adults, particularly lower-paid families, to the elderly.

Far more important are the effects of the UK's June 2016 vote to leave the European Union, with departure to take effect in March 2019. The significance of the Brexit vote can hardly be overstated and is likely to reshape the UK in the years to come. Its significance has three dimensions.

First, the vote to leave the EU revealed a deep social cleavage that has subsequently deepened. At least in England and Wales, "Leave" voters were generally older (age 49 or older), less well-off, and from less well-off parts of the UK—in particular, smaller towns that were badly affected by deindustrialization. "Remain" voters were younger, better off, and lived mainly in larger cities. (In London, 60 percent of voters voted Remain; only a slightly smaller percentage in the West Midlands voted Leave [see Clarke, Goodwin, and Whiteley 2017].) To a substantial degree, globalization's losers voted against its winners. Since those winners are also the most economically productive members of British society, generating the income that is redistributed to losers in the form of public services and welfare benefits for which their taxes cannot pay, the vote raises the longer-term question of why the winners should continue to do so. This question goes to the heart of the social basis for redistribution through public services and taxation. In addition, younger people face very high housing costs, large levels of graduate debt, and limited occupational opportunities compared to their parents' or grandparents' generations in an economy that is growing more slowly than in the past. If, as many expect, leaving the EU adversely affects the British economy for some time to come, these difficulties will be compounded. In such straits, younger people are likely to be less and less willing to see their stretched incomes taxed to pay for those who have made them worse rather than better off.

Second, Brexit will have direct effects on public services. While the form Brexit will take remains quite unclear, there is no doubt that these effects will be substantial. In particular, UK economic growth is likely to be weaker, reducing tax revenues for spending on services and increasing costs in some areas. Social care and the NHS depend heavily on staff from overseas, particularly from EU countries. Limiting migration is key part of the Brexit proposal, so the UK may have increasingly difficulty recruiting from EU countries as people from abroad may be more reluctant to work in the UK because it has become more hostile to foreigners. In such circumstances, public services will become more and more stretched.

Third, Brexit will affect the UK's territorial politics. While the UK as a whole voted to leave the EU, neither Scotland (where 62 percent of voters sought to remain) nor Northern Ireland (56 percent) did. Attempts by the Scottish National Party to exploit the difference in the vote to bolster the case for independence or trigger another independence referendum have to date come to nothing, but that may change. Such differences certainly create a basis for pushing for independence if Brexit works out badly. In Northern Ireland, the concern of the Republic of Ireland's government with protecting the Good Friday Agreement and avoiding a "hard border" have been supported by other EU member states, and both UK and the EU-27 have agreed that those concerns should form part of the parameters for Brexit, but the exact means of doing so remain unclear. Since July 2017, the reliance of the UK's minority Conservative government on parliamentary support from the only Northern Ireland party committed to leaving the EU (the hard-line Democratic Unionist Party) makes this more acute.

In the past twenty years, the UK has embarked on extensive devolution, with profound effects on public services. It now faces leaving the EU with consequences for large areas of public services and for the state as a whole that cannot be calculated or even roughly estimated. Its tolerance of anomalies, public policies that are frequently altered against a backdrop that can only be explained historically, and large territorial variations have led to a backlash from voters—the same voters whose support for leaving the EU reflected much wider discontents.

NOTES

1. While processes of devolution have occurred within England since 1999, they have been more limited. The 1997–2010 Labour governments had plans for elected regional assemblies, but with the exceptions of the London mayor and Assembly, they stalled by 2005. The post-2010 Conservative/Liberal Democrat coalition has developed an agenda focused on certain enlarged "city regions" and a "Northern Powerhouse," which started with an agreement for Greater Manchester in 2014. The directly elected element of these schemes is limited, and they have responsibility for planning-related functions and are intended to spur economic growth, but they have no fiscal powers and limited powers with regard to the welfare matters that are the concern of this project.

2. Devolved government in Northern Ireland is only Strand 1 of the Belfast Agreement. Strand 2 consists of all-Ireland arrangements for a range of specified matters, and Strand 3 is arrangements for the archipelago embracing the Irish and UK governments, the Crown dependencies in the Isle of Man and the Channel Islands, and the Scottish and Welsh devolved administrations.

3. In partial redress of these anomalies, procedures in the House of Commons were altered in 2015 to enable only English MPs to consider some stages of legislation relating only to England.

4. This has already happened in one policy area: tuition fees for higher education. The UK government's decision to abolish the "teaching grant" for humanities and social science courses in English universities and require tuition fees to increase to £9,000 per year beginning in September 2012 to cover teaching costs meant reductions in the block grants to Scotland, Wales, and Northern Ireland as well.

5. The treasury carried out a review in 1993, but it was not published at the time and came to light only in 2008 (House of Lords Select Committee on the Barnett Formula 2009, 20).

6. Both Scotland and Wales are establishing their own agencies to collect the land taxes for which they are responsible.

7. Such private finance initiative plans became a common part of British public policy in the 1990s, particularly in the health and education sectors. They would typically involve a private-sector contractor undertaking to build a facility and operate and maintain it (providing building management services, cleaning, and so forth) for a period usually of 25 or 30 years, charging an annual fee to the responsible public-sector body. Such plans generated controversy because the interest costs incurred would be several times the rate at which the public sector could borrow money but had the advantage of keeping such borrowing off the public sector's balance sheet.

8. This results in the anomaly that tuition at Scottish universities is also free for students from other EU member states but students from other parts of the UK must pay.

9. The UK acknowledges a distinction between *nursing care* and *personal care* for those unable to wash, dress, or otherwise care for themselves. In essence, "nursing" care is that identified as required by a doctor, while "personal" care is not, although the care involved is often exactly the same and the difference is hard to explain or justify. In England and Wales, nursing care is provided free, but personal care is not despite a recommendation by an expert commission that both should be free (Royal Commission on Long Term Care 1999). In what was regarded as a landmark innovation, the Scottish Parliament decided to follow the recommendation and make both free, but doing so required that care be delivered through local authorities, creating some significant anomalies in delivery (Simeon 2003).

10. Scotland's population is significantly older than the UK average and is continuing to age. Both Wales and Northern Ireland are weak economic performers and are prone to the outmigration of working-age adults, meaning that they have higher proportions of younger and older people. Moreover, Wales constitutes a popular retirement destination for pensioners from elsewhere.

REFERENCES

Bevan, G., M. Karanikolos, J. Exley, E. Nolte, S. Connolly, and N. Mays. 2014. *The Four Health Systems of the United Kingdom: How Do They Compare?* London: Health Foundation and the Nuffield Trust.

Bingham Centre for the Rule of Law. 2015. *A Constitutional Crossroad: Ways Forward for the United Kingdom: Report of an Independent Commission.* London: British Institute for International and Comparative Law.

Birrell, D. 2009. *The Impact of Devolution on Social Policy.* Bristol: Policy Press.

Bradshaw, J., L. Sturman, H. Vappula, R. Ager, and R. Wheater. 2007. *Achievement of 15-Year-Olds in England: PISA 2006 National Report* (OECD Programme for International Student Assessment). Slough: National Foundation for Educational Research.

Checkland, S. 1985. *British Public Policy, 1776–1939: An Economic, Social, and Political Perspective.* Cambridge: Cambridge University Press.

Clarke, H. D., M. Goodwin, and P. Whiteley. 2017. *Brexit: Why Britain Voted to Leave the European Union.* Cambridge: Cambridge University Press.

Commission on Devolution in Wales. 2012. *Empowerment and Responsibility: Financial Powers to Strengthen Wales.* Cardiff: Commission on Devolution in Wales.

Commission on Funding of Care and Support. 2011. *Fairer Care Funding: The Report of the Commission on Funding of Care and Support*. London: Department of Health.

Commission on Scottish Devolution. 2009. *Serving Scotland Better: Scotland and the United Kingdom in the 21st Century: Final Report*. Edinburgh: Commission on Scottish Devolution.

Connolly, S., G. Bevan, and N. Mays. 2010. *Funding and Performance of Healthcare Systems in the Four Countries of the UK before and after Devolution*. London: Nuffield Trust.

Department of Finance and Personnel Northern Ireland. Various. *Northern Ireland Net Fiscal Balance Report*.

Esping-Andersen, G. 1989. *The Three Worlds of Welfare Capitalism*. Oxford: Polity Press.

Greer, S. L. 2004. *Territorial Politics and Health Policy: The United Kingdom in Comparative Perspective*. Manchester: Manchester University Press.

Greer, S. L., ed. 2009. *Devolution and Citizenship Rights in the United Kingdom*. Bristol: Policy Press.

Heald, D. 1980. *Territorial Equity and Public Finances: Concepts and Confusion*. Glasgow: Centre for the Study of Public Policy, University of Strathclyde.

Heald, D., and A. McLeod. 2002. "Beyond Barnett? Funding devolution." In *Devolution in Practice: Public Policy Differences within the UK*, ed. J. Adams and P. Robinson, 147–75. London: ippr.

Heald, D., and A. McLeod. 2005. "Embeddedness of UK Devolution Finance within the Public Expenditure System." *Regional Studies* 39 (4): 495–518.

HM Treasury. 1979. *The Assessment of Public Expenditure Needs in England, Scotland, Wales, and Northern Ireland*. London: HM Treasury.

HM Treasury. 1999. *Funding the Scottish Parliament, National Assembly for Wales, and Northern Ireland Assembly: Statement of Funding Policy*. London: HM Treasury.

HM Treasury. 2015. *Statement of Funding Policy: Funding the Scottish Parliament, National Assembly for Wales, and Northern Ireland Assembly*. 7th ed. London: HM Treasury.

HM Treasury. Various. *Public Expenditure Statistical Analyses*. London: HM Treasury.

House of Lords Select Committee on Economic Affairs. 2015. *A Fracturing Union: The Implications of Financial Devolution to Scotland*. First report of session 2015–16. HL Paper 55. London: HMSO.

House of Lords Select Committee on the Barnett Formula. 2009. *The Barnett Formula*. First report of session 2008–9. HL Paper 139. London: HMSO.

House of Lords Select Committee on the Constitution. 2015. *The Union and Devolution*. Tenth report of session 2015–16. HL Paper 149. London: HMSO.

Independent Commission on Funding and Finance for Wales. 2010. *Fairness and Accountability: A New Funding Settlement for Wales*. Cardiff: Welsh Government.

Jackson, A. 2012. *The Two Unions: Ireland, Scotland, and the Survival of the United Kingdom, 1707–2007*. Oxford: Oxford University Press.

Keating, M., ed. 2007. *Scottish Social Democracy: Progressive Ideas for Public Policy*. Brussels: Peter Lang.

Lodge, G., and A. Trench. 2014. *Devo More and Welfare: Devolving Benefits and Policy for a Stronger Union*. London: Institute for Public Policy Research.

Marshall T. H. [1950] 1992. *Citizenship and Social Class*. London: Pluto.

McEwen, N. 2002. "State Welfare Nationalism: The Territorial Impact of Welfare State Development in Scotland." *Regional and Federal Studies* 12 (1): 66–90.

McLean, I. 2005. *The Fiscal Crisis of the United Kingdom*. Basingstoke: Palgrave.

McLean, I., C. Wlezien, and S. N. Soroka. 2003. *Identifying the Flow of Domestic and European Expenditures into the English Regions*. Final Report for Office of the Deputy Prime Minister, London.

Mitchell, J. 2006. "Undignified and Inefficient: Financial Relations between London and Stormont." *Contemporary British History* 20 (1): 57–73.

Mitchell, J. 2007. "The United Kingdom as a State of Unions: Unity of Government, Equality of Political Rights, and Diversity of Institutions." In *Devolution and Power in the United Kingdom*, ed. A. Trench, 24–47. Manchester: Manchester University Press.

OECD. 2016. *OECD Reviews of Health Care Quality: United Kingdom 2016: Raising Standards*. Paris: OECD.

OECD Programme for International Student Assessment. 2017. *Results from PISA 2015 Country Note: United Kingdom*.

Royal Commission on Long Term Care. 1999. *With Respect to Old Age: Long Term Care—Rights and Responsibilities*. London: HMSO.

Scottish Conservatives. 2014. *Commission on the Future Governance of Scotland*. Edinburgh: Scottish Conservatives.

Scottish Executive. 2007. *Choosing Scotland's Future: A National Conversation: Independence and Responsibility in the Modern World*. Edinburgh: Scottish Executive.

Scottish Executive/Government. Various. *Government Expenditures and Revenues Scotland*. Edinburgh: Scottish Executive/Government.

Scottish Government. 2009. *Your Scotland, Your Choice: A National Conversation*. Edinburgh: Scottish Government.

Simeon, R. 2003. "Free Personal Care: Policy Divergence and Social Citizenship." In *The State of the Nations 2003: The third year of devolution in the United Kingdom*, ed. R. Hazell, 215–35. Exeter: Imprint Academic.

Smith Commission. 2014. *Report of the Smith Commission for Further Devolution of Powers to the Scottish Parliament*. Edinburgh: Smith Commission.

Trench, A., ed. 2007a. *Devolution and Power in the United Kingdom*. Manchester: Manchester University Press.

Trench, A. 2007b. "The Politics of Devolution Finance and the Power of the Treasury." In In *Devolution and Power in the United Kingdom*, ed. A. Trench, 86–112. Manchester: Manchester University Press.

Trench, A. 2013. *Funding Devo More: Fiscal Options for Strengthening the Union*. London: Institute for Public Policy Research.

Germany

The Rise of Territorial Politics?

Niccole M. Pamphilis, Simone Singh, Charlie Jeffery, and Michael Slowik

Like the other countries examined in this volume, Germany is a federal system. Based on the country-level Regional Authority Index (RAI) dataset, it has the strongest decentralized system examined in this volume, trailing only Belgium during a short period of time between 1989 and 1994 (Hooghe, Marks, and Schakel 2010). However, the findings based on the institutional features measured in the index are challenged by a preexisting paradigm in the literature on Germany that argues that the overlapping and interconnectedness of different levels of government and party system actually produce a "unitary federal state" (Scharpf, Reissert, and Schnabel 1976; Scharpf 2009; Hesse 1962; Wheare 1953; Abromeit 1992; Burkhart 2008; Scheller and Schmid 2008). In practice, however, research has revealed that the variation expected across regions in a federal system do exist in Germany (Mintzel 1977; Schmidt 1980; Benz 1985; Schmid 1990; Götz 1992; Jeffery 1999; Sturm 1999; Jun, Haas, and Niedermayer 2008; Bräuninger and Debus 2012; Debus and Müller 2013; Müller 2013; Seher and Pappi 2011; Benz 1999; Auel 2010; Jeffery and Rowe 2014; Jeffery et al. 2014). This clash in expectations in the literature makes Germany an interesting case with respect to the provision of welfare policy: specifically, are provisions and outcomes in line with the proposition of uniformity or in line with the expectations of a federal system?

Germany is composed of 16 states (*Länder*) of varying sizes, populations, and economic resources (table 1). The smallest of the *Länder* is the city-state of Bremen, with an area of 420 square kilometers, while the largest is Bavaria, at more than 70,500 square kilometers. The city-states of

Berlin, Bremen, and Hamburg represent the most densely populated *Länder*. Bremen, the smallest of the three, has roughly three times as many people as the next most densely populated *Land*. Resources also vary dramatically across the *Länder*, with GDP per capita (at current prices) in 2014 ranging from €22,964 in Mecklenburg-Vorpommern to €54,526 in Hamburg. While the initial context for policy actions varies across the *Länder* and we would anticipate that this variation would produce differences in policy inputs and outcomes, a strong political climate favors equality of living conditions. This preference is embedded within the German constitution, the Basic Law (Article 72).[1]

The German federal system also follows a model of cooperative federalism, or *Politikverflechtung* (Gunlicks 2005). Although the Basic Law grants residual powers (i.e., all power not explicitly granted to the federal government) to the *Länder*, after controlling for the powers exclusively granted to the federal government (foreign affairs, defense, citizenship, migration, currency, transportation, and communications), concurrent powers and framework legislation (an additional 37 areas), and all areas the federal government believes to be under its purview to ensure the

TABLE 1. Area and Population of *LÄNDER*

Land	Total Area (km²)	Population	Population Density
Baden-Württemberg	35,751.41	10,486,660	293.32
Bayern	70,550.19	12,397,614	175.73
Berlin	891.75	3,292,365	3,692.03
Brandenburg	29,483.98	2,455,780	83.29
Bremen	419.24	650,863	1,552.48
Hamburg	755.30	1,706,696	2,259.63
Hessen	21,114.76	5,971,816	282.83
Mecklenburg-Vorpommern	23,194.18	1,609,982	69.41
Niedersachsen	47,613.60	7,777,992	163.36
Nordrhein-Westfalen	34,097.72	17,538,251	514.35
Rheinland-Pfalz	19,854.13	3,989,808	200.96
Saarland	2,568.73	999,623	389.15
Sachsen	18,419.83	4,056,799	220.24
Sachsen-Anhalt	20,450.29	2,287,040	111.83
Schleswig-Holstein	15,799.57	2,800,119	177.23
Thüringen	16,172.50	2,188,589	135.33
Total	357,137.17	80,209,997	224.59

Source: Statistisches Bundesamt n.d.
Note: Population data from 2011 census.

maintenance of equal living conditions (per Article 72), few exclusive domains remain (Jeffery 1998).

The relationship between the *Länder* and federal governments is further complicated or predicated on cooperation as a consequence of the role of the *Länder* in the Bundesrat, which offers the *Länder* a venue in which to represent their opinions at the federal level. The Bundesrat carries veto power over legislation produced by the Bundestag and absolute veto power over legislation with implications for the administration of the *Länder*, resulting in a high level of interdependence in lawmaking (Jeffery 1998; Moore, Jacoby, and Gunlicks 2013).

To help promote each *Land's* ability to achieve equal living conditions, fiscal equalization redistributes revenue equitably across the *Länder*. The *Länder* have three main sources of income: tax revenue, fiscal equalization, and additional subsidies provided through supplementary federal grants. The *Länder* have no real autonomous tax authority and predominantly voice opinions and concerns regarding tax legislation (limited to revenue volume) through the Bundesrat. Income tax, corporate taxes, and value-added taxes are controlled at the federal level and are divided between the federal, *Land*, and municipal governments. After tax revenues are distributed, fiscal equalization measures redistribute resources based on the assumption of equal need per inhabitant across the *Länder*.[2] *Länder* deemed to be below the average financial requirements receive additional funds, while those who are above the average contribute to the redistributed funds. The amount of money reallocated varies drastically (table 2) and has resulted in tensions among the *Länder*, particularly those that are fiscally sound and are consistently contributors to equalization instead of beneficiaries.[3]

Germany's 1990 reunification required various political and economic barriers to be overcome. On 31 August 1990 five *Länder* from the East (Brandenburg, Mecklenburg-Vorpommern, Saxony, Saxony-Anhalt, and Thuringia) joined the eleven older *Länder* of the West. Elections were held the following December to establish the new Bundestag, which facilitated negotiations for further integration of the two policy systems. The West's social welfare system, comprising aspects of wage replacement, unemployment compensation, and social assistance, was extended into the new *Länder*. Economic integration included the reunification of the monetary systems in July 1990, with the deutsche mark introduced into the East. In addition, financial transfers were established through the German Unitary Fund (1990–94), the Solidarity Pact I (1995–2004) and the Solidarity Pact II (2005–19) to aid in economic development and the closing of disparities between the East and West. Interterritorial redistribution in the social insurance systems thus plays an important role in achieving equal living conditions across the *Länder*. Interterritorial redistribution of social insurance funds also played an important role in funding German unification. Approximately a quarter of all West–East transfers in the decade after unification (approximately DM270 billion) were borne by the social insurance schemes (Manow 2004). A Pew (2009) survey of citizens from the old and new *Länder* revealed that while those from the new *Länder* feel they are better off after reunification (63 percent), both citizens from the East (86 percent) and West (63 percent) feel that the East has still not achieved the same standard of living as the West.

In reality, because needs are not equal across the *Länder*, additional considerations are taken into account with supplemental federal grants. Starting in 1990, additional transfers were made from the western to eastern *Länder* as part of the Solidarity Pact I. These transfers were extended through 2019, with gradual reductions each year, as part of the Solidarity Pact II (German Ministry of Finance; Gunlicks 2005). Smaller *Länder* also receive additional special-needs grants to account for overhead associated with administrative costs, which are a larger relative burden for these *Länder* (German Ministry of Finance).[4]

The data for this chapter is obtained primarily from the Federal Statistics Office, with additional information taken from various other German

TABLE 2. Fiscal Equalization Allocations for *LÄNDER*, 2013

Land	Fiscal Equalization (Million €)
Baden-Württemberg	−2,429
Bayern	−4,320
Berlin	3,338
Brandenburg	521
Bremen	589
Hamburg	87
Hessen	−1,711
Mecklenburg-Vorpommern	464
Niedersachsen	106
Nordrhein-Westfalen	693
Rheinland-Pfalz	243
Saarland	138
Sachsen	1,002
Sachsen-Anhalt	563
Schleswig-Holstein	169
Thüringen	547

Source: Data from German Statistical Yearbook 2014.

government offices, including the Ministry of Finance and the *Länder* National Accounts Working Group. Information is typically available for at least the past ten years, with multiple indicators going back to 1995.

Redistribution

Many areas typically associated with social protection fall within the competency of the federal government, including pensions and unemployment. The federal government legislates in the area of health care, but it is administered and provided by the private sector. Primary education has traditionally fallen under the control of the *Länder*, with the federal government involved indirectly with educational policy at that the primary/secondary school level through associated bodies and in higher education through provision of grants and funding.

Old-Age Pensions

Pensions play a large role in maintaining a minimum standard of living in old age. The German pension system is based on a pay-as-you-go system where contributions are made by both employees and employers (European Commission 2013). Savings for individuals are amassed over their working career, and payouts are based on income levels during the work cycle. The nature of the pension system means that individuals are not guaranteed equal pension benefits at retirement. Pension benefit levels also vary based on when an individual chooses to leave the workforce. Prior to 2012, benefits were accessible starting at age 65 years and one month if an individual had contributed to the system for at least five years; however, between 2012 and 2029, the retirement age is gradually being increased to 67 years (European Commission 2013; OECD 2013). Early retirement can start at age 63, but individuals receive a penalty of a 3.6 percent reduction in benefits per year (or 0.3 percent per month) under their retirement age, while individuals who retire after the minimum age for full benefits receive a .5 percent accrued increase for additional month worked (European Commission 2013).

Some factors beyond an individual's control are seen to impact pension benefits. The pension system in based on points earned for each year worked, which is used as a multiplier for determining final benefit packages. Inequalities between income levels in the eastern and western *Länder* lead to differences in pension benefits (OECD 2013). In addition, parents who leave the workforce for a period of time to care for children also face inequalities. Parents who had children prior to 1992 could receive one point toward their pension while out on child leave; after 1992, parents who left work to care for children can claim three points (or three years of working) toward retirement benefits (OECD 2013).

Finally, periods of unemployment also limit an individual's ability to contribute to the pension system. To offset the full loss of contributions to the pension scheme, during the first 6–24 months of unemployment, unemployment insurance makes contributions into the system at the rate of 80 percent; however, when an individual moves to unemployment assistance, pension contributions cease (OECD 2013).

While the public pension system is one means of securing income during retirement, individuals also have the option of privately investing in voluntary funds through banks, insurance companies, and investment funds. This approach further separates those who are in a position to save from those who lack the resources to do so. However, individuals who are unable to save during their working years have access to means-tested benefits through the social assistance program (OECD 2013).

In addition to the pension system, citizens are able to draw on long-term care (LTC) insurance funds, which were established in 1994 to help individuals defined as "frail" and requiring a minimum of six months of assistance to perform day-to-day activities. While accessible to the non-elderly population, this program is of particular relevance for individuals in old age who require additional services in the form of domestic assistance for daily life activities or nursing care. LTC operates in a similar manner to Germany's other insurance plans, and any individual enrolled in a health insurance program is automatically enrolled in a LTC plan. The program is financed by a contribution of 1.7 percent of income for individuals with children and 1.95 percent for childless individuals; since 1995, this contribution has been divided equally between employees and employers.[5] Dependent members of a family who do not work receive coverage through contributing family members, while the elderly are required to contribute directly out of pocket (Arntz et al. 2007). Overlap in coverage between areas of LTC and health insurance means that LTC sees a large share of high-cost items shifted from health insurance coverage to LTC.

Unemployment Benefits

Unemployment benefits are handled by the federal government and are divided into unemployment insurance and unemployment assistance. To access the first level of benefits, unemployment insurance, an individual must have worked at least 360 days in the past three years, contributed into the insurance system, be between the ages of 18 and 65, and have filed as unemployed and looking for work. Varying levels of benefits are provided based on prior income level (which is associated with level of contribution) and number of dependents. Benefit levels are typically 60 percent of an individual's prior income level for those with no dependents and 67 percent for individuals with at least one dependent (European Commission 2013).

Individuals can claim unemployment insurance benefits for varying durations contingent on age and years worked. Individuals who have contributed to the insurance plan for at least 12 months can receive 6 months of benefits, while individuals who have contributed for 48 months can receive 24 months of benefits (European Commission 2013). Differences also exist in the maximum amount of benefits: residents of the western *Länder* can receive as much as €5,800 per month, while those in the eastern *Länder* are limited to €4,900 per month (European Commission 2013).

Individuals who are close to retirement may move from unemployment insurance benefits directly to the pension system. Individuals may qualify if they are over the age of 60: women over 60 with at least 15 years of work experience can to claim their full pension benefits (OECD 2005). Individuals who have not returned to the workforce when their eligibility for unemployment insurance ends can move to the second level of unemployment benefits: unemployment assistance.

There is no limit on how long an individual can claim unemployment assistance. As of 1 January 2015, minimum standard benefit levels across the German *Länder* stood at €399 per month for lone individuals, with increases based on the number and ages of children as well as partners (Federal Employment Agency 2017).

Health

The German social health insurance (SHI) system guarantees access to comprehensive health benefits for almost 70 million German residents, or 87 percent of the population (GKV-Spitzenverband 2014), with others finding coverage through supplemental and private funds. Federal law requires that all residents who earn below a government-specified annual income (€53,550 in 2014 [Euraxess Germany n.d.]) become members of one of approximately 130 "sickness funds" (GKV-Spitzenverband 2014). Individuals who earn above the minimum level can opt out of the compulsory insurance system and have the option of voluntarily enrolling in a

SHI fund or obtaining full coverage through a private fund. Furthermore, substitute plans are available for additional fees for those who desire options not covered by the SHI funds, such a single-occupancy hospital rooms. Insured members and their dependents have access to preventative care, medicine, therapeutic aids, dental services, inpatient treatments, and domestic nursing care (provided through practitioners associated with an individual's SHI plan) (European Commission 2013). Most services are free at the point of service or require a small copayment (e.g., prescription drugs and durable medical equipment).

The German SHI system includes features of interpersonal redistribution stemming from social policy decisions. Most important, the system is based on the principle of social solidarity, which implies that all members of society should have access to health care regardless of ability to pay (Graig 1999). This principle is achieved by relying on income-based contributions. By design, the uniform income-related contribution rate results in substantial interpersonal redistribution of financial resources from wealthy individuals to the less-well-off. In 2014, the national contribution rate was 15.5 percent, with employees paying 8.2 percent and employers paying 7.3 percent (GKV-Spitzenverband 2014).

Another important feature of the SHI system is that members' dependents are covered at no additional cost. As a result, financial resources are redistributed from singles and childless families to families with children. Finally, variations in use of health care services mean that the system redistributes across gender (women on average use more services than men) and age brackets (the elderly incur higher health care costs than do the young) (Moog and Raffelhueschen 2006). The SHI system fund can also be seen as producing intertemporal transfers over a normal work/life cycle, where individuals contribute more relative to use early in life and pay less relative to use later (Hinrichs 2002).

Both interpersonal and interorganizational redistribution result in substantial interterritorial redistribution of financial resources through the SHI system. Regions where members contribute more to the SHI system than they use in services support regions where members contribute less than they use (Droessler et al. 2011). Some regions within each *Land* contribute more to the SHI system than they use in services, while other regions contribute less. None of the *Länder* consists only of regions that contribute more than they receive or vice versa; therefore, in addition to redistribution across the *Länder*, substantial redistribution of financial resources occurs within each *Land*.

Evidence of interterritorial redistribution has also been found in other parts of the German social insurance system—most notably, the social unemployment and pension insurance plans (Koller, Schiebel, and Stichter-Werner 2003; Zarth, Schnitzlein, and Bruckmeier 2009). Social unemployment insurance creates substantial interterritorial redistribution from regions with low unemployment to regions with high unemployment (Koller, Schiebel, and Stichter-Werner 2003). Regions with high unemployment not only use substantially more services than regions with low unemployment but also generate fewer contributions. Koller, Schiebel, and Stichter-Werner (2003) estimate that in 2001, net transfers from the western and eastern *Länder* amounted to €12.5 billion, more than twice the amount transferred as part of the fiscal equalization scheme during the same time period.

Education

The educational policy domain belongs to the *Länder*. Consequently, there is no national framework for curriculum decisions, assessment methods, recruitment of staff, or even duration and timing of the school year (Riggall and Sharp 2008). Although the *Länder* have the right and ability to deviate in almost all aspects of their educational systems, a need for some degree of uniformity was recognized early on, resulting in the creation of various governing bodies that provide venues for policy discussion. The Ministry of Education and Cultural Affairs, established in 1948, has addressed the coordination of specific topics covered in class and the start and end of compulsory schooling. The ministry is the primary path through which the federal government interacts with educational policy decisions at the *Land* level (Welsh 2014). Although educational policy is an exclusive competency of the *Länder*, funding is a combination of public and private resources. In the 2010–11 fiscal year, 65 percent of all education, research, and science expenditures were based on public funding (13 percent federal government, 40 percent *Land* governments, and 11 percent municipalities) (Welsh 2014).

While schooling is compulsory for children for nine or ten years beginning at age six,[6] the results of the 2000 Programme for International Student Assessment (PISA) showed a large degree of variation in schoolchildren's abilities. Differences in achievement were more highly correlated with children's socioeconomic status than in any other industrialized nation involved in the testing (Martens and Niemann 2013).[7] Immigrant students far underperformed native German students. Furthermore, differences in test scores were observable across schools, which place students on tracks for higher education and vocational careers early in the schooling system. Noticeable gaps in performance also were evident between the *Länder*, with Baden-Württemberg and Bayern scoring above the OECD average and Sachsen-Anhalt and Bremen scoring well below (Baumert et al. 2001). The poor results of the 2000 PISA testing resulted in changes to the primary and secondary educational system that narrowed the achievement gaps related to immigrant status and socioeconomic background, and these improvements constituted the primary factor in the subsequent rise in Germany's overall test ranking (OECD 2011).

Educational expansion and change have been limited within the federal system as a result of the public demand for uniformity of outcomes and the limited and unreliable access to future funding (Welsh 2014). Education funding is in part contingent on federal grants, which are time-based and constantly in renegotiation, limiting the time horizon over which planning and changes can be made. The constant negotiations also limit policy changes as a result of conflict over whether the federal or *Land* governments will be responsible for carrying the burden of payments (Welsh 2014). However, grants instituted in response to Germany's performance on the 2000 PISA assessments include an excellence initiative fund to strengthen research and graduate training (75 percent funding from the federal government); the Higher Education Pact 2020, to address larger university cohorts (equally funded between the federal and *Land* governments); and the Quality Pact for Teaching (90 percent of funding from the federal government). In addition, since 2015, the federal government has covered all student financial assistance, allowing the *Land* governments to use the savings in other areas of educational spending (Welsh 2014).

Change

Federal reforms took place in 2006 and 2009. The earlier reforms attempted to reduce the level of interdependence between the *Land* and federal governments by clarifying the legislative powers of the two levels and by reducing the amount of federal legislation requiring approval by the Bundesrat (Moore, Jacoby, and Gunlicks 2013). In addition, the 2009 reform promoted a more stable financial future by regulating the debt levels of the *Länder*. However, while helping to clarify the policy competencies of the *Länder*, the changes did not extend to policies surrounding social protection or welfare. Instead, the ongoing changes regarding social policy at the federal level have predominantly been a product of addressing increasing financial burdens instead of *Land* preferences or growing social inequalities, though changes in education policy may constitute a slight exception.

Old-Age Pensions

Like many other societies, Germany faces a growing population over the age of 65, a common benchmark for retirement in industrialized states. The increasing size of the elderly population and increased life expectancies have forced governments to seek methods of maintaining the viability of pension systems (table 3). Since 2012, the German pension system has been gradually shifting the retirement age to 67, a process that will be complete by 2029. For those born prior to 31 December 1947, the retirement age to access pension benefits without penalty remains 65. For each year after 1947 in which they were born, individuals born between 1 January 1948 and 31 December 1958 have an additional month added to their retirement age, meaning that those born in 1958 can retire at 66; individuals born between 1 January 1959 and 31 December 1963 must add two months to their retirement age per year. For individuals born after 31 December 1963 now can retire at 67.

TABLE 3. Proportion of *LÄNDER* Population over Age 65

Land	2000 (%)	2011 (%)	Change (%)
Baden-Württemberg	15.86	19.41	3.55
Bayern	16.22	19.48	3.26
Berlin	14.61	19.27	4.66
Brandenburg	15.56	22.60	7.04
Bremen	18.40	21.17	2.77
Hamburg	16.89	18.98	2.09
Hessen	16.54	19.76	3.22
Mecklenburg-Vorpommern	15.24	22.13	6.89
Niedersachsen	16.91	20.77	3.86
Nordrhein-Westfalen	16.97	20.26	3.29
Rheinland-Pfalz	17.41	20.35	2.94
Saarland	18.29	22.05	3.76
Sachsen	18.61	24.81	6.20
Sachsen-Anhalt	17.54	24.31	6.77
Schleswig-Holstein	16.79	21.68	4.89
Thüringen	16.86	23.24	6.38

Source: Data from Statistisches Bundesamt n.d.

The LTC insurance system is relatively new, with legislation introduced in 1994. However, changes to contribution rates have occurred and the elderly are now required to cover their contributions into LTC plans; however, prior to 2004, contributions by the elderly were covered by subsidies from the pension system. In addition, prior to 2005, the 1.7 percent contribution rate was applied uniformly across individuals; since 2005, however, childless individuals over age 22 have contributed at a rate of 1.95 percent (Arntz et al. 2007).

Unemployment

Prior to the 2004 Hartz IV reforms, individuals received unemployment assistance of between 53 percent and 57 percent of their prior income level (OECD 2005) for an indefinite period of time. Some observers argued that this level of compensation did not encourage individuals to return to the workforce. The Hart IV reforms therefore implemented a means-tested benefit level based on a single flat-rate payment based on an individual's number of dependents (*Economist* 2003).

Initial payments under the Hartz IV reforms differed between the western *Länder* (€345 per month) and their Eastern counterparts (€331 per month), but the payment rates were equalized starting on 1 January 2015 (€399 per month).

Health

The German social health insurance system originated in the Health Insurance Act of 1883, which provided health insurance to blue-collar workers; it has since undergone numerous reforms. West Germany, which had maintained a system similar to the original compulsory one, made changes during the 1970s and 1980s to contain costs, but they typically provided only short-term relief. In East Germany, health care services had been nationalized and brought under state control. After reunification, the West's health care system was extended into the new *Länder*. The next decade saw federal reforms regarding access to SHI systems and contribution rates.

The Health Reform Act of 1993 targeted citizens' access and risk equalization. While health insurance was and is compulsory for individuals who are employed, unemployed, retired, students, or farmers, the selection of SHI funds in which to enroll was limited prior to 1996 based on factors such as location and occupation. Consequently, some SHI funds benefited from their locations in wealthier areas or from members with occupations that carried lower health risks, allowing such funds to provide lower contribution rates. After 1996, citizens could switch plans on an annual basis, and most SHI funds were required to accept members regardless of location or profession (though restrictions were still permitted for funds that catered to particular crafts or industries) (Henke, Ade, and Murray 1994). This shift helped to equalize a disparity between blue- and white-collar workers, where previously only white-collar workers typically had the luxury of mobility (Buchner and Wasem 2003).

The 1993 reforms also introduced risk structure equalization to help prevent SHI funds from targeting young, healthy, low-risk members. Starting in 1994, SHI funds that did better on average regarding costs and profits were required to subsidize SHI funds that carried a portfolio of members with high risks and/or lower incomes (Henke, Ade, and Murray 1994). Although risk adjustment was introduced in the 1993 reforms, prior to 1999 the East and West used different mechanisms to determine the financial stability of SHI funds and need based on risks. Not until 2000 did all of Germany take a unified approach to interorganizational redistribution based on risk structures (Buchner and Wasem 2003).

Starting in January 2009, federal legislation changed how contributions into SHI funds were collected and distributed. Previously, each SHI fund had set and collected its own contributions from members. Contribution rates were consistent within a fund but varied across funds (Buchner and Wasem 2003; Henke, Ade, and Murray 1994). In the early 1990s, contribution rates ranged between 8.5 percent and 16.6 percent, averaging 13.1 percent (Henke, Ade, and Murray 1994). As of January 2009, the federal government set a standard across-the-board contribution rate of 15.5 percent. The German Federal Insurance Authority now collects contributions into a central pool (*Gesundheitsfonds*—literally "health funds") and pays a lump sum amount to SHIs for its registered members (Gaskins and Busse 2009). Furthermore, to more accurately capture each member's risk, payments distributed to SHI funds now factor in 80 morbidity criteria rather than only past expenditures and demographic information, as was previously the case (Gaskins and Busse 2009).

Access to health insurance coverage is universal within the German system. Coverage provided by the funds does not vary substantially, as the compulsory insurance benefits structure is set by federal law and determines roughly 95 percent of the items provided, including hospital care, ambulatory physician services, prescription drugs, and dental care (Buchner and Wasem 2003). Despite strides toward equalizing citizens' contribution rates, SHI funds still have incentives to lower costs by targeting the young and healthy and excluding higher-risk/lower-income individuals: the morbidity calculations focus on only 80 diseases and ignore a range of chronic issues that increase costs of coverage (Gaskins and Busse 2009).

Education

Changes in pensions, unemployment benefits, and health care have faced varying degrees of political resistance but have not directly contended with the *Land* governments. However, because decision making regarding education policy belongs to the *Länder*, policy changes in this arena have led to at times heated debates, most notably surrounding the financing of government policies (Welsh 2014). Reforms to the education system have occurred primarily during the 1970s, based on a study by Georg Picht, and during the 2000s, in the wake of Germany's poor performance in the first round of PISA assessments.

The 1970s reforms focused on including the middle class in the education system and ensuring equal opportunities for students of all backgrounds (Welsh 2014). The post-2000 reforms were aimed at school structures, the learning process, early education/school enrollment, all-day schooling, joint educational standards, and assisting underprivileged children (Wolf and Kraemer 2012; Martens and Niemann 2013; OECD 2011). The Ministry of Education and Cultural Affairs also introduced common standards or assessments: German and math for Grade 4 (2003–4); German, math, foreign language, and science for Grades 9–10 (2003–4) and upper secondary school (2007) (OECD 2011).

Various funding agreements were concluded to carry out these reforms, with the federal government covering the majority of the funding. In addition, the federal government attempted to tackle the language barrier for immigrant students by providing affordable and high-quality language training at the kindergarten level so that they started primary school with the same level of language mastery as native speakers (OECD 2011). Preschool services were also improved so that children age one to three years old were guaranteed access to early learning, which had previously been available only to families in higher socioeconomic groups (OECD 2011).

The education reforms appear to have improved student performance on the PISA tests: Germany now ranks above the OECD average in all three categories—reading, math, and science. The increased scores attributed primarily to improved scores by previously underperforming groups, including those who were less well off in socioeconomic terms and immigrants (OECD 2011).

Conclusions

Do Germany's welfare policies reflect the essence of a unitary system or a federal system? The answer is *both*, depending on the lens through which those policies are examined.

From the perspective of legislation and decisions regarding welfare policies, Germany reflects a unitary system. The nature of federal systems means that various policy responsibilities are necessarily delegated to the federal- and regional-level governments. However, a few policy domains belong exclusively to the German *Länder*: matters surrounding culture, education, universities, local authority issues, and the police. The majority of policy issues commonly included as aspects of welfare (excluding education) are controlled predominantly by the federal government, leaving little room for legislative deviation and in essence creating a unitary system.

However, from the perspective of welfare policy outputs and outcomes, Germany behaves much more like a federal system. Variations exist primarily as a product of preexisting disparities between East and West Germany prior to reunification, inequalities based on sociodemographic traits, and differences in access to funding. And although steps have recently been taken to equalize differences in *Land* benefit levels, including the standardization of unemployment payments, parity has not yet been achieved.

NOTES

1. Article 72 allows the federal government to legislate on matters argued to have passed "a 'national interest' test which justifies legislation wherever it is deemed necessary to maintain 'equivalent living conditions' through the federation" (Jeffery 1998, 2).

2. The city-states (Berlin, Bremen, and Hamburg) receive an additional 35 percent increase in their population size for calculation purposes (German Ministry of Finance).

3. The horizontal fiscal equalization from the rich *Länder* to the poorer *Länder* has not been maintained without challenges from the *Länder*. In 1952, Finance Equalization Case I was brought before the Constitutional Court, which ruled that horizontal equalization was compatible with the Basic Law. However, in 1986, Finance Equalization Case II found multiple parts of the existing equalization law to be invalid and in violation of Article 107(2) of the Basic Law, which requires that the fiscal equalization measures place reasonable fiscal demands on wealthier *Länder*. Furthermore, in 1999, three of the wealthiest *Länder*—Bayern, Baden-Württemberg, and Hessen (consistent payers into the equalization scheme)—petitioned the Constitutional Court on the grounds that fiscal equalization had become excessive. The 1999 case resulted in the lowering of the average level of equalization and consequent reduction in the level of contribution required from the wealthier *Länder* (Choudhry and Perrin 2007). The wealthy *Länder*

have repeatedly sought adjustments to fiscal equalization, with Hessen and Bayern filing another case with the Constitutional Court in 2013 regarding overburdening payments.
 4. The need for these grants is reviewed every five years.
 5. In Saxony, employers contribute 1.35 percent and employees contribute only 0.35 percent (Arntz et al. 2007).
 6. All *Länder* require nine years of schooling except for Berlin, Brandenburg, Bremen, Nordrhein-Westfalen, and Sachsen-Anhalt, which require ten (EURORAI n.d.).
 7. Only about 10 percent of students whose families belonged to the highest socioeconomic group performed at the lowest levels of reading comprehension, compared to about 40 percent of students whose families were categorized as unskilled or semiskilled workers (Baumert et al. 2001).

REFERENCES

Arbeitsgruppe Gesundheitsoekonomische Gesamtrechnungen der Laender. 2014. http://www.ggrdl.de/ggr_laenderergebnisse.html#GAR

Arntz, Melanie, Ralf Sacchetto, Alexander Spermann, Susanne Steffes, and Sarah Widmaier. 2007. *The German Social Long-Term Care Insurance: Structure and Reform Options*. IZA Discussion Paper No. 2625; ZEW Discussion Paper No. 06–074. http://ssrn.com/abstract=944780

Auel, K. 2010. "Between Reformstau and Länder Strangulation? German Co-Operative Federalism Reconsidered." *Regional and Federal Studies* 20 (2): 229–49.

Baumert, J., E. Klieme, M. Neubrand, M. Prenzel, U. Schiefele, W. Schneider, P. Stanat, K.-J. Tillmann, and M. Weis, eds. 2001. *PISA 2000: Overview of the Study, Design Method, and Results*. German PISA 2000 Consortium.

Benz, A. 1985. *Föderalismus als dynamisches System: Zentralisierung und Dezentralisierung im föderativen Staat*. Opladen: Leske und Budrich.

Benz, A. 1999. "From Unitary to Asymmetric Federalism in Germany: Taking Stock after 50 Years." *Publius: The Journal of Federalism* 29 (4): 55–78.

Bräuninger, T., and M. Debus. 2012. *Parteienwettbewerb in den deutschen Bundesländern*. Stuttgart: VS Verlag.

Buchner, Florian, and Jürgen Wasem. 2003. "Needs for Further Improvement: Risk Adjustment in the German Health Insurance System." *Health Policy* 65 (1): 21–35.

Burkhart, S. 2008. *Blockierte Politik: Ursachen und Folgen von "Divided Government" in Deutschland*. Frankfurt: Campus.

Choudhry, Sujit, and Benjamin Perrin. 2007. "The Legal Architecture of Intergovernmental Transfers: A Comparative Examination." In *Intergovernmental Fiscal Transfers: Principles and Practices*, ed. Robin W. Boadway and Anwar Shah, 259–92. Washington, DC: International Bank for Reconstruction and Development/World Bank.

Debus, M., and J. Müller. 2013. "The Programmatic Development of CDU and CSU since Reunification: Incentives and Constraints for Changing Policy Positions in the German Multi-Level System." *German Politics* 22 (1–2): 151–71.

Droessler, S., J. Hasford, B. M. Kurth, M. Schaefer, J. Wasem, and E. Wille. *Evaluationsbericht zum Jahresausgleich 2009 im Risikostrukturausgleich*. http://www.bmg.bund.de/fileadmin/dateien/Publikationen/Gesundheit/Forschungsberichte/Evaluationsbericht_zum_Jahresausgleich.pdf

The Economist. 2003. "Germany's Federal Constitution: Untangling the System." 6 November.

Euraxess Germany. N.d. *Health Insurance.* https://www.euraxess.de/germany/information-assistance/social-security/health-insurance

European Commission. 2013. "Your Social Security Rights in Germany."

European Organisation of Regional External Public Finance Audit Institutions (EURORAI). N.d. *Germany.* http://www.eurorai.org/PDF/pdf%20seminar%20Karlsruhe/Karlsruhe-Situation%20in%20DEUTSCHLAND-definitiv_EN.pdf

Federal Employment Agency. 2017. *Unemployment Benefits II.* http://www.arbeitsagentur.de/web/content/EN/Benefits/UnemploymentBenefitII/index.htm

Gaskins, Matthew, and Reinhard Busse. 2009. "Morbidity-Based Risk Adjustment in Germany: Long in Coming, but Worth the Wait?" *Eurohealth* 15 (3): 29–31.

German Ministry of Finance (Bundesministerium der Finanzen). *The Federal Financial Equalization System in Germany.* Berlin: Bundesministerium der Finanzen.

GKV-Spitzenverband. 2014. *Zahlen und Grafiken.* http://www.gkv-pitzenverband.de/presse/zahlen_und_grafiken/zahlen_und_grafiken.jsp#lightbox

Götz, K. 1992. *Intergovernmental Relations and State Government Discretion: The Case of Science and Technology Policy in Germany.* Baden-Baden: Nomos.

Gunlicks, A. 2005. "German Federalism and Recent Reform Efforts." *German Law Journal* 6 (10): 1283–96.

Henderson, Ailsa, Charlie Jeffery, and Daniel Wincott. 2013. *Citizens after the Nation State: Regionalism, Nationalism, and Public Attitudes in Europe.* Basingstoke: Palgrave Macmillan.

Henke, Klaus-Dirk, Claudia Ade, and Margaret A. Murray. 1994. "The German Health Care System: Structure and Changes." *Journal of Clinical Anesthesia* 6 (3): 252–62.

Hesse, K. 1962. *Der unitarische Bundesstaat.* Karlsruhe: Müller.

Hinrichs, Karl. 2002. "Health Care Policy in the German Social Insurance State: From Solidarity to Privatization?" *Review of Policy Research* 19 (3): 109–40.

Hooghe, Liesbet, Gary Marks, and Arjan H. Schakel. 2010. *The Rise of Regional Authority: A Comparative Study of 42 Democracies (1950–2006).* London: Routledge.

Jeffery, Charlie. 1998. *Multi-Layer Democracy in Germany: Insights for Scottish Devolution.* London: Constitution Unit. https://www.ucl.ac.uk/political-science/publications/unit-publications/26.pdf

Jeffery, Charlie. 1999. "Party Politics and Territorial Representation in the Federal Republic of Germany." *West European Politics* 22 (2): 130–66.

Jeffery, Charlie, N. Pamphilis, C. Rowe, and E. Turner. 2014. "Regional Policy Variation in Germany: The Diversity of Living Conditions in a 'Unitary Federal State.'" *Journal of European Public Policy* 21 (9): 1350–55.

Jeffery, Charlie, and C. Rowe. 2014. "The Reform of German Federalism." In *Developments in German Politics,* ed. S. Padgett, W. Paterson, and R. Zohlnhoefer, 35–56. 4th ed. Basingstoke: Palgrave.

Jun, U., M. Haas, and O. Niedermayer, eds. 2008. *Parteien und Parteiensysteme in den deutschen Ländern.* Wiesbaden: VS Verlag.

Koller, Martin, Winfried Schiebel, and Albert Stichter-Werner. 2003. "Der heimliche Finanzausgleich." *IAB Kurzbericht.* http://doku.iab.de/kurzber/2003/kb1603.pdf

Martens, Kerstin, and Dennis Niemann. 2013. "When Do Numbers Count? The Differential Impact of the PISA Rating and Ranking on Education Policy in Germany and the US." *German Politics* 22 (3): 314–32.

Mintzel, A. 1977. *Geschichte der CSU: Ein Überblick,* Opladen: Leske und Budrich.

Moog, S., and B. Raffelhueschen. 2006. *Sozialpolitisch motivierte Umverteilungsstroeme in der Gesetzlichen Krankenversicherung—eine empirische Analyse.* http://www.fiwi1.uni-freiburg.de/publikationen/138.pdf

Moore, Carolyn, Wade Jacoby, and Arthur Gunlicks. 2013. "Introduction: German Federalism in Transition?" In *German Federalism in Transition: Reforms in a Consensual State,* ed. C. Rowe and W. Jacoby, 393–407. London: Routledge.

Müller, J. 2013. "On a Short Leash? Sub-National Party Positions between Regional Context and National Party Unity." *Journal of Elections, Public Opinion, and Parties* 23 (2): 177–99.

OECD. 2005. *Germany.* http://www.oecd.org/els/soc/29730499.PDF

OECD. 2011. *Lessons from PISA for the United States, Strong Performers and Successful Reformers in Education.* https://www.oecd.org/pisa/46623978.pdf

OECD. 2013. *Pensions at a Glance: Country Profiles—Germany.* Paris: OECD.

Pew Global. 2009. "Views of Germany Reunification." In *Two Decades after the Wall's Fall: End of Communism Cheered but Now with More Reservations.* http://www.pewglobal.org/2009/11/02/chapter-5-views-of-german-reunification/

Riggall, A., and C. Sharp. 2008. *The Structure of Primary Education: England and Other Countries.* Cambridge: University of Cambridge Faculty of Education.

Scharpf, Fritz W. 2009. *Föderalismusreform: Kein Ausweg aus der Politikverflechtungsfalle?* Frankfurt: Campus.

Scharpf, Fritz W., Bernd Reissert, and Fritz Schnabel. 1976. *Politikverflechtung: Theorie und Empirie des kooperativen Föderalismus in der Bundesrepublik.* Kronberg: Scriptor.

Scheller, H., and J. Schmid, eds. 2008. *Föderale Politikgestaltung im deutschen Bundesstaat: Variable Verflechtungsmuster in Politikfeldern.* Baden-Baden: Nomos.

Schmid, J. 1990. *Die CDU: Organisationsstrukturen, Politiken, und Funktionsweisen einer Partei im Föderalismus.* Opladen: Leske und Budrich.

Schmidt, M. 1980. *CDU und SPD an der Regierung: Ein Vergleich ihrer Politik in den Ländern.* Frankfurt: Campus.

Seher, N. M., and F. U. Pappi. 2011. *Politikfeldspezifische Positionen der Landesverbände der deutschen Parteien.* Mannheim: Mannheimer Zentrum für Europäische Sozialforschung.

Statistische Ämter des Bundes und der Länder. https://www.statistikportal.de/

Statistisches Bundesamt. N.d. www.destatis.de

Sturm, R. 1999. "Party Competition and the Federal System: The Lehmbruch Hypothesis Revisited." In *Recasting German Federalism: The Legacies of Unification,* ed. Charlie Jeffery, 197–216. London: Pinter.

Welsh, Helga A. 2014. "Education, Federalism and the 2013 Bundestag Elections." *German Politics* 23 (4): 400–414.

Wheare, K. 1953. *Federal Government.* 3rd ed. Oxford: Oxford University Press.

Wolf, Frieder, and Andreas Kraemer. 2012. "On the Electoral Relevance of Education Policy in the German Länder." *German Politics* 21 (4): 444–63.

Zarth, M., D. D. Schnitzlein, and K. Bruckmeier. 2009. "Eine regionale Betrachtung der Sozialverischeurng und raumwirksamer Bundesmittel: Wer partizipiert wie?" In *Oeffentliche Finanzstroeme und raeumliche Entwicklung,* ed. H. Maeding, 105–34. Hannover: Verlag der ARL.

Federalism Shaping Social Policy in Austria

Birgit Trukeschitz and Elisabeth Riedler

The allocation of legal responsibilities and financial powers across different governmental levels significantly influences social policy in two ways. On the one hand, it sets the framework for social protection against social and economic risks. On the other hand, the allocation of competencies has an impact on the effectiveness and efficiency of policy interventions.

Austria, with 8.7 million residents as of 2016,[1] is organized as a federal country, with a central government and regional governments in nine provinces (*Laender*). In international comparisons, Austria has been characterized as "over-centralized" because the regional governments have little authority and financial power and decreasing policy responsibilities (Braun 2011, 43). Looking at different policy areas, however, reveals that Austria's federal system seems to struggle with the fragmentation of competencies. Critics note the lack of common policy aims, indicators for outcome measurement, and institutions for exchange as well as its heterogeneity in benefits and services across the *Laender* (Rechnungshof 2011, 25; Rechnungshof 2016).

In Austria, policymakers as well as experts are well aware of the shortcomings of the constitutional allocation of regulatory and financial powers (e.g., Schratzenstaller 2008; Rechnungshof 2016). The relationships between different governmental levels, parafisci or parafiscal entities (self-governed public bodies with their own sources of income), and funds have gained complexity over time. More than half of tax revenues are distributed between and within different levels of government, including funds and social insurance. Intergovernmental transfers (i.e., transfers across different levels of government and between government bodies and parafiscal entities) have increased from €24 billion in 1995 to €43 billion in 2011 (Bauer et al. 2012, 945). Few if any experts understand the system in detail (Bröthaler et al. 2011). Complexities and lack of transparency imply that efficiency and effectiveness can hardly be assessed. As a result, substantial changes seem difficult to implement and policies seek to find quick fixes to satisfy urgent needs, particularly for coordinating common tasks of the central state and regional authorities.

Austria's social safety net is structured as a two-tiered system. The majority of responsibilities for social security and social protection, known as the first safety net, have been assigned to the central level (central state and social security fund). However, for important areas of social policy— for example, long-term care services, poverty policy, health policy, and housing—extensive legislative and executive competencies remain with the *Laender*.[2] For education, a complex allocation of responsibilities between the different levels of government applies. In recent years, policy changes have sought to better coordinate central and regional governmental welfare activities.

We focus on four areas of social policy that are jointly organized by Austria's federal and regional governments: (1) family policy, highlighting the importance of policy coordination and common outcome indicators for identifying redistributive effects; (2) education policy, exemplifying a policy area where the shortcomings of allocating responsibilities between the central government and the *Laender* are well known but change has proven difficult, (3) long-term care, an emerging policy field in aging societies; and (4) poverty policy, particularly the means-tested minimum income scheme (Bedarfsorientierte Mindestsicherung [BMS]), to show that coordinated policy efforts can improve living conditions of vulnerable people regardless of where they live but are sensitive to external shocks.

This chapter does not cover social policy areas that relate to the Austrian social insurance system. In Austria, health insurance, pensions, and accident insurance are not) funded primarily by central or regional governments but are governed by federal laws and organized as parafisci, allowing them to act independently of the central budget. Redistributive effects may occur as a consequence of differences in eligibility criteria for regional social health insurance agencies, for example. However, this system was originally designed for different occupational groups, and its redistributive effects result mainly from such occupational differences rather than from different regional policy approaches. Thus, a detailed analysis of redistributive effects of parafiscal federalism is left for future research. In 2018, the central government took the first steps toward a standardization of the social insurance system. (For federalism and health policy until 2018, see Trukeschitz, Schneider, and Czypionka 2013.)

Allocation of Responsibilities for Social Policy

The Austrian Constitution assigns roles and responsibilities for social policy to both the central government and the nine regional governments. These roles as well as the scope of responsibilities depend, however, on the areas of social policy.[3] For some areas, the central state bears sole responsibility for legislation as well as execution. Fields of social protection regulated at the central level comprise the social insurance system[4] (including health care, pensions, and accident benefits), unemployment insurance, parts of the public health system, long-term care allowances, and specific family benefits (e.g., family allowances). For other areas—mainly social welfare (*Armenwesen*), hospitals, and nursing homes—each of the nine *Laender* makes, implements, and executes laws within guidelines imposed by the central state. If such guidelines, however, are missing or are not comprehensive, regulation and funding schemes vary across the nine Austrian *Laender*. Education features a particularly complex allocation of responsibilities between the different tiers of government.

In many areas of social policy, the *Laender* offer support on a complementary and mainly means-tested basis. Means testing implies that eligibility for benefits (cash, in kind, and services) is restricted to people who lack sufficient means to secure subsistence. Means testing characterizes the "second social safety net" maintained by the *Laender*. In some social policy fields, the second social safety net is linked to the first social safety net. People with less income or benefits from the first safety net rely more on regional support, particularly in the case of low net-replacement rates of unemployment benefits or low pensions.

Coordination of central and regional competencies can be organized via constitutional agreements known as Article 15a agreements from the applicable section of the Austrian Federal Constitutional Law. These agreements influence the design of federal and regional laws and often have an impact on funding responsibilities. Article 15a agreements have recently been used in different areas of social policy, such as long-term care and the needs-based minimum income scheme.

Table 1 gives an overview of the Austrian social benefit system by social risk and government subsector responsible for providing/funding these benefits. The table shows that social benefits at the regional level cover a great variety of target groups and social risks, indicating the important complementary role of *Laender* and communities in providing social protection and support. The *Laender*'s core program, the BMS, and other means-tested benefits at the regional and local levels contribute to social security.

TABLE 1. Provision of Social Infrastructure and Social Benefits by Level of Government, 2016

Education	Under 65 (Nonpension) Benefits and Services			
Pre-Primary, Primary, Secondary, and Higher	Sickness	Family & Children	Unemployment	Accident and Occupational Disability, Invalidity
Social Insurance, Unemployment Insurance				
	Social health insurance	Family-related benefits in the different branches of the insurance systems	Unemployment insurance	Social insurance against accidents and occupational illnesses
Central State				
Depending on types of schools: regulation of organizational matters (including maintenance); teachers pay; regulation and funding of public universities; cofunding for universities of applied science		Family allowance Child care allowance		
Laender / Communities				
Child care facilities Depending on types of schools: regulation of organizational matters; teachers' pay; cofunding of some universities of applied science	Contribution to social health insurance for BMS recipients Health care benefits, contributions to the health care system Public health offices	Family benefits Youth welfare programs	Additional regional labor market benefits	

Source: Based on MA 24 2012, 12f.

	Under 65 (Nonpension) Benefits and Services (cont.)				Pensions and Long-Term Care	
Disability	Housing	Securing subsistence	Other Benefits	Old Age	Long-Term Care	
		Selected cash benefits		Pension insurance		
Benefits of the federal state	Housing benefits			Pensions for civil servants (Beamte)	Long-term care cash allowance Cofunding for 24-hour care Contribution to the long-term care fund	
Benefits of the Laender	Rent subsidies for BMS recipients Housing benefits Assistance to the homeless Assistance to people at risk of losing their homes	Means-tested minimum income scheme (BMS)	Addiction prevention and care Debt counseling Other counseling services	Pensions for civil servants (Beamte) of the *Laender*	Long-term care services Cofunding for 24-hour care Contribution to the long-term care fund	

*Fiscal Regulation and Social Protection: Expenditure Patterns
by Levels of Government*

In addition to the allocation of competencies between different governmental levels, fiscal regulations, determining level and structure of revenues may shape how social policy interventions are designed and take effect. In Austria, basic principles of taxation and fiscal relations are written
down in a separate constitutional law governing fiscal matters (Finanz-
Verfassungsgesetz). Although this law provides the framework for the allocation of taxation competencies, actual fiscal relations are regulated by a
simple federal law, the law governing fiscal equalization (Finanzausgleichsgesetz). The fiscal equalization plan is temporary (usually limited to
four years) and thus periodically negotiated by the Ministry of Finance as
representative of the federal state, the governors of the *Laender*, and representatives of the Austrian Association of Municipalities (Österreichischer Gemeindebund) and the Austrian Association of Cities (Österreichischer Städtebund).

In 2016, tax revenues (excluding social insurance) accounted for 28
percent of Austria's GDP (Statistics Austria 1). On average, more than 90
percent of taxes are collected by the central government, with the remainder collected by the *Laender* and communities. Thus, transfers from the
central state to the regional governments via the fiscal equalization plan
play a major role in funding regional (social) policy. However, not all welfare benefits are financed by taxes; substantial benefits are provided by
parafiscal entities (social insurance) governed by federal laws and funded
mainly by contributions of employers and employees or by funds governed by federal or regional laws.

To assess how much the different tiers of the Austrian government
spend on social policy, we used international data on the Classification of
the Functions of Government (COFOG).[5] COFOG provides expenditure
data split by government subsector (social security funds, central government, regional governments, and local governments) (EU 2011, 23f). At
COFOG's top level, total public expenditure is split into 10 divisions (EU
2011, 14), of which 3 are particularly relevant here: health (division 7,
comprising medical products, appliances and equipment, outpatient services, hospital services, public health services, R&D health, and health not
elsewhere classified); education (division 9, including pre-primary and
primary education; secondary, postsecondary nontertiary, and tertiary
education; education not definable by level; subsidiary services to education; R&D education; and education not elsewhere classified); and social

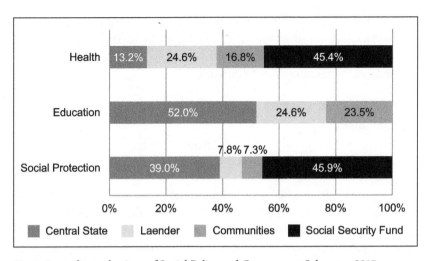

Fig. 1. Expenditures by Area of Social Policy and Government Subsector, 2017
Source: Based on Statistics Austria 2018.

protection (division 10, comprising sickness and disability, old age, survivors, family and children, unemployment, housing, social exclusion not elsewhere classified, R&D social protection, and social protection not elsewhere classified). These data, however, have two main limitations. First, further details on public spending within these divisions in Austria would give more insight but are not available. Second, transfers between different tiers of government within a functional group have not been consolidated at the government subsector level. This implies that transfers between different governmental levels thus appear both in both sides of the transaction of the government subsectors. Hence, COFOG data give only a first impression of the shares of social-policy-related spending by different governmental levels in Austria (figure 1).

In 2017, expenditures for health, education, and social protection accounted for 65 percent of all public expenditures in Austria. In total, 16.5 percent of public expenditures were allocated to health, 9.3 percent to education, and 39.2 percent to social protection. Social security funds contribute to 45 percent of total public spending for health expenditures and to 46 percent for social protection (Statistics Austria 2018). Whereas the central government played a comparatively minor role in health spending (13 percent) in 2017, it is responsible for 52 percent of education expenditures and 39 percent of social protection expenditure. *Laender* contributed 25 percent of health spending and another 25 percent of education spending but only 8 percent of social protection spending. The share of local community spending was slightly lower than the share of the *Laender* for all three functional groups (17 percent, 24 percent, 7 percent, respectively) (Statistics Austria 2018).

Redistribution

Social Policy in Austria and Reduction of Inequality

Among the goals of social policy is avoiding or reducing inequality (Barr 2012, 10ff; Badelt and Österle 2001, 9ff). Benefits designed to tackle absolute inequality usually focus on ensuring a certain standard of living. They aim to guarantee citizens a minimum income to stabilize their purchasing power and enable them to take part in social and cultural life. A more indirect approach to reducing absolute inequality is free compulsory schooling (Badelt and Österle 2001),[6] which grants every child access to education, irrespective of parental wealth. These approaches seek to influence vertical equality by reducing the difference between poor and rich. Benefits to overcome relative inequality, however, relate to criteria other than income. They link to sociodemographic characteristics such as sex, age, health status, or family size to positively affect horizontal equality by improving these people's relative position in society. Absolute and relative equality are important objectives for social policy interventions but might also be indirectly influenced by the way authority and funding are allocated to central and regional tiers of government.

Austrian social benefits have traditionally been designed to reduce vertical inequity (poverty in particular) and horizontal inequity (inequity between different groups, irrespective of income). Benefits to lower poverty comprise the BMS, which replaced social assistance in 2011. The BMS and specific social insurance benefits (e.g., the *Notstandshilfe und Ausgleichszulagenrichtsatz*) seek to prevent incomes from dropping below certain thresholds. In addition, labor market mechanisms such as minimum wages also contribute to eliminating absolute poverty. Although Austria has no legally mandated minimum wage, wages negotiated by unions and company representatives (*Gehälter laut Kollektivvertrag*) introduce a kind of minimum wage for many industries. These policies have an important impact on income distribution in Austria. Social policy instruments that aim at reducing *relative* inequity improve people's living conditions in particular circumstances. They are manifold and support a range of different target groups, such as families with dependent children, older people in need of care and their relatives, people with learning disabilities, and homeless people.

Both the central level and the regional and local levels are responsible for tackling vertical and horizontal inequity, but they do so via different instruments. On the central level, social insurance and universal benefits as well as a comprehensive labor market policy offer social protection for a broad range of people, generally regardless of income and wealth. Furthermore, the national income tax system is a major tool for redistributing income. Regional and local governments also construct the second social safety net to tackle poverty and reduce vertical inequity as well as to reduce horizontal inequity by providing both social infrastructure (e.g., long-term care services) and additional benefits for specific groups.

Effectiveness of Redistributive Policies

The global financial and economic crisis of 2007 did not affect Austria as drastically as it did other European countries (BMASK 2012, 16). Although unemployment increased, the country had one of the lowest unemployment and long-term unemployment rates among EU member states, and Austria's long-term unemployment rate had increased only marginally (EU 2013, 51). As a consequence of these comparatively good labor market outcomes, Austria was one of four member states that experienced a decrease in the proportion of people living in poverty or social exclusion from 2008 to 2011 (EU 2013, 23). About 16 percent of the Austrian population was at risk of poverty or social exclusion in 2011, one of the lowest rates in Europe (EU 2013, 24f). However, Austria was less successful in preventing those at risk from falling below the poverty threshold. According to this indicator, the persistence and depth of poverty substantially increased (EU 2013, 29).

Policies to stabilize the economy included a set of measures in different fields, mainly economic policy and fiscal and labor market policies. Furthermore, social expenditures helped to minimize the effects of the economic crisis (BMASK 2012, 16). All of these measures but particularly wage, tax, and social transfer policies helped to stabilize mass purchasing power and thus supported economic recovery and resilience (BMASK 2012, 22).

In general, redistribution in Austria is achieved through government expenditures rather than through taxes (Guger et al. 2009). Consumption taxes and contributions to social insurance are known to work regressively—that is, they impose a higher burden on people with lower incomes than on those who earn more. Conversely, income tax is considered a progressive tax, taking more from higher-income groups than from poorer ones. Since revenues from contributions to social insurance and the consumption tax account for slightly more than half of total revenues, the revenue system has no distributive effects (Mühlberger et al. 2008, 28f).

Government expenditures support more poor households than those who are better-off in Austria and thus contribute to vertical equity. This is remarkable, since social expenditures result mainly from transfers that are conditional to characteristics other than income (i.e., universal welfare benefits or social insurance benefits designed to improve horizontal equity). In 2001, only 4 percent of all social protection expenditures were income-tested (BMASK 2012). Over the past 15 years, the progressive effect of public transfers has increased. (BMASK 2012)

The total progressive effect of policy interventions is revealed by the difference between the primary distribution of income (created solely by market transactions) and the distribution of the disposable income (income after taxes and transfers). Regional differences in primary household income totaled €5,300. In 2016, the highest primary household income was in Vorarlberg, the most westerly *Land*, bordering Switzerland, Liechtenstein, and Germany, whereas the lowest primary household income was in Carinthia, bordering Slovenia and Italy. These differences reflect the varying economic strengths of the *Laender*. In contrast, the difference between the *Lands* with the highest and lowest disposable household incomes was just €1,900. This implies that in general, public policy reduced differences in income between *Laender*.

Figure 2 ranks the *Laender* by disposable household income and compares those figures with the previous primary household income after taxes and transfers. Although some *Laender* changed their relative positions, most did not. Only Burgenland improved its position, while Tirol and Vorarlberg lost ground. The fact that two-thirds of the *Laender* maintained their relative positions implies that policies implemented by both the central state and the *Laender* had little relative effect.

The differences in disposable household income between the *Laender* dropped from €3,400 in 1995 (when Austria joined the EU) to €1,900 in 2016. Furthermore, Austria's nominal primary income declined in 2009 as a result of the economic crisis, whereas disposable household income overall remained constant. Minor declines in disposable household income were recorded for only four *Laender*. All policy interventions and

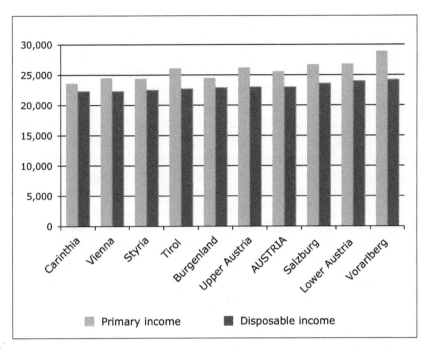

Fig. 2. Nominal Primary and Disposable Household Incomes across *Laender*, 2016 (in euros)

Note: Change in ranking = change in a *Land*'s ranking in disposable household income compared to its relative position in primary household income; arrow to the left indicates a better ranking of this *Land* for disposable income than for primary income; arrow to the right indicates a lower ranking for this *Land* in disposable income than for primary income.

Source: Data from Statistik Austria, Regionale Gesamtrechnungen, issued on 6 December 2017; author's own calculations and display.

the general line of policy thus seem to have absorbed at least some of the negative implications of the most recent global economic crisis.

Family Benefits: Effective Redistribution Requires Policy Coordination and Outcome Measurement

Family benefits illustrate that effective redistribution requires more than targeting national and regional benefits to specific groups. A range of different family-related cash benefits have developed at the regional level. However, coordinated family policy—between the central state and the regional governments as well as between regional governments—is missing, which results in unintended und undesired effects, such as double funding. Austria's expenditures for family policy are above the OECD average, whereas the effects of family policy—for example, on fertility rates or child poverty rates—have remained modest (Schratzenstaller 2014). Moreover, the combined distributional effects of federal and regional benefits remain unclear, which does not contribute to informed decision making in times of dwindling resources.

One of the core aims of the Austrian family policy is to support households with children (Rille-Pfeiffer et al. 2014, 31). The Austrian Constitution assigns legal competencies and the role of implementing population policies—child-care allowances (*Kinderbeihilfe*) and different types of family support (*Lastenausgleich im Interesse der Familie*)—to the central state (Article 10 Abs. 1 Z 17 B–VG). Furthermore, the central state sets objectives for family policy, which the *Laender* implement, with or without modification. However, if these measures do not correspond to the *Laender* aims, implementation may progress at a very slow pace. Whereas the *Laender* play a rather passive role for family-related cash benefits, they gain more responsibility for institutional child care and day care for children. However, investments in child care facilities were enabled by special federal funding programs (*Kindergartenmilliarde*), implying that the central state exerts regulatory influence on the type of child care; legal competencies and implementation of provisions of the laws for these benefits fall into the realm of the *Laender* (Article 14 Abs. 4 lit. b B–VG). Thus, both the central state and the regions take on legal and funding responsibilities for family policy.

To influence living conditions of families with dependent children, the Austrian central government and the regional governments use different types of policy instruments. On the central level, family benefits include universal cash benefits and to a much smaller extent tax allowances. Universal cash benefits aim to reduce the financial burden on all families with children, regardless of income. In 2009, about 70 percent of all family-related benefits were funded by the National Family Benefits Fund (*Familienlastenausgleichsfonds* [FLAF]) (Rechnungshof 2011), financed mainly by employer contributions and managed by the Austrian Ministry of Finance as earmarked funds from the central governments' budget. On the regional levels, the *Laender* provide tax-financed benefits in kind, particularly child care facilities; some *Laender* also offer substantial means-tested cash benefits. While the national state follows primarily strategies of horizontal equity[7] by granting access to benefits regardless of income, the *Laender* combine objectives of horizontal and vertical equity by providing family-related income-dependent cash and in-kind benefits and tying access to these benefits to parental income.

Linking family-related expenditures to the national and regional GDP and the total government budgets again brings out the importance of national spending and the heterogeneity of regional spending. In 2009, about 3.1 percent of the GDP (11 percent of the central government's total budget) was spent on family benefits. The three *Laender* for which we have data spent between 0.01 percent of GDP (0.11 percent of the total regional budget) (Salzburg) and 0.10 percent of GDP (0.69 percent of the total regional budget) (Carinthia) (Rechnungshof 2011). Overall, spending on family-related benefits varies considerably among *Laender* but is not very high.

The number, generosity, and eligibility criteria of family benefits differ substantially across the nine *Laender*. Regional expenditures for family-related cash benefits also differ substantially among *Laender* with respect to number and level of benefits. In 2011, the Austrian Court of Audit examined family-related benefits in Salzburg, Carinthia, and Upper Austria and found that in 2009, Salzburg provided 18 types of family-related benefits, while Upper Austria offered 27 such benefits (Rechnungshof 2011, 45). The *Laender* generally focus on a few important cash benefits and a large number of small-scale benefits (Rechnungshof 2011, 45). Family-related benefits are means-tested and targeted at low-income families. However, income thresholds and eligibility criteria differ not only among *Laender* but also within a *Land* (Rechnungshof 2011, 17). A child in Carinthia, for example, received on average three times more benefits than a child in Upper Austria and approximately six times more than a child in Salzburg. Although these regional differences seem massive, they do not affect much of an average family's budget. Regional cash benefits amounted to €21 per child per month in Salzburg and €125 per child in Carinthia, while the central government (financed by the FLAF) spent €4,845 per child aged 26 or younger (Rechnungshof 2011, 13). However, regional family-related cash benefits depend on the parents' income, implying that the redistributive effects of the *Laender* benefits would have been more visible if the total expenditures were divided by the number of children who received the benefit rather than the number of children living in the province. Thus, as the numbers provided by the Austrian Court of Audit suggest, the vertical redistributive effect would be expected to be higher.

Access to child care facilities depends on the regulations imposed by the particular *Land*. Vienna, for example, offers the most generous access to child care services: free full-time child care for all children up to the age of six. Other *Laender*, however, restrict free child care to specific groups of children (e.g., those aged two or older), to certain hours (e.g., a half day), or based on parental income. However, the *Laender* are legally bound to provide free half-day child care for each child aged five. This regulation assures that each *Land* offers a de facto minimum amount of child care, which is subsidized by the federal state. Compared to the central state and the regions (*Laender*), communities have no legal competencies but still have some leeway to act according to their local preferences and budgets— for example, by adjusting the number of places or opening hours of child care facilities (BMWFJ 2010, 835) or by deciding on additional benefits, such as a free lunch at child care facilities.

There is no reconciliation of family-related benefits between the different tiers of governments, a situation that contributes to duplications of benefits and overlaps in support. In 2009, ten national-level benefits were offered in the area of birth and pregnancy, with four others in Carinthia and two more in Salzburg (Rechnungshof 2011, 11).

Given the significant differences in regional family benefits, overall redistributive effects are not easy to estimate. The Austrian Court of Audit noted in 2011 that there are no records on the types and levels of benefits a family receives. Consequently, it is not clear how much families take advantage of national and regional benefits (Rechnungshof 2011, 11). Although a national database for family-related benefits has now been established, it still does not provide information on the effects of such benefits on families' living conditions (Rechnungshof 2014b, 436). Thus, it remains difficult to learn more about the impact of central and regional family policy interventions.

Change

Challenges in providing an effective and efficient system of social security and protection result not only from opposing political preferences but also from the design of these systems and the distribution of powers among the different tiers of government. Meeting these challenges requires linking the problem to the allocation of these responsibilities, which are deeply rooted in the constitution. Because a constitution is a historically developed regulatory framework, it is "not always capable of coping with the requirements of modern government and administration" (Schäffer 1992, 45). Attempts to address changes and to fulfill constitutional requirements may result in rather complex solutions and represent compromises or political horse-trading instead of addressing the root of the problem (Schäffer 1992).

Education: Changing in Responsibilities between Governmental Levels Proves Difficult

Federalism has always strongly shaped the Austrian education system. After long and difficult negotiations between the central state and the *Laender* after the Second World War, Article 14 of the Federal Constitution Act allocated the responsibilities between the different levels of government (Juranek 1999, 86f). The legal basis for the Austrian education system (excluding universities and universities of applied sciences) is the Schulgesetzwerk 1962, the body of law that reorganized the school system (see Geschichte online 1). The complex allocation of responsibilities between the central state and the *Laender* still shape political processes and regulation in the Austrian education system.

General compulsory schools (*Allgemeinbildende Pflichtschulen*), including primary schools and some types of secondary schools such as the "new secondary schools" (*Neue Mittelschulen*), are characterized by a particularly complex allocation of responsibilities across different governmental levels (Bock-Schappelwein 2010, fig. 4.1). The central state is responsible for the basic legislation of framework school organization, such as the establishment and maintenance of the schools. The *Laender* regulate organizational details and are responsible for their implementation. Maintenance of school facilities is conducted by local communities, municipal organizations, or the *Laender* according to the laws of the *Laender*. Responsibility for some secondary schools that are not part of the general compulsory schools group is either shared between the *Laender* and the central state or is solely the purview of the central state (Bock-Schappelwein 2010).

Splitting responsibilities for the employment of teachers and funding of their salaries is a well-known cause of inefficiency. For general compulsory schools, the central state covers the costs of teacher salaries, whereas the *Laender* act as employers. They may, however, transfer this task to the central government (Bock-Schappelwein 2010).

In contrast, the central state bears sole responsibility for legislation and implementation related to higher education. Since the 2002 implementation of the Federal Act on the Organization of Universities and Their Studies, public universities are legally independent units. They receive funding from the central government and are subject to legal supervision by the

Austrian Federal Ministry of Education, Science, and Research. Public university colleges of teacher education are funded by the central state and are legally part of the central state. (Kasparovsky and Wadsack-Köchl 2016). Universities of applied sciences, conversely, are only partly funded by the central government according to a standard cost model. In addition to funds from the central state, universities of applied sciences may receive funding from the *Laender*, local communities, companies, or other legal entities (Österreichischer Wissenschaftsrat 2012).

Primary and secondary schooling are characterized by a highly complex allocation of responsibilities between different levels of government. This split of competencies and its consequences have led to debate regarding the system's efficiency. According to a working group composed of representatives from several expert organizations, the complex distribution of responsibilities is a major cause of inefficiencies in funding and maintenance (Rechnungshof 2010a).

However, reducing these inefficiencies seems difficult. Both the central government and the *Laender* play important roles in the educational decision-making process but differ in their views and objectives (Rechnungshof 2010a). In June 2014, a parliamentary committee on a reform of the school system, supported by representatives of the *Laender* and experts on these topics, was established to work on simplifying administration, clarifying the role of local communities in school maintenance, and defining responsibilities concerning teaching staff (Republik Österreich Parlament 2014).

In 2017, the law on the education reform (Bildungsreformgesetz 2017) prepared the ground for changes slated to take place from 2018 to 2020 (and later). Schools receive increased autonomy in such areas as recruiting teachers, developing human resources, developing lesson plans, organizing classes, and pursuing teaching methods.[8] Schools are also allowed to create clusters, which share services and specialist classes. In addition, as of 2019, the law establishes a new educational authority (*Bildungsdirektion*) that combines federal and regional educational interests and provides consistent structures and clear chains of command is most remarkable.[9]

Although efforts to change the Austrian schooling system have long been stuck, policymakers hope that this reform will help to produce a more flexible, effective, and efficient educational system. Furthermore, coordination between the national and regional governments may lead to cost reductions that would permit the reallocation of resources to produce additional improvements to educational quality.

Long-Term Care: Clarifying Competencies Reduced Administrative Complexity, Yet Regional Differences in Services Remain

Long-term care (LTC) is an emerging social policy field in many countries. In Austria, LTC policy has recently been improved by changes in the allocation of competencies between the central and regional levels. By elucidating legal and financial responsibilities, these reforms produced a more efficient system of public support for people in need of long-term care as well as their informal caregivers. LTC policy serves as an example of how economic pressure as a result of demographic change on the one hand and recommendations by the Austrian Court of Audit on the other have made central and regional tiers of government rethink their traditional allocation of competencies.

Austria's LTC regulatory framework dates back to 1993 and builds on the Austrian Constitution, allocating responsibilities to the central state and to the *Laender*. In general, the federal state is responsible for framework legislation for social welfare and nursing homes; each *Land* is entitled to implement and execute laws within this broader framework. Establishing a regulatory framework necessitated coordinating the competencies of all levels of government via an Article 15a agreement (Trukeschitz, Schneider, and Czypionka 2013, 156, 164) By 2018, three such agreements had slowly built the regulatory framework for LTC.

Until 2012, the Article 15a agreement on the provision of LTC allowances and services assigned legal and financial responsibilities for the LTC allowance (a universal cash benefit) for 80 percent of care-dependent people to the central state. Those not covered by the regulation of the central state became the responsibility of the *Laender*. The Austrian LTC allowance was thus regulated by 10 laws—a federal law and nine *Laender*-level regional laws. Although the central state and the *Laender* standardized their LTC allowance laws, a few *Laender* deviated somewhat from the federal law by offering slightly more generous benefits. The fragmentation of the LTC allowance regulation was criticized in 2010, mainly for allocative reasons (Rechnungshof 2010b).

Contrary to LTC cash benefits, LTC service regulation remained the sole responsibility of the *Laender*. As the Austrian Constitution assigns responsibility for social welfare to the regional governments, regional responsibility for LTC services has always been part of the means-tested social assistance logic, which has often been criticized (Rechnungshof 2014a, 22). Moreover, each *Land* devised different regulations for LTC services, leading to a patchwork of services, prices, and eligibility criteria.

Communities and *Laender* have faced considerable challenges in financing long-term care. On the one hand, demographic changes such as the increase in the number of people who need care and the need to invest in facilities for institutional care and in the training of care workers have driven up care-related expenditures. On the other hand, the economic downturn reduced the revenues shared between the central, regional, and local governments (*Ertragsanteile*) as well as tax receipts. New ways of funding were required, and the division of legal and financial responsibilities between the levels of government needed to be rethought.

Two political decisions led to some reallocation of legal and fiscal competencies in the social policy field of LTC. First, legal responsibility for providing the LTC allowance was assigned solely to the central government, meaning that the number of laws regarding eligibility criteria and levels of allowance dropped from 10 to 1. In addition, the number of public entities in charge of administering the LTC allowance was reduced from 280 to 7 (BMASK 2014b, 151).

Second, a new LTC fund (*Pflegefonds*) was established within the Austrian Federal Ministry of Social Affairs in 2011, changing the way LTC services are funded by channeling revenues into the LTC system that are not for general use but for specific regional LTC-related tasks. The LTC fund is financed from tax revenues (*Vorwegabzüge*) collected by the central state to be shared with other levels of government (*gemeinschaftliche Bundesabgaben*). The central state contributes two-thirds of the funding, while the *Laender* and communities contribute the remainder. Thus, the LTC fund contains earmarked financial transfers (*Zweckzuschüsse*) that can only be used for improving and expanding the *Laender*'s LTC services.

The LTC fund seeks not to cover all regional LTC-service costs but rather to support *Laender* and communities by contributing to meeting the costs of LTC service provision. Such LTC funds transfers cover 10–15 percent of total LTC-related net expenditures (BMASK 2014a, 2). The LTC fund thus does not change the *Laender*'s core responsibility for funding of LTC services. LTC services comprise in-home care, semi-institutional care (such as day care), institutional care (such as care homes and nursing homes), short-term care in institutions, case and care management, and alternative forms of housing. In addition, these funds can be used for LTC-service-related initiatives such as quality assurance and for innovative projects. The LTC funds are transferred to the *Laender* based on population, and the *Laender* must pass the funds along to the communities according to their LTC-related net expenditures. Thus, communities profit indirectly from the LTC fund contributions (Köfel 2012, 5).

The creation of the LTC fund also involved standardizing LTC service provision and facilitating LTC service use. First, various LTC services were defined, reducing regional variation in service names and types and producing a more homogenous and transparent system. Second, all people in need of care, regardless of where they live, now have access to case-management services to help them find the optimal care arrangement.

Finally, an LTC database was established to facilitate public authorities' care planning. Run by Statistics Austria, the Richtverordnungsgrad indicates the share of LTC allowance recipients who receive LTC services. In 1993, the first LTC agreement between the central state and the *Laender* committed them to reporting on the unmet LTC needs and development of LTC infrastructure (*Bedarfs- und Entwicklungspläne*), but data on LTC service use were not publicly accessible. The new database was intended to help remedy that problem. The Richtverordnungsgrad was 50 percent for 2011–13, 55 percent from 2014–2016, and was targeted at 60 percent for 2017–21. However, the Austrian Court of Audit concluded that this new indicator is not suitable for planning institutional care and needs to be complemented by regulations on quality of care—mainly care outcomes and care structure (e.g., staff and infrastructure) (Rechnungshof 2014a, 19, 23). More generally, the court stated that Austria still needs a LTC planning strategy on which all governmental levels agree as well as data and techniques to inform such a planning strategy. In light of the aging of the society, such planning tools are essential for evidence-based policy-making (Rechnungshof 2014a, 19).

The LTC fund does not address the issue of regional differences in service prices (Rechnungshof 2014a, 20). Prices of care homes vary substantially between and within the *Laender* to a degree that cannot be justified. Within a *Land*, prices for publicly subsidized care differ substantially—as much as €669 in Tyrol and €488 in Carinthia, for example (Rechnungshof 2014a, 21). In both Carinthia and Tyrol, these prices did not relate to proven costs or specified norm costs but rather resulted from negotiations that considered the available financial means and actual costs of providers (Rechnungshof 2014a, 21). Because not only quality improvements but also the level of negotiated prices may drive care-related expenditures and thus the amount of LTC funds transferred to the *Laender*, the central state should be more aware of and interested in the reasons for price increases and pricing practices (Rechnungshof 2014a, 21). The policy goal of treating people equally by offering the same prices for comparable LTC services across all *Laender* has thus not been achieved.

The LTC fund was designed as a temporary solution (Rechnungshof

2014a, 21) but has now been extended through 2021 (§ 2 Pflegefondsgesetz). It does not change the general responsibilities of the central state and *Laender* that are assigned in the Austrian Constitution but increases the central state's financial responsibility.

A 2018 change in LTC policy added some momentum to the effort to redesign the central state and *Laender*'s LTC policy responsibilities. Care home residents, their relatives, or their heirs are no longer obligated to repay public support for services (*Abschaffung des Pflegeregresses*). From a social policy perspective, this implies that LTC service provision and its funding have left behind the often-criticized social assistance logic and have taken the first steps toward a system that regards LTC as a social risk rather than an individual risk. Whether this policy change will work in the long run, however, depends on the policy solutions for LTC funding. If the central state and the *Laender* both set up stable funding arrangements and further develop LTC services, policy will reach another milestone.

Although LTC policy has made progress over the years, the allocation of responsibilities between the central state and the *Laender* remains complex, and detailed data on policy indicators and outcomes remain lacking, hobbling efforts to improve in LTC provision. However, recent LTC policy changes offer a window of opportunity to start a more general process of rethinking responsibilities, governance, and benefit design.

Minimum Standards and Regional Variation

The *Laender* have always been responsible for a very important field of social policy, the second safety net to assist deprived people in living decent lives. However, regulations on social assistance varied considerably among the *Laender* in such areas as eligibility criteria, types of benefits, and levels of support (*Sozialhilferichtsatz*) as well as in support for specific groups (e.g., pregnant women) and in repayment of benefits. In addition, social assistance differed across the *Laender* (Pfeil 2001). A 2011 review of the legislation on regional social assistance concluded that the *Laender* had only marginally responded to the societal and economic changes since 1970s. This applies to material security (*materielle Existenzsicherung*), although not as drastically to social care and social planning (Pfeil 2001, 413). Policy approaches needed to be coordinated to ensure a transparent, effective, and efficient support system. Expert recommendations dating back to the early 2000s emphasized that a key goal of social policy was to reconcile the nine regional laws regarding social assistance (Pfeil 2001, 434).

Since 2010, an Article 15a agreement between the central state and the *Laender* on the core issues of the BMS has provided the constitutional basis for laws of the central state and the *Laender* on this issue. The new means-tested minimum income scheme was designed as a cash benefit for people who lack sufficient means to lead decent lives and/or to care for their dependents. BMS recipients of working age and without care obligations (for children younger than age three or for people with high care needs) must be willing to accept any suitable employment or benefit levels may be cut by as much as half. One of the core aims of the BMS is re(integrating) deprived people into the labor market. Thus, BMS recipients are eligible for extra support from the Public Employment Service (Arbeitsmarktservice). Furthermore, after successful integration into the labor market, long-term BMS recipients may keep at least part of the BMS benefit to provide an incentive for employment. BMS recipients are included in the e-card system, meaning that they can access any health service without being recognized as recipients of social assistance, an important improvement to reduce stigmatization.

In force since October 2011, the BMS came with a set of regulations that reduced disparities among the earlier regional income-related social assistance benefits (BMASK 2014b, 180ff). The different regional benefit levels (*Sozialhilferichtsätze*) were replaced by a common minimum level of support equal to the minimum pension.[10] The cash benefit covered subsistence—the cost of food, clothing, personal care, furniture, heat, and electricity. It also included a contribution to housing costs and covered medical care for illness, pregnancy, and childbirth (BMASK 2010, 6). The *Laender* retained some leeway for responding to political preferences (e.g., greater support of children) and to market characteristics (e.g., differences in housing costs).

In addition, impoverished single mothers and fathers received higher benefit levels regardless of where they lived. Single parents (mostly mothers) and their children account for more than one-fifth of all BMS recipients. Application procedures were standardized to ensure that all persons have equal access to the BMS. Finally, there is a common, nationwide, definition of assets that must be used up before people become eligible for BMS (BMASK 2014b, 180ff).

The old social assistance program was designed as an interest-free loan, implying that people had to repay their benefits when their financial situation improved. Repayment requirements have now been abolished in all *Laender*.

The BMS briefly demonstrated that concerted policy efforts on the central and regional levels could result in minimum standards and major improvements. It was regarded as an important step toward a modern social policy, although regional differences persisted and affected access to the benefit and chances of recovery.

However, the 2015–16 wave of refugees affected Austrian social policy in general and BMS in particular. During this period, more than 2.6 million people sought asylum in the European Union (Eurostat 1), with about 155,000 settling in Austria alone from 2015 to 2017 (Statista 2018). Most of the asylum seekers had left southern and western Asia (mainly Syria and Afghanistan) due to civil war and catastrophic economic and living conditions. This migration posed an enormous challenge for Europe-wide and national policies and led to a rise in right-wing political parties. In Austria, some *Laender* adapted eligibility criteria for the BMS, aiming to lower support for asylum seekers or refugees and thereby restoring discrepancies in eligibility criteria and benefit levels in the *Laender*. In 2018, however, the central government again attempted to reconcile the BMS across the nine *Laender*, with lower benefit levels for migrants.

Conclusion

The Austrian constitutional laws allocate legislative, executive powers, and decisions on public finance to the central state and its constituent units; jurisdiction, however, remains solely with the central state. Depending on the area of social policy, either the central state or the *Laender* have legal responsibilities. Local and municipal governments administer regulations and contribute to financing social policy interventions.

Revenues are channeled to the *Laender* via the fiscal equalization scheme, which is periodically negotiated between the central state and the *Laender*. Transfers between governmental sectors are the main source of revenue for regional and local governments. Autonomous *Laender* and community taxes are very low (Schratzenstaller 2008; Bröthaler et al. 2011). Extra funding requirements, for example, are fulfilled via special agreements. In the case of LTC, for example, the *Laender* received extra earmarked funding for service provision.

Article 15a agreements have become a popular solution for coordinating responsibilities across different governmental levels. In case of both the BMS and LTC, such solutions seem to work by improving the allocation of competencies. However, such agreements channel money to different actors, avoiding the mechanisms of the fiscal equalization system and thus further decreasing the transparency of the financial streams.

Redistribution results from public expenditures rather than from taxes or contributions to social insurance. Analyses of the redistributive effects of the *Laender*'s policy interventions are not available, meaning that the redistributive impact of federal and regional benefits could not be measured.

The allocation of competencies between the central state and the *Laender* do not facilitate policy coordination between the two. Although Article 15a enables agreements between the federal state and the *Laender*, the general allocation of competencies does not work effectively for a variety of reasons. The Ministry of Family and Youth, for example, argued that the Austrian Constitution does not permit the central state to coordinate the *Laender*'s family policies (Rechnungshof 2011, 58). As a result, the central level rarely engaged in these activities.

A holistic view of the possible impact of both central and regional social policy interventions on living conditions would be essential for identifying effective and efficient policy instruments. However, the prerequisites for such comprehensive analysis are missing, and the systems are complex, lack transparency, and can often be understood only by legal experts. Data on benefits and living conditions of benefit recipients are often not available for comparative analyses. Measures to increase transparency of regional policies and to avoid duplication of benefits have already been recommended (see, e.g., Rechnungshof 2011, 59), but they cannot take effect unless they are complemented by a strategic outcome-oriented policy approach.

Since 2013, the Austrian central state has been working to define the goals and outcomes of policy interventions (*Wirkungsorientierte Budgetpolitik*) so that scarce public resources can be used more effectively and efficiently. Thus, outcomes of policy interventions and their relations to costs have increasingly become key issues. An Article 15a agreement between the central state and the *Laender* on the principles of sound financial management includes clauses intended to spread the idea of outcome-oriented policy to the regional levels. Further agreements to strengthen outcome-related regional policy are in process with the goals of improving exchanges between units both within and between governmental levels and of increasing policy learning (Geppl 2013, 9).

Changes in the allocation of responsibilities between the central state and the *Laender* have been driven by demographic challenges—mainly the aging of the population and migration and their resulting financial pressures—as well as by repeated critiques and recommendations from the Austrian Court of Audit. The lack of transparency and coordination in regional social policy has prevented learning from different modes of social policy intervention from taking place.

Different areas of social policy change seem to feature different drivers. For LTC, for example, the need to find a sustainable mode of financing led to joint efforts of the central state and the *Laender*. The financial agreements seem to have acted as a lever to promote policy coordination and transparency, but evidence-based policymaking is still in its infancy, with a lack of comparative data on LTC service provision and its costs at the *Laender* level.

The BMS demonstrates that a coordinated effort between the central state and the *Laender* can improve support for impoverished people, but outside pressures, such as those imposed by the wave of refugees, can hamper that progress. If preferences vary across regions, a federal system providing different solutions to social challenges can be perceived as an asset for two reasons. First, central state and regional governments have the opportunity to develop different types of support and to decide at which level this support is most effective and can best be organized. Second, different solutions to the same social problem can work as regional models and contribute to identifying the best solution to tackle social challenges. However, creating such a system requires a federal system to promote transparency, political and social conditions for policy learning, and mechanisms for policy coordination among governments and agencies. Thus, regional variations in social policy must provide evidence that they improve people's living conditions, particularly in a country as small as Austria.

NOTES

We acknowledge the valuable contributions of Alan Trench and Ulrike Schneider (WU Vienna University of Economics and Business, Research Institute for Economics of Aging). Any errors remain our responsibility. This work has been funded by WU Vienna and the Fonds Soziales Wien.

1. https://www.statistik.at/web_de/statistiken/menschen_und_gesellschaft/bev oelkerung/index.html

2. Local and municipal governments do not have legislative power but contribute to the administration and financing of social policy interventions.

3. Our examples refer primarily to under-65 (nonpension) transfer benefits and services, pensions, and primary, secondary, and higher education.

4. The branches of Austria's social insurance system are self-governed public entities funded by their own sources of income. Unemployment insurance, however, is part of the central government's budget.

5. Developed by the OECD, COFOG uses three levels (divisions, groups, and classes) and is based on standardized principles of the System of National Accounts.

6. In Austria, compulsory schooling lasts nine years. Since July 2017, parents have been responsible for ensuring that their children undergo further training or education until the age of 18.

7. Research shows that FLAF affects vertical equity and that lower-income groups benefit more than higher income groups.

8. https://bildung.bmbwf.gv.at/schulen/autonomie/ap/index.html

9. https://bildung.bmbwf.gv.at/schulen/autonomie/bdir/index.html (15 March 2018).

10. Austria has no minimum pension as such; rather, all pensions below a certain threshold (*Ausgleichszulagenrichtsatz*) are raised to this threshold. The *Netto-Ausgleichszulagenrichtsatz* represents the level of support for BMS recipients.

REFERENCES

A. Legal Acts

Bildungsreformgesetz 2017: Bundesgesetz, mit dem das Bundes-Verfassungsgesetz, das Bundesverfassungsgesetz, mit dem das Bundes-Verfassungsgesetz in der Fassung von 1929 hinsichtlich des Schulwesens geändert wird, das Bundesverfassungsgesetz über die Begrenzung von Bezügen öffentlicher Funktionäre, das Unvereinbarkeits- und Transparenz-Gesetz, das Verwaltungsgerichtsverfahrensgesetz und das Verwaltungsgerichtshofgesetz 1985 geändert werden, ein Bundesgesetz über die Einrichtung von Bildungsdirektionen in den Ländern erlassen wird, das Ausschreibungsgesetz 1989, das Schulorganisationsgesetz, das Land- und forstwirtschaftliche Bundesschulgesetz, das Pflichtschulerhaltungs-Grundsatzgesetz, das Schulzeitgesetz 1985, das Minderheiten-Schulgesetz für das Burgenland, das Minderheiten-Schulgesetz für Kärnten, das Bundesgesetz BGBl. Nr. 420/1990, das Schulunterrichtsgesetz, das Schulunterrichtsgesetz für Berufstätige, Kollegs und Vorbereitungslehrgänge, das Hochschulgesetz 2005, das Schulpflichtgesetz 1985, das Berufsreifeprüfungsgesetz, das Pflichtschulabschluss-Prüfungs-Gesetz, das Schülerbeihilfengesetz 1983, das Privatschulgesetz, das Religionsunterrichtsgesetz, das Bildungsdokumentationsgesetz, das Schülervertretungengesetz, das BIFIE-Gesetz 2008 sowie das Bildungsinvestitionsgesetz geändert werden, das Bundes-Schulaufsichtsgesetz aufgehoben wird und das Beamten-Dienstrechtsgesetz 1979, das Gehaltsgesetz 1956, das Vertragsbedienstetengesetz 1948, das Bundeslehrer-Lehrverpflichtungsgesetz, das Landeslehrer-Dienstrechtsgesetz, das Land- und forstwirtschaftliche Landeslehrer-Dienstrechtsgesetz, das Landesvertragslehrpersonengesetz 1966, das Land- und forstwirtschaftliche Landesvertragslehrpersonengesetz, das Bundes-Personalvertretungsgesetz und das Unterrichtspraktikumsgesetz geändert werden, BGBl. I. Nr. 138/2017

Bundes-Verfassungsgesetz (B-VG), BGBl. Nr. 1/1930 (WV) idF BGBl. I Nr. 194/1999 B-VG, zuletzt geändert BGBl. I Nr. 22/2018

Finanz-Verfassungsgesetz: Bundesverfassungsgesetz über die Regelung der finanziellen Beziehungen zwischen dem Bund und den übrigen Gebietskörperschaften (Finanz-Verfassungsgesetz 1948), BGBl. Nr. 45/1948 idF BGBl. I Nr. 194/1999, zuletzt geändert BGBl. I Nr. 51/2012

Finanzausgleichsgesetz 2008: Bundesgesetz, mit dem der Finanzausgleich für die Jahre 2008 bis 2016 geregelt wird und sonstige finanzausgleichsrechtliche Bestimmungen getroffen werden, BGBl. I Nr. 103/2007, zuletzt geändert BGBl. I Nr. 118/2015

Finanzausgleichsgesetz 2017: Bundesgesetz, mit dem der Finanzausgleich für die Jahre 2017 bis 2021 geregelt wird und sonstige finanzausgleichsrechtliche Bestimmungen getroffen werden, BGBl. I Nr. 116/2016, zuletzt geändert BGBl. I Nr. 30/2018

Pflegefondsgesetz: Bundesgesetz, mit dem ein Pflegefonds eingerichtet und ein Zweckzuschuss an die Länder zur Sicherung und zum bedarfsgerechten Aus- und Aufbau des Betreuungs- und Pflegedienstleistungsangebotes in der Langzeitpflege für die Jahre 2011 bis 2021 gewährt wird (Pflegefondsgesetz), BGBl. I Nr. 57/2011, zuletzt geändert BGBl. I Nr. 22/2017

B. Databases and Websites

Eurostat 1: Asylum in the EU Member States, http://ec.europa.eu/eurostat/documents/2995521/7921609/3-16032017-BP-EN.pdf/e5fa98bb-5d9d-4297-9168-d07c67d1c9e1

Geschichte online 1: https://www.univie.ac.at/gonline/htdocs/site/browse.php?a=2752&arttyp=k

Statista 2018: Anzahl der Asylanträge in Österreich von 2018 bis 2018, https://de.statista.com/statistik/daten/studie/293189/umfrage/asylantraege-in-oesterreich/

Statistics Austria 1: http://www.statistik.at/web_de/statistiken/wirtschaft/oeffentliche_finanzen_und_steuern/oeffentliche_finanzen/steuereinnahmen/019086.html

C. Literature

Badelt, Christoph, and August Österle. 2001. *Grundzüge der Sozialpolitik: Sozialökonomische Grundlagen: Allgemeiner Teil.* 2nd ed. Vienna: MANZ.

Barr, Nicholas. 2012. *The Economics of the Welfare State.* 5th ed. Oxford: Oxford University Press.

Bauer, Helfried, Peter Biwald, Karoline Mitterer, Johann Bröthaler, Michael Getzner, and Margit Schratzenstaller. 2012. *Transferbeziehungen im Bundesstaat: Status und Reformperspektiven.* WIFO.

BMASK (Bundesministerium für Arbeit, Soziales, und Konsumentenschutz). 2010. *Bedarfsorientierte Mindestsicherung (BMS): Fragen und Antworten.* Vienna.

BMASK (Bundesministerium für Arbeit, Soziales, und Konsumentenschutz). 2012. *Sozialbericht 2011–2012.* Vienna.

BMASK (Bundesministerium für Arbeit, Soziales, und Konsumentenschutz). 2014a. *1865/AB XXV. GP—Anfragebeantwortung zu 2251/J (XXV.GP).* Vienna.

BMASK (Bundesministerium für Arbeit, Soziales, und Konsumentenschutz). 2014b. *Sozialbericht 2013–2014.* Vienna.

BMWFJ (Bundesministerium für Wirtschaft, Familie, und Jugend). 2010. 5. *Familienbericht 1999–2009: Die Familie an der Wende zum 21. Jahrhundert, Band 1*. Vienna.

Bock-Schappelwein, Julia. 2010. "Schulwesen und Kinderbetreuung." In *Verwaltungsmodernisierung als Voraussetzung für nachhaltige Effizienzgewinne im öffentlichen Sektor*, edited by Hans Pitlik, Julia Bock-Schappelwein, Heinz Handler, Werner Hölzl, Andreas Reinstaller, and Angelika Pasterniak, 107–36. Vienna: Österreichisches Wirtschaftsforschungsinstitut.

Braun, Dietmar. 2011. "How Centralized Federations Avoid Over-Centralization." *Regional and Federal Studies* 21 (1): 35–54. https://doi.org/10.1080/13597566.2010.507401

Bröthaler, Johann, Michael Getzner, Hans Pitlik, M. Schratzenstaller-Altzinger, Peter Biwald, Helfried Bauer, U. Schuh, and Ludwig Strohner. 2011. *Grundlegende Reform des Finanzausgleichs: Reformoptionen und Reformstrategien*. Vienna: Technischen Universität Wien/WIFO/KDZ/IHS.

EU, European Commission—Directorate-General for Employment, Social Affairs, and Inclusion. 2013. *Social Europe: Current Challenges and the Way Forward: Annual Report of the Social Protection Committee 2012*. http://ec.europa.eu/social/main.jsp?catId=738&langId=en&pubId=7405

EU, European Commission—Eurostat. 2011. *Manual on Sources and Methods for the Compilation of COFOG Statistics: Classification of the Functions of Government (COFOG)*. https://doi.org/10.2785/16355

Faludi, Andreas. 1998. "Planning by Minimum Consensus: Austrian "Co-Operative Federalism" as a Model for Europe?" *European Planning Studies* 6 (5): 485–504. https://doi.org/10.1080/09654319808720477

Geppl, Monika. 2013. "Umsetzung der Wirkungsorientierung auf Bundesebene: Erste Erfahrungen und Anknüpfungspunkte für Länder und Gemeinden." *KDZ Forum Public Management* 4:8–10.

Guger, Alois, Martina Agwi, Adolf Buxbaum, Eva Festl, Käthe Knittler, Verena Halsmayer, Hans Pitlik, Simon Sturn, and Michael Wüger. 2009. *Umverteilung durch den Staat in Österreich*. Vienna: WIFO.

Juranek, Markus. 1999. *Schulverfassung und Schulverwaltung: Band 1, Das österreichische Schulrecht*. Vienna: Verlag Österreich.

Kasparovsky, Heinz, and Ingrid Wadsack-Köchl. 2016. *Österreichisches Hochschulsystem*. Vienna: Bundesministerium für Wissenschaft, Forschung, und Wirtschaft.

Köfel, Manuel. 2012. "Wer finanziert die Pflege? Pflegefinanzierung in Österreich aus kommunaler Perspektive." *KDZ Forum Public Management* 2:4–7.

MA 24. 2012. *Wiener Sozialbericht 2012: Geschäftsgruppe Gesundheit und Soziales, Wiener Sozialpolitische Schriften Band 6Magistratsabteilung 24: Gesundheits- und Sozialplanung*.

Mühlberger, Ulrike, Alois Guger, Käthe Knittler, and Margit Schratzenstaller. 2008. *Alternative Finanzierungsformen der Pflegevorsorge*. Vienna: WIFO.

Österreichischer Wissenschaftsrat. 2012. *Fachhochschulen im österreichischen Hochschulsystem: Analysen, Perspektiven, und Empfehlungen*. Vienna.

Pfeil, Walter J. 2001. *Vergleich der Sozialhilfesysteme der österreichischen Bundesländer*. Vienna: Bundesministeriums für soziale Sicherheit und Generationen.

Rechnungshof. 2010a. *Arbeitsgruppe Verwaltung neu, Arbeitspaket 3, Schulverwaltung*. Vienna: Österreichisches Institut für Wirtschaftsforschung, Institut für Höhere Studienund Zentrum für Verwaltungsforschung.

Rechnungshof. 2010b. "Vollzug des Pflegegeldes." In *Rechnungshofberichte Reihe Bund*. Vienna.

Rechnungshof. 2011. *Bericht des Rechnungshofes: Familienbezogene Leistungen des Bundes und ausgewählter Länder*. Vienna.

Rechnungshof. 2014a. *Bericht des Rechnungshofes: Altenbetreuung in Kärnten und Tirol*. Vienna.

Rechnungshof. 2014b. *Bericht des Rechnungshofes: Reihe Bund 2014/3, III-53 der Beilagen zu den Stenographischen Protokollen des Nationalrates XXV*. Vienna.

Rechnungshof. 2016. *Positionen für eine nachhaltige Entwicklung Österreichs*. Vienna.

Republik Österreich Parlament. 2014. *Heinisch-Hosek will mit Bundesländern an Schulreform feilen*. https://www.parlament.gv.at/PAKT/PR/JAHR_2014/PK0605/

Rille-Pfeiffer, Christiane, Sonja Blum, Olaf Kapella, and Sabine Buchebner-Ferstl. 2014. Konzept der Wirkungsanalyse "Familienpolitik." In *Österreich: Zieldimensionen— Bewertungskriterien—Module*. ÖIF Forschungsbericht Nr. 12, Vienna.

Schäffer, H. 1992. "Bestandsaufnahme und weitere Wege der kooperativen Föderalismusreform (1963–1991)." In *Neue Wege der Föderalismusreform (Schriftenreihe des Instituts für Föderalismusforschung)*, edited by P. Pernthaler. Vienna: Wilhelm Braumüller Universitäts-Verlagsbuchhandlung.

Schratzenstaller, Margit. 2008. "Der neue Finanzausgleich 2008 bis 2013: Grundsätzliche Reform wieder verschoben." *WIFO-Monatsberichte* 1:35–42.

Schratzenstaller, Margit. 2014. *Familienpolitik in ausgewählten europäischen Ländern im Vergleich*. Vienna: WIFO. http://www.wifo.ac.at/wwa/pubid/50840

Trukeschitz, Birgit, Ulrike Schneider, and Thomas Czypionka. 2013. "Federalism in Health and Social Care in Austria." In *Federalism and Decentralization in European Health and Social Care: Competition, Innovation, and Cohesion*, edited by Joan Costa Font and Scott L. Greer, 154–89. Cambridge: Cambridge University Press.

Switzerland (The Swiss Confederation)

Stefan Felder and Gebhard Kirchgässner[†]

Since the founding of the modern federal state in 1848, Switzerland has been one of the world's most highly decentralized countries. Switzerland's form of federalism has proven highly successful not only from an economic point of view but also with respect to its social policy and political interests. The welfare state is still very well financed, and the country's extensive cultural diversity, which is reflected in the four national languages, does not inhibit national cohesion. It is hardly conceivable that Switzerland could have survived over the past 160+ years without any major problems if its subfederal units had possessed any less autonomy.

The Swiss experience shows that contrary to textbook wisdom, interpersonal redistribution is possible at the cantonal level and that sustainable fiscal policy is possible at the level of subfederal units without necessitating direct intervention by the federal government. The institutional conditions that are crucial to the success of such a system are substantial fiscal autonomy combined with a credible no-bailout rule as well as an effective fiscal equalization system.

The Swiss Confederation consists of 26 cantons: 4 French-speaking, 1 Italian-speaking, 17 German-speaking, 3 bilingual (German-French), and 1 trilingual (German-Rhaeteromanic-Italian). A population of 8.33 million lives in more than 2,255 municipalities. Zurich, the largest canton, has 1.47 million inhabitants, while Appenzell Inner-Rhodes, the smallest canton, has only 16,000 inhabitants. Diversity does not refer only to lan-

---

†Gebhard Kirchgässner (15 April 1948–1 April 2017) passed away during the preparation of this manuscript. He was a towering figure in the German Economic Association with broad interests that spanned the philosophy of science, sociology, public choice, public finance, and econometrics.

193

guage: in 2014, 37.9 percent of the Swiss population was Roman Catholic, 25.5 percent Protestant, 5.7 percent of other Christian denominations, 5.1 percent Muslim, and 1.5 percent other religions. The remainder either said they had no religion or did not respond to the question. Moreover, 24.6 percent of the Swiss population is foreign-born (Swiss Federal Statistical Office, 2015).

Swiss federalism evolved historically in a bottom-up process. In 1848, following a short civil war the preceding year, the Swiss cantons decided to form a confederation. Since that time, the cantons, not the confederation, have remained the main level of government. In principle, the confederation bears responsibility only for those tasks explicitly assign in the federal constitution, while the cantons exercise fundamental governing responsibilities. However, many joint responsibilities have emerged over time, though some have been disentangled again by a 2008 fiscal reform.

As in other countries, defense and foreign policy are federal responsibilities. The police force, however, is the sole responsibility of the cantons, with the federal police subsidiary to the cantonal forces. Joint responsibilities include social security and education. Primary schools are governed at the community level, while the cantons legislate and execute governance of secondary schools. Aside from the Swiss Federal Institutes of Technologies in Zurich and Lausanne, universities are financed by the host cantons and by subsidies from other cantons and the federal government. Research, conversely, is a federal task, organized and financed by the Swiss National Science Foundation. Social security is legislated at the federal level and executed by the cantons.

A key feature of the Swiss institutional setting is its decentralized tax system. The cantons have the basic power to tax income, wealth, and capital. Municipalities levy a surcharge on the cantonal tax. The federal government relies first on indirect (proportional) taxes, a VAT, and specific excise taxes such as those on minerals and oil and on tobacco. A small albeit highly progressive federal income tax contributed about one-third of the total federal tax revenues in 2016. Cantons and municipalities rely on income and property taxes (including corporate income taxes) for about 52 percent of their total revenue and 88 percent of their tax revenue. Altogether, Switzerland thus has 27 different income tax regimes.

The decentralized tax system generates strong competition regarding public-sector performance. At the same time, it also reduces a canton's revenue-raising power in tax increases create incentives for the wealthy to move to other cantons with lower taxes. Thus, the system restricts the government's capacity to spend on public goods and redistribution (see Feld and Kirchgässner 2001; Feld et al. 2010). Social transfers are less decisive than are locally determined marginal tax rates in conditioning a citizen's choice of residence. Tax competition is strong among the cantons and in some cases even stronger among municipalities.

Switzerland's extensive fiscal decentralization relative to many other federal systems is, however, only one major aspect of the Swiss political system. The second and no less important element is Switzerland's direct democracy: citizens have the right to launch initiatives and referenda at all government levels. These popular rights to propose or challenge legislation are important for the stability of the Swiss nation, which has neither a common language nor a common culture. Although these initiatives and referenda are not universally considered essential elements of the electoral process, they are very important institutions of Swiss suffrage and contribute to national cohesion.

Federalism and direct democracy have a strong impact on the distribution of tasks among the different levels of government and on the scope of democratic policy. Both federalism and direct democratic rights are sometimes accused of hindering political change. Empirical evidence shows, for example, that redistribution is generally more common in unitary states than in federal states. Nevertheless, Switzerland has a well-developed welfare state that has undertaken important reforms in recent decades.

Redistribution

Discussing redistribution in a federal state requires distinguishing between two target recipients: redistribution among individuals and redistribution among subfederal units—in particular, states (regions, cantons). While government expenditure and (progressive) taxes are the main instruments for redistributing funds among the former, redistribution among subfederal units is mainly performed by a system of fiscal equalization.

Redistribution among Individuals

Discussions about redistribution in federal systems often address only problems of (progressive) taxation. Public expenditures are, however, of no less importance. According to Kirchgässner and Pommerehne (1996), government expenditures are responsible for about two-thirds of redistribution in Switzerland, while the remainder results from progressive taxation.[1] The major components of redistribution among individuals are:

(1) Switzerland provides high-quality public primary and secondary schools with no or very low tuition. Thus, there is no need to send children to expensive private schools. Moreover, fees for university education are also quite moderate, at least in comparison to Anglo-Saxon countries. In contrast, however, child care is private and often rather expensive, though low-income parents receive subsidies.

(2) The welfare state—in particular, the first pillar, old-age insurance—is well developed. (For an overview, see Federal Social Insurance Office 2015.) It is a pay-as-you-go system financed by payroll contributions and backed by the federal government, and it is highly redistributive: Contributions are proportional to total labor income (without no limits or exemptions), while the maximum monthly pension in 2017 was CHF 2,350 for singles and CHF 3,525 for couples. About 60 percent of all senior citizens receive these maximum payments, a share that is steadily increasing. Those who earn less than the subsistence level receive additional subsidies.[2]

(3) Unemployment insurance is also a federal responsibility. Up to a certain limit, benefits depend on a person's previous earnings and the total duration of past employment. By international standards, benefits are comparatively high. They may last up to two years.

(4) Health insurance is mandatory. The federal government defines the basic health insurance basket to be provided by every insurer.[3] The standard is very high, and insurers must accept every application. Community rating applies at a regional level, with no risk differentiation at the client level. A retrospective risk-adjustment plan controls for gender, age, hospitalization in the previous year, and canton. Because poor people cannot afford the high health insurance premiums, the government pays for those receiving social benefits and subsidizes those with low incomes. Nevertheless, those with low incomes spend a rather high share of their income on health insurance, a situation that has been criticized (see, e.g., OECD 2011). Subsidies are paid by the cantons, but the cantons receive (unconditional) grants from the federal government for this purpose.

(5) The federal government is responsible for individual disability insurance payments, while the cantons are responsible for building and maintaining residential homes.

(6) Finally, a system of social assistance covers individuals ith no or extremely low incomes. Traditionally a task of the local communities, this has now become mainly a task of the cantons.

All in all, a large portion of education and social insurance expenditures are paid by the cantons, while the federal government allocates a smaller portion to the cantons. Most of the funding comes from (cantonal) taxes, especially income and property taxes. According to conventional economic wisdom, to prevent a race to the bottom, redistribution should take place at the federal level. Thus, progressive income taxes, the main tax instrument for redistribution, should be assigned to the federal government, while state and local governments should be financed by indirect taxes, property taxes, fees, or proportional income taxes.

The Swiss case, however, is quite different from this textbook model. Progressive income taxes are the responsibility of the cantons.[4] The small size of the country and its subfederal units mean that private and corporate taxpayers can easily move to places with low tax burdens. In theory, therefore, tax competition should occur, along with its negative consequences—in particular, a race to the bottom that would considerably impede redistribution. In Switzerland, however, considerable disparities exist among the cantons. In 2016, for example, a married couple with two children and a gross labor income of CHF 100,000 would have paid CHF 1,159 in income tax in Zug, while in Delémont, in canton Jura, the tax would have been CHF 8,675. With a gross labor income of CHF 1 million, the relative difference would become smaller, but the absolute difference— CHF 144,050—would grow (Département Fédéral 2017, 21).[5] Despite the fact that the tax burden is so much higher, per capita cantonal and local tax revenue in 2012 was considerably smaller in canton Jura (CHF 7,228) than in canton Zug (CHF 10,103) (Federal Finance Administration).

The total burden of cantonal, local, and church taxes can be illustrated by the exhaustion rate of taxable income. The values for 2014, presented in table 1, reveal substantial discrepancies. The exhaustion rate ranges between 10.4 percent in Schwyz, the canton with the lowest (average) tax burden, and 34.5 percent in Génève, the canton with the highest tax burden. The situation is even more differentiated at the municipality level. Zug, for example, features only minor differences between its communities. Schwyz, however, with a rather loose communal equalization system, allows some of its local communities to have even lower tax rates than communities in neighboring Zug. These low-tax and mostly rich cantons and local communities contrast with the relatively poor cantons and communities of Génève, Jura, Bern, Neuchâtel, Vaud, and Basel-Stadt, where the tax burden is at least 15 percent above the national average.

Despite such large differences in the tax burdens and economic potential of the cantons (and in some cantons between different local communities), considerable redistribution occurs within the cantons and local communities. According to Feld (2000), excluding the impact of the Swiss pension system, two-thirds of the redistribution occurs at the subfederal level through progressive income and property taxes.

Nevertheless, the Swiss posttax income distribution is somewhat more unequal than in other European countries (especially Scandinavia and the Benelux countries), but in the same range as the southern European coun-

TABLE 1. Per Capita Taxable Income and Exhaustion Rate, by Canton, 2014

Canton	Taxable Income (CHF)	Exhaustion Rate (%)	Index
Génève	66,378	34.5	137.1
Vaud	42,392	33.0	131.0
Jura	37,758	31.7	125.8
Neuchâtel	36,974	30.5	121.2
Bern	59,774	29.6	117.6
Valais	59,774	28.2	112.0
Basel-Stadt	38,001	27.6	109.4
Solothurn	41,155	26.2	104.2
Ticino	32,494	26.1	103.8
Basel-Landschaft	37,067	25.7	102.1
Fribourg	39,787	25.5	101.3
Graubünden	30,859	25.3	100.5
St. Gallen	44,338	24.7	98.2
Zürich	42,392	22.4	88.8
Aargau	36,207	22.2	88.2
Appenzell Ausserrhoden	39,532	22.1	87.7
Schaffhausen	42,039	21.8	86.8
Thurgau	57,155	21.8	86.7
Glarus	46,671	20.3	80.6
Luzern	36,974	19.8	78.7
Appenzell Innerrhoden	39,769	19.7	78.3
Uri	66,378	18.5	73.5
Obwalden	38,522	16.3	64.6
Nidwalden	47,182	11.9	47.2
Zug	38,742	11.8	46.9
Schwyz	37,758	10.4	41.3
Switzerland	42,741	25.2	100.0

tries or the United Kingdom and Ireland (see Atkinson 1996). Thus, the special design of the Swiss federal system does not inhibit income redistribution, which is comparable to other European countries. Switzerland's institutional framework ensures that high-income individuals also must contribute:

1. The federal income tax is highly progressive, and 30 percent of the revenue is paid back to the cantons, either directly or via the fiscal equalization system.
2. There is a federal withholding tax of 35 percent on interest and dividend income.
3. The first pillar of the old-age insurance, which is strongly redistributive, is a federal task.
4. There is a fiscal equalization system.

Conversely, the possibility that high-income earners can move to cantons with low taxes has a flattening effect on Switzerland's tax progressivity. Because tax differences are partly capitalized in house prices and apartment rents, a move to a low-tax canton is usually attractive only for people with very high incomes.[6]

In addition, direct democracy also helps to secure the system. Because the electorate decides on public issues and particularly issues related to the tax burden, people are more willing to accept the decision outcome and to contribute their share. There is clear evidence that tax evasion declines when people have more direct political rights (see Pommerehne and Weck-Hannemann 1996; Feld and Frey 2001).

Fiscal Equalization

In a system with tax competition, if all subfederal units were of similar size and similar economic power, there would be no need for a fiscal equalization plan, and the potential efficiency losses connected with such a system could be avoided. Problems usually arise with disparities— that is, in asymmetric situations—whether they result from to different locational conditions (as emphasized by the new economic geography) or from different sizes of governmental units (highly relevant to the case of Switzerland). Buchovetsky (1991) and Wilson (1991) have shown that small units can have a comparative advantage over large units in the tax competition game.

Starting from the situation of a social optimum with identical tax rates, a small canton such as Zug can benefit from a reduced tax rate, attracting additional taxpayers. If the neighboring large canton, Zürich, reduced its taxes to the same extent, no one would win: residents would stay where they are and pay lower taxes in both cantons. The large canton will not fully adjust, however. It will reduce its tax rates to a smaller extent, since it has to take into account that it will lose a substantial amount of tax revenue from existing residents and will—in relative terms—gain little from new residents. The opposite holds for the small canton. In the new equilibrium, both cantons will end up with lower tax rates, but the tax rate for the smaller unit will be lower than that for the larger unit.[7] Moreover, despite the lower tax rate, the smaller unit will have higher public expenditures per capita and higher welfare expenditures relative to the larger canton, and the welfare gains of the smaller unit cannot compensate for the losses of the larger one. As figure 1 shows, the rich Swiss cantons spend more money per capita but nevertheless have a smaller government share and accordingly lower tax rates.[8]

The discrepancies between rich and poor cantons have increased in recent years. Holding Switzerland together has required introducing a new system of fiscal equalization. The old Swiss fiscal equalization system was highly inefficient and failed to serve its purpose. The reform went into effect in 2008 and had six objectives:

1. to strengthen the financial autonomy of the cantons;
2. to reduce the differences in the cantons' fiscal potential;
3. to preserve the national and international competitiveness of the Swiss cantons (mainly with respect to their tax systems);
4. to provide the cantons with an effective but minimal financial infrastructure;
5. to equalize excessive financial burdens resulting from socioeconomic and geographical conditions; and
6. to negotiate an appropriate strategy for burden sharing among the cantons.

The new fiscal equalization plan has four main elements (for a more detailed description see, e.g., Kirchgässner 2012):

1. Some tasks and financial responsibilities that were the joint responsibility of the confederation and the cantons have been separated. Some tasks, however, are still shared jointly.
2. New elements of collaboration between the federal and cantonal

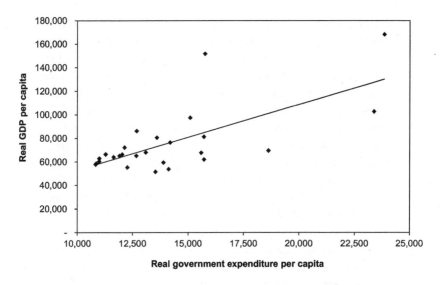

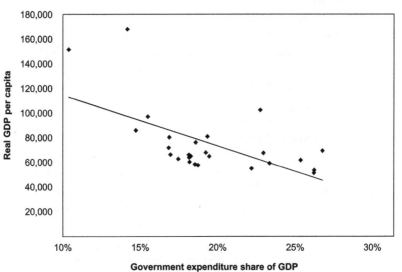

Fig. 1.

governments and financing strategies have been introduced. The traditional system of matching grants was replaced by a system where the cantons obtain all the financial means necessary for those tasks, but the confederation is in charge of strategic issues and the cantons are in charge of implementation. The objectives of these tasks are stipulated in an intergovernmental contract.

3. New forms of collaboration between the cantons, with cost compensation, have been introduced. If several cantons agree to collaborate on a task that they cannot perform by themselves (e.g., because they are too small), and if their activities benefit other cantons, the federal government can require reluctant cantons to participate if at least half of the cooperating cantons ask for such an intervention. The idea is to prevent free-rider behavior.

4. The fiscal equalization system (in the narrow sense) has been reformed. The new system consists of three building blocks. First, revenue equalization seeks to provide all cantons with at least 85 percent of the average financial means calculated across all cantons. About 70 percent of the transfers that "poor" cantons receive is provided by the federal government, while the remainder is contributed by the "rich" cantons.[9] Second, there is a cost-equalization plan, financed by the confederation: for geographic as well as sociodemographic burdens. Third, there is "hardship compensation" so that "no canton with a weak financial capacity that today benefits from equalization should suffer from worse conditions under the new plan" (cited in Dafflon 2004, 45). Two-thirds of this fund's money comes from the confederation, and one-third comes from the cantons. Full payment occurs for the first eight years, followed by a decrease of 5 percent per year for twenty years. Thus, this transition fund will remain in place for 28 years.

The new system offers a greater division of power between the different levels of government and stricter correspondence between the cantons' tasks and their financial means. In addition, the new plan strengthens incentives for the cantons to strategically manage their own tax bases—for example, by attracting new firms. Efficiency gains, therefore, might eventually lead to a reduction in the tax burden.

In November 2004, Swiss voters approved the constitutional changes necessary for this reform by a substantial popular majority as well as a majority of the cantons.[10] In 2007, the parliament adopted the necessary additional legislation, and the reform went into effect in 2008.

The new system was evaluated after 2011 to see whether it achieved its objectives. Most important, the reform sought to raise the resource endowment of each canton to a minimum of 85 percent of the national average, an objective that was achieved in 2008. In 2010, the picture differed somewhat: Valais, Jura, and Uri had resource endowments slightly below this threshold (see Conseil Fédéral Suisse 2010, 74f.). As a consequence, the transfers were altered slightly for the second period, 2012–15, and in 2014, all three cantons had endowments above 85 percent (see Conseil Fédéral Suisse 2010, 74f.). Conversely, the major donor cantons made rather moderate payments that did not impair their position, since their endowments largely remained above the national average.

Another objective was to improve the efficiency of public services, which is difficult to assess. The Federal Roads Office evaluated the efficiency of that sector. In the old system, the cantons owned and operated the highways, while the federation paid up to 97 percent of the cost. Today, the federation bears the entire responsibility with the exception of the completion of the highway network, which is a joint task of the federation and the cantons. According to the Federal Roads Office, this new arrangement resulted in efficiency gains of between CHF 100 and 250 million in 2008 (see Conseil Fédéral Suisse 2014, 235). Thus, while it is still too early to draw definite conclusions, the evidence available so far is promising.

Aside from the general fiscal equalization system based on the federal constitution, subsidiary arrangements based on contracts exist between cantons. For example, university financing beyond the moderate tuition is shared between cantons that have universities and those that do not in keeping with a concordat requiring cantons to pay a fee of between CHF 10,000 and CHF 25,000 per scholar, depending on the discipline. Redistribution thus occurs among the subunits of a federal state without federal involvement.

Fiscal equalization systems also exist within individual cantons. These arrangements are, as is usual in Switzerland, very different from canton to canton. Some are rather strict, while others—for example, Schwyz—allow large discrepancies within the canton.

Political Reforms

Whether a federal system is more or less open for political reforms is (theoretically) an open question that generally cannot be answered. On the one hand, a federal system can be seen as a laboratory where different institutional experiments can be performed in different subfederal units. Depending on the outcome, reforms might be transferred to other units or canceled. In this respect, a federal system is more innovative than a unitary state. On the other hand, if a (qualified) majority or even all sub-federal units must agree before a reform can be implemented, doing so might become rather difficult. Switzerland has experienced both out-comes. In some cases, the federal structure has enabled successful reform projects in individual cantons to be transferred to other cantons, while unsuccessful reforms have been abandoned. In other cases, the federal structure has prevented the implementation of reforms. In addition, direct democracy plays a role in Swiss reforms.

At the federal level, two kinds of reforms exist: (minor) reforms that require only a new law or a modification of an existing law, and (major) reforms that require a change in the constitution. Minor reforms are sub-ject to referenda if 50,000 signatures are collected within 100 days. The federal structure is hardly relevant for such reforms. Major reforms are subject to mandatory referenda and go into effect only if a majority of the electorate as well as a majority of the cantons approve.

Direct democracy is generally seen as an impediment to Swiss political reform, as, for example, in the February 1, 1959, referendum in which male voters rejected women's suffrage. (Women finally gained the right to vote in a February 1, 1971, referendum.) But that popular viewpoint is not necessarily accurate: the Swiss system includes both referenda and initia-tives, and while referenda tend to impede political reforms, initiatives may accelerate them. Switzerland has gained a reputation as a pioneer in envi-ronmental policy after a February 18, 1979, initiative regarding whether to phase out nuclear energy. Although the electorate rejected the initiative by a small margin, the public discourse on the risks of atomic energy that oc-curred in Switzerland did not begin until much later (if at all) in other European countries such as Germany, Austria, and France.

However, referenda, which are less radical, are more frequent than ini-tiatives, a situation that is not surprising in view of Switzerland's conserva-tive culture. Nevertheless, Switzerland seems to have been more open to reforms than many of its neighbors—Germany, France, Italy, and Austria—and particularly in contrast to the unitary state, France. These countries have considerably fewer direct political rights and much less well developed federal structures (if any). Neither of these two basic ele-ments of direct democracy stands in the way of major reform.

The new fiscal equalization system exemplifies an important Swiss re-form (see, e.g., Braun 2009), far more extensive than the two small reforms of the German federal system in the early 21st century. But the Swiss reform demanded substantial time and effort from the authorities who promoted and implemented it—approximately16 years.

Serious consideration of and planning started at the Federal Finance Administration in 1992. The first concrete proposal was presented in 1999, at which point the general structure that ultimately went into effect was present. The constitution's provisions regarding consultation were followed, and the proposal, with all comments, was published in March 2000. In August 2001, the cantons' finance ministers accepted the proposal after additional discussions and the inclusion of the hardship compensation.

Then the parliamentary process started. The first step was to pass the necessary constitutional amendment. The federal government presented its proposal in November 2001. Parliament accepted the reform with some minor revisions in October 2003, leading to intense public discussions and ultimately to the referendum. Swiss citizens approved the reform by a rather large majority, bringing to a close the most important part of the reform—after around 13 years. Another three years passed as the necessary law was enacted and the corresponding government and parliamentary decrees were issued. The new system went into effect on 1 January 2008.

The fact that this process took so long resulted in part from the constitutional rule that a majority of the people as well as a majority of the cantons must agree constitutional changes. The inclusion of the hardship compensation was necessary to satisfy this condition. Although such a mechanism might be considered inefficient from a purely economic point of view, from a political point of view, the cost of inefficiency can be considered a necessary for a smoothly functioning Swiss federal system.

In some cases, the majority of (smaller) cantons have opposed a reform and thereby in essence overruled the popular will. For example, on June 6, 1994, 52.8 percent of the electorate people voted in favor of relaxing the conditions under which young foreigners can gain Swiss citizenship, but 13 of 23 cantons opposed the plan. The opposite scenario is also possible—a majority of the cantons could agree to a proposal but a majority of the people rejects it—though no such instances have occurred over the past two decades. The small agrarian cantons situated mostly in central Switzerland are rather conservative, while the larger, more industrialized cantons are more progressive. Thus, proposals to restrict the welfare state are usually supported by the cantons rather than by the electorate, while the reverse holds for proposals to expand the welfare state. Nevertheless, the Swiss welfare state is well developed.

In a federal system, however, all subfederal units do not need to implement a reform at the same time. In such situations, cantons use concordats. And while the concordat for university education includes all cantons, such is not the case for HARMOS, an agreement to harmonize primary school education (see *Harmonisation* n.d). HARMOS was concluded by the cantonal ministers of education on 14 June 2007 and came into effect on 1 August 2009, when Ticino became the 10th canton to ratify it. In June 2014, 16 of the 26 cantons had ratified it, and 7 cantons had referenda where the constituency voted against HARMOS. These 7 cantons can choose to join later or to retain their old system, which, of course, poses an obstacle to the movement of pupils between cantons and causes problems regarding standards.

At the cantonal level, the Swiss system works as a laboratory. One experiment that failed was the early 1990s introduction of tradable permits to reduce emissions in Basel Town and Basel County. The attempt completely failed for several reasons and was canceled after a few years. The costs of the failure were limited to these two cantons and would have been far higher had a broader trial been undertaken.

A much more positive example of a staggered fiscal reform was the introduction of debt breaks at the cantonal and federal levels (see Feld and Kirchgässner 2007; Kirchgässner 2013). Introduced in 1928 in canton St. Gallen, this reform sought to decide on expenditures and then adjust tax rates to limit a possible deficit. This idea provides incentives for cantons to accumulate savings during economic upswings that can later be used to finance deficits during economic downturns. Thus, a medium-term balanced budget is combined with possibilities for anticyclical fiscal policy. This plan proved very effective. Though St. Gallen is relatively poor, it is nevertheless de facto clear of debt: its interest payments are more than outweighed by revenue from investments, particularly its share in the cantonal bank.

This debt brake provided a guide for other cantons. Fribourg followed in 1960, and other cantons have followed suit since the mid-1990s. Today, only five cantons have not adopted a debt brake or a similar instrument. The flexibility of Swiss federalism enables every canton to have its own institutions, and large differences consequently exist between the debt brakes. (For a detailed description of the rules introduced before 2000, see Stauffer 2001; for more recent overviews, see Konferenz der Kantonalen 2010; Yerly 2013.)

In the 1990s, Switzerland had the lowest economic growth of all OECD countries, which caused a large federal budget deficit and subsequently a dramatic increase in public debt (at least by Swiss standards). After several unsuccessful attempts to stabilize the federal budget, the idea of a debt brake was taken up. Because the cantonal solution to this problem, achieved by fixing expenditures and adjusting tax revenue, is not possible at the federal level, only the reverse solution was possible: citizens decide on the revenue, and parliament adjusts expenditures accordingly. The federal debt brake was approved by 84.7 percent of voters in a 2 December 2001 referendum, and after a transition period, it went into effect on 1 January 2007. Despite the financial and economic crisis that started in 2008, the debt brake proved very effective, enabling the fiscal debt (in relation to GDP) to be reduced to 1993 levels by 2013. Even the recent financial and economic crises could be managed without violating the rules of the debt brake.

Two conditions ensured the success of this debt policy. First, tax autonomy allows the cantons to adjust revenue to (planned) expenditures. Second, a credible no-bailout rule applies. Aside from transfers via the fiscal equalization system, cantons in financial crises cannot expect help from other cantons or the federal government. Although they must solve their fiscal problems on their own, they have the means to do so.

The Swiss experience with debt brakes demonstrates that in a federal system, not only can the subfederal units learn from each other, but the federal government can learn from subfederal solutions. In addition, the example of debt brakes shows that given appropriate institutions, fiscal sustainability can be achieved at a subfederal level without the intervention of the federal government. Central intervention is not necessary to induce cantons to pursue responsible and successful fiscal policies. Moreover, even for common objectives, each canton has the authority to implement its own solution depending on its specific situation and the preferences of its population. Wherever rules do not necessarily have to be identical in all subfederal units, federal systems allow a flexibility that unitary systems cannot offer. And while it might be more difficult to promote national reforms under federal systems, they are more innovation-friendly with respect to reforms at subfederal levels.

Conclusions

The Swiss are not alone in considering their nation a role model for other countries and for the European Union, demonstrating that different cultures with different languages can coexist in one country without major conflict. Switzerland also demonstrates the viability of a well-developed welfare state in a federal country. Switzerland's example, however, must be viewed with caution. Political theory tells us that it is not possible to implant a whole system on another country or to replicate single elements without taking the whole context into account.

The debt brake again offers a good example. Germany took the Swiss federal-level debt brake as a role model for legislation, applying nearly identical debt brakes at the federal level and for the *Länder*. After a transition period beginning in 2020 and aside from a business-cycle adjustment, the *Länder* will no longer be allowed to have deficits. But the *Länder* lack sufficient revenue leeway for such a system to function well, and some *Länder* are expected to be unable to meet this condition. In that case, Germany's implementation of this system will be called into question and completely reviewed.

More important, however, the introduction of debt brakes in the Swiss cantons was a bottom-up process: the (citizens of the) cantons themselves introduced and designed the brakes in accordance with their preferences. Germany, in contrast, took a top-down approach, imposing the same design on all the *Länder*, regardless of their preferences or special situations. When difficulties arise, the likelihood that institutions imposed from above will survive and be effective is rather low.[11] In a democracy, political institutions can play their role efficiently only if they are supported by a majority of the citizens, a rule that holds for the institutions of federalism in the same way that it holds for all other political institutions.

NOTES

1. Though these data refer to 1977, today the situation should not be very different, because no changes in the basic structure of the federal system have had any major impact in this respect. The new health insurance law, introduced in 1996, might even have increased expenditures' role in redistribution.

2. A second mandatory pillar of the old-age pension system seeks to enable individuals to maintain their standard of living after retirement.

3. The law does not differentiate between sickness funds and for-profit health insurers.

4. Despite being highly progressive, revenues from the direct federal income tax are much smaller than those from cantonal taxes. Moreover, only in the second half of the 20th century did the federation become entitled to tax income, and voters must periodically reauthorize this entitlement via referendum. Although no one believes that the direct federal income tax will ever be abolished, the mandated referendum offers a regular opportunity for a discussion of the subject.

5. Without the federal income tax, the tax burden (cantonal, local, and church taxes)

for an income of CHF 100,000 is approximately 7.5 times higher in Delémont than it is in Zug; for an income of CHF 1,000,000, it is about 2.5 times higher.

6. As a consequence, Swiss income taxes are in some respects regressive: high incomes are taxed less in some cantons than middle incomes in other cantons (Schmidheiny and Hodler 2006).

7. Since the 1990s, Zug and Schwyz have followed such a low-tax strategy. For the extent of tax competition in Switzerland, see Kirchgässner and Pommerehne 1996.

8. Data are averages of the 26 cantons from 1981 to 2001.

9. A total of 30 percent of the federal income tax is redistributed to the cantons: 13 percent remains with the relevant canton, while 17 percent covers the rich cantons' fiscal-equalization contribution.

10. Zurich accepted the new system even though it will pay more into the system in the future: it is also one of the main beneficiaries of the new fund for sociodemographic burdens.

11. This is particularly true for institutions in the eurozone member countries via the European Fiscal Compact.

REFERENCES

Atkinson, A. B. 1996. Income Distribution in Europe and the United States. *Oxford Review of Economic Policy* 12:15–28.

Braun, D. 2009. Constitutional Change in Switzerland. *Publius: The Journal of Federalism* 39:314–40.

Buchovetsky, S. 1991. Asymmetric Tax Competition. *Journal of Urban Economics* 30:167–81.

Conseil Fédéral Suisse. 2010. *Rapport sur l'Évaluation de l'Efficacité de la Péréquation Financière entre la Confédération et les Cantons 2008–2011*. 31 March; https://www.admin.ch/ch/d/gg/pc/documents/1855/Vorlage1.pdf

Conseil Fédéral Suisse. 2014. *Rapport sur l'Évaluation de l'Efficacité 2012–2015 de la Péréquation Financière entre la Confédération et les Cantons*. http://www.efv.admin.ch/f/downloads/finanzpolitik_grundlagen/finanzausgleich/revisionp_grundlagen/Beilage_01_Wirksamkeitsbericht_FR.pdf

Dafflon, B. 2004. *Federal-Cantonal Equalization in Switzerland: An Overview of the Present System and Reform in Progress*. BENEFRI Centre for Studies in Public Sector Economics, Working Paper No. 356, Updated Version, May 2004.

Département Fédéral des Finances. 2017. *Charge Fiscale en Suisse: Chefs-Lieux des Cantons—Chiffres Can0tonaux 2016*. Neuchâtel.

Federal Finance Administration. *Financial Statistics: Reporting*. https://www.efv.admin.ch/efv/de/home/themen/finanzstatistik/kennzahlen.html

Federal Social Insurance Office. 2015. *Overview of Social Security in Switzerland*. https://www.bsv.admin.ch/bsv/en/home/social-insurance/ueberblick.html

Feld, L. P. 2000. Tax Competition and Income Redistribution: An Empirical Analysis for Switzerland. *Public Choice* 105:125–64.

Feld, L. P., and B. S. Frey. 2001. Trust Breeds Trust: How Taxpayers Are Treated. *Economics of Governance* 2:87–99.

Feld, L. P., and G. Kirchgässner. 2001. Income Tax Competition at the State and Local Level in Switzerland. *Regional Science and Urban Economics* 31:181–213.

Feld, L. P., and G. Kirchgässner. 2007. On the Effectiveness of Debt Brakes: The Swiss Experience. In: *Sustainability of Public Debt*, ed. J.-E. Sturm and R. Neck, 223–55. Cambridge: MIT Press.

Feld, L. P., G. Kirchgässner, and C. A. Schaltegger. 2010. Decentralized Taxation and the Size of Government: Evidence from the Swiss State and Local Governments. *Southern Economic Journal* 77:27–48.

L'Harmonisation de la Scolarité Obligatoire. N.d. http://www.edk.ch/dyn/11737.php

Kirchgässner, G. 2007. Swiss Confederation. In *The Practice of Fiscal Federalism: Comparative Perspectives*, ed. A. Shah, 318–43. Montreal: McGill–Queen's University Press.

Kirchgässner, G. 2008. Direct Democracy: Obstacle to Reform. *Constitutional Political Economy* 19:81–93.

Kirchgässner, G. 2012. The Effectiveness of the 2008 Reform of Fiscal Federalism in Switzerland: Record of the First Period, 2008–2011, and Expectations for the Second Period, 2012–2015. *Cuadernos Manuel Giménez Abad* 3:8–25.

Kirchgässner, G. 2013. Fiscal Institutions at the Cantonal Level in Switzerland. *Swiss Journal of Economics and Statistics* (*Schweizerische Zeitschrift für Volkswirtschaft und Statistik*) 149:139–66.

Kirchgässner, G., and W. W. Pommerehne. 1996. Tax Harmonization and Tax Competition in the European Union: Lessons from Switzerland. *Journal of Public Economics* 60:351–71.

Konferenz der Kantonalen Finanzdirektorinnen und Finanzdirektoren. 2010. *Finanzpolitische Regeln der Kantone: Ausgaben-, Defizit-, und Schuldenbremsen.* http://www.fdk-cdf.ch/121218_hh-regeln_update_def_d.pdf

OECD. 2011. *OECD Review of Health Systems: Switzerland.* OECD Publishing.

Pommerehne, W. W., and H. Weck-Hannemann. 1996. Tax Rates, Tax Administration, and Income Tax Evasion in Switzerland. *Public Choice* 88:161–70.

Schmidheiny, K., and R. Hodler. 2006. How Fiscal Decentralization Flattens Progressive Taxes. *Finanzarchiv* 62:281–304.

Swiss Federal Statistical Office. 2015. *Statistical Yearbook of Switzerland.* Bern: Federal Statistical Office.

Stauffer, T. 2001. *Instrumente des Haushaltsausgleichs: Ökonomische Analyse und Rechtliche Umsetzung.* Basel: Helbing und Lichtenhahn.

Wilson, J. D. 1991. Tax Competition with Interregional Differences in Factor Endowments. *Regional Science and Urban Economics* 21:423–51.

Yerly, N. 2013. The Political Economy of Budget Rules in the Twenty-Six Swiss Cantons. PhD diss., University of Fribourg.

Australia

Scott Brenton

Australia is a case of weak federalism, where interventionist courts and a strong two-party system have had a more significant influence than has federalism on the size and redistributive capacity of the welfare state. Courts have mandated higher living wages than exist in many other countries and have empowered the federal government to gain more political and financial clout than was intended at federation. Most social policy questions are decided at the national level, where the two main parties, traditionally based on class cleavages, have alternated between welfare state development and dismantlement. However, the states continue to deliver most social services and maintain significant public education and health systems and therefore act as an important advocate for the public sector.

Australia has a liberal welfare state, which, like other English-speaking advanced economies spends less on social welfare than do Western European countries and strongly embraced the neoliberal agenda in the 1980s. Yet unlike in the United States and Canada, Australia has a very high degree of redistribution between regions, consistent with an egalitarian tradition. Australia is in many ways closer to the devolved United Kingdom, where the central government is the center of political power and controls most of the resources. Further, as in New Zealand, Australia consistently emphasizes government performance and outcomes. Similarly, the biggest social policy challenge is in closing the gap between indigenous and non-indigenous citizens on a range of health, educational, and other social outcomes.

The Australian welfare state is lean and acts as a safety net, with a relatively large private sector providing many social services. Unlike many other countries, Australia did not experience a recession during the global financial crisis, and the government opted for economic stimulus rather than austerity given its healthy financial position. Australia had previously produced a series of budget surpluses and had no net debt.

Federalism has influenced the welfare state's priorities and scope by empowering the central government to act when the regional governments are absent or are underperforming in the delivery of social services. Yet this is a complex story—more complicated than this chapter can detail. What can be easily observed is that the Australian federation and welfare state have become highly centralized over the past century, assisted by the High Court, social democratic Commonwealth governments, a high degree of vertical fiscal imbalance and a strong commitment to horizontal fiscal equalization.

Unlike many other federations, Australia's regions have no significant cultural, linguistic, or identity-based differences. There are some broad political differences—some states are more progressive or conservative than others—but it is difficult to clearly articulate distinctive state interests (Brenton 2015). This uniformity and egalitarian traditions facilitate centralized welfare provision, a contrast to federalism's supposed penchant toward diversity and potential inequalities.

Redistribution

The Commonwealth of Australia was formed in 1901 with the six self-governing British colonies becoming states (New South Wales, Victoria, Queensland, Western Australia, South Australia and Tasmania) in a federal system of government based on a written constitution inspired by the United States. The Commonwealth government's powers are listed in Section 51 of the Constitution (table 1), with the intention that the states would share some of those powers in addition to having responsibility for anything not listed. However, the Commonwealth government took over all income tax collection during wartime, and a series of High Court cases affirmed the central government's right to withhold grants to any state that reimposed its own income tax. No state has done so. As Stewart (2011, 157) observes, "This unique Australian history provides a striking contrast with developments in most other federations, in particular the Anglo federations of Canada and the United States, where states hold tightly their income tax bases."

The Commonwealth levies uniform personal income, company, and sales taxes, among many others. State and local governments raise only about a fifth of total taxes yet account for about half of total government expenditure and are dependent on the Commonwealth government for about half of their revenue (Stewart 2011). The Commonwealth government gives the states a range of restricted and restricted grants, including all the revenue (less administration costs) from a 10 percent goods and services tax (GST), which is a broad-based consumption tax. Yet Australia is the only federation that attempts to systematically and fully equalize the regions' revenue and expenditure capacity; it now does so by redistributing the GST differentially (Garnaut and FitzGerald 2002).

Galligan (2007) argues that with the adoption of the postwar welfare state in the mid-twentieth century, left-wing progressives criticized federalism as an obstacle to social policy development, reform, and innovation. Yet more recent scholarship has emphasized the complexity and variability associated with the timing, institutional arrangements, political actors, and pressure groups, which can slow both the adoption of welfare policies and the dismantling of the welfare system (Galligan 2007).

Australia has had a strong and stable two-party system at both tiers of government (despite the legislative presence of several minor parties and independents), historically characterized by a class divide. The left-wing, union-based Labor Party has often favored increased centralization of power and expansion of the welfare state, while the right-wing, business-

TABLE 1. Powers of the Australian Commonwealth Government

- International and domestic trade and commerce
- Taxation, customs, and excise
- Nationally uniform production and export subsidies
- Borrowing money, currency, banking, and insurance (other than intrastate services)
- Communication services
- Defense, command of railways for naval or military transport
- Maritime safety, astronomical and meteorological services, fisheries, quarantine
- Census, statistics, weights and measures
- Corporations, bankruptcy and insolvency, copyrights, patents, and trademarks
- Immigration and citizenship
- Marriage, divorce, parental rights, custody, and guardianship
- Invalid and old-age pensions, maternity allowances, widows' pensions, child endowment, unemployment, pharmaceutical, sickness and hospital benefits, medical and dental services, benefits to students, and family allowances
- Race-based laws
- Foreign affairs
- Acquisition of property on just terms
- Railway construction with consent of state
- Conciliation and arbitration of industrial disputes extending beyond one state

friendly Liberals have preferred the opposite. The Liberals have been more electorally successful, governing at the federal level for about two-thirds of the time since 1945. Yet although Labor governments have been in place for less time, they shaped much of the current welfare state by introducing bold social policies that garnered widespread popular support and thus became politically difficult to reverse.

Constitutionally, the Commonwealth government has always had responsibility for invalid and old-age pensions (Section 51xxiii). During the 1940s, the Commonwealth government began providing social benefits outside this narrow scope, and the provision of pharmaceutical benefits was ultimately challenged in the High Court and found unconstitutional. The government then embarked on changing the Constitution, receiving the necessary double majority—majorities of both total voters and voters in a majority of states. This threshold has proven difficult to cross: only 8 of the 44 attempts to amend the Constitution have succeeded.

In 1948 the Labor government introduced the Pharmaceutical Benefits Scheme, which provided free medicines to pensioners and others. Today, the plan lists certain medicines, and the government negotiates a price with pharmaceutical companies. Patients who are prescribed listed medicines contribute a small copayment, with the government covering the rest of the cost. In the 1970s and 1980s, federal Labor governments used the power under the constitutional amendment to introduce a universal public health insurance system, now known as Medicare. Queensland had previously been the only state to provide universal access to free public hospital treatment, a policy initiated by a Labor government. Medicare provides free or subsidized primary health care from doctors, including specialists and optometrists; free treatment and accommodation in public hospitals; some subsidized treatment in private hospitals; and access to public health systems in certain other countries.

Liberal governments have often introduced social policy reforms to subsidize individuals using private-sector services, arguing that doing so relieves pressure on the public system and that the subsidies are less than the full cost of public services. Since 1964, the Liberal government has become more directly involved in school funding, using Section 96 of the Constitution to "grant financial assistance to any State on such terms and conditions as the Parliament thinks fit" (Harrington 2013a).

The funding began with small amounts of capital assistance for infrastructure and operations and became recurrent grants to Catholic schools. Beginning in 1973, funding was extended to all schools, including public and other independent private schools, using various formulas on the basis of need. In practice, most state government funding went to public schools, while most Commonwealth government funding went to non-government schools. Australia now has one of largest nongovernment primary and secondary education sectors in the OECD. Only about two-thirds of Australian school students attend fully government-funded public schools (69 percent primary; 64 percent lower secondary; 65 percent upper secondary), well below the OECD averages of 81–89 percent. Constitutionally, state governments (not local governments) are responsible for primary and secondary education, although the Commonwealth government is increasingly using its financial resources to impose national regulations and common testing of all students.

In 1999, a Liberal government introduced a private health insurance rebate. It is means-tested, and a loading is charged for each year a person waits to take out private health insurance after the age of 30. Now, almost half the population has private health insurance for hospital treatment.

For ideological reasons, Commonwealth governments of both political persuasions have used their financial resources to encroach into areas of state government responsibility such as health and education. The states continue to run public hospitals and ambulance services and to fund some dental and mental health services, community and preventative health programs, drug and alcohol treatment programs, rural and indigenous health services, disability services, and aged care. However, many of these areas are increasingly shared with the Commonwealth as a consequence of state-level funding shortfalls. Commonwealth governments often pursue national reforms, seeking uniformity or regulatory oversight in response to public demands for improved services.

Most Australian universities are established under state government legislation and are publicly funded. Over the past century, the Commonwealth government has become the chief source of funding, supplemented by student fees, particularly from a large international-student market. Qualified Australian students are generally subsidized by the Commonwealth government. The additional fees are regulated by the government and can be paid with interest-free deferred loans funded by the Commonwealth government and repaid through the tax system when income reaches a certain level. The system was designed by a Labor government (reversing an earlier Labor government decision to abolish fees) to ensure equal access to higher education regardless of background and capacity to pay up front. However, the Liberal government has signaled its intention to have universities set their own fees as the share of public funding declines in the future.

The states have largely funded vocational education, primarily through institutes of technical and further education. The Commonwealth government has recently become more involved in skills and training.

While both the Commonwealth and state governments are involved in providing social welfare, the Commonwealth centrally controls and administers direct welfare payments to citizens. Most social service delivery is the constitutional responsibility of the states. Funding for service delivery is shared between the tiers of government, and the Commonwealth's superior financial position has forced the states to cede some control in recent decades. Outcomes thus are largely uniform across Australia, with the exception of the Northern Territory, which has a large proportion of disadvantaged indigenous Australians.

Today, the Commonwealth government is responsible for most social welfare benefits and services, including paid parental leave (up to 18 weeks of minimum wage); widows' allowances; child care rebates; family tax benefits (payments to taxpayers with children); unemployment benefits and employment services; government monopsony purchasing of pharmaceuticals and subsidies to citizens; disability support pensions; sickness allowances; universal public health care through Medicare (although the states and territories operate hospitals and provide some health services); rebates for private health insurance premiums; dental services for children; student and youth allowances; and veterans' benefits. The Commonwealth government provides the same levels of benefits to eligible citizens regardless of state of residence.

Pensions have always been the Commonwealth's responsibility. They are means-tested and act as a safety net, with most Australians expected to cover their own retirements through employer-funded superannuation schemes. Australians are encouraged to make voluntary contributions, with a range of Commonwealth government copayments and tax concessions.

Table 2 shows the average distribution of social welfare benefits to each household within each state along with average household incomes and income taxes, and "equivalized" (made equivalent) figures to take account of different household sizes. Western Australia has experienced strong economic growth due to a mining boom, while the smallest states, South Australia and Tasmania, have the least developed and least diverse economies and lower average incomes. However, they are compensated with higher-than-average Commonwealth cash benefits, which are aimed at lower-income recipients such as pensioners and the unemployed as well as people caring for dependents. With a progressive income tax system, these states also contribute less on average in income tax; after these factors are taken into account, the final differences between the states are less pronounced.

State social benefits in kind include the education and health services previously detailed along with housing assistance and small concessions for pensioners using electricity (because energy companies are or used to be owned by state governments). State and Commonwealth social benefits in kind are services shared between the tiers of government, while Commonwealth social benefits are primarily for tertiary education, pharmaceuticals, and rebates for private health insurance.

Redistribution also occurs at a regional level to achieve horizontal fiscal equalization, which is the goal of equalizing the fiscal capacities of each state and territory government to provide public services in the face of inequalities arising from geography, demography, natural resources, and economies. The Commonwealth Grants Commission, an independent statutory body, makes a recommendation to the Commonwealth treasurer about how to distribute the GST revenue to achieve horizontal fiscal

TABLE 2. Average Weekly Household Income, Taxes, and Benefits, 2011–12 (AU$)

State:	AUS	NSW	Vic	Qld	WA	SA	Tas
Private income	1,754	1,821	1,674	1,692	2,053	1,462	1,294
Equivalized private income	1,038	1,068	987	1,002	1,212	903	807
Social assistance benefits in cash (C'wlth)	194	204	195	195	159	206	236
Gross income	1,948	2,025	1,868	1,887	2,212	1,668	1,530
Taxes on income (C'wlth)	297	309	267	292	396	226	184
Disposable income	1,651	1,717	1,601	1,595	1,816	1,442	1,346
Equivalized disposable income	970	1,000	987	940	1,066	882	832
State social benefits in kind	144	136	135	150	139	165	147
State and C'wlth benefits in kind	121	122	111	124	137	115	123
C'wlth benefits in kind	144	156	145	135	131	140	146
Total	**409**	**414**	**391**	**409**	**407**	**420**	**416**
Total Income	**2,060**	**2,131**	**1,993**	**2,004**	**2,223**	**1,862**	**1,763**
Equivalized Total Income	**1,220**	**1,250**	**1,174**	**1,191**	**1,316**	**1,147**	**1,093**

Source: Data from Australian Bureau of Statistics.
Note: Abbreviations as follows: C'wlth = Commonwealth; NWS = New South Wales; Vic = Victoria; Qld = Queensland; WA = Western Australia; SA = South Australia; Tas = Tasmania.

equalization. During the first few decades after its establishment in 1933, the commission simply assessed the smallest states' claims for special grants. Beginning in 1978, the Commission moved away from this partial form of equalization and toward full equalization; the largest states, New South Wales and Victoria, have always been donor states in that they receive less than their population share.

The commission applies a complex formula to account for the state's efforts to raise revenue from its own sources, the level of service delivery efficiency, the cost of delivering services to certain population groups, and wage pressures, among other factors. The Commonwealth Grants Commission consults with each state government but does not negotiate over the distribution of the GST, and state governments lack a veto power. Table 3 shows how much GST revenue each state receives as a proportion of how much it would receive if funds were distributed solely according to population share.

Resource-rich Western Australia loses the most GST revenue on a per capita basis, while New South Wales and Victoria, which have more developed and diverse economies and more comprehensive revenue bases, see smaller losses. Western Australia's proportion of its per capita entitlement is the lowest of any state since the adoption of full equalization—as low as 30 percent. Western Australia has understandably become one of the most vocal critics of the current system, but it has only recently become a donor state and long benefited from higher than per capita shares. Supporters of the system thus point to Western Australia as evidence that recipients can use equalization payments to develop their economies. Queensland has also been critical after briefly becoming a donor in the 2000s before returning to recipient status, again demonstrating how relativities change over time. However, in 2015 the Commonwealth government gave Western Australia an extra AU$499 million

TABLE 3. Goods and Services Tax Distribution to the States, 2013–14

State	Population	Proportion of per Capita Entitlement (%)
New South Wales	7,386,994	97
Victoria	5,766,257	91
Queensland	4,699,864	106
Western Australia	2,531,150	45
South Australia	1,671,669	127
Tasmania	515,689	162

Source: Data provided to author from the Commonwealth Grants Commission.

in compensation. The finance minister and deputy leader of the Liberal Party were from Western Australia.

New South Wales and Victoria do not oppose the provision of extra support to the smaller states but do not see GST redistribution as the best means of doing so because it is unrestricted funding. Overall, 64 percent of transfers to recipient states are unrestricted, meaning that states can use the money in any way they choose, whereas only 52 percent of donor-state funding is unrestricted (Victorian Government 2011). These two states argue that the extra funding should be tied to address the particular needs that are being subsidized, such as improved outcomes for indigenous residents.

The other area of contention with the current system is that the GST and other sources of state revenue are not increasing at the same rate as spending demands, and state governments are becoming even more dependent on the Commonwealth government. When the GST was introduced in 2000, revenue was projected to grow by an average of 6 percent per year (GST Distribution Review). While the first few years saw growth rates of well above 6 percent, revenues fell by 2.7 percent with the onset of the global financial crisis, and future projections show growth below 6 percent. GST is not levied on fresh food, education, or health services, yet these forms of consumption are growing at a faster rate than taxable forms of consumption. Furthermore, over the first twelve years of the GST, state expenditures grew at an average rate of 7.1 percent per year.

Change

Since the transfer of exclusive income tax collection to the Commonwealth government in 1941, Australia has become a more centralized federation. The Commonwealth government has gained financial control and fostered dependency by exercising control over how the states spend money. Although it has not been a consistent trajectory toward greater centralization at all times, short-lived Labor governments have tended to accelerate centralization, and even recent Liberal governments have been centralists in some areas.

While the global financial crisis signaled the end of the resources-led economic boom and "rivers of gold" to government coffers, the immediate response was not austerity, as in other developed economies, but rather stimulus. The Labor government had embarked on significant reforms to federal-state financial relations as the effectiveness of federalism in service delivery became a major political issue even prior to the crisis. While a change of government to the Liberals in 2013 has seen attempts at austerity, reform of the federation and taxation arrangements has remained a prominent issue. Both reforms have effectively been abandoned, particularly after the government changed prime ministers.

Australia experienced austerity and a contraction of the welfare state in the late 1980s and early 1990s, with major budgetary reforms commencing in anticipation of a recession and a move toward more user-pay services and individual responsibility for social insurance. Australia embraced neoliberal policies centered on containing and reducing both spending and taxation as a proportion of GDP, delivering budget surpluses and repaying debt along with reducing the public sector and rationalizing the public provision of services. Alongside New Zealand, Australia was one of the pioneers of new public management reforms and one of its most radical adherents.

Both Labor and Liberal governments pursued fundamental budgetary reforms and emphasized budget discipline (Wanna, Kelly, and Forster 2000; Hawke and Wanna 2010). New public management reforms delegitimized debate about how to spend money and instead elevated the "guardians" (agencies and ministers with economic oversight) and focused on cuts and restraint as well as ideas of "reciprocity" from citizens (Kelly and Wanna 2001). Since the late 1980s, Australia has recorded 13 budget surpluses, with observers coining the term *surplus fetish* to describe the phenomenon. Many of the early surpluses were achieved when the Commonwealth government cut grants to the states (Robinson 1996). During the 1990s, many state governments espoused the "balanced budget doctrine," with a focus on eliminating debt and no net borrowings and even proposing constitutional amendments to enshrine the principle (Robinson 1996).

By the early 2000s, surpluses in excess of 1 percent of GDP were achieved at the national level. In 2005, the government's net debt was eliminated after sustained budget surpluses and asset sales, placing Australia in an enviable position compared to other OECD countries. Thereafter, surpluses were placed in off-budget sovereign wealth funds to pay for unfunded future public-sector pension liabilities and specified infrastructure, such as that for higher education and research. Australia avoided recession in 2008–9 via a substantial economic stimulus—2.6 percent of GDP, the largest of all OECD countries (Wettenhall 2011). Subsequent political debate has focused on when the budget will return to surplus and when debt will be repaid, with elements of austerity despite Australia's strong financial position relative to other OECD countries.

The global financial crisis coincided with a change of government from a long-serving Liberal government to a new Labor government that had elevated federal-state financial relations as a major issue while in opposition. During the same period, Labor had more electoral success at the state level and was governing in most jurisdictions. Labor claimed that citizens were unsure which tier of government was responsible for what, leading governments to blame each other for failings, and that the states were not financially strong enough to improve services unilaterally. Labor advocated "cooperative" federalism, and for a brief period, all jurisdictions had governments from the same party, the first time that had ever occurred.

In 2009, the country's peak intergovernmental forum, the Council of Australian Governments (COAG), agreed to an overarching framework on federal financial relations. The Intergovernmental Agreement on Federal Financial Relations is one of the most significant reforms in regulating Commonwealth government payments to state and territory governments. There are now three broad forms of payments: national specific-purpose payments, national partnership payments, and general revenue assistance.

The specific-purpose payments must be spent in six key areas of social policy, each of which is subject to an individual agreement: health, education, skills and training, disability services, housing, and "closing the gap" in indigenous disadvantage. The agreements specify objectives, outcomes, outputs, and performance indicators, but the states have flexibility in how they spend the funds as long as they do so in the specified policy area and achieve the mutually agreed objectives and outcomes. Similarly, partnership payments are tied to specified objectives and outcomes but in relation to major reforms or projects. General revenue assistance is unrestricted funding and is mainly GST revenue.

Health was one of the most contentious reform areas. Former Labor prime minister Kevin Rudd pledged to "end the blame game" and at one stage threatened a Commonwealth takeover of hospitals to improve performance. However, the final National Health Reform Agreement maintained that the states would continue to manage their public hospital systems and that joint funding would continue. Instead, since 2012 there has been increased transparency regarding funding sources, appropriate costs for efficient services, and performance. The Commonwealth had agreed to take a greater share of funding the growth in the efficient cost of services beginning in 2017, but the current Liberal government reduced the Commonwealth share from 50 to 45 percent between 2017–18 and 2019–20, with COAG to renegotiate a future agreement.

The agreement also provided that the Commonwealth would take over full responsibility for aged care and continue the establishment of local primary health care centers so that patients could access health services and after-hours care normally provided a public hospitals. Again, the Liberal government criticized Labor's initiative regarding local primary health care centers but pursued a similar concept. Many Australians currently access hospital emergency departments because they are free and are open 24 hours, with the costs borne by state governments. However, this practice is neither efficient nor cost-effective.

As part of the National Partnership Agreement on Early Childhood Education, the Commonwealth government is providing extra funding to the states to ensure that all Australian children have access to at least 15 hours a week or 600 hours a year of preschool. States and territories had previously provided different levels of access, with each regional government operating its own system. The Commonwealth government also completely took over the licensing and accreditation of child care and early childhood workers, a responsibility previously shared with the states and differing across jurisdictions.

The Commonwealth became much more involved in education, using the global financial crisis to inject billons of dollars of economic stimulus into upgrading school infrastructure. Through COAG agreements with the states, the Commonwealth established national accreditation standards for teachers and began working toward a national curriculum. It also provided additional funding to improve teacher quality, promote student literacy and numeracy, operate trades training centers, and support students from low socioeconomic backgrounds and students with disabilities. Similarly, the Commonwealth assumed greater responsibility for vocational education and training under a framework of national accreditation and regulation of qualifications and service provision as well as increased funding and training facilities.

Two of the signature policies of the previous Labor government were the National Plan for School Improvement and the National Education Reform Agreement, with all states except for Queensland and Western Australia (which had conservative governments at the time). The billion-dollar reform package lifted the Commonwealth's share of recurrent government funding to all schools from about one-third to almost two-thirds and indexed its funding at a higher rate than the states and territories (see Harrington 2013b). All schools, government or nongovernment, are funded at a per student rate, although nongovernment schools will be assessed according to their capacity to contribute. There will also be loadings for students with disabilities, aboriginal and Torres Strait Islander students, students from low socioeconomic backgrounds, students with low English proficiency, and to account for school size and location.

The nonparticipating states initially continued under a modified version of the former system of funding. However, the Liberal government initially provided more funding to Queensland and Western Australia and committed to the agreements with the other states and territory for only one year. After widespread criticism from across the political spectrum, the government retreated, pledging to honor the agreement for four years (still down from the original six years).

The current system is based on a school resource standard—a base amount for every primary and secondary student. This is then discounted based on the school's "capacity to contribute," which uses each student's residential address and other data from the Australian Bureau of Statistics to calculate a socioeconomic status score for the school. Then the loadings are applied based on nationally consistent definitions that replaced the earlier state/territory-based conceptions of disability or English proficiency, for example. The process is overseen by a new independent National School Resourcing Board. The Commonwealth will fund on average 20 percent of the school resource standard for government schools by 2027 (up from 17 percent in 2017) and 80 percent of the standard for nongovernment schools (up from 76.2 percent in 2017). While these figures reflect the Commonwealth government's historical status as the minority funder of government schools, the Liberals have traditionally favored large subsidies for nongovernment schools, arguing that doing so is ultimately cheaper for government as enrollments gradually shift to the nongovernment sector.

One of the other signature policies of the previous Labor government was a reform of disability services and the progressive introduction of a National Disability Insurance Scheme (NDIS). It has been designed to replace the current patchwork system of shared provision and funding of disability services, which has for decades been criticized as inadequate. Under the scheme, funding and governance are still shared between the Commonwealth and the states, but the Commonwealth takes on overall coordination and will impose a 0.5 percent levy on all taxpayers (with some exemptions and concessions) to meet some of the costs. To meet projected increased demand and funding shortfalls, the Liberal government increased the levy by another 0.5 percent beginning in 2019.

The scheme is being progressively rolled out, with full coverage beginning in 2016 and national coverage by 2019, though some states and territories will reach that goal sooner. Western Australia did not initially commit and did not sign a bilateral agreement with the Commonwealth until in 2017 (after the election of a new state Labor government), with a national agency taking control in 2018. The National Disability Insurance Scheme provides individualized, long-term funding for a range of support services and costs associated with living with a disability and receiving care. The money is available until the recipient reaches age 65 or enters the aged care system. The Commonwealth government will be responsible for just over half the cost of the scheme.

The final recent landmark social policy with significant implications for federal-state relations is "closing the gap," which refers to the range of measures of (in)equality between aboriginal and Torres Strait Islanders on the one hand and other Australians on the other. About 85 percent of Torres Strait Islanders live in New South Wales, Queensland, Western Australia, or the Northern Territory; the latter three jurisdictions have vast remote areas where is the cost of delivering services is extremely high. The most important measures are life expectancy (closing the gap in life expectancy by 2031); infant mortality (halving the mortality rate for Torres Strait Islander children under five years of age by 2018); access to early childhood education (all Torres Strait Islander four-year-olds in remote communities to have access by 2013); literacy and numeracy (halving the gap in achievement by 2018); Year 12 or equivalent educational attainment (halving the gap by 2020); and employment outcomes (halving the gap by 2018). These goals are underpinned by a range of national agreements focused on reform in this specific area as well as sections of most of the other national agreements.

Conclusions

While the 1940s was the most significant decade in terms of shaping the Australian federation and welfare state, the early 21st century has been eventful in terms of reform and containing welfare expenditures and the balance of political power between the different tiers of government. Four major developments have occurred during this period: financial and budgetary reforms with cuts to welfare spending and grants to the states to balance Commonwealth budgets as well as greater reliance on user fees; the institutionalization of COAG as the forum for intergovernmental negotiations and reform; the introduction of the GST and the recalibration of state dependency on equalization payments; and the streamlining of federal-state financial relations and improvement of accountability and efficiency through "cooperative" federalism. A fifth major development could occur if the shift toward decentralization and "competitive" federalism proceeds. Most of these developments contain a partisan element, although it is not always consistent, and prime ministers from both major parties have, not surprisingly, been attracted to increased power.

Beginning in the late 1980s and strengthening from the mid-1990s, a broad bipartisan consensus has emerged in favor of pursuing budget surpluses and reducing government spending and levels of taxation. This has had two main effects on fiscal federalism and the welfare state: first, Australia's high vertical fiscal imbalance makes cutting grants to states or failing to maintain funding at appropriate levels an easy way for the Commonwealth to balance its budget; second, welfare has become more of a safety net with less universality and a greater expectation that individuals will provide for themselves privately or pay user fees for public services. Thus, private health insurance has grown, access to free primary health services has been restricted, the nongovernment school sector has grown, tertiary education fees have been reintroduced and have increased, and compulsory superannuation has been introduced. A focus on government spending masks fundamental shifts toward private-sector provision of services and also obscures differing levels and quality of services dependent on user fees.

Many formal and informal forums for intergovernmental dialogue and agreements have emerged over the years, but COAG has become the most enduring and all-encompassing. COAG began in 1992 and has since become the only arena for formal intergovernmental negotiations. Its members include the prime minister and first ministers from each state and territory as well as the president of the Australian Local Government Association. However, the prime minister determines the meeting schedule and agenda, and long periods have passed with no meetings. In addition, although meetings have been frequent in recent years, the federal government is not bound to incorporate the positions of the other participants. States often must choose to either accept or reject the federal government's offer without the opportunity to significantly influence the agenda. The Commonwealth government under both Labor and Liberal administrations has increasingly tied its grants to the states to particular spending priorities or key performance measures and to greater accountability from the states, particularly for outcomes.

The GST has been a perennially contentious issue in Australian politics because it is criticized as regressive. The Liberals lost the 1993 election by campaigning for a 15 percent GST, and when they returned to government, they changed the proposal by lowering the rate to 10 percent. The party only narrowly retained government with that proposal and had to exempt a range of goods and services to get it through the Senate. The Liberals pledged that it would be a state tax and would change only with the approval of the states, though this was not technically true. There is now some political pressure to increase the rate and scope of the GST (which does not apply to fresh food and health and education services) to provide more revenue for the states. The distribution of this revenue also receives criticism, with Western Australia's share starkest. The fiscal differences between the states have become more pronounced, and whereas the largest two states previously were the only donors, more states have now or recently assumed that status.

While Australia will likely never retreat from a comprehensive equalization system, increased attention is being given to how to also fairly treat donor states. Some observers have called for the states to reclaim their income tax power, but the idea appears to have little support, if only because of the administrative costs of having different rates in a country of Australia's size. Similarly, efficiency gains result from national uniformity in a range of other areas, and this is often prioritized over the possibility of increased innovation in decentralized settings. This may be achieved by untying more grants from the Commonwealth.

The most recent reforms to federal-state financial relations under a Commonwealth Labor government have simplified what nevertheless remains a complex system while upholding a high degree of vertical fiscal imbalance and a strong commitment to horizontal fiscal equalization. Direct welfare payments to citizens remain centralized, some services have become more centralized, and the Commonwealth has taken a larger funding and regulatory role in areas of joint responsibility. It is too early to evaluate the effectiveness of these changes, and the change of government has resulted in modifications to many of the agreements. The Liberal government shifted more toward competitive federalism, but critics argue that it merely constitutes an extension of the neoliberal agenda and a race to the bottom. Despite the supremacy of the Commonwealth, it still must work with the states to make these changes.

The High Court has remained active in the area in a series of landmark cases in which the Commonwealth's power has been challenged, often by citizens rather than state governments. While the High Court supported the Commonwealth's ability to enact controversial workplace relations legislation and direct payments to citizens as economic stimulus, it did rule that the Commonwealth could not directly fund religious chaplains in schools. Citizens generally have supported the principle that all Australians are entitled to the same level of services regardless of where they live. This is not to suggest that inequalities and differences in outcomes do not exist among the states. Legacies of colonialism and entrenched indigenous disadvantage affect some parts of Australia more than others, while economic prosperity differs significantly by region.

Galligan (2015, 90) identifies several "myths" or untested ideals that have developed over time and previously inhibited a return of power to the states: that centralism, uniformity, and Commonwealth intervention are desirable; that federalism is inefficient and encourages costly duplication; and that the Commonwealth is best able to discern the national interest and respond to globalization. While these attitudes are unlikely to change in the immediate future, there are no serious proposals to abolish the states, and the Commonwealth is not necessarily seen as more efficient or more capable of delivering better services. The states still constitute important veto points and an accountability counterbalance, while many states have been less fervent adherents to the neoliberal agenda, continuing to support the public sector in social policy domains.

The relationship between federalism and the welfare state is not clear-cut and is difficult to determine without a counterfactual. If Australia had started as a unitary system, especially with a unicameral parliament or weak upper house like the United Kingdom, the welfare state likely would be less developed because non-Labor parties have been more dominant at the national level while state parliaments have provided Labor with resources and vital political platforms. Furthermore, the lower house has been more advantageous to conservative parties, while the upper house has had more progressive majorities in recent decades. Federalism has facilitated powerful and influential institutions that regularly consider social policy issues, such as the High Court and intergovernmental forums. Federalism has also fostered a culture of egalitarianism. Thus, while Australia is highly centralized and liberal, the importance and influence of federalism cannot be discounted.

REFERENCES

Australian Bureau of Statistics. 2012. *State and Territory Statistical Indicators*, 1367.0, ABS, Canberra.

Australian Bureau of Statistics. 2013. *Household Income and Income Distribution, Australia: Government Benefits, Taxes, and Household Income, Detailed Tables, 2011–12*, 6523.0, ABS, Canberra.

Australian Bureau of Statistics. 2014. *Life Tables: States, Territories, and Australia, 2011–2013*, 3302.0.55.001, ABS, Canberra.

Australian Government. 2014. *Fiscal Equalisation*. Canberra: Commonwealth Grants Commission. https://www.cgc.gov.au/index.php?option=com_content&view=article&id=37&Itemid=153

Brenton, S. 2015. "State-based Representation and National Policymaking: The Evolution of the Australian Senate and the Federation." *Journal of Legislative Studies* 21 (2): 270–80.

Commonwealth of Australia Constitution Act 1900 (Imp) 63 & 64 Vict., c 12, s 9.

Galligan, B. 2007. "Federalism." In *Oxford Companion to Australian Politics*, ed. B. Galligan and W. Roberts, 202–5. Oxford: Oxford University Press.

Galligan, B. 2015. "Challenges in Reforming Australian Federalism." *Australian Journal of Public Administration* 74 (1): 87–92.

Garnaut R., and V. FitzGerald. 2002. *Review of Commonwealth-State Funding Final Report: A Review of the Allocation of Commonwealth Grants to the States and Territories*. Melbourne: Committee for the Review of Commonwealth-State Funding, Governments of New South Wales, Victoria, and Western Australia.

Harrington, M. 2013a. *Australian Government Funding for Schools Explained*. Canberra: Parliamentary Library, Department of Parliamentary Services.

Harrington, M. 2013b. *Funding the National Plan for School Improvement: An Explanation*. Canberra: Parliamentary Library, Department of Parliamentary Services.

Hawke, Lewis, and John Wanna. 2010. "Australia after Budgetary Reform: A Lapsed Pioneer or Decorative Architect?" In *The Reality of Budgetary Reform in OECD Nations: Trajectories and Consequences*, ed. John Wanna, Lotte Jensen, and Jouke de Vries, 65–90. Cheltenham: Edward Elgar.

Kelly, Joanne, and John Wanna. 2001. "Are Wildavsky's Guardians and Spenders Still Relevant? New Public Management and the Politics of Government Budgeting." In *Learning from International Public Management Reform*, ed. Lawrence Jones, James Guthrie, and Peter Steane, 589–614. Bingley: Emerald Group.

Robinson, Marc. 1996. "The Case against Balanced Budgets." *Australian Journal of Public Administration* 55 (1): 48–62.

Stewart, M. 2011. "Australia." In *Tax Aspects of Fiscal Federalism: A Comparative Analysis*, ed. G. Bizioli and C. Sacchetto, 137–85. IBFD.

Victorian Government. 2011. *Submission to the GST Distribution Review*.

Wanna, John, Joanne Kelly, and John Forster. 2000. *Managing Public Expenditure in Australia*. Sydney: Allen and Unwin.

Wettenhall, Roger. 2011. "Global Financial Crisis: The Australian Experience in International Perspective." *Public Organization Review* 11 (1): 77–91.

Canada

Provincial Autonomy, Policy Fragmentation, and Fiscal Redistribution

Daniel Béland and Heather Elliott

Canada is the second-largest country in the world (after Russia), and federalism has been one of its most central institutional features since 1867, when the country was created. That year, the British North America Act created four provinces out of existing British colonies: New Brunswick, Nova Scotia, Ontario, and Quebec. Five other provinces were added over the next three and a half decades: Manitoba (1870), British Columbia (1871), Prince Edward Island (1873), Alberta (1905), and Saskatchewan (1905). Finally, in 1949, after much debate and two referenda, Newfoundland (known as Newfoundland and Labrador since 2001) became the 10th and last province. In addition, Canada has three large yet sparsely populated territories: Northwest Territory (created in 1870), Yukon (1898), and Nunavut (1999).

It is impossible to study social policy in Canada without paying close attention to federalism, territorial politics, and the central role of the provinces in the provision of welfare. Canada is one of the most decentralized federal countries in the world, a reality apparent in its fragmented social policy system, in which the provinces play a central role. Despite this high average level of decentralization, however, the federal government is a key fiscal actor through its block grants and equalization program. Moreover, the government is involved in the direct provision of social benefits and services to aboriginal peoples and members of the armed forces. The federal government also distributes major family, pension, and unemployment benefits to the general Canadian population. Yet the 10 provinces are the most crucial policy actor in Canada, which explains why provinces, especially Quebec, have developed unique social programs that reflect their needs and politics (Béland and Lecours 2008; Van den Berg et al. 2017). Nevertheless, Ottawa should continue to play a key fiscal and social policy role (Atkinson et al. 2013). Simultaneously, although federalism may have slowed down social policy development in Canada up to the Second World War, such has hardly been the case since the 1940s, as competitive state building (Banting 1995) between Ottawa and the provinces stimulated welfare state expansion in areas such as pensions and health care (Maioni 1998; Simeon 1972). In other words, there is no evidence that federalism in itself has been a key obstacle to social policy expansion in Canada during the postwar era and beyond (Théret 2002).

Compared to provinces, territories have limited constitutional autonomy and depend much more on federal fiscal transfers. From a constitutional standpoint, municipalities are pure creatures of the provincial governments, with limited fiscal autonomy, and—with a few exceptions like social assistance delivery in Ontario—limited involvement in social policy, at least compared to the situation prevailing in other federal countries. The analysis in this chapter excludes both the territorial and municipal governments from consideration. (For a similar approach and an overview of Canadian federalism and the role of the provinces within it, see Atkinson et al. 2013.)

Although the federal government received jurisdiction over issues such as national security and aboriginal peoples, the British North America Act granted provinces most powers we associate today with social policy, including health and education (Banting 1987; Théret 2002). Over the years, however, the federal government has used its spending power to enter key provincial jurisdictions. In some cases, this situation has proved contentious, particularly because the federal spending power is not mentioned in the Constitution. The federal spending power is consequently an ongoing source of discussion among legal and policy experts (Telford 2003).

Starting during World War II, the federal government entered a number of traditional provincial jurisdictions, partly through unilateral decisions such as the enactment of family allowances in 1944 and partly as the result of constitutional amendments negotiated with the provinces. These amendments resulted in the adoption of unemployment insurance (known as employment insurance [EI] since 1996) in 1940 and old-age security in 1951, thereby creating political and territorial tensions that proved especially strong in the French-speaking province of Quebec, where a strong substate nationalist movement has long opposed federal "intrusion" in provincial jurisdictions (Béland and Lecours 2008). In other policy areas such as health care, however, provinces took the lead and pushed the federal government to provide funding while allowing the provinces to preserve much of their policy autonomy. As a result of this push for provincial state building (Banting 2005), by the early 1970s, all provinces featured a single-payer, universal health care system cofinanced by the federal government (Boychuk 2008; Maioni 1998). Finally, in a crucial area such as education, the provinces have largely preserved their strong policy autonomy: Canada, unlike other federal countries including Australia and the United States, does not even have a federal department of education (Wallner 2014).

Long political and territorial struggles have led Canada to develop three main types of social programs from a territorial standpoint (Banting 2005, 95). The first type includes purely federal (EI) or provincial (workers' compensation) policies, for which only one level of government is responsible, both constitutionally and fiscally. Second is shared-cost programs managed by the provinces but fiscally supported by the federal government (currently mainly through block grants), such as health care and social assistance for the nonelderly. Finally, under what Keith Banting (2005, 95) calls "joint decision federalism," the Canada Pension Plan (CPP) is an earnings-related retirement program adopted in the mid-1960s that cannot be revised by the federal government without explicit and formal support of at least two-thirds of the provinces representing at least two-thirds of the Canadian population. (This program covers workers in all provinces except Quebec, which operates the similar but not identical Quebec Pension Plan.)

We gathered basic expenditure data, at both the provincial and federal levels for 2000–2013. Some data, however, including data on aboriginal peoples, were available only in select years. Expenditure data were gathered for the following categories: total health expenditures, combined public and private expenditures on education, public expenditures on education, educational attainment of the population aged 25–64 (includes off-reserve aboriginal population as well as nonaboriginal population), total social services expenditures, total housing expenditures, unemployment, aboriginal-identifying population, and persons in low-income families (before tax). While data for pensions were available, public old-age security programs are quite uniform across Canada (despite the existence of provincial top-ups for low-income seniors) and therefore were not included in these analyses. Data on provincial-level spending as well as federal expenditures in these areas are largely comparable across years.

Territorial Redistribution

The fact that the provinces have full or principal jurisdictions over many key social programs and policy areas (with the exception of fields such as employment insurance, public pensions, and aboriginal policy, where the federal government is either in charge or dominant) does not mean that they are on their own from a fiscal standpoint. For example, Ottawa supports provincial efforts through two large transfers (operating as block grants) for health and social matters. First, the Canada Social Transfer provides funding to provinces for higher education, social assistance, child care, and other childhood-related policies. For the 2013–14 fiscal year, the Canada Social Transfer allocated more than Can$12 billion in total to the provinces (Department of Finance Canada 2013). Second, the larger of these federal programs, the Canada Health Transfer, allocated more than Can$30 billion to the provinces for the 2013–14 fiscal year (Department of Finance Canada 2013). Health care is by far the largest source of spending in the provinces, and the Canada Health Transfer covers only about 20 percent of provincial health expenditures, a proportion that is set to decline slightly over time (Matier 2012). This means that the provinces have to finance the large majority of their own health expenditures.

In exchange for federal funding, the provinces have to follow the five broad principles embedded in 1984 Canada Health Act: public administration; comprehensiveness; universality; accessibility; and portability of health coverage from province to province (Health Canada 2012). From a redistributive standpoint, the recent shift announced by the Conservative Harper government (2006–15) to "a pure per capita funding formula . . . will have an even more negative impact on the ability of most provinces to finance necessary health care. As it turns out, only one province, Alberta, will benefit from the new funding formula" (Marchildon and Mou 2013). Considering that Alberta has by far the highest fiscal capacity of all provinces, this Conservative decision seems quite regressive from a fiscal federalism standpoint (Marchildon and Mou 2013). More broadly, disparities among provinces in health care spending are significant but relatively moderate in scope considering the high level of provincial autonomy in that policy area. Overall, poorer provinces do not necessarily spend less on health care than wealthier ones (Canadian Institute for Health Information 2014).

In contrast to the United States but similar to other advanced industrial federations, Canada operates a federal equalization program. Its main goal, reducing horizontal fiscal disparities among the provinces, has indirect yet clear implications for social policy financing (Théret 2002). Unlike the model adopted in Australia and other federal countries, Canada's equalization program calculates transfers to lesser-off provinces purely on the basis of average fiscal capacity, without assessing variations in social and economic need. Created in 1957, equalization is enshrined in the 1982 Constitutional Act, Subsection 36(2): "Parliament and the government of Canada are committed to the principle of making equalization payments to ensure that provincial governments have sufficient revenues to provide reasonably comparable levels of public services at reasonably comparable levels of taxation." Despite this strong constitutional stance, equalization became increasingly contentious in the mid-2000s, in part because of the way natural resources are taken into account in measuring provincial fiscal capacity. More generally, the status within equalization of the oil-rich province of Alberta, which has not received equalization payments since the early 1960s, is especially contentious from both policy and political standpoints (Lecours and Béland 2010).

Because only provinces falling below a changing national average receive equalization payments, the number of provinces accessing them and the amount to which each of these provinces is entitled changes from year to year. Historically, the four Atlantic provinces (New Brunswick, Nova Scotia, Prince Edward Island, and Newfoundland and Labrador) typically received proportionally larger payments on a per capita basis. Quebec, until recently the most populous province to receive equalization money (industrial decline in Ontario made that larger province eligible for payments for the first time in 2009–10), has long received the most equalization money in absolute terms (Lecours and Béland 2010). During the 2017–18 fiscal year, total equalization payments amounted to about Can$18.3 billion, with Can$11.1 billion going to Quebec, Can$1.8 billion to Manitoba, and Can$1.4 billion to Ontario. That year, four provinces did not qualify for benefits: Alberta, British Columbia, Saskatchewan, and Newfoundland and Labrador. The excluded provinces are energy-rich jurisdictions (British Columbia has relatively little oil but is a large natural gas producer). The fact that the most populous province, Ontario, is now receiving equalization payments is an ongoing source of concern for the long-term fiscal sustainability of the federal equalization program.

Beyond fiscal transfers and equalization payments to the provinces, purely federal programs may have a strong redistributive-territorial component to them. This is the case of EI, a program under which workers living in regions of the country with higher unemployment have faced less stringent eligibility criteria since 1977. Currently, Canada has 52 EI regions, and most people need to work between 420 and 700 hours to qualify for benefits, depending on the EI region in which they live (table 1).

Workers and employers from all across the country pay the same EI contribution rate, and the existence of EI regions further amplifies redistributive effects related to the simple fact that some regions of the country face much higher unemployment rates than do others. Although clear differences exist among provinces and regions (unemployment is much higher on average in the four Atlantic provinces than in the four western provinces), major socioeconomic discrepancies exist within each province, which has clear implications for EU benefits and eligibility criteria.

Table 1 demonstrates that within Saskatchewan, which has barely one million people, workers in one EI region could access benefits after only 420 hours (Northern Saskatchewan), while those elsewhere would have to work at least 700 hours to qualify for EI benefits. Disparities in EI eligibility criteria as well as massive regional inequalities both within and among provinces create enduring political and territorial tensions, even though EI is entirely managed by the federal government and provinces have no formal veto point over its reform, unlike that of CPP. To a certain extent, variable eligibility criteria are a form of political accommodation of higher-unemployment regions and provinces. People from regions such as eastern Quebec and most of Atlantic Canada tend to mobilize politically to preserve such favorable criteria. Premiers and federal members of parliament representing economically disadvantaged districts are central to this type of mobilization, which can mean electoral losses for parties who dare to cut EI benefits, as the Liberals learned firsthand during the 1997 federal election, for example (Béland and Myles 2012; Hale 1998).

TABLE 1. Number of Hours of Insurable Employment Required to Qualify for Benefits

Regional Rate of Unemployment	Hours Required over the Past 52 Weeks
6% or less	700
6.1–7%	665
7.1–8%	630
8.1–9%	595
9.1–10%	560
10.1–11	525
11.1–12%	490
12.1–13%	455
13.1% or more	420

Source: Employment and Social Development Canada 2012, http://www.esdc.gc.ca/eng/jobs/ei/reports/mar2011/chapter1.shtml

Disparities in per capita spending exist among purely provincial programs but are less dramatic than might be expected. The existence of federal transfers and especially the federal equalization program helps less-well-off provinces choose to offer more adequate benefits and services to their population (Théret 2002). For example, in K–12 education policy, disparities among provinces in terms of services and spending patterns are relatively limited in scope. In 1999–2000, for example, combined provincial public and private education spending per K–12 student ranged from Can\$8,432 in Manitoba to Can\$6,239 in Prince Edward Island (in constant 2001 dollars) (Wallner 2014, 43). Looking at the evidence on provincial education spending in Canada, Jennifer Wallner (2014, 43) concludes that when all relevant factors are considered, "the provinces match one another's educational investments. Canadian variation is on par with unitary England and is considerably less than its federal counterparts, Germany and the United States, even though both are considered to be more centralized federations than Canada." Overall, as Wallner points out, the absence of a federal department of education in Canada has not created massive interprovincial inequalities in education spending in part because of the role of broad fiscal factors such as the federal equalization program, which provides special funding to less-well-off provinces.

Regarding social assistance, the Canada Assistance Plan provided a relatively loose federal fiscal and policy framework for provincial welfare programs from 1966 to 1995. Under the plan, Ottawa typically paid for 50 percent of provincial welfare benefits as long as the provinces met some broad conditions: "that need must be the sole basis for determining eligibility for income support, that provincial residency rules are prohibited, that there be an appeals system on social assistance decisions, that the provinces and the territories commit to data reporting and sharing, and that the federal transfers go only to supporting nonprofit provision of social services" (Prince 1998, 829 n. 5). The Canada Assistance Plan was abolished in 1996 and replaced by a block grant known today as the Social Transfer. Through this move, Ottawa removed all but one of the federal requirements for receiving money under the plan (the surviving condition involves residency). This change was intended to appease the provinces, especially Quebec, which was facing major cuts in federal transfers (Baker 1997).

The dismantlement of the Canada Assistance Program led to speculation about the possibility of an imminent race to the bottom among the provinces in welfare benefits. As Gerard Boychuk suggests (2015), however, there is no strong evidence that the elimination of most federal norms in itself affected provincial assistance in a strong negative way;

rather, the most important determinant of social assistance benefits over time is simply the fluctuation in unemployment rates. Overall, social assistance rates vary significantly from one province to another depending on the category of beneficiaries. Typically, parents and people with disabilities receive higher benefits on average than single, employable individuals. For example, in wealthy yet politically conservative Alberta, able-bodied individuals have long received lower benefits than in many other provinces, but the permanently disabled can now access the most generous payments in the country (Wood 2015). Overall, although social assistance benefits are generally meager and do not lift welfare recipients above existing poverty lines (Kneebone and White 2015), clear disparities across provinces are evident in the field of social assistance.

One policy area where the level of social protection offered is particularly uniform across the country is old-age security, in part because of the existence of Old-Age Security (OAS) as well as the Guaranteed Income Supplement (GIS). These purely federal social assistance programs were created in 1967 and apply to all citizens and permanent residents regardless of where they live. The CPP and Quebec Pension Plan (QPP) offers very similar benefits, including the same replacement rate of 25 percent of eligible wages, which is low by international standards. Beyond large federal programs such as OAS, GIS, and the CPP and QPP, which are by far the main source of public retirement security in Canada, provinces offer pension supplements for low-income seniors who qualify for GIS payments. Because provinces are free to set the levels of their pension supplements, they vary greatly, ranging from up to Can$280 per month in Alberta to only Can$33 per month in New Brunswick (Marier and Séguin 2015). It is not surprising that the wealthiest province, Alberta, spends the most on these pension supplements. Despite provincial variations in pension supplements and the strong reliance on private pension benefits unavailable to many workers, however, Canada has dramatically reduced its rate of senior poverty since the 1970s through the GIS, among other factors (Wiseman and Yčas 2008).

In some policy areas, constitutional autonomy has enabled some provinces to innovate, developing unique programs without direct equivalents in other provinces. Quebec, for example, implemented a universal child care program in the late 1990s, and it remains unique in North America. This program is based on a subsidy model, according to which most parents pay a flat fee of Can$7 per day for a child care spot, regardless of their income. Despite issues such as waiting lists, this program has proved popular in Quebec, where substate nationalist politicians tend to claim their province is more egalitarian while pushing for profamily policies aimed at increasing fertility to protect the demographic integrity of the province's French-speaking majority (Béland and Lecours 2008). Quantitative evidence suggests that Quebec has adopted more generous social programs in a number of policy areas such as labor-market activation and family benefits, resulting in social democratic spending patterns that are not observed in Alberta, British Columbia, and Ontario, other populous provinces that clearly remain within the liberal logic (Bernard and Saint-Arnaud 2004; Van den Berg et al. 2017).

Regarding territorial inequality and redistribution, the widely disadvantaged status of aboriginal peoples is a central social policy concern. From a socioeconomic standpoint, factors such as colonial legacies, discrimination, and geographical isolation have meant that aboriginal peoples, who comprised 4.3 percent of the population in 2011 (HRSDC 2014), face lower life expectancies, poorer health status, and much higher than average unemployment and poverty rates. The data regarding the educational outcomes of aboriginal people illustrate this disadvantage, which is especially striking for those who live on reserves: "more than 50 per cent of registered Indians living on reserve fail to complete high school, compared to 29 per cent of registered Indians living off-reserve, who are therefore educated in the provincial systems, and 10 per cent of the non-Aboriginal population" (Wallner 2014, 273 n. 4). Constitutionally, the Indian Act of 1876 grants the federal government jurisdiction over "status Indians" and "Indian reserves," which means it must fund education, housing, health care, and social assistance benefits for aboriginal people living on reserves. In the area of social assistance, federal payments adopt the benefit structure of the province in which the reserve is located. This policy, which is seldom debated, allows the federal government to offer aboriginal social assistance benefits that vary widely from one province to another (Papillon 2015).

The provinces play a greater role in social policy affecting aboriginal peoples, a growing percentage of whom (currently more than 40 percent) live outside the reserve system. Considering higher-than-average fertility rates and rising rates of urbanization among aboriginal peoples, provinces must step up their efforts to improve the education level and the health and socioeconomic profile of this growing segment of the Canadian population. This situation is particularly essential in the Prairie Provinces, Manitoba and Saskatchewan, in which aboriginal people represent more than 15 percent of the population, a share that is climbing. Paradoxically, these provinces are among those in which provincial social policy efforts targeting the aboriginal population are the least developed and most problematic (Laroque and Noël 2013).

Policy Change

From a historical standpoint, the institutional configuration of Canadian federalism helped slow down the development of the welfare state, especially with regard to countrywide programs (Banting 1987). The creation of several key federal social programs such as Unemployment Insurance and OAS became possible only after the enactment of a constitutional amendment and the resulting direct negotiations between Ottawa and the provinces. Yet there is another side to this story, as pressures from the provinces and the political dynamics of federal-provincial relations sometimes favored the expansion of the federal role in social policy financing (Théret 2002). This dynamic played a key role in the advent of the CPP and the creation of federal funding for hospital insurance in 1957 and for health insurance in 1966. In the case of health care, Saskatchewan and other provinces pressured Ottawa for financing help, and the federal government agreed in part because of the high level of party competition, which led to minority governments and the unusual political clout wielded by the Co-Operative Commonwealth Federation (the social democratic party) in the House of Commons in 1961 (Maioni 1998). Strong evidence indicates that pressure created by Quebec premier Jean Lesage's alternative proposal pushed the federal government to increase the CPP's proposed replacement rate from 20 to 25 percent as well as to make other changes (Babich and Béland 2009). This debate led to the creation of both CPP and QPP, with pension surpluses invested in the province's economy in the name of the statist form of substate nationalism that emerged in the province during the 1960s (Béland and Lecours 2008).

Thus, federalism has not been a key obstacle to welfare state development in and of itself in Canada since the 1940s. In fact, Canada's decentralized constitutional design and provincial veto points that prevented the creation of particular social programs before the Second World War sometimes later favored the expansion of federal social programming (Théret 2002). In 1937, for example, the Privy Council struck down federal legislation enacted two years earlier that would have created a national unemployment insurance system. This decision, which declared the legislation to be "beyond the powers of the federal government as grounded in the Constitution," forced the federal government to bargain with the provinces over the constitutional amendment that finally allowed Ottawa to implement a centralized unemployment insurance system (Rice and Prince 2013, 56). Conversely, during the 1960s, key policy decisions that expanded federal fiscal support to the provinces while preserving most of their policy autonomy were the product of intergovernmental relations that created a race to the top rather than the bottom, at least in policy areas such as health care and pensions (Simeon 1972; Théret 2002).

The contemporary territorial politics of social policy in Canada began in 1977 with the bold attempt to control federal spending in health care. No single pattern of change has subsequently emerged, in part because each policy area and even program tends to feature particular institutional design and territorial logics. A suitable way to illustrate this institutional diversity is to explore three episodes of policy change affecting distinct programs that belong to different types of territorial governance (Banting 2005).

First, the level of territorial conflict varies greatly from case to case in purely federal programs. On one hand, programs such as OAS lack a strong, explicitly territorial component as far as the politics of policy change is concerned. On the other hand, in part because of regional variation in eligibility criteria introduced in 1977, EI is a purely federal program that is a recurrent source of territorial conflict, at least when the federal government seeks to control costs and promote activation for the unemployed (Béland and Myles 2012). A striking example of this territorial politics of federal social policy is the major reform of unemployment benefits that took place in the mid-1990s. Jean Chrétien's Liberal government sought to cut social spending to balance the federal budget. In 1996, Unemployment Insurance officially became Employment Insurance, a new terminology reflecting a logic of activation characterized by benefit cuts and more stringent eligibility criteria (Campeau 2005).[1]

Although EI is a purely federal program, the benefit cuts in the 1996 reform created much political protest against the Chrétien government in high-unemployment regions, especially in the four Atlantic Provinces, where rates typically are significantly higher than the national average (MacDonald 1998). This backlash translated in major electoral losses for the Liberal Party during the 1997 federal election, thereby convincing the Chrétien government to reduce the negative impact of the 1996 EI reform on seasonal workers, who are overrepresented in the Atlantic Provinces (Clarkson 2001).

From a territorial and political standpoint, the 1996 EI reform is important not only because of the backlash it created in certain parts of the country but also because it did not dismantle the variable entrance requirement, which that creates uneven eligibility criteria across the 52 EI regions. The system makes territorial redistribution explicit while generating significant opposition in western provinces, where the unemployment rate is lower on average (with the exception of sparsely populated EI regions in northern Manitoba and Saskatchewan). The institutional legacies of EI, the constituencies the variable entrance requirement created over time, and ultimately strong political opposition to EI's dismantlement in certain regions of the country likely explains the resilience of this problematic unemployment insurance system (Béland and Myles 2012), an explanation consistent with the institutional institutionalist perspective on policy feedback (Pierson 1994).

Second, in the area of shared-cost programs, health care financing has been the most contentious issue in Canada for decades. Starting in 1977, the federal government moved from a 50–50 cost-sharing arrangement to a block-grant logic that throughout most of the 1980s and 1990s gradually reduced the percentage of health care spending for which Ottawa compensates the provinces. An especially dramatic episode was the 1995 federal budget, which dramatically slashed federal health and social transfers. This unilateral federal decision, which forced provincial governments to scramble to fill this large, sudden gap in anticipated transfers from Ottawa, triggered a strong provincial backlash against the Chrétien government (Béland and Lecours 2008).

This reaction ultimately created a provincial push for the formulation of what became known the Social Union Framework Agreement, an accord signed in February 1999 between Ottawa, the three territories, and 9 of the 10 provinces. Quebec decided to opt out of this intergovernmental framework, which it found overly centralizing and blind to the province's distinct cultural and political identity (Facal 2005). While the agreement represented a provincial attempt to reduce the level of federal unilateralism in fiscal and social policy matters, Quebec's exclusion from the agreement led to what Alain Noël (2000) has labeled "collaborative federalism with a footnote," a form of collaboration between Ottawa and the provinces in which Quebec does not participate. This logic exacerbates the asymmetrical nature of Canadian federalism, which has been based since the 1960s on Quebec's repeated withdrawal from federal initiatives with full fiscal compensation (Béland and Lecours 2008).

In the late 1990s and early 2000s, a new era of budget surpluses, the federal government increased health care funding while consulting with the provinces. That process peaked with the 2004 Health Accord, a 10-

year, Can$40-plus billion financing deal between Ottawa and the provinces that featured strategies to tackle pressing problems like excessive waiting times in exchange for the extra funding. Once again, this logic did not apply to Quebec, which received "federal funding with no real strings attached" after cleverly bargaining a special deal with rookie Liberal premier Paul Martin, who had replaced Chrétien in late 2003 (Gregg 2005).

When the time came to allocate federal health spending after the 2004 Health Accord expired, the Stephen Harper's Conservative government adopted a unilateral approach similar to the one adopted as part of the 1995 Liberal federal budget. Refusing to bargain over health funding with the provinces, and adopting a strict logic of territorial governance known as "open federalism" that downplays executive federalism in the name of a stricter division of functions between Ottawa and the provinces, the Harper government slowed down the anticipated increase in federal health funding over the 2004–14 period. Although provinces voiced their strong dissatisfaction with this return of pure federal unilateralism, the Harper government's decision regarding health funding, which was announced in 2011, had no strings attached, which seems consistent with the "open federalism" creed (Department of Finance Canada 2011). Shortly after taking office in early November 2015, the Justin Trudeau government (2015–) initiated consultations with the provinces with the aim of crafting a new health care funding framework. Although the federal government and the provinces ultimately failed to reach an agreement on a new framework, over time, Ottawa signed separate agreements with each of the provinces to moderately boost their federal health care funding on a case-by-case basis (Galloway 2017).

Finally, the main example of "joint decision federalism" (Banting 2005) is the mid-1990s reform of CPP. Facing growing demographic and fiscal challenges related to aging, federal and provincial officials began to work together on a reform aimed at restoring long-term fiscal balance in the CPP trust fund while maintaining future payroll contributions below 10 percent. A provision adopted a decade earlier required Ottawa and the provinces had to address CPP reform every five years (Jacobs 2011; Little 2008). In the name of intergenerational equity, Ottawa and most of the provinces agreed on an increase in CPP contribution rates, which gradually climbed by more than 50 percent to reach 9.9 percent in 2003. The increase allowed the accumulation of larger trust fund reserves to be invested through the newly created CPP Investment Board, an arms-length public organization whose main goal is to increase returns on investment to improve CPP's long-term sustainability. These measures and a number of indirect benefit cuts put the CPP back on track, from an actuarial standpoint, as the program is now projected to remain fiscally sound for at least 75 years.

The large increase in payroll contributions associated with the 1997 CPP reform did not generate a strong political backlash against the Chrétien government and the premiers who agreed on it, in part because the intergovernmental agreement leading to the reform helped federal and provincial officials to both share and diffuse potential blame for unpopular decisions (Béland and Myles 2012; on the politics of blame avoidance, see Weaver 1986 and Pierson 1994). Quebec agreed to implement a QPP reform modeled on the CPP one in order to maintain the high level of coordination that has existed between CPP and QPP since their inception in the mid-1960s (Tamagno 2008).[2] These examples point to a variety of institutional, territorial, and political patterns of policy change within Canada's asymmetrical, fragmented, and multilevel welfare state.

Conclusion

Canada is a highly decentralized federal country, a reality apparent in its fragmented social policy system, in which provinces play a central role. However, historical evidence suggests that since the 1940s, federalism has not posed a strong obstacle to welfare state expansion because competitive state building (Banting 1995) between Ottawa and the provinces stimulated the advent of a decentralized yet substantial welfare state (Maioni 1998; Théret 2002). Quebec has played a central role in these struggles, and the province has developed the country's most comprehensive set of social programs (Béland and Lecours 2008; Bernard and Saint-Arnaud 2004; Van den Berg et al. 2017). More specifically, Quebec has embraced a social-investment approach that has resulted in policies promoting activation and work-life balance that have resulted in both a significant reduction in family poverty and a transformation of the provincial welfare regime in the sense of a social-democratic logic distinct from the liberal logic that remains dominant in the other provinces (Van den Berg et al. 2017).

Despite the high average level of policy decentralization, the federal government is a key fiscal actor through its block grants and equalization program (Théret 2002). Moreover, that government is involved in the direct provision of social benefits and services to aboriginal peoples and members of the armed forces. The federal government also distributes major family, pension, and unemployment benefits to the general Canadian population. In a context of growing income inequality (Banting and Myles 2013) and under the Liberal government of Justin Trudeau (2015–), the federal government can still play a leadership role, but it must work with the provinces, which remain the most crucial policy actors in this decentralized polity (Atkinson et al. 2013).

NOTES

For comments and suggestions, the authors thank Scott Greer, André Lecours, Charles Plante, Alan Trench, Brad Pickard, and the participants in the University of Michigan workshops related to this volume. Daniel Béland acknowledges support from the Canada Research Chairs Program.

1. Simultaneously, the federal government put forward training and job creation measures. In 1997, it reached administrative agreements with five provinces, allowing them to manage employment measures financed through the federal EI fund (Campeau 2005). The five remaining provinces signed similar agreements with the federal government in the mid- to late 2000s.

2. In 2016, the federal government and most of the provinces agreed to modestly expand CPP benefits (with the replacement rate moving from 25 to 33.3 percent) through a gradual increase in payroll contributions. The following year, Quebec decided to increase QPP benefits along the same lines (Béland and Weaver 2017).

REFERENCES

Atkinson, Michael, Daniel Béland, Gregory P. Marchildon, Kathleen McNutt, Peter W.B. Phillips, and Ken Rasmussen. 2013. *Governance and Public Policy in Canada: A View from the Provinces*. Toronto: University of Toronto Press.

Babich, Kristina, and Daniel Béland. 2009. "Policy Change and the Politics of Ideas: The Emergence of the Canada/Québec Pension Plans." *Canadian Review of Sociology* 46 (3): 253–71.

Baker, Maureen. 1997. *The Restructuring of the Canadian Welfare State: Ideology and Policy*. Sydney: Social Policy Research Centre.

Banting, Keith. 1987. *Welfare State and Canadian Federalism*. Rev. ed. Montreal: McGill-Queen's University Press.

Banting, Keith. 1995. "The Welfare State as Statecraft: Territorial Politics and Canadian Social Policy." In Stephan Leibfried and Paul Pierson, eds., *European Social Policy: Between Fragmentation and Integration*, 269–300. Washington, DC: Brookings Institution.

Banting, Keith. 2005. "Canada: Nation-Building in a Federal Welfare State." In Herbert Obinger, Stephan Leibfried, and Frank G. Castles, eds., *Federalism and the Welfare State: New World and European Experiences*, 89–137. Cambridge: Cambridge University Press.

Banting, Keith, and John Myles, eds. 2013. *Inequality and the Fading of Redistributive Politics*. Vancouver: University of British Columbia Press.

Béland, Daniel, and André Lecours. 2008. *Nationalism and Social Policy: The Politics of Territorial Solidarity*. Oxford: Oxford University Press.

Béland, Daniel, and John Myles. 2012. "Varieties of Federalism, Institutional Legacies, and Social Policy: Comparing Old-Age and Unemployment Insurance Reform in Canada." *International Journal of Social Welfare* 21 (S1): S75–S87.

Béland, Daniel, and R. Kent Weaver. 2017. "Fork in the Road for Canada and Quebec Pension Plans." *Policy Options*, August 18. http://policyoptions.irpp.org/magazines/august-2017/fork-road-canada-quebec-pension-plans/

Bernard, Paul, and Sébastien Saint-Arnaud. 2004. *More of the Same? The Position of the Four Largest Canadian Provinces in the World of Welfare Regimes*. Ottawa: Canadian Policy Research Networks. http://www.cprn.org/documents/32764_en.pdf

Boychuk, Gerard W. 2008. *National Health Insurance: Race, Territory, and the Development of Public Health Insurance in the United States and Canada*. Washington, DC: Georgetown University Press.

Boychuk, Gerard W. 2015. "The Histories of Provincial Social Assistance, 1985–2013." In Daniel Béland and Pierre-Marc Daigneault, eds., *Welfare Reform in Canada: Provincial Social Assistance in Comparative Perspective*. Toronto: University of Toronto Press.

Canadian Institute for Health Information. 2014. *National Health Expenditure Trends, 1975 to 2014*. Ottawa: Canadian Institute for Health information. https://www.cihi.ca/en/nhex_2014_report_en.pdf

Clarkson, Stephen. 2001. "The Liberal Threepeat: The Multi-System Party in the Multi-Party System." In Jon H. Pammett and Christopher Dornan, eds., *The Canadian General Election of 2000*, 13–58. Toronto: Dundurn Press.

Department of Finance Canada. 2011. *Harper Government Announces Major New Investment in Health Care*. December 19. Ottawa. http://www.fin.gc.ca/n11/11-141-eng.asp

Department of Finance Canada. 2013. *Federal Support to Provinces and Territories*. Ottawa. http://www.fin.gc.ca/fedprov/mtp-eng.asp

Employment and Social Development Canada. 2012. *Employment Insurance Monitoring and Assessment Report 2011*. http://publications.gc.ca/collections/collection_2012/rhdcc-hrsdc/HS1-2-2011-eng.pdf

Facal, Joseph. 2005. *Social Policy and Intergovernmental Relations in Canada: Understanding the Failure of SUFA from a Quebec Perspective*. Regina: Saskatchewan Institute of Public Policy (Public Policy Paper 32). http://www.uregina.ca/sipp/documents/pdf/PPP32_Facal.pdf

Galloway, Gloria. 2017. "Health Accord Nearly Sealed as Ontario, Quebec, Alberta Reach Deals." *Globe and Mail*, March 10. https://www.theglobeandmail.com/news/politics/ontario-quebec-alberta-reach-health-deals-with-ottawa/article34264300/

Gregg, Allan. 2005. "Quebec's Final Victory." *The Walrus*, February. http://walrusmagazine.com/articles/2005.02-politics-health-care-problem/

Hale, Geoffrey E. 1998. "Reforming Employment Insurance: Transcending the Politics of the Status Quo." *Canadian Public Policy* 24 (4): 429–51.

Health Canada. 2012. "Canada's Health Care System." http://www.hc-sc.gc.ca/hcs-sss/pubs/system-regime/2011-hcs-sss/index-eng.php

HRSDC. 2014. *Canadians in Context: Aboriginal Population*. Ottawa: Employment and Social Development Canada. http://www4.hrsdc.gc.ca/.3ndic.1t.4r@-eng.jsp?iid=36

Jacobs, Alan M. 2011. *Governing for the Long Term: Democracy and the Politics of Investment*. New York: Cambridge University Press.

Kneebone, Ronald, and Katherine White. 2015. "An Overview of Social Assistance Trends." In Daniel Béland and Pierre-Marc Daigneault, eds., *Welfare Reform in Canada: Provincial Social Assistance in Comparative Perspective*, 53–92. Toronto: University of Toronto Press.

Larocque, Florence, and Alain Noël. 2013. "Kelowna's Uneven Legacy: Federalism and Aboriginal Poverty in Canada." Paper presented at the annual meeting of the Canadian Political Science Association, University of Victoria, June 4.

Lecours, André, and Daniel Béland. 2010. "Federalism and Fiscal Policy: The Politics of Equalization in Canada." *Publius: The Journal of Federalism* 40 (4): 569–96.

Little, Bruce. 2008. *Fixing the Future: How Canada's Usually Fractious Governments Worked Together to Rescue the Canada Pension Plan*. Toronto: University of Toronto Press.

MacDonald, Maureen. 1998. "The Impact of a Restructured Canadian Welfare State on Atlantic Canada." *Social Policy and Administration* 32 (4): 389–400.

Maioni, Antonia. 1998. *Parting at the Crossroads: The Emergence of Health Insurance in the United States and Canada*. Princeton: Princeton University Press.

Marchildon, Gregory, and Haizhen Mou. 2013. "The Funding Formula for Health Care Is Broken: Alberta's Windfall Proves It." *Globe and Mail*, October 9.

Marier, Patrik, and Anne-Marie Séguin. 2015. "Aging and Social Assistance in the Provinces." In Daniel Béland and Pierre-Marc Daigneault, eds., *Welfare Reform in Canada: Provincial Social Assistance in Comparative Perspective*, 339–52. Toronto: University of Toronto Press.

Matier, Chris. 2012. *Renewing the Canada Health Transfer: Implications for Federal and Provincial-Territorial Fiscal Sustainability*. Ottawa: Office of the Parliamentary Budget Officer. http://www.pbo-dpb.gc.ca/files/files/Publications/Renewing_CHT.pdf

National Health Expenditure Trends, 1975 to 2014. 2014. Ottawa: Canadian Institute for Health Information. https://www.cihi.ca/en/nhex_2014_report_en.pdf

Noël, Alain. 2000. *Without Quebec: Collaborative Federalism with a Footnote?* Montreal: Institute for Research on Public Policy.

Papillon, Martin. 2015. "Playing Catch-Up with Ghosts: Income Assistance for First Nations on Reserve." In Daniel Béland and Pierre-Marc Daigneault, eds., *Welfare Reform in Canada: Provincial Social Assistance in Comparative Perspective*, 323–38. Toronto: University of Toronto Press.

Pierson, Paul. 1994. *Dismantling the Welfare State? Reagan, Thatcher, and the Politics of Retrenchment*. New York: Cambridge University Press.

Prince, Michael J. 1998. "Holes in the Safety Net, Leaks in the Roof: Changes in Canadian Welfare Policy and Their Implications for Social Housing Programs." *Housing Policy Debate* 9 (4): 825–48.

Rice, James J., and Michael J. Prince. 2013. *Changing Politics of Canadian Social Policy*. 2nd ed. Toronto: University of Toronto Press.

Simeon, Richard. 1972. *Federal-Provincial Diplomacy: The Making of Recent Policy in Canada*. Toronto: University of Toronto Press.

Tamagno, Edward. 2008. *A Tale of Two Pension Plans: The Differing Fortunes of the Canada and Quebec Pension Plans*. Ottawa: Caledon Institute. http://www.caledoninst.org/Publications/PDF/667ENG.pdf

Telford, Hamish. 2003. "The Federal Spending Power in Canada: Nation-Building or Nation-Destroying?" *Publius: The Journal of Federalism* 33 (1): 23–44.

Théret, Bruno. 2002. *Protection Sociale et Fédéralisme: L'Europe dans le Miroir de l'Amérique du Nord*. Montreal: Presses de l'Université de Montréal and Peter Lang.

Van den Berg, Axel, Charles Plante, Christine Proulx, Hicham Raïq, and Samuel Faustmann. 2017. *Combating Poverty: Quebec's Pursuit of a Distinctive Welfare State*. Toronto: University of Toronto Press.

Wallner, Jennifer. 2014. *Learning to School: Federalism and Public Schooling in Canada*. Toronto: University of Toronto Press.

Weaver, R. Kent. 1986. "The Politics of Blame Avoidance." *Journal of Public Policy* 6 (4): 371–98.

Wiseman, Michael, and Martynas Yčas. 2008. "The Canadian Safety Net for the Elderly." *Social Security Bulletin* 68 (2): 53–67. www.ssa.gov/policy/docs/ssb/v68n2/v68n2p53.pdf

Wood, Donna E. 2015. "The State of Social Assistance in Alberta." In Daniel Béland and Pierre-Marc Daigneault, ed., *Welfare Reform in Canada: Provincial Social Assistance in Comparative Perspective*, 161–76. Toronto: University of Toronto Press.

Fiscal Federalism and Redistribution in Mexico

Alberto Díaz-Cayeros

Fiscal federalism in Mexico has been designed to ensure cohesion among unequal constituent units (both states and municipalities) through a mildly redistributive system of revenue sharing and relatively large social expenditure transfers for education, health, and social infrastructure provided by the federal government. However, the Mexican transfer system is not particularly redistributive. It does not achieve anything resembling a German *Finanzausgleich* or the equalization grants that underpin Canada's social union. State governments also do not provide a subnational welfare state. Notwithstanding the massive intergovernmental transfers and federal programs aimed at poverty alleviation, Mexico one of the most unequal federations in the world in terms of both regional inequality and personal income distribution. After the transition from hegemonic party rule to democracy in 2000, the system of federal transfers grew but did not become more redistributive. Despite decades of reform to fiscal federalism, regional inequality across states remains virtually unchanged.

That neither fiscal equalization (revenue sharing) nor federal social expenditures has done much to reduce personal income and regional inequality is intrinsically related to Mexican politics. Political institutions ensured that territorial interests have weak channels for representation, even under democratic rule. Politically, fiscal federalism has been used to play states against each other on the premise that any effort at redistribution involves a zero-sum game. A system of representation that until 2018 did not allow for reelection produced weak linkages between local and state politicians and their citizens. States had no incentive to innovate in exercising spending powers or to reassert authority over tax collection. State public finances are almost completely dependent on federal revenue sharing and social transfers. Although some of the most critical social expenditures for health, education, and local public goods provision have been decentralized to subnational governments, local authorities perceive these services not as requiring responsiveness to local constituencies but rather as forms of administrative delegation of functions they would rather not undertake. In short, the federal fiscal architecture produces little accountability to citizens, and transfers are driven primarily by a bureaucratic effort to provide resources through administrative devolution rather than by the goal of strengthening state autonomy with a supplementary federal compensatory role. (For a good framework for understanding this type of arrangement in Latin America, see Falleti 2010.)

The Mexican Fiscal Federalism Pact

Since its inception, the Mexico's federal system has been more centralized than other federations around the world. This does not mean, however, that Mexican states have not asserted their regional autonomy. Regional tensions do not surface often, but states and governors have been critical veto players throughout the country's history despite a high degree of fiscal centralization. The federal arrangement is not simply a copy of the U.S. model, as many critics have suggested, but is deeply rooted in regional differences exhibited since colonial (and perhaps even pre-Hispanic) times. Mexican states originated in the restructuring of colonial subnational administrative units by the Bourbon reforms of the 1760s, which created the system of *intendencias* (Pietschmann 1996). That system, in turn, led through the Cadiz Constitution to the provincial deputies of 1808. When the country achieved independence in 1821, the territorial map of the federal system basically followed those colonial subdivisions. Admiration for the U.S. federal model loomed large in debates between centralist and federalist factions during the newly independent country's first decades. However, contrary to an often-quoted misconception, the federal arrangement was not an artificial liberal imposition but rather was in keeping with the previous political traditions of regional autonomy and indirect rule, both under Spanish colonialism tutelage of Spain (Benson 2010) and after independence.

Fiscal centralization increased throughout the 19th century (Carmagnani 1994), with federal control of customs duties and the elimination of domestic taxes on trade (the *alcabala*) in 1857. Analogous processes of fiscal centralization occurred in Europe and the rest of Latin America.

But over the 20th century, the Mexican federal government's tax and spending powers grew enormously, making the states and municipalities highly dependent on federal transfers. Innovations in fiscal technology, such as income taxation in the 1930s, a national sales tax in 1954, and the introduction of the value-added tax in 1980, coupled with the bonanza coming from oil revenues in the late 1970s, shifted the fiscal system to one where the federal government collected almost all taxes while states and municipalities financed public goods and services through transfers from higher levels of government (Díaz-Cayeros 2006). Transfer dependence of subnational governments is arguably the most distinctive trait of the Mexican arrangement, and it has occupied most of the debates regarding decentralization and federalism since the 1990s (Courchene and Díaz-Cayeros 2000).

Figure 1 shows the evolution of revenue-sharing and expenditure-transfer funds in Mexico over the past two decades. The increase in the size of the transfers is briefly interrupted by major macroeconomic crises in 1995 and 2009. Most of the significant increase in transfers after 1997 resulted from conditional federal transfers that were not formally decentralized by law. The sustained increase in federal funding available to the states can be traced back to processes that began in the 1980s but became particularly significant in the 1990s, a decade of decentralization and democratization that culminated in the first partisan alternation in presidential control in 2000.

Fiscal federalism in Mexico is not a zero-sum game, even though from a static perspective state finance ministers and governors often conceive it in those terms. Figure 1 shows that in inflation-adjusted pesos, the size of the fiscal pie available to states has increased almost every year. Incremental resources could have allowed shifts in the design of the federal transfers over those decades, but the system's overall fiscal architecture has changed very little in the past three decades. Even the 1995 reforms, which ushered in far-reaching changes to federal transfers, did not fundamentally modify the terms of the federal fiscal arrangement. Almost all revenue is collected by the federal government, while states finance most of their own budget spending from a mix of unconditional and conditional federal transfers.[1]

The Ley de Coordinacion Fiscal (LCF) is the most important legal provision determining the architecture of fiscal federalism in Mexico. In contrast to constitutional provisions, no special majority is required to change that law. Although the precedents of revenue sharing date back to the 19th century, the current law came into force only in 1980, with the introduc-

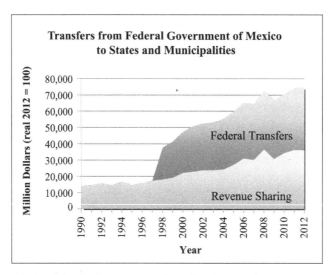

Fig. 1. Trend of Fiscal Transfers in Mexico (in deflated pesos of 2012, measured in U.S.$ for the sake of international comparability)

tion of the value-added tax. The legislature has modified the LCF to allow new funds to be added in various budgetary rounds since 1995. The most important legal amendment occurred in 1998, when the law was expanded to include not only revenue sharing but also expenditure transfers for education, health, and social infrastructure. Recent amendments have added federal funds for public safety. But the reforms have never questioned the overall logic of fiscal federalism. Revamping the revenue-sharing law to allow states greater fiscal authority—changing the inertia in the distribution of funds across states—has proved politically difficult. Governors have articulated a rhetoric that assumes that any change in the system of fiscal federalism is zero-sum. This has meant that some majority of states has usually opposed any reform that would threaten their historically allocated revenue shares. Adding new funds has been easy; changing the existing ones has proven all but impossible.

States are part of the revenue-sharing system based on a contract, the *convenio de adhesion*, that establishes that they voluntarily join the revenue-sharing system. This means that the fiscal federal arrangement is not established at the constitutional level but emerges as a voluntary agreement between states and the federal government. Although states could, in principle, exit the revenue-sharing system, the LCF contains a provision that makes withdrawing prohibitively costly: federal taxes would continue to be levied in these states that exited the system, so revenue shares are calculated as though the state were still in the system, and residual revenue remains with the federation. Exiting thus implies an increase in the tax burden for citizens in the exiting state and smaller federal transfers for all remaining states. Threats to abandon the revenue-sharing system hence are not particularly credible. States and local-government dependence on federal transfers may be reformed on if a substantial number of states coordinate to threaten a simultaneous withdrawal from the system. But such coordination is unlikely given cross-cutting divisions among states in levels of wealth, exposure to trade, and partisan alignments.

The LCF establishes revenue and social expenditure funds that constitute the fundamental basis of the Mexican federal fiscal architecture:

- Fondo General de Participaciones, which receives 20 percent of the federal shareable revenue (most tax revenue, excluding extraordinary oil rents) and is allocated to states via a complex formula that includes a marginal reward for tax-collection efforts.
- Fondo de Fomento Municipal, which receives 1 percent of the federal shareable revenue, to be allocated directly by the federal government to the municipalities.
- Fondo de Aportaciones para la Nomina Educativa y Gasto Operativo, an education transfer determined in the annual federal budget according to a formula dominated by the appropriations from the previous year.
- Fondo de Aportaciones para los Servicios de Salud, a health transfer, also determined in the annual federal budget.
- Fondo de Aportaciones para la Infraestructura Social, which receives 2.5294 percent of the federal shareable revenue, is to be used for local public works, and is determined by a formula based on social-deprivation indicators.
- Fondo de Aportaciones para el Fortalecimiento de los Municipios y de las Demarcaciones Territoriales del Distrito Federal, which receives2.5623 percent of the federal shareable revenue; is to be used for debt relief, public security, and other local (municipal) priorities; and is allocated in proportion to population.
- Fondo de Aportaciones Múltiples, which receives 0.814 percent of federal shareable revenue and is used for social assistance, including school lunches.

- Fondo de Aportaciones para la Educación Tecnológica y de Adultos, a small fund appropriated in the annual federal budget.
- Fondo de Aportaciones para la Seguridad Pública de los Estados y del Distrito Federal, a fund for public safety appropriated in the annual federal budget, similar in size to the Fondo de Aportaciones para la Infraestructura Social, and allocated according to a formula that includes indicators of efforts to reduce crime and improve safety.
- Fondo de Aportaciones para el Fortalecimiento de las Entidades Federativas, an open-ended fund that can be used for public works, pension reform, public security, science and technology, and other state priorities.

With only a few exceptions, the constitution does not establish exclusive tax powers for any level of government. The federal government has exclusive power to impose taxes related to foreign trade and oil revenues. Municipalities have exclusive authority to levy property taxes. Most such taxes are urban, since no taxes can be levied on *ejidos*, the collectives that account for the majority of rural landholdings. Hence, income and sales taxes are, from a constitutional standpoint, based on concurrent authority. Revenue collected from these taxes is shared with states and municipalities. However, the provision establishing that oil revenues are exclusively levied by the federal government has very important implications for the revenue-sharing system.

States and municipalities have shared in the windfalls of natural resource rents through the revenue-sharing and expenditure-transfer systems. These rents lie at the core of the fiscal bargain. This is not a constitutional bargain established at the time of the foundation of the federation but a political equilibrium maintained during decades when the price of oil was high. Municipalities are guaranteed revenue shares at the constitutional level, which means that states cannot freely determine all aspects of municipal regulation. There are no explicit constitutional restrictions to state or municipal debt. However, the fact that local and state governments are highly dependent on federal transfers limits their capacity to access debt through financial markets. The constitution contains no explicit provisions regarding subsidiarity. The distributive characteristics of the system are determined primarily by the formulas through which revenue sharing is allocated to the states and municipalities and the formulas for the allocation of the large array of social funds in the LCF involving various degrees of redistribution.

Redistribution in Mexican Federalism

Mexico is marked by a large degree of regional and personal inequality. The simplest measure of personal inequality is the widely used Gini coefficient. Gini indexes are not particularly sensitive to changes in the extremes of the distribution (neither the highest incomes nor the households in extreme poverty).[2] One of the best cross-national reconstructions of Gini coefficients around the world is provided by Solt (2016), who assembled all available information over long periods of time, providing both point estimates and confidence intervals for the calculation of inequality measures.

Figure 2 shows the evolution of personal inequality in Mexico since the 1960s. The 95 percent confidence intervals shown in the graph suggest the existence of substantial uncertainty regarding the true measure of inequality in Mexico before the 1990s. Income distribution surveys have improved to the point where one can be quite confident in assessing that inequality grew more or less steadily until a peak in 2000 but has subsequently decreased, stabilizing at around 0.46.

The figure also shows the existence of a wedge between market and net income after 2000, presumably driven by the state's redistributive role in various forms of social spending, particularly the emergence of conditional cash transfer programs that comprise a sizeable part of the net income of households in the lowest deciles of the income distribution. Although the reduction in inequality has been good news for the poor not just in Mexico but throughout Latin America (Lustig, Lopez Calva, and Ortiz Juarez 2013), these levels of Gini coefficients remain among the world's largest.

Esquivel (2015) succinctly analyzes some of the reasons behind the persistent inequality, including the trends toward concentration of wealth in the top 1 percent, an extremely low minimum wage, ethnic discrimination, the dismal social conditions faced by indigenous peoples, forced migratory pressures induced by criminal violence, and the education attainment gap generated by insufficient funding to public schools.

Panel B in figure 2 shows a different dimension of inequality—that is, the territorial dispersion of wealth across states. The horizontal axis shows the non-mining (i.e., excluding oil and other extractive activities) per capita GDP of each state, calculated in 2003. The size of each state is represented by its population.[3] The vertical axis is the growth rate for the economy of each state, as an annual rate, for the period 2003–2011. The literature on economic growth uses such graphs depicting countries ordered according to the initial level of development as a means of indicat-

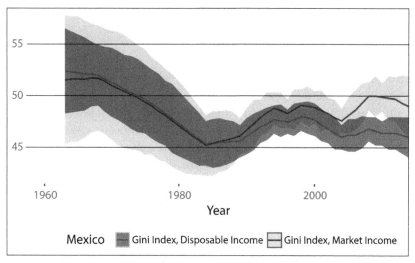

A) Personal Income Inequality (Gini Index)

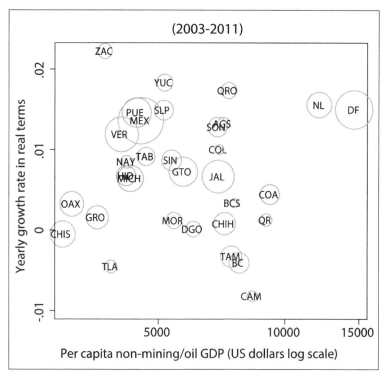

B) Regional Inequality

Fig. 2. Evolution of Personal and Regional Inequality in Mexico

Source: Data for (A) Gini index from SWIID (Solt 2016); (B) GDP per capita and growth rates are own calculations based on data from INEGI.

ing a trend toward economic convergence. If this type of convergence exists—that is, if poorer countries (states or regions) grow at faster rates than rich ones—the graph slopes downward. Figure 2 suggests that Mexico has not trended toward regional convergence over the past decade.

This persistence of territorial inequality has received some attention but has usually been regarded as a temporary phenomenon. Observers at least as far back as Simon Kuznets have argued that market forces will eventually generate some equalization across regions as resources, labor in the form of migration, and financial capital through investment flows. Furthermore, frequent arguments contend that government interventions in the provision of public goods at a national level will push toward regional equalization. However, Beramendi, Díaz-Cayeros, and Ziegler (2016) have suggested that Latin American federations are characterized by a tension between horizontal and redistributive pressures, meaning that transfers tend to become allocated between regions rather than redressing the (highly unequal) personal distribution of income. When poor regions receive transfers, they are often captured by the rich and consequently fail to generate greater equality. Hence, Latin American fiscal federalism transfer systems have tended to perpetuate rather than reduce inequality. Furthermore, the Latin American federations are not redistributive as a consequence of intrinsic links to political institutions and the system of representation.

Mexico's federal system is in large part a result of pre-1898 political hegemony, in which one political party controlled all levels of government. The structure of representative institutions weakens the expression of the interests of poor citizens in the states. Governors have had little incentive to promote territorial claims. From 1929 to 1989, the Partido Revolucionario Institucional (PRI) controlled all governorships, the majority in all the legislatures, and virtually all municipal governments. The party line and the priorities of the federal administration, embodied in the president, powerfully determined the shape of the fiscal system. Although party hegemony is now a thing of the past, legislative institutions still reflect this weak territoriality.

The Senate, which should ideally be well suited to represent the states, has no role in passing the revenue side of the budget bill (i.e., only the lower house votes on the Ley de Ingresos). And the rules for the Senate composition are more likely to represent partisan rather than regional interests. One-quarter of the Senate's members are elected from a national-level party list through proportional representations, while the remainder comprises three members from each state. This binomial formula with a single fused ballot establishes that the first two senators go to the party that won a majority in each state, while the third seat goes to the first losing party. Political parties control the candidate nominations. Hence, candidates at the top of a state formula or in a highly ranked position in the proportional representation list are likely to be beholden to partisan rather than regional interests. The majority of the senators owe their seats to the party's positioning rather than to the popular vote (Díaz-Cayeros 2005).

The lower house also does not represent the interests of poor voters. Proportional representation candidates elected through five regional lists account for two-fifths of the members of the Chamber of Deputies, while the remainder come from single-member districts. Without the possibility of reelection, members of Congress have been more interested in advancing their political careers representing broad groups within their parties rather than catering to territorially concentrated interests in the poor states. The 2013 political reforms permit deputies, senators, and mayors to seek reelection starting in 2018, a change that will likely have a major impact on incentives for territorial representation. But even the reelection reforms envisage term limits, which probably imply that the territorial incentives for representation of local interests will remain somewhat muted.

The previous absence of reelection at all levels of government constituted a path-dependent outcome from a process that was integral to the stability of the hegemonic party regime that controlled Mexican politics for almost 70 years. In 1928, one of the revolutionary leaders sought reelection notwithstanding the fact that the civil war had been fought precisely to prevent any single individual from taking up permanent residence in the presidential palace. The revolutionary leader became president-elect but was then murdered, sinking the country into a deep political crisis. Revolutionary leaders subsequently became convinced that forbidding reelection would allow political elites to circulate through office yet ensure that the party could control nominations. This rule became an integral part of party discipline in the legislature, within a fragmented federal system, since all politicians from the hegemonic party, the PRI, knew that their career advancement depended on obeying party lines. The prohibition on reelection was a foundational piece of the regime, bringing substantial stability even though it reinforced many of the system's nondemocratic features. Power became concentrated in the figure of the president, who controlled nominations. This control was particularly stark in the case of governors, who depended on the presidential nomination for their posts. The PRI often committed electoral fraud and suppressed the opposition, so a gubernatorial nomination was equivalent to a direct presidential appointment (Díaz-Cayeros 2016).

Despite the muted constitutional provisions for territorial representation, after 1989 democratically elected governors have increasingly played a prominent role in the federal pact. Governors are directly elected in their states and since the onset of democratization have been actively involved in the debates regarding fiscal federalism, influencing state legislators to advance territorial interests. The revenue-sharing law provides for regularly scheduled meetings of state finance ministers throughout the year (the Reunion de la Comision Permanente de Funcionarios Fiscales), although such gatherings are often dominated by federal government officials. The agreements and decisions reached in these meetings are not binding. But there is a far more powerful organization of governors, the Conferencia Nacional de Gobernadores. Though initially started by opposition governors, as a means to present a unified front vis-à-vis the federal government, the Conferencia has become a forum where governors from all parties gather regularly to discuss issues of fiscal federalism. This organization has no binding authority or in fact any legal standing at a constitutional level. But lacking senatorial representation, states exert pressure as an organized interest group on the federal government through this body. Some of the changes in fiscal federalism—in particular, the creation of new transfer funds—can be directly attributed to pressure exerted by the group.

Dynamics of Change in Mexican Fiscal Federalism

The Mexican Constitution establishes a concurrent character for all levels of government on most policy areas and spending responsibilities. But because revenue authority is concentrated with the federal government, it controls social spending. Mexico is a centralized federation with limited state autonomy, particularly on the revenue side. Despite a comprehensive system of intergovernmental transfers, centralization was enhanced by federal government's political dominance in determining spending priorities for the states. This does not mean, however, that the system is static.

Centralization in Mexico is a consequence not of specific constitutional provisions but of political bargains that can shift over time. States have the constitutional authority to levy income, consumption, and sales taxes. Furthermore, both municipalities and states are free to manage their own budgets. States have not exercised autonomous fiscal authority because of an implicit fiscal bargain struck with the federal government, gradually throughout the 20th century and more decisively when the current revenue-sharing law (the LCF) was passed in 1979. The LCF is primarily a political agreement between states and the federal government in which politicians at the local level agreed to forgo their capacity to tax in exchange for transfers from the top (Díaz-Cayeros 2016). The credibility of this transfer system hinged on a particular configuration of Mexican politics, where the hegemonic party, the PRI, controlled all public offices and political careers. The availability of oil revenue rents made this deal attractive to the states.

Despite the centralization of Mexican federalism during much of the 20th century, recent decades have seen a trend toward decentralizing reforms in 1983–84 and 1994–98. Reforms have left tax centralization untouched and hence have mechanically increased states' and municipalities' dependence on federal transfers. This has been a consequence not of constitutional rigidities or special majorities necessary to change the constitution but rather of the reluctance of local and state decision makers to pay the political costs of collecting more revenue along with an unwillingness by the federal government to make agreements involving tax sharing on the basis of a unified national administration of the main federal taxes. But the reforms have increased substantially the resources available to local and state governments for the provision of education, health, social infrastructure, and public safety, to name some of their largest expenditures.

The main thrust for reform in the federal system is related to a change in the political regime. As democratization advanced in the 1990s, the federal system became stressed, with states and municipalities demanding greater decentralization. The federal government dealt with these pressures by increasing federal expenditure transfers while promoting decentralization in health, education, public works, and citizen safety spending.[4] The federal government had the fiscal space to increase expenditure funds to states while continuing to control the overall patterns of spending to a large extent because of the fiscal system's reliance on oil revenue, which is fully controlled by the federal government.

The credibility of the current transfer system no longer depends on partisan attachments but rather hinges on a complex set of rules and regulations contained in secondary law. Although specific revenue-sharing provisions for some taxes are embedded in the constitution, revenue-sharing funds are distributed across states and municipalities not so much on the basis of a derivation principle as on equal per capita terms. This reflects strong norms among all political actors. They agree on the desirability of keeping a mildly redistributive system in place and making only marginal changes, consequently leaving the overall distribution of revenue-sharing funds across states relatively unchanged over the past three decades.

The Mexican Constitution does not include a subsidiarity clause. Residual powers are in fact vested in the states unless explicitly granted to the federal government. The redistributive character of the Mexican system is a consequence of political forces, not institutional ones. Federal transfers coming from revenue sharing are determined by a formula that is proportional to population (and the inertia of past revenue shares and the initial revenue collected by the states when the system was established in 1979). The other federal social transfers on the expenditure side are driven by formulas specific to each policy area (through specific funds for education, health, basic infrastructure, and public safety, among others). The distribution of each fund reflects deals reached between the states and the federal government when the funds were created. Those usually were not determined on a state-by-state basis but rather emerged from negotiations involving the representatives in the Chamber of Deputies.

In addition, rents from natural resources, specifically oil, are not shared in a particularly progressive way. Revenue-sharing funds comprise 21 percent of federal shareable revenue—the personal and corporate income tax, value-added tax, and most oil rents. Around one-fifth of these funds are transferred directly to municipalities, which means that states cannot reduce the funds available to that level of government out of the federal revenue sharing, although states can determine how those funds are distributed among municipalities via to state level revenue-sharing formulas.

On the expenditure side, the largest federal fund was created with the decentralization of education in 1994. Education transfers are primarily driven by the size of decentralized teacher payrolls and the historic presence or absence of state-level school systems (Hecock 2006). States have historically varied on whether they appropriate funds from their own budgets to pay for elementary and secondary school systems due to path-dependent processes that have received relatively little scholarly attention. At the beginning of the 20th century, most elementary schools were operated either by states or by municipalities (usually the capital cities of each state). With the expansion of federal education after the 1920s, some states abandoned their education systems, while others maintained their own schools for at least five or six more decades. Municipal schools were eventually absorbed by the states, but by the 1990s, some rich states (e.g., Nuevo Leon) provided around half of the school enrollments, while many poor states basically relied on federal schools and teachers. (Oaxaca, for example, had no state educational system.) There is no evidence that the relative weight of the state educational systems on the overall enrollment had any effect on student performance, but it does mean that the transfers provided by the federal government for education are unequal, reflecting the variation in the compensatory role federal expenditures played in each state (Merino 1999).

Health transfers emerged from two processes of decentralization—a failed one in 1984, and a more successful one in the 1990s (Homedes and Ugalde 2006). The distribution of health transfers depends on the clinics and health facilities transferred to the states with the decentralization processes of 1996. Since 1998, social infrastructure transfers depend on poverty formulas calculated at the municipal level. Additional transfers are allocated for public safety, school construction, debt relief, and other local government functions. These funds were consolidated into a single federal budgetary item (Ramo 33) and incorporated as an additional chapter of the revenue-sharing law in 1998.

An important effort at reform was made in the 1980s. As oil prices collapsed, Mexico was saddled with debt and experienced a profound recession. While the federal government continued to play a major role in steering economic affairs, some decentralization was attempted in the health sector, and municipal governments received greater autonomy than ever before. The health decentralization failed because around half of the states were unwilling to take over the health sectors offered by the federal government. But the municipal reform was largely successful. While in principle municipalities controlled the property tax, in practice many states had taken over this crucial source of local taxation. The reform ensured that municipalities would control the property tax and could henceforth use the flow of their own revenue (rather than revenue shares) more effectively as a guarantee for municipal debt. There was also a lack of clarity regarding the functions municipalities were expected to perform. The constitution clarified these functions, empowering mayors vis-à-vis their governors.

Another far-reaching process of decentralization took place between 1994 and 1996 and first involved the decentralization of education services and schools (usually referred in Mexico by the misnomer *federalización educativa*) to the states and then involved an effort to fix the aborted decentralization of health services and clinics to the states. Those reforms succeeded in the sense that they represented a very large inflow of resources to the states, but they also carried a mandate to provide services, without the freedom to change many of the existing structures in the education or health sectors as a consequence of the concurrent character of these responsibilities envisaged in the constitution (Falleti 2010). Compounding the weak authority of the states on health and education policy, teacher, doctor, and nurse salaries continued to be negotiated with the powerful national unions at the central level. Thus, the decentralization of these services did not mean a greater opportunity for innovation and reform in the provision of these services.

The most comprehensive institutional reform of expenditure transfers occurred in 1998, when all the various expenditure-transfer funds were concentrated under a new budgetary item and regulated explicitly in a new chapter of the LCF. The driving force for the reform was political. In 1997, the PRI lost the control of the federal legislature it had maintained for almost 70 years. Though no political party had a majority, the opposition parties saw an opportunity to modify the way in which budgetary decisions had been traditionally made. Since Mexico does not have a clear reversion point for what might happen if no federal budget is passed, the legislators did not want to jeopardize passage of a federal budget with distributive debates regarding fiscal federalism. The debate consequently shifted away from the budgetary allocations for each year and toward the creation of transparent and easily reproducible formulas for the distribution of the most important federal transfers. The new chapter of the LCF and the creation of a new type of fund (*aportaciones*) was meant to clarify and coordinate expectations regarding the distribution of federal funds. Health and education funds would primarily be distributed according to the shares that had historically been received by each state. Other funds such as the Fondo de Fortalecimiento de los Municipios were created to be distributed on a per capita basis to municipalities. The Fondo de Infraestructura Social was established on the basis of poverty formulas to provide resources for public works in the municipalities. And new funds were established for public safety (Sabet 2012).

The system of fiscal transfers after democratization has evolved with increases in funding to the states. Figure 3 offers greater insight into the distributive effects of those increases. The vertical axis shows the yearly growth, in real terms, of revenue sharing and conditional transfers granted to Mexican states over two presidential administrations covering the period between 2000 and 2012. The horizontal axis shows the per capita allocation that each state was receiving at the beginning of each presidential term. The bubbles are the states, proportional to their population, shown in two administrations, the one for Vicente Fox (2000–2006) and the one of Felipe Calderón (2006–12). The slight downward slope suggests that transfers have tended to equalize across states. The convergence is very

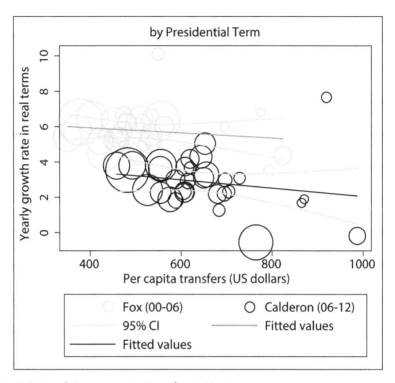

Fig. 3. Regional Convergence in Transfers in Mexico

mild, but a state with higher transfers per capita tends to have smaller increases than a state with lower levels of transfers at the beginning of an administration. But the largest difference between the Calderón and Fox administrations lies in the fact that with such large increases in the transfers received by every state, almost no overlap in the data points occurs. All states start at far higher points during the Calderón administration, but growth was less impressive and two states even saw no increase. Nevertheless, there is no question that during the decade after democratization, all states benefited from increases in their available funds.

Table 1 provides a statistical model that summarizes the general patterns of the main transfers within the federal fiscal arrangement. The table demonstrates that despite the rhetoric regarding the reform of fiscal federalism, the system is highly inertial and redistribution remains relatively limited.

TABLE 1. Inertia and Redistribution in Regional Transfers in Mexico, 2000–2013

Variables	(1) Revenue Sharing	(2) Transfers	(3) Health	(4) Education	(5)[a] Infrastructure
Lag	0.826***	0.947***	0.934***	0.931***	1.020***
	(0.0199)	(0.0130)	(0.0216)	(0.0122)	(0.0117)
Old Age (share)	0.0346	0.0293	0.0160	0.0206	−0.00544
	(0.0258)	(0.0274)	(0.0123)	(0.0152)	(0.00543)
GDP per capita	−0.0113***	−0.00571**	−0.00297***	−0.00400***	−0.000104
	(0.00273)	(0.00276)	(0.00114)	(0.00151)	(0.000486)
Constant	0.00545***	0.000646	0.000604	0.000559	0.000231
	(0.00177)	(0.00162)	(0.000696)	(0.000881)	(0.000312)
Observations	382	414	414	410	399
Number of st_id	32	32	32	32	31

Note: Standard errors in parentheses. Pooled time series OLS regressions with one lag of the dependent variable. Some observations lost due to incomplete data in some years.

[a]Model 5 drops the Federal District because it previously did not receive social development transfers due because of its unique structure, with no municipal governments.

***$p < 0.01$, **$p < 0.05$, *$p < 0.1$

Conclusion

Perhaps the most important lesson that can be learned from the Mexican fiscal constitution is political. Not even in the context of a hegemonic party system, where one party had the majorities to change the constitution at will during 70 years, was it easy redistribute resources. The federal government had the most leverage (in the direction either of centralization or of decentralizing reforms) when it provided political guarantees that the reforms would include safeguards that would protect regional leaders' interests and that distributional consequences would be only marginal. The system thus has always been highly inertial in its distribution, ensuring that any changes do not result in massive dislocations in local and state finances. Change in Mexican federalism has been slow and promises to remain so in the future.

Data Sources

The most important data source for information on transfers in the Mexican Fiscal Federal System is provided by the Secretaria de Hacienda y Credito Publico through its Unit of Coordination for Federated Entities. Some additional data is collected by the Conferencia Nacional de Goberandores, the Instituto Nacional para el Federalismo y el Desarrollo Municipal (INAFED), and the Instituto Para el Desarrollo Tecnico de las Haciendas Publicas (INDETEC). The Federal Health Ministry's Direccion General de Informacion de Salud has compiled detailed information on state expenditures in health, but such systematic information is not available for primary and secondary education. Data on higher education has not been consolidated into a national registry. States spend substantial parts of their budgets in support of state universities, but that information could not be readily collected for all jurisdictions.

Population—CONAPO projections, Consejo Nacional de Poblacion. From 1990 to 2010, these are the official revised figures for population by state, based on demographic models and census data; after 2010 they are the official projections.
http://www.conapo.gob.mx/es/CONAPO/Proyecciones_Datos
Debt—SHCP, Secretaria de Hacienda y Credito Publico. http://obligaciones_entidades.hacienda.gob.mx/en/OBLIGACIONES_ENTI DADES/2015
Transfers—SHCP, Secretaria de Hacienda y Credito Publico. http://finanzaspublicas.hacienda.gob.mx/es/Finanzas_Publicas/Estadisti cas_Oportunas_de_Finanzas_Publicas
INAFED (Instituto Nacional para el Federalismo y el Desarrollo Municipal).
http://www.inafed.gob.mx/es/inafed/inafed_Sistema_de_Informa cion_Hacendaria
Health—Secretaria de Salud. Gasto en Salud por Fuente de Financiamiento y Entidad Federativa.
http://www.dgis.salud.gob.mx/contenidos/sinais/gastoensalud.html
Public Finances—INEGI (Instituto Nacional de Estadistica, Geografia, e Informatica). Estadísticas de finanzas públicas estatales y municipales
GDP—INEGI (Instituto Nacional de Estadistica, Geografia, e Informatica). Sistema de Cuentas Nacionales de México. GDP per capita, 1993–2004 (in 1993 pesos), was calculated by the Centro de Estudios de las Finanzas Públicas de la H. Cámara de Diputados, with data from INEGI, Sistema de Cuentas Nacionales, Producto Interno Bruto por Entidad Federativa; Conteo de Población y Vivienda 1995, and Censo General de Población y Vivienda 2000 y 2005.

Mexico General Information

	Population[a]	GDP per capita[b]	Unemployment (%)	Age 0–19	Age 16–65	Age 65+
Aguascalientes	1,184,996	7,838.9	4.19	374,237	746,380	60,347
Baja California	3,155,070	7,305.9	3.45	901,886	2,075,134	140,625
Baja California Sur	637,026	7,867.3	4.05	178,472	421,998	27,219
Campeche	822,441	7,916.9	1.58	236,538	533,014	46,500
Coahuila	2,748,391	9,259.3	4.64	797,175	1,756,839	1,564,17
Colima	650,555	7,143.1	2.88	177,605	424,730	40,373
Chiapas	4,796,580	2,947.1	1.32	1,645,047	2,860,151	234,982
Chihuahua	3,406,465	7,385.5	4.79	982,401	2,127,341	193,183
Distrito Federal	8,851,080	16,157.4	3.72	1,937,538	6,027,661	687,855
Durango	1,632,934	6,079.0	3.10	495,733	1,003,805	104,988
Guanajuato	5,486,372	5,971.7	2.98	1,707,187	3,416,330	331,702
Guerrero	3,388,768	3,691.0	1.34	1,124,584	2,010,149	234,427
Hidalgo	2,665,018	4,360.4	2.41	789,409	1,678,211	176,239
Jalisco	7,350,682	7,175.5	3.28	2,136,416	4,666,739	460,858
México	15,175,862	5,120.9	3.95	4,353,914	9,890,102	745,298
Michoacán	4,351,037	4,462.1	1.79	1,304,279	2,681,245	316,176
Morelos	1,777,227	5,451.6	2.42	490,064	1,138,000	124,274
Nayarit	1,084,979	4,642.1	2.27	315,295	684,927	77,322
Nuevo León	4,653,458	13,350.5	4.26	1,259,253	3,056,492	274,671
Oaxaca	3,801,962	3,230.4	1.64	1,187,395	2,295,889	296,077
Puebla	5,779,829	4,910.7	2.52	1,799,744	3,560,275	363,871
Querétaro	1,827,937	8,117.7	3.74	545,065	1,176,541	93,390
Quintana Roo	1,325,578	9,117.4	3.27	381,532	885,368	39,487
San Luis Potosí	2,585,518	5,642.2	2.39	786,125	1,590,938	185,016
Sinaloa	2,767,761	6,063.1	2.32	787,536	1,786,281	183,131
Sonora	2,662,480	7,483.5	4.42	767,802	1,715,956	158,431
Tabasco	2,238,603	4,773.5	3.95	669,529	1,427,895	116,201
Tamaulipas	3,268,554	7,338.2	3.67	902,528	2,068,899	195,331
Tlaxcala	1,169,936	3,753.2	3.75	358,037	736,760	69,699
Veracruz	7,643,194	4,504.6	1.80	2,132,581	4,856,797	558,859
Yucatán	1,955,577	5,988.4	1.87	534,918	1,273,159	134,902
Zacatecas	1,490,668	4,485.0	3.16	455,971	910,417	111,062

Source: Data from the online database of the Government of Mexico: datos.gob.mx

[a] Population according to the 2010 Census.

[b] GDP per capita calculated by INAFED excluding mining and oil activity for 2010 (in US dollars).

Revenue Sharing and Transfer Dependence

	State Tax Revenue (% GDP)	Transfers Dependence (% State Expenditure)	Revenue Sharing (% State Expenditure)	Transfers (% State Expenditure)	Indebtedness (% GDP)
Aguascalientes	0.38	91.56	32.74	58.82	1.92
Baja California	0.48	86.32	39.24	47.08	2.98
Baja California Sur	0.51	71.88	30.35	41.52	2.01
Campeche	0.12	85.13	35.00	50.13	0.12
Coahuila	0.20	41.30	17.85	23.45	7.88
Colima	0.57	84.32	28.51	55.81	2.79
Chiapas	0.53	80.96	28.77	52.18	5.53
Chihuahua	0.47	73.01	29.45	43.57	4.01
Distrito Federal	1.18	56.02	40.10	15.92	2.11
Durango	0.37	91.20	27.10	64.10	2.33
Guanajuato	0.34	88.56	34.98	53.58	1.50
Guerrero	0.50	96.29	24.52	71.77	1.45
Hidalgo	0.36	88.82	29.21	59.61	1.63
Jalisco	0.29	89.45	40.26	49.19	2.84
México	0.52	79.45	32.92	46.53	2.90
Michoacán	0.27	80.36	27.48	52.87	4.60
Morelos	0.25	79.06	30.43	48.63	1.81
Nayarit	0.63	83.61	27.83	55.79	6.72
Nuevo León	0.45	64.84	32.14	32.70	3.62
Oaxaca	0.25	81.86	22.39	59.47	2.31
Puebla	0.47	92.69	32.15	60.54	1.97
Querétaro	0.68	86.67	34.72	51.95	0.73
Quintana Roo	0.52	50.21	20.65	29.56	6.55
San Luis Potosí	0.25	93.56	30.77	62.79	1.69
Sinaloa	0.24	91.80	35.33	56.48	1.86
Sonora	0.35	74.16	31.69	42.47	4.03
Tabasco	0.26	92.47	44.64	47.83	0.51
Tamaulipas	0.33	84.19	33.98	50.21	2.26
Tlaxcala	0.32	83.93	33.51	50.41	0.08
Veracruz	0.37	76.56	29.30	47.27	4.72
Yucatán	0.50	85.28	31.63	53.66	1.20
Zacatecas	0.23	82.00	26.00	56.00	4.40

Redistributive Transfers as Percentage of Regional GDP, 2000–2013 (Average)

	Regional Spending	Health	Education	Benefits
Aguascalientes	9.56	0.97	2.19	0.11
Baja California	8.04	0.57	1.81	0.07
Baja California Sur	10.37	0.95	2.68	0.07
Campeche	3.85	0.34	0.83	0.11
Chiapas	23.67	2.65	5.82	2.20
Chihuahua	10.36	0.68	1.87	0.21
Coahuila	8.17	0.41	1.72	0.08
Colima	12.24	1.51	2.99	0.13
Distrito Federal	5.50	0.64	1.22	0.00
Durango	12.29	1.37	3.45	0.42
Guanajuato	9.32	1.12	2.10	0.42
Guerrero	19.02	2.38	5.96	1.65
Hidalgo	13.93	1.71	4.09	0.70
Jalisco	8.43	0.73	1.58	0.16
México	12.08	1.23	1.99	0.28
Michoacán	14.66	1.38	3.99	0.72
Morelos	11.62	1.29	2.86	0.28
Nayarit	18.45	1.73	4.66	0.44
Nuevo León	6.40	0.29	0.93	0.05
Oaxaca	22.23	2.66	6.44	1.93
Puebla	12.37	1.22	2.65	0.77
Querétaro	8.13	0.75	1.69	0.23
Quintana Roo	9.58	0.72	1.73	0.16
San Luis Potosi	11.38	1.10	3.26	0.61
Sinaloa	11.32	0.96	2.52	0.24
Sonora	9.90	0.69	1.80	0.11
Tabasco	13.25	1.22	2.11	0.38
Tamaulipas	9.13	0.82	2.15	0.17
Tlaxcala	19.14	2.27	4.51	0.50
Veracruz	13.04	1.15	3.07	0.74
Yucatán	10.47	1.19	2.49	0.50
Zacatecas	16.78	1.57	4.71	0.69

NOTES

1. The Mexican federation does not establish fiscal rules or provisions limiting state indebtedness. But subnational debt is relatively modest (Hernandez Trillo and Jarillo 2008). Local and state budgets are thus highly dependent on the federal transfers, with no interference by the federal government in state budgetary processes. The Supreme Court has tended to uphold interpretations of the constitution that provide greater power and authority to the federal government over those transfers, in keeping with the federal origin of funds for state and local public spending.

2. Income distribution surveys also vary in their quality over time based on how the data are collected, their territorial reach, the match between consumption and income, the measurement of nonmonetary income, and the inclusion of financial flows and government transfers, among other factors.

3. Mining and oil production are excluded to have a better indicator of per capita GDP reflecting well-being.

4. Pressure also came from municipal governments, which demanded a more prominent role as democratization advanced.

REFERENCES

Bednar, Jenna. 2011. The political science of federalism. *Annual Review of Law and Social Science* 7:269–88.

Benson, Nettie Lee. 2010. *The provincial deputation in Mexico: Harbinger of provincial autonomy, independence, and federalism.* Austin: University of Texas Press.

Carmagnani, Marcello. 1994. *Estado y mercado: La economía pública del liberalismo mexicano, 1850–1911.* El Colegio de México.

Díaz Cayeros, Alberto. 1995. *Desarrollo económico e inequidad regional: Hacia un nuevo pacto federal en México.* Fundación Friedrich Naumann.

Díaz-Cayeros, Alberto. 2005. "Endogenous institutional change in the Mexican Senate." *Comparative Political Studies* 38 (10): 1196–1218.

Díaz-Cayeros, Alberto. 2016 [2006]. *Federalism, fiscal authority, and centralization in Latin America.* Cambridge: Cambridge University Press.

Falleti, Tulia G. 2010. *Decentralization and subnational politics in Latin America.* Cambridge: Cambridge University Press, 2010.

Giugale, Marcelo, and Steven Benjamin Webb, eds. 2000. *Achievements and challenges of fiscal decentralization: Lessons from Mexico.* World Bank Publications.

Hecock, R. Douglas. 2006. "Electoral competition, globalization, and subnational education spending in Mexico, 1999–2004." *American Journal of Political Science* 50 (4): 950–61.

Hernandez-Trillo, Fausto, and Brenda Jarillo-Rabling. 2008. "Is local beautiful? Fiscal decentralization in Mexico." *World Development* 36 (9): 1547–58.

Homedes, Nuria, and Antonio Ugalde, eds. 2006. *Decentralizing health services in Mexico: A case study in state reform.* San Diego: Center for US-Mexican Studies, UCSD.

Lustig, Nora, Luis F. Lopez-Calva, Eduardo Ortiz-Juarez, and Célestin Monga. 2016. "Deconstructing the decline in inequality in Latin America." In *Inequality and growth: Patterns and policy,* edited Kaushik Basu and Joseph E. Stiglitz, 212–47. London: Palgrave Macmillan.

Merino, Gustavo. 1999. "Federalism and the policy process: Using basic education as a test-case of decentralization in Mexico." PhD diss., Harvard University.

Pietschmann, Horst. 1996. *Las reformas borbónicas y el sistema de intendencias en la Nueva España: Un estudio político-administrativo*. Trans. Rolf Roland Meyer Misteli. Mexico City: Fondo de Cultura Económica.

Sabet, Daniel. 2012. *Police reform in Mexico: Informal politics and the challenge of institutional change*. Stanford: Stanford University Press.

Solt, Frederick. 2016. "The Standardized World Income Inequality Database." *Social Science Quarterly* 97 (5): 1267–81.

Wibbels, Erik. 2006. "Madison in Baghdad? Decentralization and federalism in comparative politics." *Annual Review of Political Science* 9:165–88.

United States

Territory in a Divided Society

Heather Elliott, Scott L. Greer, and Amanda Mauri

At first blush, the United States looks like strong confirmation of the thesis that federalism is not compatible with social democracy. It is a federal country with a relatively weak and partial welfare state whose expenditure is not always redistributive. Its political history is full of failed efforts at social democracy that were in some way foiled by its many veto points and state governments. Furthermore, its federalism is interlaced with an ugly politics of racial privilege and economic exploitation so that invocation of "states' rights" has usually been the argument of racists.

Nonetheless, federalism is not the main story of the American welfare state or the weakness of American social democracy. Rather, history, programmatic analysis, and expenditure data suggest that veto points within governments, particularly the federal government, have been the main way in which redistributive and universal—that is, social democratic—policies have been blocked. The United States has many veto points, but the key ones are not in its federal political institutions; rather, they are in the federal government. States vary within the space allotted them by federal legislation, and the weakness of social democracy in the United States relative to the other nations evaluated in this book is best explained through and on the federal level. That federal level is where the underlying politics of region, race, and class play out most consequentially and where strategic politicians use greater or lesser federal action and constraint of states as a way to pursue their own policy goals. The shape of American federalism is settled in Washington, DC.

The United States is a very old federation, constituted in the eighteenth century with its current constitution only slightly amended since. It is a classic coming-together federation in Stepan's (2001) terms. The unity of the original thirteen colonies was made necessary by the military difficulties of coping with the British empire. The price paid for a stronger federal state that could cope with the British threat was a federal government that so divided and set against itself that it would be unlikely to engage in tyranny of a faction or of a majority. Given a deeply rooted suspicion of government (Bailyn 1967), the result was a characteristic American form of government described in the *Federalist Papers* that sought to prevent the corruption and corresponding tyrannical activity of colonies' governors through a variety of mechanisms that would check their power, limit their tenure, divide their accountability, and set them against each other.

One of the most salient results of this history is that the United States has a strong separation-of-powers model within each government.[1] With minor exceptions, enacting a policy at any particular level of government requires passage of two independently elected legislative houses and an executive as well as judicial review and possible challenge in referenda; state policies can also be challenged in federal courts. Each legislator and executive has his or her own electoral mandate, divided powers are common, and formal shared rule between the federal and state levels is minimal. As a result, the United States or any given U.S. state is at the far upper end in any tally of legislative veto points (Stepan and Linz 2011). The essentially Westminster-model governments of Canada provide a telling contrast. In Canada, federal-provincial relations are a major veto point for policy (Maioni 1998). In the United States, federal-state relations may constitute a veto point for a given policy but are generally much less important than interbranch veto points (Greer 2009). The Senate has state-level electoral circumscriptions that overrepresent thinly populated rural states, but it does not represent state governments per se. Senators, like members of the House of Representatives, will often try to steer benefits to their states, but that is not the same thing as representing the state governments.[2]

For a long time, the fragmentation of U.S. politics was joined with fragmented parties whose members could substantially overlap in policy preferences. The result was a political system with a substantial transactional element, filled with side payments and ad hoc coalitions discussed in much classic political science. Since the 1980s, the country has also seen a steady development of party uniformity and polarization on the federal and now state levels. Its combination of increasingly unified parties, a veto-ridden institutional setup, and declining use of side payments has produced a situation of gridlock and effective supermajority requirements on the increasingly large number of issues that are subject to party polarization.

Federalism in the United States is also salient for its lack of formal interterritorial redistribution. Federal programs aimed at particular parts of the population (children, the elderly) or purposes (the military) have pronounced interterritorial distribution effects, and politicians are very capable of articulating what a military base, agricultural subsidy, grant, or federal facility will do for their constituents. But since the Reagan administration ended a short-lived program known as "revenue sharing," states per se receive no money to carry out their normal functions, which include most areas of domestic policy, such as health, education, security, infrastructure, and local government. There is simply no general revenue-sharing or equalization arrangement.

Instead, U.S. states are expected to raise their own funds for their own general spending. Forty-nine states have balanced budget provisions, though they vary in stringency and enforcement mechanism. The fact that states with balanced budget provisions also have debt ratings and debt suggests what students of Europe might expect: balanced budget rules are a real but loose constraint on policymaking, and efforts to game them make state budgets and finances opaque (Kelemen and Teo 2012). The effect of the constraint is predictable: states are procyclical forces that increase spending and lower taxes when the economy is doing well and cut spending and raise taxes when the economy is doing badly (Greer and Jacobson 2010).

Balanced budget provisions, rather than interstate economic competition, may explain why states are historically so good at innovation in social policy yet are unlikely to sustain an innovation, particularly an expansion, over business cycles. It is not clear, for example, that the Massachusetts health coverage expansion, which was the model for federal health care reform under Barack Obama, would have survived the 2008 recession had the federal government not generalized the Massachusetts model to the rest of the country with appropriate assistance for states. Contemporary observers were doubtful about the Massachusetts expansion's survival in light of the long track record of state health initiatives that foundered at a downturn in the business cycle (Jacobson and Braun 2007).

The United States extensively uses all three of the categories of expenditure explored in this project. Federal programs in the United States are principally targeted at the elderly. Two giant expenditure categories aimed at the elderly are Medicare (universal health insurance) and social security (a baseline old-age pension). For retired persons in the United States, the welfare state is substantially a federal government enterprise. There are a wide variety of "tax expenditures" not counted in this study by which the federal government rewards certain middle- and upper-class preferences—most notably, subsidies for buying houses with mortgages, saving for college, and tax refunds for low- and middle-income working people (Howard 1999; Mettler 2010). The most visible federal welfare state is directed at the elderly. Otherwise, in many cases the U.S. federal government serves many Americans through a series of federal-state programs in which the federal government essentially strikes a bargain with states and private or nonprofit providers, cofinancing services and leaving administration to others.

This distribution of resources means that the United States does not, on paper, have a clearly dominant source of funding in the way many other countries in our sample do. The scale of American federal social policy expenditure suggests that the federal government is a much bigger actor in U.S. social policy than it is often credited as being.

Programs

Social policy in the United States is frequently more complex and fractured than in other countries. This is the result of interactions between and within different branches of different governments, with policies produced by variable coalitions within and between different parts of the political system.

The veto points built into American politics have made the policies less coherent than they might otherwise have been. The history of any given piece of legislation in the United States tends to start with a coherent idea, but the initial legislative proposal is generally less coherent because it reflects compromises necessary to make it politically plausible. By the time multiple committees and floor votes in both houses have taken place, almost any given piece of legislation will have become quite incoherent in its ability to fulfill its original intent. More often than not, final legislation contains short descriptions with much ambiguity in policy specifics. Delineation is left to actors not involved in the legislative process, creating inconsistency among policy intent, design, and implementation.

Primary and secondary education is, in organization and financing, primarily a responsibility of local governments, which are creatures of states. A slow but steady leakage of authority and responsibility upwards has occurred, increasing since the 1970s, with many states taking on some role in financing, often with redistributive intent, and the federal government contributing some funds. The organization of schools and their educational outputs has also become somewhat more centralized, with states taking an interest in education (particularly the creation of testing regimes and support for private provision), and the federal government substantially supporting them since the landmark No Child Left Behind legislation (Manna 2006). Because so much finance remains local, primary and secondary education is an efficient device for the production and reproduction of inequality. Interventions by state and federal governments try to specify quality while having some redistributive effects and can be surprisingly influential given the relatively small amount of money involved (Manna 2006; McGuinn 2006). Overall, though, education is a local function with some roles for the state and for federal financing.

Higher education is a diverse sector with both public and private provision and a variety of funding sources. States finance the bulk of the system in the form of public universities and colleges: together public two- and four-year institutions educated 15.7 million students in 2013, but there is also a large nonprofit sector and a smaller but booming for-profit sector. Public universities and some nonprofit universities receive direct if diminishing support from states. The federal government and sometimes state governments finance research and support college saving tax credits. Tuition has been rising as states reduce funding to public universities, and students finance much of their education with federally backed loans.

Health includes a variety of programs. Medicare is a universal, federal health care program for people over age 65. The federal Veterans Administration directly provides health care to former soldiers with war injuries. Veterans can also receive private insurance through a federally run program, Tricare. Medicaid is a joint federal-state program, with the federal government cofinancing qualifying state programs. After the Supreme Court eliminated a state Medicaid expansion mandate in a 2010 decision, some states offer generous Medicaid for poor adults defined solely by income, while others have the prereform system which basically provides care for mothers, children, indigent elderly, and a very few other poor people. This variation has significant effects on expenditures, health care access, and redistribution between states but is not reflected in our data. Finally, the Children's Health Insurance Program (CHIP) involves federal cofinancing. These federal and federal-state programs, expenditures for which make up our categories, collectively absorb bad risks and thereby support what is supposedly the core of the system, the employer-provided sector, in which health insurance is treated as a component of employee compensation in the interests of firms' recruitment and retention strategies. The Patient Protection and Affordable Care Act (commonly known as the ACA as well as the PPACA or Obamacare) made a wide variety of changes, including a large expansion of Medicaid and a new mandate for the individual purchase of health insurance, coupled with subsidies.

The ACA is the major health care reform enacted by the U.S. federal government in 2012. It is a large and complex bill whose contents have been discussed and analyzed elsewhere (Béland, Rocco, and Waddan 2016; Jacobs and Skocpol 2010; McDonough 2011; White 2013). Its future seems relatively secure in the wake of the collapse of the 2017 Republican effort to repeal it, even if the administrative discretion of the Trump administration and the complex federal politics of the law still permit shifts in its meaning.

The law was shaped by the internal veto points of the U.S. political system, including by the short duration of the Democratic Senate supermajority that allowed the bill to pass: the particular legislative mechanics used to push the bill through meant that the final legislation was poorly drafted and had a bigger role for the states than would have been the case if the voters of Massachusetts not unexpectedly elected a Republican senator.

The law's broad contents ranged from student loan policy to taxes on paper mills and drug patents, but the core features for health expenditure are the following:

- A mandate for every citizen above 138 percent of the federal poverty line to have health insurance (with some exceptions). The mandate was structured as a tax, which saved it from Supreme Court challenge (the Court's conservatives might have regarded it as an overreach of the Commerce Clause) but made it vulnerable to repeal under budget reconciliation, which is a procedure for avoiding a Senate supermajority rule on budget bills. As a result, the Republican-led Congress repealed the tax penalty in 2017, with negative effects on the number of people who purchased coverage.
- Public marketplaces set up by states or the federal government on which citizens not otherwise insured, by employers or government could buy insurance.
- Subsidies so that poorer citizens could afford insurance on marketplaces.
- Expansion and standardization of the joint federal-state Medicaid program to cover everyone earning below 138 percent of the federal poverty line.

The Supreme Court took several unusual cases challenging the ACA. In the most important ruling, *NFIB v. Sebelius*, it ruled that states did not need to expand Medicaid. Meanwhile, an impressive Republican backlash meant that many states chose not to expand Medicaid or establish their own exchanges (Jones, Bradley, and Oberlander 2013). If a state did not establish an exchange, the federal government created the exchange and paid the subsidies. If a state did not expand Medicaid, people under 138 percent of the poverty line who were not previously insured saw no benefit from the ACA. The federal government and states can negotiate waivers for demonstration, a freedom that Republicans use to enable states to make health care access harder.

In other words, the interaction of partisanship, veto points, and federalism produced the actual ACA. Partisanship and veto points produced a complex and flawed piece of legislation. Partisanship, including the Supreme Court's Republican bent, interacted with federalism so that the ACA's effects produced as well as reduced territorial inequalities in expenditure and health care coverage. Both states and branches of the federal government became sites for a larger partisan war over the ACA and the Obama presidency.

Assistance to able-bodied people under age 65 in the United States is not generous and has always been focused on those perceived as "deserving"— essentially, temporarily unemployed mothers and the disabled. The disabled receive cash benefits from a pair of federal programs linked to social security (Berkowitz and DeWitt 2013; Erkulwater 2006). Out-of-work parents are eligible for the federal-state Temporary Assistance for Needy Families (TANF), which provides limited-duration help and can include requirements for job searches and, less frequently, training.

Finally, the public pension system is relatively simple: Almost everyone who is legally present in the country and worked or was married to a worker can receive social security starting in their 60s. Social security is a purely federal program. The main exception is that states and local governments have some employees who were never part of the social security system and depend on those governments for their pensions. Government employee pension liabilities are a separate problem in some places and a politically contentious issue almost everywhere. We do not discuss public employee pensions, since they are better viewed as deferred compensation than as a welfare state program.

In other words, each policy area contains a variety of programs, some federal, some federal-state, and some state-led. The logic of American politics cross-cuts policy areas: broadly, the federal government takes on the worst risks while the state and local government support other risks and make social investments.

Expenditure Patterns

The expenditure data show that the federal role is quite considerable: the states are relatively small actors relative to the federal government and are smaller still in light of the fact that much state expenditure is matching federal conditional grants (meaning that federal Medicaid policy can drive state Medicaid expenditure).

Some states tend to be outliers in terms of the federal expenditure that they draw. North Dakota, Alaska, Montana, Louisiana, and Vermont, for example, all have years in which they receive notably large federal grants in a given policy area. In no case is there a clear reason relating to the basic design of the programs. Given some of the variation, such as Louisiana receiving substantially more conditional education funding than most states in 2008, substantially less in 2009, and substantially more in 2010, it is likely that fluctuation at the extremes is a result of grant programs or accounting practices that place expenditures in one year or another.

Insofar as these outliers are not a function of accounting changes, the most likely explanation draws on the fact that they are small (so special treatment for them does not have big overall effects) and politically over-represented in the Senate. As a result, pivotal or senior senators have an opportunity to shape programs in a way that benefits the states. Even if there are undeniable arguments for the distinctiveness of policy problems in an island state such as Hawaii or a sparsely populated Plains state such as North Dakota, those claims for a distinctively high share of federal expenditure had to have been mediated through a federal political system that overrepresents inhabitants of small states and allows their senators, if they choose, to direct resources.

The impressive federal role in social policy is in keeping with basic theories of both fiscal federalism and American politics (Adolph, Greer, and Massard da Fonseca 2012; Oates 1999; Peterson 1995). However, this role does not fit with the widespread perception that American states are substantial social policy actors in their own right. What explains the differences? Inequality is built into American federal social policy in two ways. First, there is inequality in basic design: Who is included in federal programs? Even today, after the ACA, nearly unconditional access to health care is still confined to people who are over 65, and there is no federal income support for able-bodied men between ages 18 and 65 who have exhausted any unemployment insurance. Second, what do states do for those outside federal programs? To some extent, states compensate for gaps in federal expenditure, expanding the scope of benefits and thereby creating some divergence. Whether state governments choose to do so and which gaps they fill, is up to them. The decision space of states in social policy is the key driver of territorial variation in redistributive social policy. Less state decision space reduces variation in redistribution between states.

Implementation

Major programs that involve large amounts of federal money, such as higher education, TANF, Medicaid, and to a considerable extent primary and secondary education, are not just cofinanced by states but are implemented by states, which can therefore insert their own priorities and ideas. Just as the U.S. federal government delegates much of its policy administration in areas such as student loans or Medicare to private companies, it delegates joint federal-state programs to states. All of this delegation results in a putative loss of accountability and efficiency that outrages critics on the left (Morgan and Campbell 2011), on the right (DiIulio 2014), and in the center (Kettl 1988).

States have a great deal of variation within conditional grants. Federal legislation sets out the terms of federal-state cooperation on a program-by-program basis that requires consultation to understand state latitude in each case. Politicians are strategic in how they delegate, supporting federal power when they do not trust their state governments and vice versa (McCann 2015). The ACA shows the complexity and importance of such intergovernmental delegation decisions (Béland, Rocco, and Waddan 2016; Greer 2018). Further, the use of waivers—provisions that allow the federal government to agree with a particular state government on alteration of some aspect, such as program management, generosity, or coverage, of a federal-state program—has steadily increased.

Waivers are most significant in health policy but were extensively used by the Obama administration in education policy. Health care policy waivers have allowed the states to engage in a variety of experiments with Medicaid and CHIP. Arizona did not join Medicaid until it received a waiver, thereby allowing its politicians to save face by arguing that they were not being subordinated to federal priorities (Brecher 1984). The Obama administration used waivers to attract states to the ACA's Medicaid expansion (Jones, Singer, and Ayanian 2014). This policy flexibility is matched by a shift in politics that comes with waivers (Thompson 2012; Thompson and Gusmano 2014). On one hand, waivers substitute executive action for legislative compliance, shifting the United States toward more executive federalism. On the other, they give state governments considerable leverage, since they can condition participation on modification of objectionable legislative provisions. States might not have much ex ante influence over federal legislation, but waivers and noncooperation give them powerful ex post tools to modify policy (Dinan 2014; Ryan 2012). The result is a higher degree of shared-rule federalism than most international comparisons would suggest.

Programmatic design tends to reflect the redistributive nature and target populations of different programs. Programs for whiter and better-off citizens tend to be delegated to the private sector, disguising their governmental nature. These submerged state policies, such as the home mortgage interest deduction, child and dependent tax credit, and earned income tax credit, channel public resources to individuals indirectly through subsidies for private activities, leaving unemployed and minority peoples more likely not to receive benefits from private social policy (Mettler 2011). Programs for the poor are historically delegated to state and local governments and emphasize their governmental nature while sometimes humiliating their clients (Mettler 2010). Lieberman (1998, 2011; see also Lieberman and Lapinski 2001), Katznelson (2005, 2013), and other scholars have documented how race and to a lesser extent parochial urban machine preferences drove this system of "race-laden" policies. Passing programs based in social insurance through a legislative process dominated by southerners required the inclusion of initial conditions that largely excluded black Americans, principally by exempting domestic and farm work, the main occupations of blacks, from social insurance programs such as social security and Medicare. Passing unconditional programs for the poor, such as Aid for Dependent Children (the forerunner of TANF) required allowing state and local governments to discriminate and consequently support the local racial and economic order. This logic is also visible in the distinction between the social health insurance program Medicare, which is federal, and the Medicaid program for the poor, which has much more state administration and a bigger state role in setting parameters.

Scholars are not unanimous about the racist intent of such programmatic design, pointing to other reasons for local administration or particular eligibility criteria as well as disputing the legislative histories and influence of southern Democrats on the various laws (Béland 2005; Davies and Derthick 1997; DeWitt 2010). In particular, the big health programs of Medicare and Medicaid, while they share the basic relationship between lower-status, nonwhite clients and state administration, had very different legislative histories with far less southern Democratic support. Many countries without the particular racial politics of the United States also decentralize social care and services for vulnerable populations (but see Lieberman 2011). Regardless of this understandably contested history, federal-state partnerships often create a role for states and state politics in precisely the areas of policy where the clients are most likely to be poor or nonwhite.

Redistribution

The United States does not have an explicit and general interterritorial redistribution system: states receive no baseline allocation, and there is no equalization formula for states per se. Federal-state programs such as Medicaid can allow for an element of redistribution by altering cofinancing rates; the federal government gives poorer states in some programs more money in support of agreed-upon policy goals. Such formulas are set program-by-program, and there is no guarantee any particular formula will effectively redistribute between states. Between the larger population of retirees and the poor in poorer states (including people who took early retirement or whose ill health put them out of the workforce), federal programs and federal-state programs generally redistribute from richer states to poorer states (Richardson 2009).

The context is a large and diverse country, with Gini coefficients suggesting the range of variation. New York has the highest Gini coefficient of personal income, and it is therefore not surprising that the U.S. county with the highest estimated Gini coefficient is New York County (Manhattan, with a coefficient of 0.59940 and a margin of error of +/− 0.00380). Morgan County in Utah has the lowest Gini coefficient, at 0.33220 (margin of error +/− 0.0314). These two areas have vastly different economic and political profiles as well as cultural differences that contribute substantially to income inequality. Many states are congeries of very different economies and societies: parts of Florida, Michigan, California, Connecticut, and New York are very unlike other parts of those states. The old chestnut that the southern states are different also remains important in understanding state politics, policy choices, and the federal policies that southern states influence. Southern elites in the twentieth century typically supported financial transfers to their states but opposed limits on those states' abilities to maintain inegalitarian and often racist political systems. Since the realignment of southern politics to the Republican party began in the wake of the 1960s federal legislation that enfranchised many blacks, the explicitly racist elements of southern politics have been much reduced—as has support for government programs to reduce poverty in the South and elsewhere.

Despite this regional variation, the United States tends to have debates about interpersonal rather than interterritorial redistribution. The form these debates take, the budgetary arguments on each side, and the outcomes differ territorially, but territoriality generally does not structure them.

Interterritorial redistribution mechanisms hidden within the interpersonal redistribution mechanisms increase the extent to which people who live in poorer states receive more interpersonal aid. The most notable cases are Medicaid matching formulas that give more aid to poorer states. Given that it is unlikely that Medicaid crowds out hypothetical expenditures by poorer and often more conservative states on health care for the poor, the result seems to be higher overall expenditures than those states would otherwise have.

With control over their own taxes and spending, states have some ability to redistribute across ages (e.g., taxing for education) and income (e.g., taxing for social assistance). American states have a median population of about five million and range from Wyoming, with fewer than half a million, to California, with more than 33 million. Many if not all states are thus big enough to engage in substantial internal redistribution: the median EU member state, Sweden, has a population of about 9 million, and the poorest U.S. state, Mississippi, has about the same GDP per capita as much more redistributive New Zealand. Given the dominance of the federal government in pensions and health care for the elderly and the major federal role in support for the indigent, states' autonomous redistributive effects are focused on education at all levels and secondarily on assistance to those under age 65. Especially since the ACA, health spending is much more a federal-state expenditure and is dominated by conditional programs (Medicaid and CHIP).

Our data show that in the areas where states dominate, the coefficient of variation of total expenditure is very large, as can be found in some international comparisons. For example, the coefficient of variation for regional spending on people 65 years of age and older is 52 percent, while the coefficient of variation for central spending on the same population is

7 percent. In the area of health, similar results are seen. For people under 18 years of age, the coefficient of variation for states is 59 percent, while for people 65 and older, the coefficient of variation for central spending is a striking 66 percent. The coefficient of variation for federal via state expenditure on health is 42 percent for people 65 and older and 49 percent for people under 18. This demonstrates that the coefficient of variation is less for federal via state expenditure than for pure state expenditure and is still less for purely federal programs, which essentially use the same rules everywhere. States vary when they have latitude, but federal decisions constrain that latitude.

States, then, also vary substantially in the management and programmatic design of much of what they do—not surprisingly, given that there are fifty different political systems, each with its own agendas and complex electoral and institutional politics. Governors seek and receive or reject federal grants in keeping with their own politics, and Democrats are more likely to pursue and accept grants with a redistributive effect (Nicholson-Crotty 2015). The design of the federal contribution as a federal matching grant with programmatic requirements or a block grant/per capita cap with significantly more federal devolution to the states also influences state support or rejection of federal programs. Likewise, states at times have strikingly different approaches to taxation, with a mixture of tax bases (including states with no income tax or no sales tax), variable but often regressive income tax rates, and highly varied use of fees and supplementary taxes.

As a result, American states and their policies vary in expenditures, fiscal resources, and management. They are more or less constrained by working with the federal government in joint federal-state programs but are substantially free to determine their own spending levels in other areas, to dramatic effect. (Kansas simply eliminated its arts budget in 2011.) Balanced budgets and interstate competition for lower taxes produce a constant downward pressure on welfare programs and social investment by states that, over time and in bad times, can be expected to make the federal programs proportionately more important.

Change

Compared to some other countries discussed in this project, U.S. federal social policy and the allocation of authority is at the moment quite stable. A veto-filled political system with high levels of discipline in two roughly equally matched parties would suggest as much: either party can block the other. Even in the remarkable conditions of 2017 (Republican majorities at the federal level and in most states), the null hypothesis for U.S. social policy expenditures is only incremental change, since the price of such majorities tends to be a degree of internal diversity that taxes a party's ability to maintain unity.

This stability comes after a period of change, principally driven by Obama's 2008 election to the presidency, where he could work with strong Democratic majorities in both federal houses.[3] The lasting fruit of that era is the ACA, which fulfilled decades of Democratic programmatic commitment (McDonough 2011). The ACA is particularly noteworthy because it creates a new flow of federal expenditures within the states, allowing eligible people to buy insurance with new federal subsidies. In the 28 states that had accepted Medicaid expansion as of late 2015, the ACA also substantially increased health coverage, with the expansion financed completely or 90 percent by the federal government via the state. Second, the ACA's financing was redistributive, mostly coming from a variety of taxes that affect higher-income taxpayers (Rice 2011). Third, the measure increases interstate inequality because as a result of the Supreme Court's 2010 intervention, some states have not expanded Medicaid and received additional federal revenue. Because the purchase of subsidized insurance on federal exchanges happens regardless of state resistance (focused on who would run the website and be involved in regulating the markets), the direct federal health expenditure on subsidies was unaffected by state preferences except insofar as states managed to depress acceptance of subsidies.

Within the latitude created by federal inaction or by the design of federal programs, states became increasingly divergent in the aftermath of the 2010 election. Refusal to accept Medicaid expansion (the kind of "free money" that some theories of federalism say states cannot resist) is a salient example of how strongly polarized American states have become (Jones, Bradley, and Oberlander 2013; Jones, Singer, and Ayanian 2014). States are smaller entities with weaker public spheres and cheaper politics, and a steadily increasing number have one-party rule across the legislature and executive. This means that experimentation is increasing, from Kansas (which opted for particularly deep cuts in taxes and expenditure) to Vermont (which seriously considered creating a universal public health care system on the model of Canada). It is perhaps unsurprising that states would become more polarized in their outcomes at a time of increasing party unity and polarization. Some of this polarization is evident in issues with limited expenditure consequences, such as regulation of guns (liberalized in many states) or abortion (constricted in many states), but it is also evident in expenditures over time.

Conclusion

From one point of view, the United States has a quite rational basic allocation of power and responsibility in social policy (Adolph, Greer, and Massard da Fonseca 2012; Peterson 1995). The federal government, with its enormous ability to smooth expenditures over business cycles and generations, finances the worst risks—above all the elderly, but also the very poor. State and local governments are free to make economic development investments, such as education and infrastructure, and can decide what strategy works best for them subject to the disciplines of competition. Governments that make bad investment decisions, including in education, can be punished by voters twice. The voters can cast ballots on the grounds of poor performance, and they can vote with their feet by leaving, taking their taxes with them.

From the point of view of social investment, however, the United States is almost exactly backward. Its biggest, most effective programs, carried out by its most financially stable government, are by definition the least like investments: they are aimed at the elderly and injured. Programs that might invest in a better workforce and greater human capital are decentralized to the most financially vulnerable levels of government, as are programs that sit on the border between investment and charity (e.g., CHIP and TANF). The result, in aggregate, is that the United States has a spending ratio skewed heavily in favor of the elderly at the expense of the young. This ratio is comparable to Japan or Italy, neither of which is regarded as a model of human capital investment (Greer, Elliott, and Oliver 2015; Lynch 2006). This aggregate statistic, once disaggregated, shows a country where the welfare state is federal but some states opt to make minimal investment in education and others opt to invest a great deal, which might improve the competitive chances of some states but forsakes a great deal of national potential. Federalizing old age in the American welfare state made old-age policy stable (Béland, Rocco, and Waddan 2014). The rest is subject to the vicissitudes of state politics.

This picture differs from the simple depiction of the United States as simply a fragmented state. It is indeed fragmented and filled with veto points such as bicameralism, judicial review, and in some places referenda, but that fragmentation reveals patterns that make the U.S. welfare state look distinctive. The key fragmentation is not in the federal-state relationship, as in Canada; rather, the fragmentation lies within the federal government and within the governments of the fifty states. Only rarely do states act effectively in opposition to federal action, and a number of the most dramatic assertions of federal power in American history (the Civil War, Reconstruction, the 1960s and 1970s civil rights movement and Great Society) were powerful responses to southern efforts to use states' rights in defense of local racist politics. (Southern elites have never been shy about mobilizing federal support for their local political economy.)

So, for example, the federal welfare state has a strong old-age bias. That has nothing directly to do with federalism but rather has to do with the politics within the federal government that produced federal programs there and not in areas such as higher education. Social security and Medicare, which supported sympathetic populations that were bad commercial risks, passed Washington at times of large Democratic majorities (under Franklin Delano Roosevelt and Lyndon B. Johnson, respectively).

The space left outside this federal welfare state was occupied by states, perhaps with long-standing federal encouragement, as in the case of higher education, and perhaps as a legacy antedating the rest of the welfare state, as with primary and secondary education. In those areas, variation occurred: states vary a lot when the federal government is not acting with, through, or in place of them. The obstacle to a more redistributive, centralized, or egalitarian welfare state in the United States is not so much federalism per se as it is the limitations on the federal government (Greer 2009). At times these two factors have worked together, as with the long-standing efforts of southern legislators to keep state control over programs that could be used to support the region's particular racial and economic structures. But even that need not be blamed on federalism. Powers are more separated in the United States.

Perhaps the most hackneyed term in the history of American federalism is Supreme Court justice Louis D. Brandeis's description of the states as "laboratories of democracy." We find that the states do indeed differ in expenditures and programmatic design and management. But our data also show the importance of the federal government across the American welfare state, which should direct our attention to the programs where states implement federal priorities. The U.S. welfare state's finances might be surprisingly federal, but its operation and implications reflect the use of federalism for policy ends.

NOTES

1. In keeping with standard usage for the United States, *states* refers to the fifty subnational governments, and *federal government* refers to the U.S. government.

2. Presidents also, unsurprisingly, steer benefits to core supporters and swing voters (Hudak 2014; Kriner and Reeves 2015).

3. However, the Democrats had only limited legislative power under Obama. Despite their majorities, they confronted an effective 60-vote supermajority requirement in the Senate that a unified Republican opposition used extremely well. As a result, the window in which the Democrats effectively enjoyed a legislative majority was not two years, but rather extended from July 7, 2009, when Senator Al Franken was seated, to February 4, 2010, when Republican Scott Brown won a special election to replace deceased Democratic senator Edward Kennedy. Outside that seven-month window, the Democrats had to rely on Republican defections to legislate. The ACA's legislative history and text make little sense without taking into account the Republican use of the filibuster, the need for Democratic unanimity, and the short duration of the Democratic supermajority (McDonough 2011).

REFERENCES

Adolph, Christopher, Scott L. Greer, and Elize Massard da Fonseca. 2012. "Allocation of authority in European health policy." *Social Science and Medicine* 75 (9):1595–1603.

Bailyn, Bernard. 1967. *The ideological origins of the American Revolution*. Cambridge: Belknap Press of Harvard University Press.

Béland, Daniel. 2005. *Social Security: History and politics from the New Deal to the privatization debate*. Lawrence: University Press of Kansas.

Béland, Daniel, Philip Rocco, and Alex Waddan. 2014. "Implementing health care reform in the United States: Intergovernmental politics and the dilemmas of institutional design." *Health Policy* 116 (1): 51–60.

Béland, Daniel, Philip Rocco, and Alex Waddan. 2016. *Obamacare wars: Federalism, state politics, and the Affordable Care Act*. Lawrence: University Press of Kansas.

Berkowitz, E. D., and L. DeWitt. 2013. *The other welfare: Supplemental security income and U.S. social policy*. Ithaca: Cornell University Press.

Brecher, Charles. 1984. "Medicaid comes to Arizona: A first-year report on AHCCS." *Journal of Health Politics, Policy, and Law* 9 (3): 411–25.

Davies, Gareth, and Martha Derthick. 1997. "Race and social welfare policy: The Social Security Act of 1935." *Political Science Quarterly* 112 (2): 217–35.

DeWitt, Larry. 2010. "The decision to exclude agricultural and domestic workers from the 1935 Social Security Act." *Social Security Bulletin* 70 (4): 49–68.

DiIulio, J. 2014. *Bring back the bureaucrats: Why more federal workers will lead to better (and smaller!) government*. West Conshohocken: Templeton Press.

Dinan, John. 2014. "Implementing health reform: Intergovernmental bargaining and the Affordable Care Act." *Publius: The Journal of Federalism* 44 (3): 399–425.

Erkulwater, Jennifer L. 2006. *Disability rights and the American social safety net*. Ithaca: Cornell University Press.

Greer, Scott L. 2009. "How does decentralisation affect the welfare state?" *Journal of Social Policy* 39 (2): 1–21.

Greer, Scott L. 2018. "The politics of bad policy in the United States." *Perspectives on Politics* 16 (2): 455–59.

Greer, Scott L., Heather Elliott, and Rebecca Oliver. 2015. "Differences that matter: Overcoming methodological nationalism in comparative social policy research." *Journal of Comparative Policy Analysis: Research and Practice* 17 (4): 408–29.

Greer, Scott L., and Peter D. Jacobson. 2010. "Health policy and federalism." *Journal of Health Politics, Policy, and Law* 35 (2): 203–26.

Howard, Christopher. 1999. *The hidden welfare state: Tax expenditures and social policy in the United States*. Princeton: Princeton University Press.

Hudak, J. 2014. *Presidential pork: White House influence over the distribution of federal grants*. Washington, DC: Brookings Institution Press.

Jacobs, L. R., and T. Skocpol. 2010. *Health care reform and American politics: What everyone needs to know*. New York: Oxford University Press.

Jacobson, Peter D., and Rebecca L. Braun. 2007. "Let 1000 flowers wilt: The futility of state-level health care reform." *University of Kansas Law Review* 55:1173–1202.

Jones, David K., Katharine W. V. Bradley, and J. B. Oberlander. 2013. "Pascal's wager: Health insurance exchanges, Obamacare, and the Republican dilemma." *Journal of Health Politics, Policy, and Law* 39 (1): 97–137.

Jones, David K., Phillip M. Singer, and John Z. Ayanian. 2014. "The changing landscape of Medicaid: Practical and political considerations for expansion." *JAMA: Journal of the American Medical Association* 311 (19): 1965–66.

Katznelson, Ira. 2005. *When affirmative action was white: An untold history of racial inequality in twentieth-century America*. New York: Norton.

Katznelson, Ira. 2013. *Fear itself: The New Deal and the origins of our time*. New York: Liveright.

Kelemen, R., and Terence Teo. 2012. "Law and the Eurozone Crisis." Paper presented at the annual meeting of the American Political Science Association.

Kettl, D. F. 1988. *Government by proxy: (Mis?)managing federal programs*. Washington, DC: CQ Press.

Kriner, D. L., and A. Reeves. 2015. *The particularistic president: Executive branch politics and political inequality*. Cambridge: Cambridge University Press.

Lieberman, Robert C. 1998. *Shifting the color line: Race and the American welfare state*. Cambridge: Harvard University Press.

Lieberman, Robert C. 2011. *Shaping race policy: The United States in comparative perspective*. Princeton: Princeton University Press.

Lieberman, Robert C., and John S. Lapinski. 2001. "American federalism, race, and the administration of welfare." *British Journal of Political Science* 31 (2): 303–29.

Lynch, Julia. 2006. *Age in the welfare state: The origins of social spending on pensioners, workers, and children*. Cambridge: Cambridge University Press.

Maioni, Antonia. 1998. *Parting at the crossroads: The emergence of health insurance in the United States and Canada*. Princeton: Princeton University Press.

Manna, Paul. 2006. *School's in: Federalism and the national education agenda*. Washington, DC: Georgetown University Press.

McCann, Pamela J. Clouser. 2015. "The strategic use of congressional intergovernmental delegation." *Journal of Politics* 77 (3): 620–34.

McDonough, J. E. 2011. *Inside national health reform*. Berkeley: University of California Press.

McGuinn, P. J. 2006. *No Child Left Behind and the transformation of federal education policy, 1965–2005*. Lawrence: University Press of Kansas.

Mettler, Suzanne. 2010. "Reconstituting the submerged state: The challenges of social policy reform in the Obama era." *Perspectives on Politics* 8 (3): 803–24.

Mettler, Suzanne. 2011. "20,000 leagues under the state." *Washington Monthly*, July–August.

Morgan, Kimberly J., and Andrea Louise Campbell. 2011. *The delegated welfare state: Medicare, markets, and the governance of social policy*. New York: Oxford University Press.

Nicholson-Crotty, S. 2015. *Governors, grants, and elections: Fiscal federalism in the American states*. Baltimore: Johns Hopkins University Press.

Oates, Wallace E. 1999. "An essay on fiscal federalism." *Journal of Economic Literature* 37:1120–49.

Peterson, Paul. 1995. *The price of federalism*. Washington, DC: Brookings Institution.

Rice, Thomas. 2011. "A progressive turn of events." *Journal of Health Politics, Policy, and Law* 36 (3): 491–94.

Richardson, Gary. 2009. "The truth about redistribution: Republicans receive, Democrats disburse." *Economists' Voice* 6 (10): 1–5.

Ryan, Erin. 2012. *Federalism and the tug of war within*. Oxford: Oxford University Press.

Stepan, Alfred. 2001. *Arguing comparative politics*. Oxford: Oxford University Press.

Stepan, Alfred, and Juan J. Linz. 2011. "Comparative perspectives on inequality and the quality of democracy in the United States." *Perspectives on Politics* 9 (4): 841–56.

Thompson, Frank J. 2012. *Medicaid politics: Federalism, policy durability, and health reform*. Washington, DC: Georgetown University Press.

Thompson, Frank J., and Michael K. Gusmano. 2014. "The administrative presidency and fractious federalism: The case of Obamacare." *Publius: The Journal of Federalism* 44 (3): 426–50.

White, Joseph. 2013. "The 2010 U.S. health care reform: Approaching and avoiding how other countries finance health care." *Health Economics, Policy, and Law* 8 (3): 289–315.

Conclusion

Comparative Federalism As If Policy Mattered

Scott L. Greer

This book has brought together scholars of eleven decentralized countries in an effort to go beyond the existing approaches to federalism and policy. We focus on money and policy rather than the law and constitutional politics that so often are the subject of conversations about federal design and comparative federalism. The focus on constitutional design and legal incentives often departs from the assumption that such rules determine both policy outputs and financial stability. While it would be absurd to claim that such rules are irrelevant, the guiding assumption informing the literature is woefully underexplored. Legal rules can be endogenous to the dynamics of money and policy, calling into question much of the extant literature's modeling and policy prescriptions.

Our focus on specific public policy areas and programs in comparative perspective has aligned us with issues that often matter much more to voters and politicians and has allowed us to address questions about the nature of federalism and social policy that are generally answered only with very high-level and imperfect data (e.g., correlations between veto points and expenditure) or in country-specific situations. Our approach is in keeping with the fact that policy demands govern much of what happens in politics (Hacker and Pierson 2014). It is also in keeping with the extensive focus on federal and territorial dimensions in single-country public policy literatures that are often impressive but rarely comparative.

The Politics of Missing Data

The presence, absence, and quality of data are as much a kind of data as the numbers themselves. Authors, editors, referees, and most commentators initially thought our work would be easy and had been done. Instead, it was hard and was indeed novel. We found a striking number of empty cells in our effort to collect cross-nationally comparable data—as well as patterns in what countries do or do not report. In particular, data about the territorial distribution of central government expenditures turned out to be a rare creature, and some categories such as education and transfers and benefits for the 18–65 group proved intractable as comparative data. This was not just the usual frustration. *Data turned out not to be about our dependent variable but rather a dependent variable in its own right.*

There is a large literature on the politics of numbers and data in the field of science and technology studies (Lampland and Star 2009; Crosby 1996; Bowker and Star 2000; Berg and Bowker 1997). The comparative politics of data has fallen between science and technology studies, which well understands the political nature of data but focuses elsewhere, and comparative politics, which rarely takes data as a dependent variable. This is despite the fact that publications in the space between the fields produce both substantive findings about data and methodological points about research with public data (Clasen and Siegel 2007; Danforth and Stephens 2013; Peeters, Verschraegen, and Debels 2014; Wenzelburger, Zohlnhöfer, and Wolf 2013).

We found some interesting and suggestive regularities that map onto basic theories found in comparative politics and warrant more exploration. Social insurance (Bismarckian) welfare states are notably reluctant to provide territorial breakdowns of expenditures and revenues in the social insurance system. The mechanics of collecting and disbursing money clearly mean that such states have access to data that would allow territorial breakdowns of expenditures, but the politics of social insurance apparently militate against it. As the German supreme court ruled, social insurance and federal risk sharing are very different conceptual and practical forms of decentralization (Mätzke 2013). Germany applies the logic in practice, with very good data on expenditures by different governments but very little data on the territorial distribution of expenditures in the social insurance systems. The political and perhaps moral economy logic is suggestive: social insurance combines an individual component with solidarity along occupational or social lines. Presenting data that makes social insurance appear a form of territorial redistribution, as with data that present it as intergenerational redistribution, might endanger the moral economy that supports social insurance. The result is that pensions, health, and most 18–65 benefits data for Austria, Belgium, and Germany are hopelessly partial.

Then, there is suggestive evidence of two kinds of equilibriums in data on government expenditures. On one hand, some countries put considerable effort into clear, transparent data in the apparent hope that it will enable more productive political conflict and better decisions about redistribution. Such transparency countries include Australia and the UK as well as to a lesser extent Canada, Mexico, and the United States.

On the other hand, an alternative model might be attractive to politicians who wish to claim more credit and escape more blame than transparent accounting would allow: systematic obfuscation. This appeared to be the situation in Spain (which in effect operates multiple fiscal years simultaneously) and Belgium (see Gray 2014, 2015, 2016). If any government's fiscal situation or relationship is not clear, then every politician has more opportunities to claim credit for expenditure, shift blame for lack of expenditure, and create hidden fiscal problems. Even Canada, which is clearly in a data-rich equilibrium, has essentially contested concepts such as the size of federal "points" transfers where one might prefer an internationally agreed accounting category.

Finally, any government data has flukes. One problem we encountered in the United States, for example, was that budget cuts meant that the Census of State and Local Government simply did not occur in some years. This produced an unfortunate gap covering the end of the fiscal stimulus that followed the 2008 financial crisis. (That the United States uses a questionnaire, sent out by the Census Bureau, is distinctively American and might reflect its nearly ninety thousand local governments.) Governments repeatedly change categories, so the UK's excellent PESA series on territorial public expenditure comes in five-year runs that are not comparable with each other due to changes in the categories of expenditure. Governments also make different choices in the normal course of business—for example, presenting data with different inflation weights that are not always well explained.

Data is not just about politics; it is politics. Or as Alan Trench has noted, data is comparable or useful but rarely both. The commitment to producing data on territorial expenditures clearly varies politically. As scholars of science and technology studies point out, data and the process of commensuration necessary to make comparable, manageable data, is also an exercise in power politics (Espeland and Stevens 1998; Bowker and Star

2000; Crosby 1996). The person who creates the categories and codes is making reality. Naturally, in intensely political settings such as intergovernmental finance debates, actors appreciate this and will resist and negotiate any imposed effort to create quantitative data.

Mexico, for example, had relatively clear data—better than most European countries—probably in part because of economists' long-standing role in Mexican politics (Babb 2009) and their legitimate distrust of Mexican state and local politicians. This seems to be the situation in a number of Latin American countries. But the political act of creating data shaped data in Mexico and elsewhere. An example from one of the most transparent and data-rich federal countries in the world, Brazil, is suggestive. The admirable Brazilian system of data on local and state government expenditure, which has made possible an extensive system of federal social policy through conditional grants despite a highly decentralized constitution, was set up under a military regime that was presumably frustrated by the difficulty of controlling subordinate governments. Unsurprisingly, the generals did not think to set up such a sophisticated or transparent system to monitor themselves. Subsequent democratic federal governments, frequently dealing with fiscal crises, retained the system and began to use it to circumvent the cumbersome structure of Brazilian federalism. However, they also saw no good reason to create data on their own territorial expenditures. As a result, territorial distribution of much federal money is a mystery—even though the country is an international exemplar of good data on state and local government funding.

Insofar as the problems have been overcome, they have been overcome in the interest of compliance with commitments to international organizations. The OECD and the EU seem to be the most effective, with OECD data particularly valuable in this area. The OECD's database that puts numbers to the UN's COFOG categorization of government functions, for example, is by far the best and most comparable information available on the expenditure decisions of regional governments. OECD work on the allocation of responsibilities in health care systems (part of a broader benchmarking operation) is excellent (Paris, Devaux, and Wei 2010). The politics of this kind of international data are fascinating and often understudied, but literature on the topic as well as the extensive literature on data and comparison within the EU suggest that the international organization is often being used as a lever by domestic interests such as finance departments that seek numbers to make the case for the policies they desire. Agreeing to share data with an international organization is a lever to creating or distributing that data at home. Quality and coverage can often be patchy, meaning that the commitment must be long-term and sufficient to cope with the challenges of generating and validating comparable numbers about fiscal federalism.

At a minimum, this is a cautionary tale for those who use internationally comparative data. *Someone put a great deal of effort into creating data and did so for a more applied reason than promoting scholarship.* So scholars would be wise to ask about the data's purpose and how methods, issues, and preoccupations are reflected in the data. For example, OECD data explicitly focus on fiscal sustainability, in keeping with the OECD's established approach, which is dominated by economists and often called neoliberal. There is even a small literature on the interesting soft politics of the OECD and the networks within which it operates (e.g., Radaelli 2018; Armingeon and Beyeler 2018). Other data is designed for submission to the IMF and other international financial institutions. Maybe it should not surprise us that the result is data focused on controlling the debt and fiscal behavior of regional governments. As in any adventure story, when our heroes stumble across an unguarded treasure, they might ask what kind of curse or condition comes with it.

Four Questions and Their Answers

We began this book with four questions drawn from the literature, which seemed amenable to answers using information about money and policy. What have we found?

Do Regional Welfare States Exist?

It is beyond argument that there are regional policy variations in almost every system and that in some political systems, especially those of stateless nations, social policy is used for region- or stateless-nation-building (Béland and Lecours 2008; Chaney 2017, 10). The conditions of political competition in stateless nations with nationalist parties lead other parties to follow their lead and propose nationally distinctive policies (Vampa 2016; Greer 2004). Likewise, both territorial diversity and federalism will unquestionably lead to some level of diversity in politics, policies, and outcomes (Greer 2006; Jeffery et al. 2014). This study starts to answer the question of what the payoff is: How distinctive are these regional welfare states in structure and spending priorities? Do any of them differ to the extent that we expect different countries to differ in their welfare arrangements?

The answer is *no*. In each case that we studied, regional governments resemble the governments of other regions in their country more than they resemble any other jurisdiction. The main axis of variation is not the types of policy adopted or their priorities, but money—how the strength of the underlying economy and the operation of state-level redistributive programs combine to give regional governments more or less expenditure. The Basque Country has more money than other Spanish regions, but its distribution of expenditure looks much like that of other Spanish regions. Italy, Mexico, and the United States all have steep gradients between their richest and poorest states, but the result is that richer states have more money and spend more money on the same set of programs, while poorer states spend less. The amount of divergence between regional governments does vary from country to country, but that only shows the importance of the state structure and in particular finance.

This pattern is constantly repeated. In most cases, regions vary in the method and competence of implementation rather than the priorities or the basic pattern of expenditure. Thus, for example, the Scottish welfare state differs from those of the other parts of the UK in how it carries out the same set of functions (running a highly centralized health, education, and local government system) rather than in the basic set of policies and resources allocated to those functions. Differences in actual policies are on the margin—often highlighted by politicians (Birrell 2009) but not especially impressive in a large-scale comparative analysis such as ours.

The chapters suggest that institutional, financial, political, and structural constraints limit regional government diversity. The institutional constraints are in the country's basic division of powers (Halberstam and Reimann 2014). Every country except Canada makes pensions a central responsibility, so a distinctive pension scheme is difficult to imagine for a regional government. The financial constraints flow from the constitutional limitations but also create more room for central governments to constrain or enable policy diversity. Conditional grants with loose conditions, as in Canada, permit variation, while ones with tight conditions (most common in the Western Hemisphere and Australia) do not. Overall general revenue (or equalization) payments, found everywhere except the United States, give regional governments more autonomy than do conditional grants. It does not seem to matter much whether equalization payments are associated with legislation spelling out necessary services, as in Spain, where revenue grants coexist with regional government obligations to provide certain services in certain ways but are not effectively conditional grants.

These constraints do not explain the consistency that we see, however. For a variety of political reasons, the demand for regional divergence, even in the most distinctive regions, is limited. These include the operation of statewide parties (Caramani 2004; Niedzwiecki 2016), statewide media, population mobility, and spillover between the agendas of different political systems (Boushey 2010; Baumgartner and Jones 1993). Citizens in most countries also display a measurable commitment to a level of homogeneity in standards, even if the demonstrable variation in standards within countries suggests that citizens have some trouble operationalizing this commitment (Henderson, Jeffery, and Wincott 2013). Even in countries where some regions are highly deviant from a democratic norm—the authoritarian enclaves of Mexican, American, and to some extent Spanish and Italian history—the elites of those enclaves are intensely interested in shaping a federal welfare state that will benefit them and their local political regimes (Gibson 2013).

Such mutually reinforcing political dynamics do not just happen. They suggest a final level of structural determinism. Party systems reflect social cleavages, shared economic fates, and history. The media both perpetuate and reflect a shared sense of social belonging. Even Austria, one of our younger states (an imperial residuum refashioned as a nation-state, slightly less than a hundred years old in its current borders, and younger still if we consider its problematic first three decades), shows how states bind people and parts together via ubiquitous party politics, neocorporatism, and the state's resulting economic profile. In other words, the basic argument that states shape societies is very much true.

The deviant cases reinforce this basic analysis. The hardest case is probably Quebec in Canada. It has a number of distinctive programs—most notably in child care and a pension plan that converts savings into an effective tool of developmentalist capitalism. These are both salient and meaningfully different—though the pension plan offers a different way to achieve what is an essentially typical Canadian pension outcome.

Unsurprisingly, regional governments that resemble Quebec in both autonomy and nationalist politics are the most likely to have a claim to distinctiveness in spending priorities and outcomes as well as a few particular salient policies. In all cases, the reason is that the regional governments are primarily creatures of the state-level constitutional order in which they exist. Quebec has the autonomy to be the most distinctive regional welfare state in our sample, with a high level of legislative autonomy as well as a powerful position that allows its politics and provincial government to shape Canadian federalism. That power was partly inherent in its relative size and in the power of Canadian provinces, but it was also deliberately enhanced by Quebec leaders. The mobilization of a stateless nation created some space to diverge from other parts of the country. That does not mean that any stateless nation's regional government has actually ceased to look like the other regional governments of that country.

How Much Do the Structures of Federal Welfare States Vary?

Do different states have significantly different ways of allocating power, authority, and responsibility? In a sense, the answer is obviously *yes*. Contrast the Austrian system, based on substantial social insurance and mandatory consensus, and the contentious, executive-led, Canadian or Australian systems, with their mixture of liberalism and a strong public sector. However, in terms of responsibility for finance, policy design, and policy implementation, a pattern is evident. Crudely, pensions are centralized in delivery and finance; health expenditure is decentralized (to regions or social insurance funds) but finance is generally centralized; higher education is regional; primary and secondary education are regional but in reality often local; and 18–65 benefits and services are mixed and patternless.

This arrangement happens to conform relatively well to the basic dictum of fiscal federalism that risk pooling, as with pensions and health finance, should be carried out for the largest unit possible, while delivery and investment (e.g., education) should be carried out by smaller governments with more sense of local priorities and competitive incentives to spend well. As with most economics, it is unclear whether the economic model is normative or functionalist; it argues implicitly that countries do something because to do otherwise is irrational or suboptimal for the relevant actors as is made clear by economic research. We could even ask whether decades of nearly unanimous advice by economists had some impact on policy design.

Regardless, we find that although welfare states are highly diverse, there is a clear pattern consonant with pooling risks at the highest level. The pattern would be stronger still if we were to consider social insurance plans in health, which are redistributive across territory in federal Belgium, Germany, and Austria. The further implication is that vertical fiscal imbalance (in which central states have more money and fiscal flexibility than regions) is universal. Likewise, horizontal fiscal imbalances (in which some regions have more tax resources) are universal and are to some extent addressed in every country. Even the United States, which since the Reagan years has had no formal equalization system to shore up weaker state governments (Conlan 1998), does a substantial amount of programmatic redistribution by giving more money to poorer states under conditional grant programs such as Medicaid.

There are two kinds of deviant cases. One is the countries with a strong stateless nation—Spain, Canada, Belgium, and the UK. Each of these has somewhat stronger regional governments, with more spending and (outside the UK) taxing responsibilities than might be anticipated from the examples of the other countries (Adolph, Greer, and Massard da Fonseca 2012). The other deviant case is Switzerland, which runs a more localized system in health and education than do other countries. The Swiss have developed incentives and equalization mechanisms to allow them to combine a strong welfare state with competitive mechanisms that effectively force the federal units to pursue fiscally sustainable policies. This is an important case to study, given that the role of welfare states as automatic stabilizers tends to mean that they unbalance budgets by spending more just as tax revenues drop (a problem for U.S. states, with their balanced budget rules). The Swiss welfare state is certainly expensive and not particularly focused on reducing inequalities, but that seems to be a set of characteristics the Swiss are willing to accept, and the system's design has impressive benefits. A question for further research is whether the structure of federalism alone tells us that the correct set of institutional incentives will produce a successful and fiscally decentralized welfare state, or whether Switzerland has additional characteristics that explain its success.

Is Federalism Bad for Welfare?

The existing literature strongly argues that federalism is bad for welfare. Framed in the language of self-rule and shared rule (Elazar 1987), two mechanisms might make federalism lead to less generous or at least less expensive welfare states. Via self-rule, policy divergence means that a state-level outcome is an average of divergent outcomes, so that the U.S. data average Mississippi and Minnesota. The divergence allows some jurisdictions to have weak or at least cheap welfare states and thereby to lower the whole country's average. This is almost undeniable, though the exact mechanisms of fiscal redistribution, conditional grants, and legal requirements mean that the amount of variation can vary greatly between countries. Once divergence arises, of course, interjurisdictional competition can arise for mobile factors of production, and the risk of a race to the bottom can exist. Insofar as factors of production are mobile and fiscal equalization is weak, this mechanism would produce downward competition in wages and at least some social benefits.

The more popular but weaker argument works through shared rule, apparently contending that federalism creates a veto point in the central government—for example, through a territorially apportioned Senate (Huber and Stephens 2001). The problem with this argument is that shared rule is not a necessary component of federalism. Both the United States and Australia are federal, and both have territorially apportioned upper houses that have a history of blocking legislation from the left, but neither has much shared rule. Both countries' state governments are more akin to lobbies than veto players, and the weaknesses of their welfare states lie more in the demos-constraining effects of checks and balances within their federal governments (Greer 2009; Brenton, this vol.; Greer, Elliott, and Mauri, this vol.).

The chapters in this volume contest these two arguments. While ideally we could compare more centralized countries to the ones in the sample, we can look for longitudinal data within countries and compare countries at different levels of decentralization. Overall, the chapters suggest that federalism is at best a very weak variable because it operates at the wrong level of detail. For example, shifting from tight and well-funded conditional grants to vaguer block grants, as happened with benefits to mothers in the United States and much of the Canadian welfare state in the 1990s, can lead to both greater variation in benefits and less overall generosity. Of course, the U.S. case study is somewhat hard to read because the 1990s were also a time of near-consensus across both major parties that welfare needed to be less generous and because the racial coding of "welfare" made it hard to defend such programs. Federalism is not only too broad a variable but also is not necessarily strong enough to stand out amid other trends toward less generous welfare states. From a policy design perspective, every country seems to have mechanisms to drive down expenditure by decentralizing it, but study would need to proceed on the level of those mechanisms, not on the level of federalism.

Does Austerity Recentralize or Decentralize Welfare States?

Finally, most of our countries experienced serious austerity starting in the 2008 financial crisis, and several are still experiencing very tight budgetary constraints for various reasons, including economic stagnation, eurozone membership, and right-wing government.[1] Australia, Switzerland, and Canada largely escaped the worldwide economic crisis and austerity, and the United States, Germany, and the UK recovered relatively well by 2016 even if the nature, distributional consequences, and sustainability of their recoveries can be debated. That leaves us with Belgium, Italy, and Spain as the cases of serious economic slowdowns combined with a decision to adopt austerity. Both the UK and United States chose to adopt austerity measures after 2010—a political choice by right-wing parties in both cases. What do these five cases tell us about the relationship between austerity and the allocation of authority in a given country?

The answer is *not much.* Spain, as Dubin argues, is a clear case of a central government taking centralizing measures that reduce the power of economically prostrate regional governments (Colino and del Pino 2014; Mendizabal 2014; Muro 2015). Many conditions led to this action, including the large debt loads of the Spanish regions, serious economic distortions during its years in the eurozone, and the long history of tensions related to nationality and territorial politics. In Spain, actors (central parties and a central state) had economic and political motives for centralization, and the crisis gave them an opportunity. They took it, and faced a backlash in Catalonia and elsewhere that has consequences for the stability of Spanish territorial politics now.

Other countries displayed no such pattern, though some analogies can be seen between Spanish and Italian policies (Bolgherini 2016). The UK carried out a program of fiscal decentralization to Scotland despite austerity across the country. The Scottish government now enjoys opportunities to raise taxes and fund a better welfare state if it so desires. No major change occurred in the United States, where the large stimulus and Affordable Care Act went through established intergovernmental channels. Belgium continued implementing its long series of decentralizing reforms, but the connection to austerity or economic conditions is hard to see. Italy did start a reform to its regions, but that is primarily part of a far longer story of (largely failed) efforts at territorial reform.

If we look back to economic crises and austerity before the 2008 crisis—in particular, the recession around 2000 with the end of the dot-com stock bubble—we still find no clear relationship. In Canada, the central state's withdrawal from detailed and generous conditional financing of social policies took the form of block grants to provinces that limited central government expenditure while giving provinces more autonomy and more difficult fiscal decisions. This approach continued with particular vigor under Prime Minister Stephen Harper. Germany spent much of the 2000s in the doldrums, which might have given some impetus to a federalism reform that clarified some competencies in areas such as higher education; nevertheless, it is hard to characterize that reform as centralizing or decentralizing. The United States saw a major expansion of the federal welfare state under George W. Bush with the creation of the Medicare Part D pharmaceutical plan, but that decision seems to have had little to do with federalism or economic policy. The UK, Spain, and Belgium continued to decentralize in those years. In short, there is little reason to believe that either the 2000 or 2008 economic busts led to consistent centralization or decentralization. In the one case where it did, recent Spanish history, the long history of fierce contention over the powers of regional governments seems to explain events. Crisis and austerity offered a pretext for centralization, and the weak fiscal and political positions of the regional governments made centralization easier.

Summary

Looking at federalism from a policy perspective, claims about its importance are often not well supported by our work. Regionally distinctive welfare states really do not exist because shared institutions, underpinned by shared politics and integrated economies, make building one very difficult—and regional politicians may not want to be so distinctive. The most distinctive regional welfare states are, unsurprisingly, in the most institutionally and politically distinctive regions, i.e., Quebec, the Basque Country, and Navarre. Notably, distinctive welfare states do not clearly map onto strong nationalist movements. It is much easier to focus desire for conflict with other governments on particular issues such as language or on small but highly distinctive programs and be pragmatic on big issues such as health or education policy. The structures of the welfare states—in particular, the interaction of the allocation of authority for finance and delivery—broadly conforms to what the economics of fiscal federalism would suggest, with central governments pooling risks and others delivering services. Federalism per se does not seem to lead to less generous welfare states, though mechanisms within federal systems have led to less generosity in particular areas. Every kind of regime has such mechanisms, of course, even if they operate differently. And finally, no links appear to exist between austerity, economic crisis, and the allocation of authority. Central governments pursuing austerity can centralize, can offload burdens in a decentralizing manner, or can just use some other budgetary technique. Federalism seems to be best understood as just one more institution, like bicameralism or referenda or independent central banks, that shapes politics but does not explain macrolevel outcomes.

Implications for European Integration—Or Disintegration

The chapters in this book and the larger scholarly and practitioner literatures about federalism are filled with examples of more or less dysfunctional federal arrangements, from ineffective constraints on debt to policy designs that encourage shirking to simple coordination failures across borders. While economists have written a great deal about the appropriate design of a federation, often with the help of models that assume the power of intergovernmental competition or voters' oversight, the political science literature has taken a more rounded view of federalism and its safeguards (Bednar 2009, 2011).

One particularly interesting federal state is under construction as well as in something of a crisis: the European Union. Leaving aside the rather politicized discussions of whether the EU is federal, it is easy to see how the problems of multilevel governance and intergovernmental relations in the EU are comparable to those of federal polities. Essentially, European integration is a shift in the allocation of authority between different governments, and European policymaking is about making and implementing policies in such a complex multilevel system (Marks, Hooghe, and Blank 1996; Fabbrini 2004). Its changing nature and institutional makeup and the complexities it faces make it one of the most interesting cases for the study of federal politics.

The European Union is in a turbulent period. On one hand, there are strong and clear disintegrative tendencies at work. The Brexit vote in the United Kingdom was the most prominent aspect to date of European disintegration, but the rise of the populist Right in Europe more generally means that member-state governments are increasingly inclined to turn away from the EU. The EU has not had obvious success at addressing major challenges such as conflict with Russia, migration, and economic stagnation, and leadership within the EU is uncomfortably split between weakened central institutions and member states that hesitate to provide European leadership.

On the other hand, since the crisis, member states have charged the EU with implementing a major increase in integration (Greer, Jarman, and Baeten 2016; Greer and Jarman 2018). The EU's new "fiscal governance" regime is designed to be a tough regulatory regime that will prevent member states from creating destabilizing public debt loads (as in Greece) or macroeconomic imbalances that make governments vulnerable in crisis (as in Ireland). The system involves surveillance by the EU of budgets and public policies, with a warning system and quasi-automatic fines for member states that fail to comply with budgetary rules and policy advice. The system is set up in legislation and in the Treaty on Stability, Coordination, and Growth, which all member states except the UK and the Czech Republic adopted (Greer and Jarman 2018).

This system applies the regulatory logic of the EU to the fiscal and policy decisions of the member states (Schelkle 2009; Greer and Jarman 2016). The logic of the regulatory state is that it does not directly provide services or much financing (the EU budget is capped at around 1 percent of EU GDP, and much of that goes to agricultural subsidies) (Majone 1994). Rather, the regulatory state directs the uses that member states make of their own resources. The result is a very efficient organization that essentially co-opts member states to enact policies (Page 2001) but that also is by international standards very limited in its range of policy tools.

Federations frequently are marked by some degree of this regulatory logic, in which the central government appropriates the right to make rules without necessarily helping the subordinate units fulfill their duties (Kelemen 2004). But federations also redistribute, whether between units or between people. Almost all of the countries in this study have both a formal equalization process to ensure that every federal unit has some minimal level of resources and individual-level programs such as pensions and social health insurance that redistribute from wealthier to poorer people. The closest the EU comes is its structural funds, which are for capital investment, primarily in poorer regions. While they amount to an impressive sum of money relative to the economies of some of the smaller and poorer member states, they are still no substitute for the kinds of big interpersonal and interterritorial redistributive mechanisms at work within federations.

In EU fiscal governance, the logic of the regulatory state amounts to the EU institutions being tasked with the oversight of government budgets, economic outcomes, and all the policies that might influence them, often in some detail. This suggests that EU politics are moving toward a particularly pathological form of federalism (Ziblatt 2013). The EU already pools risks at a low level (the member states, many of which are quite small and in demographic imbalance), while integration of the internal market, and eurozone, creates winners and losers that the EU does not really compensate. With the reinforced fiscal governance system, member states lose autonomy in real and symbolic ways. The compensations in law are limited—mostly access to EU funds for bailouts in future financial crises. In practice, they also include the likelihood of support from the European Central Bank in a crisis. They are nothing like the compensations operating within federal systems.

Optimists might note that the new fiscal governance regime shows signs of meeting the same fate as its predecessors—that is, it is being manipulated and undermined by member states and the commission, with decisions fudged and objectives expanded to reduce the focus on fiscal austerity (Greer and Jarman 2016; Schmidt 2016). Such an outcome would be in keeping with the failure of such balanced budget rules elsewhere (except in Switzerland). Predictably, bond markets rather than courts seem to discipline government budgets (Kelemen and Teo 2014). This is not a satisfactory situation, however. The political stakes might be too high to allow the same kind of manipulation that reduced predecessor systems of fiscal surveillance to insignificance. Creditor states, whose publics might think they have paid a great deal conditional on future good behavior by debtor states, might object to rule breaking. Even if they do not, it is a strange form of optimism that lauds mass noncompliance with rules that are probably impossible to follow.

The EU is probably hitting the end of what a regulatory polity can achieve. The regulatory state form has been the core of European integration, but it is also is built around reducing the policy space for member states to act on their own while exposing them to the pressure of Europe-wide markets. The result has been disequilibriums of all sorts, notably including the widening gaps in the economic performances of eurozone countries (Hancké 2013). Simply constraining member states without compensating them or their citizens for losses or giving them resources is a formula for building up disequilibriums and discontent. It is hard to imagine that this formula is not at the root of many of the EU's current political problems. *Not one of the states studied in this volume has adopted this model of federalism, which suggests that it is not a robust form of federalism or a viable future for the EU.*

Conclusion: Bringing the State Back In

Much of the comparative analysis of federalism to date has directed attention to purely political variables such as institutions or party systems, has discussed the intricacies of policies and politics in the context of single countries, or has focused on the fiscal balance of subnational governments. This study, in contrast, focused on social policy and its funding to address big questions about the relationship between federalism and the welfare state. In a broad sense, regional governments do not vary much, and the state they are in constitutes the key variable explaining their action or inaction. In addition, states' overall allocation of authority does not vary much, the specifics of federal arrangements rather than the mere existence of federalism shapes the impact on the welfare state, and there is no necessary relationship between austerity and allocation of authority.

We started from an interest in avoiding methodological nationalism and showing the impact and variety of regional governments (Greer, Elliott, and Oliver 2015; Jeffery and Wincott 2010) and ended by affirming the constitutive and real power of states vis-à-vis regional governments. To borrow an old phrase, the study of territorial politics and federalism could benefit from bringing the state back in (Evans, Rueschemeyer, and Skocpol 1985). There is much to be said for the evolution of historical institutionalism from the original state-focused research paradigm to a focus on institutions, but there is also much to be said for remembering that states, in constitution and in everyday politics, are both constitutive of their subnational units and able to exercise considerable power over them, whether through legislation, finance, or superior resources. When we focus on the public policies that interest most voters and politicians, the state should be at the center of our analyses.

NOTES

1. New work by Braun, Ruiz-Palmero, and Schnabel (2016) focuses on the ways federations handle fiscal consolidation pressures and decisions, framed in Bednar's (2009) terms of the robustness of the federation. Their findings appear compatible with ours.

REFERENCES

Adolph, Christopher, Scott L. Greer, and Elize Massard da Fonseca. 2012. "Allocation of Authority in European Health Policy." *Social Science and Medicine* 75 (9): 1595–1603. https://doi.org/10.1016/j.socscimed.2012.05.041

Armingeon, Klaus, and Michelle Beyeler, eds. 2004. *The OECD and European Welfare States*. Cheltenham: Edward Elgar.

Babb, Sarah. 2009. *Behind the Development Banks: Washington Politics, the Wealth of Nations, and World Poverty*. Chicago: University of Chicago Press.

Baumgartner, Frank R., and Bryan D. Jones. 1993. *Agendas and Instability in American Politics*. Chicago: University of Chicago Press.

Bednar, Jenna. 2009. *The Robust Federation: Principles of Design*. Cambridge: Cambridge University Press.

Bednar, Jenna. 2011. "The Political Science of Federalism." *Annual Review of Law and Social Science* 7 (1): 269–88.

Béland, Daniel, and André Lecours. 2008. *Nationalism and Social Policy: The Politics of Territorial Solidarity.* Oxford: Oxford University Press.

Berg, Marc, and Geoffrey Bowker. 1997. "The Multiple Bodies of the Medical Record." *Sociological Quarterly* 38 (3): 513–37.

Birrell, Derek. 2009. *The Impact of Devolution on Social Policy.* Bristol: Policy Press.

Bolgherini, Silvia. 2016. "Crisis-Driven Reforms and Local Discretion: An Assessment of Italy and Spain." *Italian Political Science Review/Rivista Italiana di Scienza Politica* 46 (1): 71–91. https://doi.org/10.1017/ipo.2015.23

Boushey, Graeme. 2010. *Policy Diffusion Dynamics in America.* Cambridge: Cambridge University Press.

Bowker, G. C., and S. L. Star. 2000. *Sorting Things Out: Classification and Its Consequences.* Cambridge: MIT Press.

Braun, D., C. Ruiz-Palmero, and J. Schnabel. 2016. *Consolidation Policies in Federal States: Conflicts and Solutions.* Milton Park: Taylor and Francis.

Caramani, Daniele. 2004. *The Nationalization of Politics: The Formation of National Electorates and Party Systems in Western Europe.* Cambridge: Cambridge University Press.

Chaney, Paul. 2017. "'Governance Transitions' and Minority Nationalist Parties' Pressure for Welfare State Change: Evidence from Welsh and Scottish Elections–And the UK's 'Brexit' Referendum." *Global Social Policy* 17 (3): 279–306.

Clasen, J., and N. A. Siegel. 2007. *Investigating Welfare State Change: The "Dependent Variable Problem" in Comparative Analysis.* Cheltenham: Edward Elgar.

Colino, César, and Eloísa del Pino. 2014. "Spanish Federalism in Crisis." In *The Global Debt Crisis: Haunting U.S. and European Federalism,* edited by P. Peterson and D. Nadler, 159–78. Washington, DC: Brookings Institution.

Conlan, Timothy J. 1998. *From New Federalism to Devolution? Twenty-Five Years of Intergovernmental Reform.* Washington, DC: Brookings Institution.

Crosby, A. W. 1996. *The Measure of Reality: Quantification and Western Society, 1250–1600.* Cambridge: Cambridge University Press.

Danforth, Benjamin, and John D. Stephens. 2013. "Measuring Social Citizenship: Achievements and Future Challenges." *Journal of European Public Policy* 20 (9): 1285–98.

Elazar, Daniel. 1987. *Exploring Federalism.* Tuscaloosa: University of Alabama Press.

Espeland, Wendy Nelson, and Mitchell L. Stevens. 1998. "Commensuration as a Social Process." *Annual Review of Sociology* 24:313–43.

Evans, P., D. Rueschemeyer, and T. Skocpol. 1985. *Bringing the State Back In.* Cambridge: Cambridge University Press.

Fabbrini, Sergio, ed. 2004. *Democracy and Federalism in the European Union and the United States: Exploring Post-National Governance.* London: Routledge.

Gibson, Edward L. 2013. *Boundary Control: Subnational Authoritarianism in Federal Democracies.* Cambridge: Cambridge University Press.

Gray, Caroline. 2014. "Smoke and Mirrors: How Regional Finances Complicate Spanish-Catalan Relations." *International Journal of Iberian Studies* 27 (1): 21–42.

Gray, Caroline. 2015. "A Fiscal Path to Sovereignty? The Basque Economic Agreement and Nationalist Politics." *Nationalism and Ethnic Politics* 21 (1): 63–82.

Gray, Caroline. 2016. *Nationalist Politics and Regional Financing Systems in the Basque Country and Catalonia*. Bilbao: Diputación de Bizkaia and Ad Concordiam Association.

Greer, Scott L. 2004. *Territorial Politics and Health Policy: UK Health Policy in Comparative Perspective*. Manchester: Manchester University Press.

Greer, Scott L. 2006. "The Politics of Divergent Policy." In *Territory, Democracy, and Justice: Regionalism and Federalism in Western Democracies*, edited by Scott L. Greer, 157–74. Basingstoke: Palgrave Macmillan.

Greer, Scott L. 2009. "How Does Decentralisation Affect the Welfare State?" *Journal of Social Policy* 39 (2): 1–21.

Greer, Scott L., Heather Elliott, and Rebecca Oliver. 2015. "Differences That Matter: Overcoming Methodological Nationalism in Comparative Social Policy Research." *Journal of Comparative Policy Analysis: Research and Practice* 17 (4): 408–29. https://doi.org/10.1080/13876988.2015.1060713

Greer, Scott L, and Holly Jarman. 2016. "Reinforcing Europe's Failed Fiscal Regulatory State." In *A Global Perspective on the European Economic Crisis*, edited by Bruno Dallago, Gert Guri, and John McGowan, 122–43. Abingdon: Routledge.

Greer, Scott L., and Holly Jarman. 2018. "European Citizenship Rights and European Fiscal Politics after the Crisis." *Government and Opposition* 53 (1): 76–103.

Greer, Scott L., Holly Jarman, and Rita Baeten. 2016. "The New Political Economy of Health Care in the European Union: The Impact of Fiscal Governance." *International Journal of Health Services* 46 (2): 262–82. https://doi.org/10.1177/0020731416637205

Hacker, Jacob S., and Paul Pierson. 2014. "After the 'Master Theory': Downs, Schattschneider, and the Rebirth of Policy-Focused Analysis." *Perspectives on Politics* 12 (3): 643–62.

Halberstam, Daniel, and Mathias Reimann. 2014. *Federalism and Legal Unification: A Comparative Empirical Investigation of Twenty Systems*. New York: Springer.

Hancké, B. 2013. *Unions, Central Banks, and EMU: Labour Market Institutions and Monetary Integration in Europe*. Oxford: Oxford University Press.

Henderson, A., C. Jeffery, and D. Wincott, eds. 2013. *Citizenship after the Nation State: Regionalism, Nationalism, and Public Attitudes in Europe*. Basingstoke: Palgrave Macmillan UK.

Huber, Evelyne, and John D. Stephens. 2001. *Development and Crisis of the Welfare State: Parties and Policies in Global Markets*. Chicago: University of Chicago Press.

Jeffery, Charlie, Niccole M. Pamphilis, Carolyn Rowe, and Ed Turner. 2014. "Regional Policy Variation in Germany: The Diversity of Living Conditions in a 'Unitary Federal State.'" *Journal of European Public Policy* 21 (9): 1350–66.

Jeffery, Charlie, and Daniel Wincott. 2010. "The Challenge of Territorial Politics." In *New Directions in Political Science: Responding to the Challenges of an Interdependent World*, edited by Colin Hay, 167–88. Basingstoke: Palgrave Macmillan.

Kelemen, R. Daniel. 2004. *The Rules of Federalism: Institutions and Regulatory Politics in the EU and Beyond*. Cambridge: Harvard University Press.

Kelemen, R. Daniel, and Terence K. Teo. 2014. "Law, Focal Points, and Fiscal Discipline in the United States and the European Union." *American Political Science Review* 108 (2): 355–70.

Lampland, M., and S. L. Star. 2009. *Standards and Their Stories: How Quantifying, Clas-*

sifying, and Formalizing Practices Shape Everyday Life. Ithaca: Cornell University Press.

Majone, Giandomenico. 1994. "The Rise of the Regulatory State in Europe." *West European Politics* 17 (3): 77–102.

Marks, Gary, Liesbet Hooghe, and Kermit Blank. 1996. "European Integration from the 1980s: State-Centric v. Multi-Level Governance." *Journal of Common Market Studies* 34 (3): 341–78.

Mätzke, Margitta. 2013. "Federalism and Decentralization in German Health and Social Care Policy." In *Federalism and Decentralization in European Health and Social Care*, edited by Joan Costa i Font and Scott L Greer, 190–207. Basingstoke: Palgrave Macmillan.

Mendizabal, Nagore Calvo. 2014. "Crisis Management, Re-Centralization and the Politics of Austerity in Spain." *International Journal of Iberian Studies* 27 (1): 3–20.

Muro, Diego. 2015. "When do Countries Recentralize? Ideology and Party Politics in the Age of Austerity." *Nationalism and Ethnic Politics* 21 (1): 24–43.

Niedzwiecki, Sara. 2016. "Social Policies, Attribution of Responsibility, and Political Alignments: A Subnational Analysis of Argentina and Brazil." *Comparative Political Studies* 49 (4): 457–98.

Page, Edward C. 2001. "The European Union and the Bureaucratic Mode of Production." In *From the Nation State to Europe: Essays in Honour of Jack Hayward*, edited by Anand Menon, 139–57. Oxford: Oxford University Press.

Paris, Valerie, Marion Devaux, and Lihan Wei. 2010. *Health Systems Institutional Characteristics*. Paris: OECD.

Peeters, Hans, Gert Verschraegen, and Annelies Debels. 2014. "Commensuration and Policy Comparison: How the Use of Standardized Indicators Affects the Rankings of Pension Systems." *Journal of European Social Policy* 24 (1): 19–38.

Radaelli, Claudio M. 2018. "Regulatory Indicators in the European Union and the Organization for Economic Cooperation and Development: Performance Assessment, Organizational Processes, and Learning." *Public Policy and Administration*, February 20, https://doi.org/10.1177/0952076718758369

Schelkle, Waltraud. 2009. "The Contentious Creation of the Regulatory State in Fiscal Surveillance." *West European Politics* 32 (4): 829–46.

Schmidt, Vivien A. 2016. "Reinterpreting the Rules 'by Stealth' in Times of Crisis: A Discursive Institutionalist Analysis of the European Central Bank and the European Commission." *West European Politics* 39 (5): 1032–52. https://doi.org/10.1080/0140 2382.2016.1186389

Vampa, D. 2016. *The Regional Politics of Welfare in Italy, Spain, and Great Britain*. New York: Springer.

Wenzelburger, Georg, Reimut Zohlnhöfer, and Frieder Wolf. 2013. "Implications of Dataset Choice in Comparative Welfare State Research." *Journal of European Public Policy* 20 (9): 1229–50.

Ziblatt, Daniel. 2013. "Between Centralization and Federalism in the European Union." In *The Global Debt Crisis: Haunting U.S. and European Federalism*, edited by P. Peterson and D. Nadler, 113–33. Washington, DC: Brookings Institution.

Contributors

Daniel Béland is Director, McGill Institute for the Study of Canada, and Professor, Department of Political Science, McGill University. A specialist in comparative fiscal and social policy, he has published more than 15 books and 125 articles in peer-reviewed journals.

Scott Brenton is a senior lecturer in political science and public policy at the University of Melbourne. He is the author of *The Politics of Budgetary Surplus: Ideology, Economic Governance, and Public Management Reform* (2016), along with several journal articles.

Alberto Díaz-Cayeros is senior fellow at the Center on Democracy, Development, and Rule of Law (CDDRL) and director of the Center for Latin American Studies at Stanford University. His research interests include federalism, poverty, indigenous governance, political economy of health, violence, and citizen security.

Kenneth Dubin received his doctorate from the University of California-Berkeley and teaches at the IE business school in Madrid. His interests include labor law, comparative politics, and Spanish politics and policy.

Heather Elliott is a doctoral candidate and research associate in the Departments of Health Management and Policy and Political Science at the University of Michigan.

Stefan Felder is professor of health economics in the Department of Business and Economics at the University of Basel. He holds a doctorate from the University of Bern.

Scott L. Greer is professor of health management and policy, global public health, and political science at the University of Michigan and senior expert adviser on health governance to the European Observatory on Health Systems and Policies. His research interests include the comparative politics of health care, welfare states and territorial politics, and the EU. He is coediting *The European Union after Brexit* with Janet Laible.

Charlie Jeffery is professor of politics and senior vice principal at the University of Edinburgh. He has published on comparative federalism and Austrian and German politics. His books include *Citizenship after the Nation State* (with Ailsa Henderson and Daniel Wincott, 2014) and *Federalism, Unification, and European Integration* (with Roland Sturm, 1993).

Gebhard Kirchgässner (15 April 1948–1 April 2017) of the University of St. Gallen, Switzerland, made numerous contributions in the fields of the philosophy of science, public choice, public finance, and time series analysis. His publications include *Homo Oeconomicus* (2008).

Janet Laible is associate professor of political science at Lehigh University. She researches territorial politics, nationalism, and social policy in the European Union, with particular interests in the United Kingdom and Belgium. She is coediting *The European Union after Brexit* with Scott L. Greer.

Julia Lynch is associate professor of political science at the University of Pennsylvania. Her research focuses on the politics of inequality and social policy in the rich democracies, particularly the countries of Western Europe.

Amanda Mauri is a doctoral student in health services organization and policy at the University of Michigan. Her research examines the politics of health care, specifically the development and effects of policies targeting behavioral health care and firearm violence.

Rebecca Oliver is assistant professor at Allegheny College. Her work examines distributional politics with a focus on labor unions, child care policy, and social spending in decentralized political contexts.

Niccole M. Pamphilis is a lecturer in quantitative social sciences at the University of Glasgow. Her work focuses primarily on the relationships between political institutions and policy.

Elisabeth Riedler contributed to this chapter when she was a Research Assistant at the Research Institute for Economics of Aging at the WU Vienna University of Economics and Business (2013–14). Today, she works in the Education, Research, Culture, Justice Division at the Federal Statistical Office of Germany.

Simone Singh is an assistant professor in the Department of Health Management and Policy at the University of Michigan. Her research focuses on financing health care and public health systems, particularly in the United States and Germany.

Michael Slowik is an adviser for inpatient care in the Department for Inpatient Care and Rehabilitation at the AOK-Bundesverband, a think tank and political umbrella organization for eleven public health insurance funds in Berlin, Germany. He previously studied health economics at the University of Bayreuth and health care management at the School of Public Health at the University of Michigan.

Alan Trench served as professor of politics at Ulster University and held research posts at University College London and the University of Edinburgh. He also served as a specialist adviser to numerous parliamentary committees in the UK.

Birgit Trukeschitz is a senior research fellow at the Research Institute for Economics of Aging at WU Vienna University of Economics and Business. An economist by training, she has conducted research in several areas of social policy, mainly related to long-term care. Her interests include the measurement of long-term care outcomes, issues related to informal elder care, and the usability and effects of smart technologies on older people's lives.

Index